Non-League FOOTBALL

POCKET ANNUAL 1993-94

Editor Bruce Smith

Copyright © Bruce Smith – Author 1993

The right of Bruce Smith to be identified as the Author of the Work has been asserted by him in accordance with the Copyright, Designs and Patents Act 1988.

3rd Year of Publication
(Previously published as *The Playfair Non-League Football Annual*)

First published in 1993
by
Words on Sport

All rights reserved. No part of this publication may be reproduced, stored in a retrieval system, or transmitted, in any form or by any means, without prior permission in writing of the publisher, nor be otherwise circulated in any form of binding or cover other than that in which it is published and without a similar condition including this condition being imposed on the subsequent purchaser.

Cover photograph: Stuart Bogg, courtesy of the Runcorn Weekly News

Runcorn v Witton FA Trophy semi-final first leg

ISBN: 1-898351-00-7

Typeset by Bruce Smith Books Ltd

Printed and bound in Great Britain

Words on Sport
Bruce Smith Books Limited
PO Box 382
St. Albans
Herts, AL2 3JD

CONTENTS

Editorial 5
About Your Annual 10

FA Competitions
FA Cup 1992-93 13
FA Trophy 1992-93 26
FA Vase 1992-93 37
FA Sunday Cup 1992-93 54
England Semi-Pro Internationals 56

GM Vauxhall Conference
Final Table and Season Review 63
Awards 66
Results Grid 68
Attendance Grids 70
Attendance Summaries 72
Drinkwise Cup 74
GMVC Club Directory 77

Diadora League
Season Review 100
Isthmian League History 102
Isthmian League Cup 103
Full Members' Cup 105
Associate Members' Trophy 106

Premier Division
Final Table and Leading Goalscorers 107
Results Grid 108
Attendance Grids 110
Attendance Summaries, Club Scorers and Awards 112
Premier Club Directory 114

Division One
Final Table and Leading Goalscorers 126
Results Grid 128
Division One Club Directory 130

Division Two
Division Two Final Table and Leading Goalscorers 136
Division Two Results Grid 138
Division Two Club Directory 140

Division Three
Division Three Final Table and Leading Goalscorers 145
Division Three Results Grid 146
Division Three Club Directory 149

Beazer Homes League
Season Review 153
Southern League History 155
Barclays Commercial Services Cup 156

Premier Division
Final Table and Leading Goalscorers 158
Results Grid 160
Attendance Grids 162
Attendance Summaries 164
Premier Division Club Directory 165

Midland Division
Final Table and Leading Goalscorers 176
Results Grid 178
Midland Division Club Directory 180

Southern Division
Final Table and Leading Goalscorers 186
Results Grid 188
Southern Division Club Directory 190

Northern Premier League
Season Review 196
Northern Premier League History and Annual Awards 197
League Cup 198
President's Cup and Division One Cup 199

Premier Division
Final Table and Leading Goalscorers 200
Results Grid 202
Attendance Grids 204
Attendance Summaries and Full Club Playing Records 206
Top Goalscorers by Club 207
Premier Division Club Directory 208

Division One
Final Table and Leading Goalscorers 220
Manager/Player of the Month Awards and Attendance Summaries 221
Results Grid 222
Division One Club Directory 224

Official Feeder Leagues – Final Tables
Diadora League Feeder Leagues 231
Beazer Homes League Feeder Leagues 240
Northern Premier League Feeder Leagues 255
Miscellaneous Leagues 273

Fixtures 1993-94
GM Vauxhall Conference 280
Diadora League Premier Division 282
Beazer Homes League Premier Division 284
Northern Premier League 286
Fixture Diary 1993-94 – FA Cup, FA Vase, FA Trophy, FA Sunday Cup 288

Editorial

It was largely the year of second comings. Wycombe Wanderers – who so narrowly missed out on promotion to the Football League last time around – achieved their goal comfortably and did so completing the Non-League double, lifting the FA Trophy at Wembley.

Bridlington returned to the hallowed turf for the second time in four seasons to lift the FA Vase defeating Tiverton Town in the Final. Brid too did their own double, running away with the Northern Premier League First Division title to move into the Premier Division for this season. Adding irony to the double theme is the fact that neither of the cup winners will be able to defend their silverware this season due to their new elevated status.

Throughout the higher echelons of the Pyramid there was also encouragement in the fact that some of the bigger names of yesteryear are starting to recapture past glories. Southport – a former Football League club who has not had the best of luck in recent years – are now just one division away from the status they left at the end of the 1977-78 season, having been run-away winners of the the Northern Premier League. In the South, Dover captured the Beazer Homes League title with equal vigour and took the place in the Conference that they were cruelly denied at the end of the 1989-90 season.

In the Diadora League Hitchin Town regained their place among the Premier elite by taking the First Division title just four minutes from the end of the season whilst Aldershot Town had a fabulous re-incarnation running away with the Division Three title in front of crowds which on occasions were the highest in the Non-League arena. How ironic that, had they had the same sort of crowds a season or two earlier, they may never have lost their Football League status. No doubt the Division Three clubs will be mourning their loss as much as the Division Two clubs will be rubbing their hands in anticipation of the increased revenue the travelling band of 900-odd Aldershot supporters will bring. It will be very interesting to see how their home attendances develop should they have an indifferent season.

It was also the year of the Tree. A 200-year old Oak Tree in the Clarence Park terracing was a lame excuse to deny St Albans City promotion to the Conference, when the same ground is used by international teams, and cup finalists prior to Wembley appearances. Of course as a vice-president of the club I have a vested and declared interest, however surely the thing that will bring families back into the grounds is the scenic settings of stadiums like Clarence Park and not the corrugated iron and concrete that seems to be the desired requirement.

City's chance only came about because of Chesham United's withdrawn application as Champions of the Diadora League. The requirements needed to meet grading criteria were clearly impossible to meet within the specified period, and so United's fabulous title win was denied its ultimate reward – promotion. Perhaps the GMVC is the loser though – both Chesham and St Albans hit over 100 goals in their league campaigns.

It was a case of happy returns for one club – Tonbridge who were relegated from the Beazer Homes League Southern Division at the end of the 1988-89 season showed that it is possible to make the return journey by winning the Winstonlead Kent League and having their application to re-join the Southern Division accepted.

One club still not sure of their status at the time of going to press are Whitby Town. On 1st May 1993 they clinched the Northern League title for the first time in their 97 year history and looked forward to Northern Premier League status for the 1993-94 season. However– to cut a long story short – the Northern League did not give their approval for the club to take promotion and this was subsequently upheld by the FA. At the time of writing, the matter is now in the hands of the FA Board of Appeals.

In the FA Cup Yeovil Town put up a brave performance against the eventual Cup winners Arsenal, whilst Marlow's run terminated at Tottenham. Marlow did lift silverware though in the form of the Diadora League Cup. However, their win was matched by the performance of First Division Molesey in reaching the final of the competition with a series of outstanding displays – not least a marvellous two leg semi-final victory over Enfield. It was a runner-up double for Molesey who finished behind Hitchin in the Diadora League. However, they ply their skills in the Premier Division next season.

Northwich Victoria achieved their first cup success in 10 years by winning 3-2 at Adams Park to take the Drinkwise Cup by the same aggregate score.

Farnborough – who shot to fame last season in the FA Cup – were relegated from the Conference on the last day of the season to complete an unhappy end to a dismal season which saw Ted Pearce – manager for 23 years and the architect of their rise from Park football in that period – resign.

The season though belonged to Wycombe Wanderers and such is the Wycombe effect that even before a ball was kicked in the new League season they were installed ats 9/2 favourites to take the Third Division title at the first attempt!

STOP PRESS: As we went to press Whitby Town were informed by the FA Board of Appeals that they would not be able to join the NPL. The NPL First Division will therefore be one club short for the 1993-94 season.

The Pyramid of Football

In a perfect world the Pyramid of Football would not need explaining. A club would simply move up and down the regional arms of the tree-like structure and, like water, find its own level as its playing resources dictated. However, it is not a perfect world and there remains a great deal of confusion about the mechanics of it all. What follows is a summary of the system as it works at the time iof going to press.

About Promotion

Simply being a champion club does not guarantee automatic promotion. A club will only be promoted to a higher division if it has a ground and facilities that are acceptable to the league or higher division which the club is proposing to join. If this is not the case, then the club will probably not be promoted even though it may have won all its games and not conceded a goal all season. Like it or not, that is generally the way it is. But clubs should not complain because these facts are normally spelled out in league rules. Now, this contentious rule – which I believe is the correct one – is sometimes bent if a club can convince the league that work required to make the grade will be in place for the start of the following season. If the champion club cannot achieve, or does not want, promotion then the invitation may be extended to another club, generally the runners-up, but not always.

The Conference champion club is invited to join the Football League Third Division. It is unlikely that the winners would ever wish to decline such an invitation, but if they did the invitation would not – unless the Football League was looking to expand its numbers – be extended to a second or third placed club.

A club coming down into the GMVC must notify the Conference of its intention to play in the Conference before the AGM. After two years without automatic relegation from the Football League as it swelled to its full complement of 94 clubs, 1992-93 saw Halifax Town exchange places with Wycombe Wanderers.

Below the GMVC, the Pyramid branches into three distinct chains. These are headed by the Northern Premier League (NPL), the Southern League and the Isthmian League. These are the correct names of the leagues as each is a limited company. However, the Southern and Isthmian Leagues are more commonly known by their sponsors' names which are currently, Beazer Homes and Diadora respectively. The Northern Premier League is currently without sponsorship although it has been generally known as the HFS Loans League for the past few seasons.

The rules of the Conference allow for a maximum of three clubs to be relegated to these three arms. In previous seasons, when no club has been relegated from the Football League only two clubs have been relegated to the lower divisions. This can, and often does, have a knock-on effect right down the leagues.

A club may also escape relegation if a side capable of being promoted does not meet the criteria for grounds and facilities as outlined. This applies all the way down the Pyramid and is one of the reasons why confirmation of promotion and relegation may not take place until two or three weeks after the end of the season.

Clubs being relegated from one league to another are normally relegated to the league from whence they came. This solves the dilemma of whether a club in the south is relegated from the Conference to either the Southern or Isthmian Leagues.

But there can be another spanner in the works here. Everything is fine so long as the bottom three clubs are ultimately dropping into the Premier Divisions of the Northern, Southern and Isthmian. But what if the bottom three clubs all come from the North? They cannot be shifted into either the Southern or Isthmian and so they can only go into the Northern Premier League. Once again, this has a knock-on effect such that clubs lower down the Pyramid may not be promoted to allow for it.

However, such drastic action may not happen because, in such a circumstance, the Joint Management Committee (made up of members of the Conference, Northern Premier, Southern and Isthmian Leagues) would almost certainly endeavour to shift other clubs sideways from one league to another.

For example, a club based in Derbyshire and playing in the Northern Premier League may be asked/compelled to play in the Southern League for the new season. A similar movement may take place between the Southern and Isthmian Leagues should relegation prove problematic.

Clearer – Just!

Below the Premier Divisions of the three major regional leagues things remain a little clearer, for a while. Firstly, promotion and relegation between the regional leagues' divisions is relatively straightforward, but again subject to ground grading.

Two clubs are transferred between the Premier and First Divisions of the NPL. In normal circumstances three clubs are transferred between the Premier Division and between Divisions One, Two and Three of the Isthmian. The champions and runners-up in the Southern League's Southern and Midlands divisions are promoted and the bottom four in the Southern League's Premier are relegated.

These relegated clubs will go into the appropriate regional division. If a club is geographically located such that it must go into the Midlands Division, for example, then it would be switched from the Midlands to the Southern Division.

From this point on there is no automatic promotion to the Southern and Isthmian Leagues. Leagues apply to be affiliated to a particular arm of the Pyramid which is normally defined by their geographical position. Feeder leagues to the Isthmian League include the South Midlands, Combined Counties, Essex and London Spartan Leagues. Clubs in these leagues – which are still classed as senior leagues – may apply to join the Isthmian League.

As two clubs only are relegated from the Isthmian League, only two of four clubs have a chance of being successful. The expectant clubs have to present their case and, of course, have the correct facilities, etc.

This set-up is mirrored for the Northern Premier and Southern Leagues. Which clubs – if any – get promoted is decided by the League. It may be that only one or perhaps none are accepted and, as such, the relegated clubs are reprieved.

Continuing the Isthmian scenario, there now comes a series of additional leagues which are not normally classified as Senior. These are the Herts County, Chiltonian, Middlesex and Surrey and clubs in these can apply to join their appropriate feeder leagues. For example, a Herts County League club might apply to join the South Midlands and a Chiltonian the Combined Counties League. The rules of acceptance are the same.

The Northern Premier League has a slightly more balanced set-up in that there is automatic promotion (grounds permitting) into the First Division from the North West Counties, Northern Counties East and Northern Leagues for one club, with three coming down from the First Division. The Northern League arm of the Pyramid only came into operation during the 1991-92 season and again there is automatic promotion for Northern Alliance and Vaux Wearside League clubs.

The application and acceptance criteria apply to the other two leagues.

Of course, not all leagues are in the system but several are looking to join as soon as possible. The Pyramid is not as clear-cut as one might have first thought and it is perhaps not surprising that there is a good deal of confusion.

About Your *Words on Sport* Non-League Annual

A lot of hard thought went into the contents of this Annual and the format of the information contained within. As a small pocket-sized book it has been designed to be an aid to the Non-League supporter on the move and, as such, much of its contents are fairly contemporary in nature. But, as an adjunct to that, we also felt it necessary to provide some historical background that would be informative, innovative and be capable of settling some of those odd, but quite friendly, arguments that raise their heads on the terraces from time to time.

Your Pocket Annual is divided into three quite distinct sections for ease of reference. Each of these is described briefly below, along with the conventions used.

FA Competitions

This section provides full match details for all the FA competitions. This includes: FA Cup, FA Trophy, FA Vase, FA Sunday Cup and the England Semi-Pro International scene. In most instances, match results and attendances are given, with scorers for the final stages of the competition. The FA Cup is covered until the Non-League interest is exhausted.

Where replay details are listed, unless otherwise specified, the replay took place at the home of the team who were originally drawn away.

Final line-ups and scorer details are provided for previous Trophy and Vase finals along with all England Semi-Pro matches.

Club Guide

The club guide is arranged by league and overall the same format is adhered to throughout. For the GMVC and all Premier Division clubs in the three feeder leagues, a brief club history is provided along with a complete five-year playing record. Thus you can see instantly how consistent a team has been in recent years.

For the Conference sides, league appearances, substitutions and goalscorers are listed along with the clubs' major achievements past and present.

In addition to acrostic results grids for all the leagues in the main Pyramid section, attendance grids are given for the GMVC and Premier Division games of the three feeders.

GM Vauxhall Conference

This section provides full details on the 1992-93 GMVC campaign. In addition to listing scorers it also provides full attendance grids. Each club is allocated a page and league appearance, substitute and goalscoring details are also listed, including those for the promoted and relegated sides. Club histories by necessity are brief. The five-year playing records provide a useful indication of recent club form and the notations used are listed below.

Beazer, Diadora, Northern Premier Leagues

Each of the three main feeders into the Conference are given similar treatment. However, club histories and five-year playing records are limited to those clubs participating in the Premier Division of each league.

League Tables

The third and final section of your Pocket Annual contains final tables from all the major regional leagues that in general supply clubs to the Beazer, Diadora and Northern Premier Leagues. There are a few exceptions to this and these tables are listed under a separate heading.

Notations Used

Five-year playing record: P, matches played; W, matches won; D, matches drawn; F, goals for; A, goals against; Pts, points; Psn, final league position; Cup, round reached in FA Cup (Pr, preliminary round; q, qualifying round); FAT, round reached in FA Trophy (Pr, preliminary round; q, qualifying round). If a club competed in the FA Vase the details appear in brackets and with a V.

Leagues: CONF, GM Vauxhall Conference; VLP, Vauxhall League Premier Division; VL1, Vauxhall League First Division; VL2S, Vauxhall League Division Two South; VL2N, Vauxhall League Division Two North; DLP, Diadora League Premier Division; DL1, Diadora League First Division; HFSP, HFS Loans Premier Division; HFS1, HFS Loans First Division; NPLP, Northern Premier League Premier Division; NPL1, Northern Premier League First Division; BHLP, Beazer Homes League Premier Division; BHLM, Beazer Homes League Midland Division; BHLS, Beazer Homes League Southern Division; NCEP, Northern Counties East League Premier Division; NWC1, North West Counties League First Division; NL1, Northern League First Division; WSX, Wessex League; MC, Midland Combination.

Ground: Where capacities are given the value in brackets is the seating capacity. With respect to records the following abbreviations are used: f.o., floodlight opening; g.o., ground opening.

Miscellaneous: na, not available; tba, to be announced.

Disclaimer

In a book of this type it is inevitable that some errors will creep in. Non-League football also suffers heavily with movement of managers, players, etc during the close season. While every effort has been made to ensure that the details given in this annual are correct at the time of going to press, neither the editor nor the publishers can accept any responsibilities for errors within.

Acknowledgments

As with previous editions of this Annual (previously published as the *Playfair Non-League Football Annual*) there are many to thank for their help. None more so than **Phil Heady** whose contribution as ever has been considerable. The club and league histories and club positions are entirely his doing and are, I believe, a major contribution to the completed product. Phil also helped research appearance details. Thank you to those club secretaries and programme editors who helped him!

Considerable thanks are also due to the various league secretaries and publicity officers and agencies for sending bulletins and information on request, in particular to Peter Hunter and Scott and Jones (GMVC), Alan Turvey and Nick Robinson (Diadora), Dennis Strudwick (BHL) and Duncan Bayley (NPL). Thanks also to Phil Bradley for the Northern Premier League report and his input to that section, Sue Thearle for her FA Trophy Final report, Steve Clark and Sue Ball at the FA Competitions Department who go out of their way to be helpful.

In house thanks go to Peter Fitzpatrick, Martin Ritchie and Mark Webb.

FA CUP 1992-93

Bucks Flying

Although not a classic year for Non-League FA Cup giant-killing action, 1992-93 nevertheless saw some stunning action and some excellent results by clubs from outside the full professional realm.

Hardly known as a hot-bed of football it was the county of Buckinghamshire who provided two of the glamour clubs of the FA Cup season in Wycombe and Marlow. Wanderers' achivements are chronicled throughout these pages but their two second round ties with Osvaldo Ardiles' West Brom side – on their way to a play-off promotion exuded everything that is exciting in football. Indeed, given a modicum of good fortune then the tie could well have been decided in their favour at Adams Park and in front of the on-looking Sky Sports audience.

Marlow – for the second successive year – made the competition proper and, drawn against the might of Tottenham Hotspur in the glamour tie of the third round, they conceded ground advantage but were not disgraced in their 5-1 defeat in front of nearly 27,000 sympathetic supporters.

The last time Arsenal played Yeovil in an FA Cup tie they went on to win the FA Cup and complete The Double. Their 3-1 defeat of Yeovil Town proved equally lucky as they again went on to complete a unique double. The Glovers used the opportunity to turn their own season around and more than one club has fallen to the goal-scoring talents of Ian Wright. Yeovil though also take with them memories of a fabulous 5-3 win at nearby Torquay in the first round and a 2-1 replay win over Hereford.

Bad weather meant that Marine and their third round opponents Crewe Alexandra went into the draw for the fourth round proper. Football is always full of funny querks and it was hardly surprising that the winners of the tie would face Kenny Daglish's Blackburn Rovers side. Hardly surprising? Marine's manager Roly Howard's window-cleaning round took in none other than the home of a certain Mr Dalglish. Such headline-grabbing novelty was short-lived though as, on a bog of a pitch the Northern Premier League side went down 3-1.

The cup was not without its less savoury moments. After a 1-1 draw at Kingsmeadow, Kingstonian travelled to Peterborough with manager Chris "The Lip" Kelly promising a big upset. Indeed there was, as the Ks went down 1-9. The game was marred by a coin-throwing incident and the FA ordered the game played behind closed doors. Although The Posh won by the only goal of the game it left an unsavoury flavour in the Kingstonian camp not least due to the unavailability of a number of players because of the FA's insistence on a mid-week afternoon kick-off.

Clubs Exempt to the Fourth Qualifying Round – 1992-93

Atherstone United	Halesowen Town	Sutton United
Aylesbury United	Hayes	Telford United
Barrow	KidderminsterHarriers	Tiverton Town
Bromsgrove Rovers	Kettering Town	Welling United
Crawley Town	Marlow	Whitley Bay
Enfield	Merthyr Tydfil	Yeovil Town
Farnborough Town	Runcorn	

Non-League Clubs Exempt to First Round Proper – 1992-93

Trophy Finalists 92-93:	Witton Albion	
Most Appropriate:	Woking	Wycombe Wanderers

Preliminary Round – 29 August 1992

Home		Away	Res	Att.	Replay	
Alfreton Town	v	Oakham United	2-1	163		
Andover	v	Ringmer	5-0	147		
Armthorpe Welfare	v	Brandon United	2-0	54		
Arnold Town	v	Liversedge	4-0	96		
(at Kimberley Town FC)						
Ashton United	v	Garforth Town	1-2	154		
Bamber Bridge	v	Prudhoe East End	4-0	275		
Banstead Athletic	v	Eastbourne United	2-1	31		
Basildon United	v	Tring Town	1-0	62		
Beckenham Town	v	Feltham & Hounslow Boro'	2-0	50		
Bedworth United	v	Walsall Wood	1-0	110		
Biggleswade Town	v	Barking	1-3	61		
(at Langford FC)						
Bilston Town	v	Newcastle Town	1-3	85		
Boston	v	Banbury United	4-1	109		
Bourne Town	v	Peterborough City	3-2	93		
Bradford Park Avenue	v	Burscough	1-1	142	2-1	146
(at Burscough FC)						
Brook House	v	Aveley	1-1	89	0-1	74
Burnham	v	Canvey Island	1-0	86		
(at Windsor & Eton FC)						
Canterbury City	v	Bracknell Town	4-1	65		
Chadderton	v	Lancaster City	2-1	173		
Chalfont St Peter	v	Hoddesdon Town	1-0	106		
Cheshunt	v	Spalding United	0-0	75	5-0	162
Chester-le-Street Town	v	Billingham Town	0-1	109		
Cinderford Town	v	Newbury Town	3-0	135		
Clevedon Town	v	Yate Town	4-1	346		
Clitheroe	v	Immingham Town	2-1	114		
Congleton Town	v	Eastwood Town	2-0	151		
Corinthian	v	Cove	1-0	26		
Crook Town	v	Norton & Stockton Ancients	0-3	36		

Home		Away	Res	Att.	Replay	
Croydon Athletic	v	Arundel	7-3	31		
Darlington CB	v	Consett	0-1	62		
Dawlish Town	v	Newport AFC	0-3	296		
Deal Town	v	Epsom & Ewell	3-0	260		
Denaby United	v	Heanor Town	2-5	111		
Dorking	v	Hythe Town	wo			
(Hythe Town withdrawn from competition)						
Easington Colliery	v	Shotton Comrades	2-1	28		
Eastleigh	v	Newport (IOW)	1-2	119		
East Thurrock United	v	Chipstead	1-0	127		
Eccleshill United	v	Harworth CI	3-2	60	3-1	29
Egham Town	v	Selsey	2-1	94		
Esh Winning	v	Alnwick Town	0-0	40	1-2	70
Exmouth Town	v	Elmore	1-2	131		
Eynesbury Rovers	v	Milton Keynes Borough	4-5	118		
Ferryhill Athletic	v	Spennymoor United	2-3	232		
Fisher Athletic	v	Brightlingsea United	2-1	114		
(at Brightlingsea United FC)						
Flackwell Heath	v	Walthamstow Pennant	2-0	50		
Fleet Town	v	Abingdon Town	1-2	82		
Flixton	v	Worksop Town	1-1	155	0-3	462
Forest Green Rovers	v	Barnstaple Town	4-2	145		
Formby	v	Bootle	1-2	90		
Gorleston	v	Clapton	5-2	139		
Gosport Borough	v	Calne Town	0-4	143		
Great Harwood Town	v	Prescot	2-1	87		
Gresley Rovers	v	Highgate United	4-2	441		
Hailsham Town	v	Steyning Town	3-1	300		
Halesowen Harriers	v	Wednesfield	2-2	110	3-2	115
Harefield United	v	Barkingside	0-1	16		
Haringey Borough	v	Bury Town	5-2	32		
Harrogate Town	v	Louth United	4-3	171		
Harwich & Parkeston	v	Leighton Town	3-3	205	0-2	525
Haywards Heath Town	v	Bedfont	0-1	101		
Hebburn	v	Annfield Plain	1-1	142	1-5	90
Herne Bay	v	Camberley Town	3-3	134	3-2†	76
Hinckley Town	v	Willenhall Town	1-1	67	2-1	110
Histon	v	Long Buckby	1-2	72		
Hitchin Town	v	Chatteris Town	3-1	276		
Horden CW	v	Darwen	1-1	39	0-5	131
Horsham YMCA	v	Eastbourne Town	4-3	67		
Hucknall Town	v	Grantham Town	2-1	481		
Ilfracombe Town	v	Truro City	3-4	160		
Ilkeston Town	v	Harrogate RA	7-0	585		
Irlam Town	v	Atherton LR	1-2	30		
Kingsbury Town	v	Oakwood	4-3	41		
Lancing	v	Littlehampton Town	2-3	185		

15

Home		Away	Res	Att.	Replay	
Leicester United	v	Dudley Town	3-0	132		
Letchworth Garden City	v	Haverhill Rovers	1-1	63	4-3†	106
Lewes	v	Leatherhead	1-0	132		
Leyton	v	Felixstowe Town	5-4	100		
Lye Town	v	Barwell	1-1	82	3-1	102
(at Dudley Town FC)						
March Town United	v	Braintree Town	1-3	252		
Melksham Town	v	Swanage Town & Herston	1-5	80		
Merstham	v	Malden Vale	0-0	60	1-3	124
Metropolitan Police	v	Ford United	0-0	50	2-0	80
Mickleover RBL	v	Belper Town	0-2	125		
Minehead	v	Lymington	2-2	120	1-2	134
Molesey	v	Northwood	3-1	80		
Nantwich Town	v	Maltby MW	1-1	140	3-2†	120
Newcastle Blue Star	v	Whickham	0-0	47	2-0	75
Newmarket Town	v	Langford	4-0	86		
Northallerton Town	v	Langley Park	6-1	88		
Northampton Spencer	v	Rushall Olympic	1-1	83	2-3†	108
Norwich United	v	Edgware Town	1-0	79		
Nuneaton Borough	v	Boldmere St Michaels	2-1	515		
Ossett Town	v	Dunston FB	1-2	132		
Oxford City	v	Devizes Town	2-3	93		
Paulton Rovers	v	Bristol Manor Farm	0-2	73		
Pelsall Villa	v	Oldbury United	0-0	352	4-4	209
					1-0†	465
Peterlee Newtown	v	Evenwood Town	1-0	42		
Petersfield United	v	Chippenham Town	0-1	70		
Poole Town	v	Abingdon United	0-1	145		
Portfield	v	Faversham Town	2-4	60		
Purfleet	v	Great Yarmouth Town	4-1	85		
Rainham Town	v	Mirrless Blackstone	2-0	98		
Raunds Town	v	Rocester	2-2	85	4-3	162
Rayners Lane	v	Ashford Town (Middx)	2-2	70	1-0	117
Redhill	v	Boreham Wood	1-5	115		
Royston Town	v	Potton United	1-2	143		
Ruislip Manor	v	Hornchurch	1-0	141		
Rushden & Diamonds	v	Desborough Town	2-0	301		
Ryde Sports	v	Southwick	1-2	104		
Salford City	v	North Ferriby United	0-1	69		
Sandwell Borough	v	Malvern Town	4-0	18		
Sheffield	v	Rossendale United	2-2	247	2-1†	247
(at Rossendale United FC)						
Sheppey United	v	Croydon	0-1	77		
Shildon	v	Blackpool (wren) Rovers	2-0	107		
Sholing Sports	v	Bemerton Heath Harlequins	1-2	65		
Shoreham	v	Witney Town	0-3	70		
Shortwood United	v	Brockenhurst	0-4	75		

Home		Away	Res	Att.	Replay	
South Bank	v	Bedlington Terriers	5-0	46		
St Blazey	v	Falmouth Town	1-4	190		
St Helens Town	v	Tow Law Town	3-2	64		
Stewart & Lloyds	v	Evesham United	4-2	47		
Stourport Swifts	v	Stourbridge	0-5	273		
Stratford Town	v	Hinckley Athletic	6-2	142		
Sutton Coldfield Town	v	West Bromwich Town	0-0	164	2-0	70
Sudbury Town	v	Saffron Walden Town	6-1	416		
Taunton Town	v	Barri	0-3	252		
Thackley	v	Radcliffe Borough	2-1	81		
Three Bridges	v	Alma Swanley	0-3	111		
Tilbury	v	Collier Row	3-2	60		
Torrington	v	Bideford	1-0	220		
Totton	v	Havant Town	0-1	101		
Tunbridge Wells	v	Margate	0-4	251		
Uxbridge	v	Southall	4-2	136		
Viking Sports	v	Bishops Stortford	0-1	140		
Ware	v	Stowmarket Town	1-2	91		
Warrington Town	v	Skelmersdale United	6-1	145		
Waltham Abbey	v	Halstead Town	1-1	100	4-3	140
(at Halstead Town FC)						
Walton & Hersham	v	Peacehaven & Telscombe	2-1	132		
Washington	v	Stockton	1-3	29		
(at Stockton FC)						
Watton United	v	Burnham Ramblers	1-0	88		
Wealdstone	v	Tiptree United	2-1	379		
Welton Rovers	v	Hungerford Town	4-1	81		
Wembley	v	Welwyn Garden City	5-0	74		
Westbury United	v	Thatcham Town	0-5	121		
West Midlands Police	v	Bridgnorth Town	5-2	76		
Whitehawk	v	Chichester City	5-2†	71	3-1	100
(Replay ordered)						
Whitstable Town	v	Sittingbourne	1-2	391		
Whyteleafe	v	Pagham	5-1	88		
Wick	v	Ashford Town	1-1	150	1-3	246
Willington	v	Whitby Town	1-5	52		
Wimborne Town	v	Bournemouth	1-1	427	3-1	368
Wisbech Town	v	Wellingborough Town	10-0	403		
Witham Town	v	Wingate & Finchley	4-3	118		
Workington	v	West Auckland Town	3-2	161		
Worthing	v	Chatham Town	8-0	190		
Worthing United	v	Langney Sports	1-4	75		
Yorkshire Amateur	v	Seaham Red Star	1-3	84		

17

First Qualifying Round – 12 September 1992

Home		Away	Res	Att.	Replay	
Abingdon Town	v	Devizes Town	4-0	145		
Abingdon United	v	Bemerton Heath Harlequins	0-5	42		
Alfreton Town	v	Stafford Rangers	0-0	381	0-3	750
Alma Swanley	v	Bedfont	1-0	70		
Alnwick Town	v	Consett	0-0	52	0-2	72
Altrincham	v	Curzon Ashton	3-0	594		
Andover	v	Hampton	0-6	170		
Annfield Plain	v	Newcastle Blue Star	0-1	96		
Arlesey Town	v	Shepshed Albion	0-1	118		
Armthorpe Welfare	v	Billingham Town	2-2	66	0-2	128
Ashford Town	v	Faversham Town	1-1	311	2-0	391
Atherton LR	v	Great Harwood Town	1-1	150	2-1	117
Bamber Bridge	v	Peterlee Newtown	1-1	380	2-0	101
Banstead Athletic	v	Herne Bay	4-1	56		
Barri	v	Clevedon Town	1-3	180		
Barton Rovers	v	Moor Green	2-3	141		
Barkingside	v	Wembley	1-3	95		
Blakenall	v	Droylsden	4-3	143		
Bognor Regis Town	v	Romsey Town	9-2	240		
Boreham Wood	v	Chesham United	2-2	272	1-9	454
Boston	v	Stourbridge	3-4	45		
Boston United	v	Kings Lynn	2-1	1013		
Bourne Town	v	Milton Keynes Borough	3-2	119		
Bradford Park Avenue	v	Belper Town	2-0	161		
Brigg Town	v	Bridlington Town	2-1	151		
Brockenhurst	v	Basingstoke Town	1-0	302		
Buckingham Town	v	Maidenhead United	1-1	181	1-2†	187
Burgess Hill Town	v	Hastings Town	0-2	306		
Burnham	v	Bishops Stortford	3-2	128		
Caernarfon Town	v	Colwyn Bay	1-4	116		
Carshalton Athletic	v	Erith & Belvedere	1-2	227		
Chadderton	v	Bootle	3-0	130		
Chasetown	v	Redditch United	1-0	110		
Chelmsford City	v	Grays Athletic	0-0	761	1-2	454
Chertsey Town	v	Gravesend & Northfleet	3-2	287		
Cheshunt	v	Chalfont St Peter	1-0	80		
Chippenham Town	v	Thatcham Town	1-2	128		
Chorley	v	Knowsley United	1-1	232	1-2	133
Clitheroe	v	Hucknall Town	1-3	240		
Congleton Town	v	Nantwich Town	0-0	190	1-2	283
Corinthian Casuals	v	Slough Town	1-1	264	3-4	518
Croydon	v	Canterbury City	0-0	25	1-2	75
			0-4	136		
Croydon Athletic	v	Dorking	1-2	64		
Dagenham & Redbridge	v	Billericay Town	1-1	963	4-1	1018

Home		Away	Res	Att.	Replay	
Dartford	v	Horsham	wo			
(Walkover for Horsham, Dartford withdrawn from Competition)						
Darwen	v	Northallerton Town	1-6	182		
Deal Town	v	Malden Vale	4-0	215		
Dunston FB	v	Norton & Stockton Ancients	7-0	68		
Durham City	v	Bishop Auckland	1-1	301	2-5	236
Easington Colliery	v	Workington	1-1	53	0-1	239
Egham Town	v	Worthing	1-1	140	1-7	276
Falmouth Town	v	Elmore	2-0	281		
Fareham Town	v	Tooting & Mitcham United	2-0	170		
Fisher Athletic	v	Stevenage Borough	1-7	569		
(at Stevenage Borough FC)						
Flackwell Heath	v	Stowmarket Town	0-5	68		
Fleetwood Town	v	Guiseley	3-2	288		
Forest Green Rovers	v	Newport AFC	1-2	419		
Frickley Athletic	v	Lincoln United	0-0	229	1-0	334
Frome Town	v	Worcester City	1-2	158		
Gateshead	v	Billingham Synthonia	3-1	173		
Glastonbury	v	Bath City	0-4	422		
Glossop North End	v	Macclesfield Town	0-1	815		
Gloucester City	v	Weston-super-Mare	2-3	509		
Goole Town	v	Horwich RMI	0-1	163		
Hailsham Town	v	Bromley	2-3	487		
Halesowen Harriers	v	Lye Town	2-1	190		
Haringey Borough	v	Gorleston	0-0	30	0-1	266
Harrogate Town	v	Warrington Town	1-2	227		
Harrow Borough	v	Berkhamsted Town	0-2	261		
Havant Town	v	Horsham YMCA	2-1	154		
Heanor Town	v	Ilkeston Town	2-1	658		
Hednesford Town	v	Tamworth	1-1	1277	4-2	1347
Hemel Hempstead	v	Solihull Borough	1-2	88		
Hertford Town	v	Hendon	0-2	188		
(at Windsor & Eton FC)						
Heybridge Swifts	v	Cambridge City	2-4	132		
Hitchin Town	v	Wisbech Town	4-2	370		
Hyde United	v	Accrington Stanley	1-5	333		
Kempston Rovers	v	Wivenhoe Town	3-4	128		
Kingsbury Town	v	Beckenham Town	2-3	65		
Kingstonian	v	Dulwich Hamlet	4-0	535		
Langney Sports	v	Littlehampton Town	3-1	176		
Leek Town	v	Burton Albion	3-2	636		
Leighton Town	v	Aveley	2-4	463		
Letchworth Garden City	v	Braintree Town	0-4	126		
Leyton	v	Lowestoft Town	4-2	128		
Long Buckby	v	Rushden & Diamonds	0-1	105		
Lymington	v	Bristol Manor Farm	3-3†	88	2-0	80
(Replay at Keynsham Town FC)						

19

Home		Away	Res	Att.	Replay	
Maine Road	v	Morecambe	2-1	108		
Mangotsfield United	v	Dorchester Town	0-1	147		
Margate	v	Corinthian	0-0	540	1-1	137
Marine	v	Emley	5-0	341		
Metropolitan Police	v	Lewes	2-1	75		
Molesey	v	East Thurrock United	4-2	63		
Mossley	v	Borrowash Victoria	0-0	240	1-0	130
Murton	v	Guisborough Town	1-2	60		
Newcastle Town	v	Gresley Rovers	0-1	315		
Newport (IOW)	v	Wimborne Town	2-3	296		
North Ferriby United	v	Garforth Town	1-0	146		
Northwich Victoria	v	Winsford United	4-1	1154		
Norwich United	v	Barking	2-1	96		
Nuneaton Borough	v	Leicester United	3-1	742		
Ossett Albion	v	Netherfield	1-3	99		
Paget Rangers	v	Gainsborough Trinity	1-3	124		
Pelsall Villa	v	Willenhall Town	1-0	347		
Penrith	v	Blyth Spartans	1-2	185		
Purfleet	v	Watton United	6-1	73		
Racing Club Warwick	v	Eastwood Hanley	0-2	108		
Rainham Town	v	Corby Town	0-1	130		
Raunds Town	v	Stratford Town	0-0	83	2-1	164
Rayners Lane	v	Uxbridge	1-1	122	1-0	156
Rothwell Town	v	Matlock Town	0-2	157		
Ruislip Manor	v	Basildon United	3-1	159		
Rushall Olympic	v	Sandwell Borough	3-0	80		
Salisbury	v	Trowbridge Town	6-2	425		
Seaham Red Star	v	Eccleshill United	3-2	110		
Sheffield	v	Thackley	3-1	120		
(at Thackley FC)						
Shildon	v	Whitby Town	0-2	157		
Slade Green	v	Harlow Town	wo			
(Harlow Town withdrawn from competition)						
South Bank	v	North Shields	wo			
(North Shields withdrawn from competition)						
Southport	v	Buxton	0-0	432	2-1	316
Southwick	v	Witney Town	2-5	55		
Spennymoor United	v	Gretna	4-0	181		
St Albans City	v	Brimsdown Rovers	3-1	440		
St Helens Town	v	Stockton	3-4	79		
Staines Town	v	Yeading	0-3	239		
Stewart & Lloyds	v	Sutton Coldfield Town	1-3	58		
Stocksbridge Park Steels	v	Stalybridge Celtic	0-4	501		
Sudbury Town	v	Potton United	3-2	430		
Swanage Tn & Herston	v	Cinderford Town	1-2	120		
Thame United	v	Bashley	2-3	119		

Home		Away	Res	Att.	Replay	
Tilbury	v	Newmarket Town	1-1	73	0-1	173
Tonbridge	v	Dover Athletic	0-0	1012	1-2†	1127
Truro City	v	Torrington	2-0	151		
VS Rugby	v	Alvechurch	wo			
(Alvechurch withdrawn from competition)						
Waltham Abbey	v	Baldock Town	2-3	178		
(at Baldock Town FC)						
Walton & Hersham	v	Wokingham Town	2-0	216		
Waterlooville	v	Cheltenham Town	0-0	204	0-2	541
Wealdstone	v	Witham Town	2-1	355		
Welton Rovers	v	Calne Town	1-4	63		
West Midlands Police	v	Bedworth United	1-2	114		
Weymouth	v	Saltash United	1-0	750		
Whitehawk	v	Sittingbourne	0-1	123		
Whyteleafe	v	Windsor & Eton	1-3	137		
Worksop Town	v	Arnold Town	5-3	448		

Second Qualifying Round – 26 September 1992

Home		Away	Res	Att.	Replay	
Abingdon Town	v	Maidenhead United	2-0	241		
Accrington Stanley	v	Bradford Park Avenue	2-0	707		
Altrincham	v	Sheffield	3-1	578		
Ashford Town	v	Windsor & Eton	2-2	325	3-2	234
Atherton LR	v	Colwyn Bay	1-2	300		
Bamber Bridge	v	Spennymoor United	0-4	590		
Bashley	v	Wimborne Town	3-1	826		
Bedworth United	v	Stafford Rangers	1-1	301	0-1	762
Berkhamsted Town	v	Beckenham Town	0-0	162	1-0	126
Blyth Spartans	v	Workington	6-0	409		
Bognor Regis Town	v	Bemerton Heath Harlequins	1-1	245	2-2	291
			1-1	386	0-1	429
Boston United	v	Aveley	1-2	882		
Bourne Town	v	Moor Green	4-8	210		
Calne Town	v	Brockenhurst	0-1	103		
Cambridge City	v	Norwich United	6-1	311		
Chasetown	v	Braintree Town	0-2	181		
Cheltenham Town	v	Cinderford Town	3-0	752		
Cheshunt	v	Solihull Borough	0-0	115	0-4	125
Consett	v	Netherfield	1-1	91	3-4	106
(abandoned after 58 minutes due to fog, replay at Consett)						
Dagenham & Redbridge	v	Stowmarket Town	6-1	868		
Dorking	v	Walton & Hersham	4-2	253		
Dover Athletic	v	Banstead Athletic	0-0	928	2-1	370
Dunston FB	v	South Bank	2-0	79		
Erith & Belvedere	v	Havant Town	1-1	245	4-5	240
Falmouth Town	v	Bath City	0-3	703		

Home		Away	Res	Att.	Replay	
Fleetwood Town	v	Northallerton Town	1-2	239		
Frickley Athletic	v	Halesowen Harriers	8-2	263		
Gateshead	v	Whitby Town	5-2	237		
Gorleston	v	Leyton	1-2	184		
Grays Athletic	v	Sudbury Town	1-0	398		
Gresley Rovers	v	Gainsborough Trinity	1-4	748		
Guisborough Town	v	Billingham Town	3-0	154		
Hastings Town	v	Canterbury City	1-2	419		
Hednesford Town	v	Rushden & Diamonds	4-1	685		
Hendon	v	Burnham	6-0	338		
Horsham	v	Deal Town	1-6	275		
Horwich RMI	v	Worksop Town	1-1	147	5-1	475
Hucknall Town	v	Macclesfield Town	1-1	1305	1-3	635
Kingstonian	v	Langney Sports	2-2	431	1-1	590
			3-1†	542		
Knowsley United	v	Stockton	0-2	100		
Leek Town	v	Rushall Olympic	0-1	418		
Lymington	v	Dorchester Town	1-1	216	4-2	502
Margate	v	Chertsey Town	1-4	565		
Marine	v	Heanor Town	2-0	306		
Metropolitan Police	v	Slough Town	0-1	340		
Molesey	v	Chesham United	0-4	222		
Mossley	v	Pelsall Villa	1-2	290		
Nantwich Town	v	Blakenall	1-0	269		
Newcastle Blue Star	v	Bishop Auckland	0-1	132		
Newmarket Town	v	Baldock Town	2-2	196	6-2	278
Newport AFC	v	Worcester City	3-0	685		
North Ferriby United	v	Brigg Town	0-2	235		
Northwich Victoria	v	Raunds Town	0-2	685		
Nuneaton Borough	v	Matlock Town	2-1	846		
Purfleet	v	Corby Town	2-2	155	0-1	261
Ruislip Manor	v	Stevenage Borough	1-3	437		
Salisbury	v	Thatcham Town	4-0	288		
Seaham Red Star	v	Maine Road	1-1	118	1-1	143
			0-5	251		
Southport	v	Chadderton	2-0	542		
Sittingbourne	v	Fareham Town	3-2	568		
St Albans City	v	Rayners Lane	5-1	681		
Stourbridge	v	Shepshed Albion	0-0	272	2-4	272
Sutton Coldfield Town	v	Eastwood Hanley	2-1	156		
VS Rugby	v	Hitchin Town	3-0	470		
Warrington Town	v	Stalybridge Celtic	0-3	638		
Wealdstone	v	Wivenhoe Town	1-1	356	2-0	302
Wembley	v	Slade Green	3-2	92		
Weston-super-Mare	v	Clevedon Town	0-4	695		
Weymouth	v	Truro City	3-2	846		
Witney Town	v	Hampton	3-1	261		

Home		Away	Res	Att.	Replay	
Worthing	v	Bromley	2-1	267		
Yeading	v	Alma Swanley	7-1	142		

Third Qualifying Round – 10 October 1992

Home		Away	Res	Att.	Replay	
Alvechurch	v	Corby Town	2-0	217		
Abingdon Town	v	Bashley	4-2	274		
Ashford Town	v	Deal Town	3-1	606		
Bath City	v	Weymouth	2-0	890		
Bishop Auckland	v	Blyth Spartans	1-3	503		
Brigg Town	v	Southport	0-1	324		
Brockenhurst	v	Salisbury	1-3	451		
Chertsey Town	v	Kingstonian	1-3	858		
Chesham United	v	Berkhamsted Town	3-0	764		
Colwyn Bay	v	Altrincham	3-3	601	1-1†	784
(Second replay at Altrincham)			1-3	805		
Corby Town	v	Aveley	4-1	321		
Dorking	v	Dover Athletic	1-0	559		
Dunston FB	v	Northallerton Town	0-3	165		
Gainsborough Trinity	v	Pelsall Villa	4-2	289		
Leyton	v	Cambridge City	3-0	303		
Lymington	v	Cheltenham Town	0-1	358		
Macclesfield Town	v	Horwich RMI	1-0	789		
Moor Green	v	VS Rugby	1-2	428		
Nantwich Town	v	Marine	0-1	382		
Netherfield	v	Guisborough Town	4-1	199		
Newmarket Town	v	Grays Athletic	1-0	350		
Newport AFC	v	Clevedon Town	1-1	723	1-1†	940
(Second Replay)			4-2	599		
Nuneaton Borough	v	Raunds Town	4-0	1206		
Seaham Red Star	v	Stockton	1-2	195		
Shepshed Albion	v	Hednesford Town	1-2	404		
Sittingbourne	v	Havant Town	3-2	682		
Slough Town	v	Yeading	2-1	930		
Solihull Borough	v	Braintree Town	4-1	291		
Spennymoor United	v	Gateshead	0-7	647		
Stafford Rangers	v	Frickley Athletic	3-0	814		
Stalybridge Celtic	v	Accrington Stanley	1-2	1323		
Stevenage Borough	v	St Albans City	3-3	1561	1-2	1781
Sutton Coldfield Town	v	Rushall Olympic	0-0	255	1-1†	280
(Second replay at Rushall)			2-1	323		
Wealdstone	v	Dagenham & Redbridge	1-6	823		
Wembley	v	Hendon	1-0	421		
Witney Town	v	Bemerton Heath Harlequins	1-0	215		
Worthing	v	Canterbury City	3-1	371		

Fourth Qualifying Round – 24 October 1992

Home		Away	Res	Att.	Replay	
Abingdon Town	v	Merthyr Tydfil	0-0	893	1-2	868
Accrington Stanley	v	Northallerton Town	3-1	1159		
Ashford Town	v	Slough Town	1-2	1051		
Barrow	v	Southport	0-0	1545	2-3†	2082
Blyth Spartans	v	Stockton	1-1	495	2-1	548
Cheltenham Town	v	Worthing	3-2	891		
Crawley Town	v	Yeovil Town	1-2	1898		
Enfield	v	Aylesbury United	0-0	942	1-2	1768
Farnborough Town	v	Dorking	1-1	1023	0-2	1207
Gainsborough Trinity	v	Altrincham	0-2	805		
Gateshead	v	Whitley Bay	3-0	652		
Halesowen Town	v	VS Rugby	1-2	1115		
Hednesford Town	v	Dagenham & Redbridge	1-3	1311		
Kettering Town	v	Corby Town	2-1	3273		
Kidderminster Harriers	v	Atherstone United	2-0	1139		
Kingstonian	v	Welling United	2-1	861		
Netherfield	v	Macclesfield Town	1-1	918	0-5	903
Newmarket Town	v	Hayes	0-2	651		
Newport AFC	v	Sutton United	1-4	810		
Runcorn	v	Marine	1-4	749		
Sittingbourne	v	Marlow	1-1	1259	1-2	701
Solihull Borough	v	Chesham United	3-1	618		
Stafford Rangers	v	Bromsgrove Rovers	3-0	1274		
Sutton Coldfield Town	v	Leyton	6-1	258		
Telford United	v	St Albans City	1-2	1132		
Tiverton Town	v	Bath City	0-0	976	1-2	869
Wembley	v	Nuneaton Borough	1-1	828	0-0†	2512
(Second replay)			1-2	551		
Witney Town	v	Salisbury	1-2	544		

First Round Proper – 14 November 1992

Home		Away	Res	Att.	Replay	
Accrington Stanley	v	Gateshead	3-2	2270		
Blyth Spartans	v	Southport	1-2	2206		
Bolton Wanderers	v	Sutton Coldfield Town	2-1	5345		
Brighton & Hove Albion	v	Hayes	2-0	5879		
Bury	v	Witton Albion	2-0	2682		
Cardiff City	v	Bath City	2-3	4506		
Chester City	v	Altrincham	1-1	4033	0-2	3000
Colchester United	v	Slough Town	4-0	3858		
Dagenham & Redbridge	v	Leyton Orient	4-5	5300		
Dorking	v	Plymouth Argyle	2-3	3200		
Exeter City	v	Kidderminster Harriers	1-0	3082		
Gillingham	v	Kettering Town	3-2	3962		

Home		Away	Res	Att.	Replay	
Lincoln City	v	Stafford Rangers	0-0	3380	1-2	2209
Kingstonian	v	Peterborough United	1-1	3826	1-9	5307
(Second replay at Peterborough behind closed doors)			1-0	–		
Macclesfield Town	v	Chesterfield	0-0	3063	2-2†	4143
(Macclesfield Town won replay 3-2 on penalties)						
Marine	v	Halifax Town	4-1	1892		
Marlow	v	Salisbury	3-3	940	2-2†	1854
(Marlow won replay 4-3 on penalties)						
St Albans City	v	Cheltenham Town	1-2	3189		
Solihull Borough	v	VS Rugby	2-2	1395	1-2†	1289
Sutton United	v	Hereford United	1-2	2749		
Torquay United	v	Yeovil Town	2-5	3453		
West Bromwich Albion	v	Aylesbury United	8-0	12337		
Woking	v	Nuneaton Borough	3-2	3280		
Wycombe Wanderers	v	Merthyr Tydfil	3-1	4322		

Second Round Proper – 5 December 1992

Home		Away	Res	Att.	Replay	
Accrington Stanley	v	Crewe Alexandra	1-6	10801		
(at Blackburn Rovers FC)						
Altrincham	v	Port Vale	1-4	3859		
Bath City	v	Northampton Town	2-2	3626	0-3	4106
Brighton & Hove Albion	v	Woking	1-1	9208	2-1	5870
Cheltenham Town	v	AFC Bournemouth	1-1	4100	0-3	4879
Hartlepool United	v	Southport	4-0	4171		
Macclesfield Town	v	Stockport County	0-2	5583		
Marine	v	Stafford Rangers	3-2	1965		
VS Rugby	v	Marlow	0-0	2258	0-2	1904
Wycombe Wanderers	v	West Bromwich Albion	2-2	6904	1-0	17183
Yeovil Town	v	Hereford United	0-0	8085	2-1	6051

Third Round Proper – 2 January 1993

Home		Away	Res	Att.	Replay
Crewe Alexandra	v	Marine	3-1	4036	
Marlow	v	Tottenham Hotspur	1-5	26636	
(at Tottenham Hotspur)					
Yeovil Town	v	Arsenal	1-3	8612	

† after extra time

VAUXHALL FA TROPHY 1992-93

Wycombe Wonders

From the moment that right-back Jason Cousins bludgeoned home a 20-yard free-kick in only the second minute of the contest, there seemed little doubt that the Vauxhall FA Trophy would end up in the Wycombe Wanderers' trophy cabinet, nestling comfortably alongside the Championship trophy to cap a wonderful season for Martin O'Neill's side.

In the final analysis the runaway winners of the Conference had just that bit more class than their worthy Runcorn opponents who, despite losing 4-1, gave the favourites some torrid moments in an entertaining clash.

Proof, if ever it were needed of O'Neill's masterful managerial style, lies in the very manner of Wycombe's victory, courtesy of three set pieces and a fortunate late effort from Dave Carroll.

Having caught Runcorn by surprise with Cousins' excellently executed free-kick, the Chairboys made it 2-0 after 21 minutes when defender Andy Kerr, one of seven players in the Wycombe side who had played against Kidderminster in the Trophy winning team of 1991, headed home a Carroll corner from eight yards.

Runcorn made a fight of it, pulling a goal back just before half-time with a brilliantly taken effort by Steve Shaughnessy and for the first 15 minutes of the second half, John Carroll's side looked capable of producing an equaliser.

But Wycombe struck the killer blow on 60 minutes when Steve Thompson, who had an outstanding match for the Blues, headed home another dangerous Carroll corner to make it 3-1.

Despite the efforts of Linnets' striker Ken McKenna, who had a header which rattled the woodwork and rolled tantalisingly along the line, and the intervention of two second-half streakers, Wycombe made the game safe in injury time when the hard-working Carroll scored a fourth goal after an error by Runcorn keeper Arthur Williams.

As the final whistle sounded the crowd of 32,968 – just short of 1991's record attendance of 34,842 – rose to salute both teams for their part in what had proved to be yet another great advert for Non-League Football.

Lke Colchester the year before, who bid farewell to the Conference with the League and Trophy double, the glory and the honours almost inevitably belonged to the amiable O'Neill who became only the third manager to complete the double and only the third to win the FA Trophy twice.

"I've had a wonderful time at Wycombe Wanderers. Don't forget that when I first came to the club my one ambition was always to manage a league club and I've done that now because Wycombe are in Division Three. I've got a great squad here and my players have given everything for me. We've won the league and the Trophy in style and I'm delighted for the fans." *Sue Thearle*

First Qualifying Round – 19 September 1992

Home		Away	Res	Att.	Replay	
Accrington Stanley	v	Whitley Bay	3-1	419		
Alfreton Town	v	Eastwood Town	2-4	205		
Alvechurch	v	Halesowen Town	wo			
(Walkover for Halesowen Town, Alvechurch withdrawn from competition)						
Andover	v	Abingdon Town	0-3	149		
Ashford Town	v	Yeading	0-0	276	2-5	151
Baldock Town	v	Barking	4-3	175		
Barri	v	Bideford	2-1	205		
(at Bideford FC)						
Boreham Wood	v	Aveley	3-1	71		
Carshalton Athletic	v	Crawley Town	1-2	427		
Chelmsford City	v	Hendon	1-3	651		
Chorley	v	Newcastle Blue Star	2-2	175	1-3	79
Congleton Town	v	Grantham Town	4-2	109		
Corby Town	v	Billericay Town	1-4	235		
Croydon	v	Dulwich Hamlet	0-1	180		
Dorchester Town	v	Waterlooville	3-1	325		
Droylsden	v	Winsford United	0-2	256		
Fareham Town	v	Margate	2-2	125	0-1	350
Gainsborough Trinity	v	Solihull Borough	1-1	270	4-4	142
(Second replay at Solihull)			4-0	168		
Hayes	v	Tamworth	6-1	243		
Heybridge Swifts	v	Cambridge City	2-1	129		
Hitchin Town	v	Bishops Stortford	3-1	371		
Leicester United	v	Worksop Town	1-1	149	5-1	310
Marlow	v	Lewes	3-2	170		
Molesey	v	Basingstoke Town	1-3	130		
Moor Green	v	Colwyn Bay	1-1	259	2-4†	152
Mossley	v	Dudley Town	6-2	173		
North Shields	v	Easington Colliery	wo			
(Walkover for Easington Colliery, North Shields withdrawn from competition)						
Peterlee Newtown	v	Guiseley	2-1	97		
Redditch United	v	Caernarfon Town	0-3	103		
Saltash United	v	Trowbridge Town	2-5	178		
Shepshed Albion	v	Bedworth United	1-0	174		
Spennymoor United	v	Brandon United	4-3	197		
Staines Town	v	Leyton	1-2	237		
Stevenage Borough	v	Harlow Town	wo			
(Harlow Town withdrawn from competition)						
Tooting & Mitcham Utd	v	Walton & Hersham	0-1	147		
Uxbridge	v	Bognor Regis Town	3-2	130		
Weymouth	v	Newport AFC	2-2	922	1-2	397
Whyteleafe	v	Hastings Town	2-2	195	1-1	306
(Second replay at Hastings)			0-3	340		

Second Qualifying Round – 17 October 1992

Home		Away	Res	Att.	Replay	
Abingdon Town	v	Marlow	2-1	211		
Accrington Stanley	v	Easington Colliery	5-0	473		
Baldock Town	v	Heybridge Swifts	0-1	215		
Barri	v	Weston-super-Mare	0-2	110		
Basingstoke Town	v	Crawley Town	2-0	415		
Billericay Town	v	Stourbridge	3-4	403		
Caernarfon Town	v	Goole Town	1-4	33		
Colwyn Bay	v	Solihull Borough	0-1	149		
Dorchester Town	v	Poole Town	1-2	371		
Fisher Athletic	v	Canterbury City	2-2	101	1-3	56
Hednesford Town	v	Halesowen Town	1-2	685		
Hendon	v	Grays Athletic	0-0	203	1-2†	178
Leicester United	v	Matlock Town	3-1	207		
Margate	v	Hastings Town	1-3	435		
Mossley	v	Eastwood Town	3-1	220		
Nuneaton Borough	v	Congleton Town	3-1	794		
Peterlee Newtown	v	Shildon	1-1	42	0-2	78
Purfleet	v	Boreham Wood	3-2	103		
Seaham Red Star	v	Spennymoor United	2-4	225		
St Albans City	v	Hayes	3-2	566		
Stevenage Borough	v	Chalfont St Peter	2-1	415		
Stockton	v	Ferryhill Athletic	10-2	33		
Sutton Coldfield Town	v	Leyton	2-1	191		
Trowbridge Town	v	Newport AFC	0-1	565		
Uxbridge	v	Dulwich Hamlet	0-2	202		
Walton & Hersham	v	Gravesend & Northfleet	2-0	196		
Warrington Town	v	Shepshed Albion	3-0	138		
Wembley	v	Hitchin Town	3-1	89		
West Auckland Town	v	Consett	1-1	56	2-2†	56
(Second replay at Consett)			1-1†	98	0-3	40
Winsford United	v	Buxton	0-0	419	3-0	468
Workington	v	Newcastle Blue Star	0-2	165		
Yeading	v	Maidenhead United	2-2	146	3-1	124

Third Qualifying Round – 28 November 1992

Home		Away	Res	Att.	Replay	
Abingdon Town	v	Dorking	2-1	188		
Accrington Stanley	v	Tow Law Town	6-0	511		
Basingstoke Town	v	Dulwich Hamlet	3-0	301		
Billingham Synthonia	v	Consett	1-1	106	6-2	82
Chesham United	v	Leicester United	7-3	391		
Emley	v	Spennymoor United	2-6	379		
Fleetwood Town	v	Blyth Spartans	1-3	240		
Goole Town	v	Bishop Auckland	0-1	238		
Grays Athletic	v	Atherstone United	2-1	248		

Home		Away	Res	Att.	Replay	
Guisborough Town	v	Shildon	2-0	168		
Harrow Borough	v	Stevenage Borough	2-2	445	0-4	361
Hastings Town	v	Wokingham Town	2-1	403		
Heybridge Swifts	v	Halesowen Town	1-0	321		
Horwich RMI	v	Winsford United	1-2	176		
Kingstonian	v	Canterbury City	5-0	375		
Morecambe	v	Southport	2-2	948		
Mossley	v	Frickley Athletic	2-4	196		
Newport AFC	v	Sutton United	1-2	400		
Northallerton Town	v	Newcastle Blue Star	2-1	81		
Nuneaton Borough	v	Burton Albion	0-0	1019	3-0	633
Poole Town	v	Bashley	1-1	402	2-2†	219
(Second replay at Poole Town)			2-4	279		
Slough Town	v	Bromley	3-1	860		
Southport	v	Morecambe	1-3	878		
St Albans City	v	Purfleet	2-0	471		
Stafford Rangers	v	Wembley	1-1	612	1-0	111
Stourbridge	v	Leek Town	1-4	245		
Sutton Coldfield Town	v	VS Rugby	1-1	263	4-5†	204
Warrington Town	v	Stockton	5-2	193		
Wealdstone	v	Solihull Borough	5-2	295		
Weston-super-Mare	v	Windsor & Eton	1-0	454		
Whitby Town	v	South Bank	2-1	281		
Worcester City	v	Salisbury	2-1	650		
Yeading	v	Walton & Hersham	3-1	231		

First Round Proper – 9 January 1993

Home		Away	Res	Att.	Replay	
Barrow	v	Billingham Synthonia	0-1	1203		
Basingstoke Town	v	Kingstonian	1-4	521		
Bishop Auckland	v	Leek Town	1-0	259		
Dover Athletic	v	Hastings Town	1-1	1129	2-0	611
Farnborough Town	v	Abingdon Town	4-0	690		
Gateshead	v	Gretna	3-0	336		
Gloucester City	bye					
Grays Athletic	v	Stafford Rangers	1-0	421		
Heybridge Swifts	v	Worcester City	4-0	328		
Hyde United	v	Runcorn	1-2	425		
Kettering Town	v	Bromsgrove Rovers	0-0	1723	1-4	1269
Kidderminster Harriers	v	Enfield	1-3	1280		
Macclesfield Town	v	Witton Albion	0-0	890	0-0	901
(Second replay at Witton Albion)			1-2	907		
Marine	v	Blyth Spartans	2-0	406		
Merthyr Tydfil	v	Wivenhoe Town	3-0	653		
Morecambe	v	Frickley Athletic	5-1	588		
Murton	v	Nuneaton Borough	1-2	253		

Home		Away	Res	Att.	Replay	
Northallerton Town	v	Whitby Town	3-0	255		
Spennymoor United	v	Boston United	1-2	431		
St Albans City	v	Weston-super-Mare	1-0	730		
Stalybridge Celtic	v	Accrington Stanley	2-0	963		
Stevenage Borough	v	Bath City	2-0	907		
Sutton United	v	Woking	3-0	1884		
Telford United	v	Northwich Victoria	2-1	1211		
VS Rugby	v	Chesham United	1-6	564		
Warrington Town	v	Guisborough Town	2-1	248		
Wealdstone	v	Bashley	1-2	274		
Welling United	v	Aylesbury United	2-1	743		
Winsford United	v	Altrincham	1-0	727		
Wycombe Wanderers	v	Cheltenham Town	3-1	3964		
Yeading	v	Slough Town	1-1	561	1-2	755
Yeovil Town	v	Dagenham & Redbridge	0-0	2973	1-2	1171

Second Round Proper – 30 January 1993

Home		Away	Res	Att.	Replay	
Billingham Synthonia	v	Winsford United	1-2	338		
Bishop Auckland	v	Warrington Town	0-1	323		
Bromsgrove Rovers	v	Dagenham & Redbridge	3-1	1711		
Chesham United	v	Dover Athletic	1-0	2055		
Farnborough Town	v	Enfield	4-0	1130		
Gateshead	v	Heybridge Swifts	3-1	367		
Gloucester City	v	Runcorn	3-3	577	2-2	618
(Second replay at Gloucester)			0-0	771	1-4	701
Kingstonian	v	Telford United	1-2	809		
Morecambe	v	Wycombe Wanderers	1-1	2196	0-2	4490
Northallerton Town	v	Bashley	1-0	317		
Nuneaton Borough	v	Marine	0-1	1165		
St Albans City	v	Witton Albion	0-2	1470		
Stalybridge Celtic	v	Merthyr Tydfil	1-1	818	0-1	704
Stevenage Borough	v	Grays Athletic	0-1	893		
Sutton United	v	Slough Town	3-1	1374		
Welling United	v	Boston United	1-2	1012		

Third Round Proper – 20 February 1993

Home		Away	Res	Att.	Replay	
Chesham United	v	Sutton United	1-3	1516		
Grays Athletic	v	Gateshead	1-1	1013	0-3	402
Merthyr Tydfil	v	Warrington Town	1-1	556	2-3†	1447
Northallerton Town	v	Farnborough Town	1-3	671		
Runcorn	v	Winsford United	1-0	1276		
Telford United	v	Boston United	1-1	1408	0-4	1626
Witton Albion	v	Marine	1-0	1171		
Wycombe Wanderers	v	Bromsgrove Rovers	2-0	4907		

Fourth Round Proper – 13 March 1993

Home		Away	Res	Att.
Boston United	v	Runcorn	0-2	2639
		Parker (51), Anderson (66 pen)		
Sutton United	v	Warrington Town	2-1	1547
Gates (47), Burn (58 pen)		Dunn (45)		
Witton Albion	v	Farnborough Town	3-2	1262
Thomas (24, 25), Burke (68)		Leworthy (17), Baker (85 pen)		
Wycombe Wanderers	v	Gateshead	1-0	4795
Guppy (90)				

Semi-Finals 1st Leg – 3 April 1993

Home		Away	Res	Att.
Runcorn	v	Witton Albion	2-0	1610
McKenna (73), Anderson (81)				
Wycombe Wanderers	v	Sutton United	2-3	5600
Guppy (18), Caroll (52)		Byrne (12), Quail (32), Browne (77)		

Semi-Finals 2nd Leg – 10 April 1993

Home		Away	Res	Att.
Sutton United	v	Wycombe Wanderers	0-4	5002
		Crossley (34, 49), Scott (46), Carroll (76)		

(Wycombe Wanderers won 6-3 on aggregate)

Witton Albion	v	Runcorn	1-0	2033
Burke (32)				

(Runcorn won 2-1 on aggregate)

Final – 10 May 1993 at Wembley Stadium

Runcorn	v	Wycombe Wanderers	1-4	32968
Shaughnessy (41)		Cousins (2), Kerr (20)		
		Thompson (58), Carroll (90)		

The Teams

Runcorn: Arthur WILLIAMS, Jamie BATES, Paul ROBERTSON, Graham HILL, Ian HAROLD (Joe CONNOR), Gary ANDERSON (Capt), Ian BRADY (Neil PARKER), Jimmy BROWN, Steve SHAUGHNESSY, Ken McKENNA, Gary BRABIN.
Wycombe Wanderers: Paul HYDE, Jason COUSINS (Capt), Geoff COOPER, Andy KERR, Matthew CROSSLEY, Steve THOMPSON, Dave CARROLL, Keith RYAN, Simon HUTCHINSON (Hakan HAYRETTIN), Keith SCOTT, Steve GUPPY. Sub not used: Kim CASEY
Referee: IJ Borrett. *Linesmen:* NS Barry and GM Lee
† after extra time

FA TROPHY FINALS 1970-1992

1970   *(Att:28,000)*
MACCLESFIELD TOWN   2   TELFORD UNITED   0
Lyons, Fidler B
Macclesfield Town: Cooke, Sievwright, Bennett, Beaumont, Collins, Roberts, Lyons, Fidler B, Young, Corfield, Fidler D
Telford United: Irvine, Harris, Croft, Flowers, Coton, Ray, Fudge, Hart, Bentley, Murray, Jagger

1971   *(Att:29,500)*
TELFORD UNITED   3   HILLINGDON   2
Owen, Bentley, Fudge   Reeve, Bishop
Telford United: Irvine, Harris, Croft, Ray, Coton, Carr, Fudge, Owen, Bentley, Jagger, Murray
Hillingdon: Lowe, Batt, Langley, Higginson, Newcombe, Moore, Fairchild, Bishop, Reeve, Carter, Knox

1972   *(Att: 24,000)*
STAFFORD RANGERS   3   BARNET   0
Williams 2, Cullerton
Stafford Rangers: Aleksic, Chadwick, Clayton, Sargeant, Aston, Machin, Cullerton, Chapman, Williams, Bayley, Jones
Barnet: McClelland, Lye, Jenkins, Ward, Embrey, King, Powell, Rerry, Flat, Easton, Plume

1973   *(Att: 23,000)*
SCARBOROUGH   2   WIGAN ATHLETIC   1 aet
Leaske, Thompson   Rogers
Scarborough: Garrow, Appleton, Shoulder, Dunn, Siddle, Fagan, Donoghue, Franks, Leaske (Barmby), Thompson, Hewitt
Wigan Athletic: Reeves, Morris, Sutherland, Taylor, Jackson, Gillibrand, Clements, Oats (McCunnell), Rogers, King, Worswick

1974   *(Att: 19,000)*
MORECAMBE   2   DARTFORD   1
Richmond, Sutton   Cunningham
Morecambe: Coates, Pearson, Bennett, Sutton, Street, Baldwin, Done, Webber, Roberts (Galley), Kershaw, Richmond
Dartford: Morton, Read, Payne, Carr, Burns, Binks, Light, Glozier, Robinson (Hearne), Cunningham, Halleday

1975   *(Att: 21,000)*
MATLOCK TOWN   4   SCARBOROUGH   0
Oxley, Dawson, Fenoughty T, Fenoughty N
Matlock Town: Fell, McKay, Smith, Stuart, Dawson, Swan, Oxley, Fenoughty N, Scott, Fenoughty T, Fenoughty M
Scarborough: Williams, Hewitt, Rettit, Dunn, Marshall, Todd, Houghton, Woodall, Davidson, Barnby, Aveyard

1976 (*Att: 21,000*)
SCARBOROUGH 3 **STAFFORD RANGERS** 2 aet
Woodall, Abbey, Marshall (pen) Jones 2
Scarborough: Barnard, Jackson, Marshall, Dunn H, Ayre (Donoghue), Dunn HA, Dale, Barmby, Woodall, Abbey, Hilley
Stafford Rangers: Arnold, Ritchie, Richards, Sargeant, Seddon, Morris, Chapman, Lowe, Jones, Hutchinson, Chadwick

1977 (*Att: 20,500*)
SCARBOROUGH 2 **DAGENHAM** 1
Dunn (pen), Abbey Harris
Scarborough: Chapman, Smith, Marshall (Barmby), Dunn, Ayre, Deere, Aveyard, Donoghue, Woodall, Abbey, Dunn
Dagenham: Huttley, Wellman, Currie P, Dunwell, Moore, Currie W, Harkins, Saul, Fox, Harris, Holder

1978 (*Att: 20,000*)
ALTRINCHAM 3 **LEATHERHEAD** 1
King, Johnson, Rogers Cook
Altrincham: Eales, Allan, Crossley, Bailey, Owens, King, Morris, Heathcote, Johnson, Rogers, Davidson (Flaherty)
Leatherhead: Swannell, Cooper, Eaton, Davies, Reid, Malley, Cook, Salkeld, Kelly, Baker, Boyle (Bailey)

1979 (*Att: 32,000*)
STAFFORD RANGERS 2 **KETTERING TOWN** 0
Wood A 2
Stafford Rangers: Arnold, Wood F, Willis, Sargeant, Seddon, Ritchie, Secker, Chapman, Wood A, Cullerton, Chadwick (Jones)
Kettering: Lane, Ashby, Lee, Eastall, Dixey, Suddards, Flannagan, Kellock, Phipps, Clayton, Evans (Hughes)

1980 (*Att: 26,000*)
DAGENHAM 2 **MOSSLEY** 1
Duck, Maycock Smith
Dagenham: Huttley, Willman, Scales, Dunwell, Moore, Durrell, Maycock, Horan, Duck, Kidd, Jones (Holder)
Mossley: Fitton, Brown, Vaughan, Gorman, Salter, Polliot, Smith, Moore, Skeete, O'Connor, Keelan (Wilson)

1981 (*Att: 22,578*)
BISHOP'S STORTFORD 1 **SUTTON UNITED** 0
Sullivan
Bishop's Stortford: Moore, Blackman, Brame, Amith (Worrell), Bradford, Abery, Sullivan, Knapman, Radford, Simmonds, Mitchell
Sutton United: Collyer, Rogers, Green, Rains J, Rains T, Stephens (Sunnucks), Waldon, Pritchard, Cornwell, Parsons, Dennis

1982   *(Att: 18,678)*
ENFIELD   **1**   **ALTRINCHAM**   **0**
Taylor
Enfield: Jacobs, Barrett, Tone, Jennings, Waite, Ironton, Ashford, Taylor, Holmes, Oliver (Flint), King
Altrincham: Connaughton, Crossley, Davison, Bailey, Cuddy, King (Whitbread), Allan, Heathcote, Johnson, Rogers, Howard

1983   *(Att: 22,071)*
TELFORD UNITED   **2**   **NORTHWICH VICTORIA**   **1**
Mather 2   Bennett
Telford United: Charlton, Lewis, Turner, Mayman (Joseph), Walker, Easton, Barnett, Williams, Mather, Hogan, Alcock
Northwich United: Ryan, Fretwell, Murphy, Jones, Forshaw, Ward, Anderson, Abel (Bennett), Reid, Chesters, Wilson

1984   *(Att: 14,200)*
NORTHWICH VICTORIA   **1**   **BANGOR CITY**   **1** aet
Chesters   Whelan
Northwich Victoria: Ryan, Fretwell, Dean, Jones, Forshaw (Power), Bennett, Anderson, Abel, Reid, Chesters, Wilson
Bangor City: Letheren, Cavanagh, Gray, Whelan, Banks, Lunn, Urquart, Morris, Carter, Howat, Sutcliffe (Westwood)

REPLAY   *(Att: 5,805)*
NORTHWICH VICTORIA   **2**   **BANGOR CITY**   **1**
Chesters (pen), Anderson   Lunn
Northwich Victoria: Ryan, Fretwell, Dean, Jones, Forshaw, Bennett, Anderson, Abel, Reid, Chesters, Wilson
Bangor: Letheren, Cavanagh, Gray, Whelan, Banks, Lunn, Urquart, Morris, Carter, Howat, Sutcliffe

1985   *(Att: 20,775)*
WEALDSTONE   **2**   **BOSTON UNITED**   **1**
Graham, Holmes   Cook
Wealdstone: Iles, Perkins, Bowgett, Byatt, Davies, Greenaway, Holmes, Wainwright, Donnellan, Graham (Cordice N), Cordice A
Boston United: Blackwell, Cassey, Ladd, Creane, O'Brien, Thommson, Lavereick (Mallender), Simpson, Gilbert, Lee, Cook

1986   *(Att: 15,700)*
ALTRINCHAM   **1**   **RUNCORN**   **0**
Farrelly
Altrincham: Wealands, Gardner, Densmore, Johnson, Farrelly, Conning, Cuddy, Davidson, Reid, Ellis, Anderson
Runcorn: McBride, Lee, Roberts, Jones, Fraser, Smith, Crompton S (Crompton A), Imrie, Carter, Mather, Carrodus

1987   *(Att: 23,617)*
KIDDERMINSTER HAR'S   **0**   **BURTON ALBION**   **0**
Kidderminster Harriers: Arnold, Barton, Boxall, Brazier, Collins (Pearson), Woodall, MacKenzie, O'Dowd, Tuohy, Casey, Davies

Burton Albion: New, Essex, Kamara, Vaughan, Simms, Groves, Bancroft, Land, Dorset, Redfern, Gauden

REPLAY	*(Att: 15,685)*	
KIDDERMINSTER HAR'S	**2**	**BURTON ALBION**	**1**

Davies 2   Groves

Kidderminster Harriers: Arnold, Barton, Boxall, Brazier (Hazelwood), Collins, Woodall, MacKenzie, O'Dowd, Tuohy, Casey, Davies
Burton Albion: New, Essex, Kamara, Vaughan, Simms, Groves, Bancroft, Land, Dorset, Redfern (Wood), Gauden

1988   *(Att: 23,617)*
ENFIELD   **0**   **TELFORD UNITED**   **0**

Enfield: Pape, Cottington, Howell, Keen, Sparrow (Hayzleden), Lewis (Edmonds), Harding, Cooper, King, Furlong, Francis
Telford United: Charlton, McGinty, Storton, Nelson, Wiggins, Mayman, Sankey, Joseph, Stringer (Griffiths), Biggins, Norris

REPLAY   *(Att: 26,912)*
ENFIELD   **3**   **TELFORD UNITED**   **2**

Furlong 2, Howell   Biggins, Norris (pen)

Enfield: Pape, Cottington, Howell, Keen (Edmonds), Sparrow, Lewis, Harding, Cooper, King, Furlong, Francis
Telford United: Charlton, McGinty, Storton, Wiggins, Mayman (Cunningham, Hancock), Sankey, Joseph, Stringer, Griffiths, Biggins, Norris

1989   *(Att: 18,102)*
TELFORD UNITED   **1**   **MACCLESFIELD**   **0**

Crawley

Telford United: Charlton, Lee, Brindley, Hancock, Wiggins, Mayman, Grainger, Joseph, Nelson, Lloyd, Stringer. Subs: Crawley, Griffiths
Macclesfield: Zelem, Roberts, Tobin, Edwards, Hardman, Askey, Lake, Hanion, Imrie, Burr, Timmons. Subs: Derbyshire, Kendall

1990   *(Att: 19,011)*
BARROW   **3**   **LEEK TOWN**   **0**

Gordon 2, Cowperthwaite

Barrow: McDonnell, Higgins, Chilton, Skivington, Gordon, Proctor, Doherty (Burgess), Farrell (Gilmore), Cowperthwaite, Lowe, Ferris
Leek Town: Simpson, Elsby (Smith), Pearce, McMullen, Clowes, Coleman (Russell), Mellow, Somerville, Sutton, Millington, Norris

1991   *(Att: 34,842)*
WYCOMBE WANDERERS   **2**   **KIDDERMINSTER HAR'S**   **1**

Scott, West   Hadley

Wycombe Wanderers: Granville, Crossley, Cash, Kerr, Creaser, Carroll, Ryan, Stapleton, West, Scott, Guppy (Hutchinson). Sub not used: Robinson.
Kidderminster Harriers: Jones, Kurila, McGrath, Weir, Barnett, Forsyth, Joseph (Wilcox), Howell (Whitehouse), Hadley, Lilwall, Humphreys.

1992 *(Att: 27,806)*
COLCHESTER UNITED 3 WITTON ALBION 1
Masters, Smith, McGavin Lutkevitch
Colchester United: Barret, Donald, Roberts, Kinsella, English, Martin, Cook, Masters, McDonough (Bennett), McGavin, Smith. Sub not used: Collins.
Witton Albion: Mason, Halliday, Coathup, McNeilis, Connor, Anderson, Thomas, Rose, Alford, Grinshaw (Connor), Lutkevitch (McCluskie).

Vauxhall Awards and Facts for 1992-93

Team of the Round

First Qualifying Round
BILLERICAY TOWN v Corby Town 4-1 (A)

Second Qualifying Round
NEWPORT AFC v Trowbridge Town 1-0 (A)

Third Qualifying Round
SPENNYMOOR UNITED v Emley 6-2 (A)

First Round
SUTTON UNITED v Woking 3-0 (H)

Second Round
NORTHALLERTON TOWN v Bashley 1-0 (H)

Third Round
WARRINGTON TOWN v Merthyr Tydfil 1-1, 3-2 (H)

Fourth Round
RUNCORN v Boston United 2-0 (A)

Highest Attendances
5600	Wycombe Wanderers v Sutton United	SF1Leg	2-3
5002	Sutton United v Wycombe Wanderers	SF2Leg	0-4
4907	Wycombe Wanderers v Bromsgrove Rovers	3rd Rd	2-0
4795	Wycombe Wanderers v Gateshead	4th Rd	1-0

FA VASE 1992-93

Bridlington's Day Out

Alan Radford, in his second season with Bridlington Town, scored the goal that took the FA Vase back to Yorkshire and helped wipe out the misery of defeat experienced three years earlier against Yeading. With goal attempts at a minimum it was always going to take something a bit special to separate the two sides. The goal on 64 minutes was just that as skipper Steve Brentano delivered a searching ball down the right which Radford took in his stride some 35 yards out and threatening no apparent danger. However, his turn of pace as he entered the area left England Under-18 international Jason Smith floundering as the Barnsley born striker cracked an unstoppable shot past Ian Nott in the Tiverton goal.

Radford was in no doubt about the moment and the day in general. "Obviously the whole thing is the highlight of my career. It's nice just coming to Wembley, but to win it and score the winning goal as well is something that will stay with me for the rest of my life. A totally fantastic feeling." At one point Radford looked like being the culprit of the afternoon a minute before the interval when Graeme Jones tapped home a rebound off an upright only to have his celebrations behind the goal cut short by a linesman's flag because Radford, whose flick had created the chance, had wandered offside.

But the final was far from a one man affair and Tiverton had their chances even if they were few and far between. They suffered badly in the first half by electing to play just Phil Everett and Kevin Smith up front against a strong Bridlington rear guard marshalled superbly by man of the match Paul Bottomley, a winner with Guiseley two years earlier.

With the Tivvy midfield and defence slow to support, Bridlington were always likely to pick up on the loose ball and come forward. It was something that Tiverton manager Martyn Rodgers was quick to pick up on and change at the turn around and for a five minute spell at the start of the second half Smith and Everett came within a whisker of giving them the lead..

But for Rodgers he had achieved the ambition he set his side. "I stated at the start of the season that I would rather go for the FA Vase than win the league and I still stand by that statement. If you ask anyone at the club whether they would have rather been here or have won the league then they would all say that they would rather be here. The prestige is second to none. Even now, if you ask me whether I would rather win the league or come back here, then it's Wembley every time."

For Bridlington manager Colin Richardson it is yet another success in a list of impressive achievements in his first season with the club. They had already clinched the Division One championship and with it a place in the Premier Division of the Northern Premier League next season.

He was delighted with his team's performance. "In the first half we had the best chances and it was just a question of keeping going from there and the boys did just that. I never felt we were in any threat and were always going to win the game. Champions and Vase winners – that cannot be bad – can it!"

Extra Preliminary Round – 5 September 1992

Home		Away	Res	Att.	Replay	
Almondsbury Picksons	v	Swindon Supermarine	3-2	32		
Amersham Town	v	Langford	1-5	29		
Armitage	v	Stourport Swifts	2-0	64		
Ash United	v	Broadbridge Heath	4-3†	34		
Atherton Collieries	v	Ayone	4-1	30		
Backwell United	v	Bishops Sutton	3-0	83		
BAT	v	Sherborne Town	3-3†	55	2-3	90
Beaconsfield United	v	Cockfosters	1-2†	45		
(at Cockfosters FC)						
Bicester Town	v	Brockenhurst	1-1†	61	0-1	148
Biggleswade Town	v	Leverstock Green	0-2	39		
Blidworth MW	v	Mickleover RBL	3-1	30		
Bloxwich Town	v	Meir KA	1-3†	10		
Bolehall Swifts	v	Holwell Sports	3-2†	85		
Bowers United	v	Hanwell Town	1-2	90		
Brackley Town	v	Stapenhill	1-4	61		
Brantham Athletic	v	Chatteris Town	0-1	50		
Brimsdown Rovers	v	Kempston Rovers	4-0	58		
Calne Town	v	Tuffley Rovers	1-4	83		
Castleton Gabriels	v	Ashville	2-3†	39		
Cheadle Town	v	Merseyside Police	0-1	46		
Cirencester Town	v	Old Georgians	2-0	100		
Clipstone Welfare	v	Hall Road Rangers	3-2	81		
Coleshill Town	v	Anstey Nomads	3-3†	37	2-5	86
Concord Rangers	v	Potters Bar Town	1-4	90		
Cradley Town	v	Northfield Town	1-2	61		
Cranleigh	v	Bedfont	4-0	60		
Cray Wanderers	v	Farnham Town	wo			
(Farnham Town withdrawn from competition)						
Crowborough Athletic	v	West Wickham	0-1	85		
Darenth Heathside	v	Petersfield United	3-2	41		
Ditton	v	Ramsgate	1-2	75		
Downham Town	v	Brightlingsea United	1-1†	120	1-1	125
(Second replay at Downham Town)			3-0	145		
DRG (FP)	v	Brislington	2-4	61		
Dunkirk	v	Nettleham	5-3	47		
Ecclesshall	v	Stewart & Lloyds	1-4	31		
Ely City	v	St Ives Town	2-1	62		

Home		Away	Res	Att.	Replay	
Fakenham Town	v	Woodbridge Town	2-1	112		
Farleigh Rovers	v	Cobham	1-4	37		
(at Cobham FC)						
Friar Lane OB	v	Immingham Town	4-2†	57		
General Chemicals	v	Wythenshawe Amateurs	1-2	25		
Glasshoughton Welfare	v	Maltby MW	2-1	60		
Godalming & Guildford	v	Slade Green	0-3	82		
Grove United	v	St Dominics	2-1	38		
Hadleigh United	v	Stansted	7-0	93		
Hamworthy United	v	Fleet Town	0-5	100		
Harpenden Town	v	The 61	6-0	50		
Hartley Wintney	v	Deal Town	2-0	97		
Hatfield Main	v	Res Parkgate	1-1†	50	3-1	70
Hillingdon Borough	v	Brook House	0-5	50		
Kimberley Town	v	Stocksbridge Park Steels	2-3†	52		
Kintbury Rangers	v	Wollen Sports	0-2†	49		
Knypersley Victoria	v	Waterloo Dock	1-5	75		
(at Waterloo Dock FC)						
Larkhall Athletic	v	Cinderford Town	1-4	51		
Liversedge	v	Hallam	1-2	56		
Long Sutton Athletic	v	Sudbury Wanderers	2-4	41		
Lutterworth Town	v	Kings Heath	0-2	47		
Maghull	v	Blackpool Mechanics	3-1	64		
Marske United	v	South Shields	2-4	47		
Mile Oak Rovers	v	Knowle	5-2	55		
Milton United	v	AFC Lymington	1-2†	43		
Moreton Town	v	Bemerton Heath Harlequins	1-2	60		
Newton (WC)	v	Westhoughton Town	2-1	19		
Newton Aycliffe	v	Walker	1-2	27		
North Leigh	v	Flight Refuelling	6-2	75		
Norwich United	v	Cornard United	2-1	62		
Patchway	v	Fairford Town	1-1†	37	1-2	50
Pegasus Juniors	v	Daventry Town	1-0	28		
Pelsall Villa	v	Birstall United	5-1	144		
Pershore Town	v	Harrowby United	1-0	170		
Ponteland United	v	Seaton Delaval Amateurs	1-0	65		
Porthleven	v	Elmore	4-2†	77		
Poulton Victoria	v	Heswall	4-3	78		
Rayners Lane	v	Long Buckby	3-4†	62		
Rossington Main	v	Priory (Eastwood)	3-5	40		
Ryde Sports	v	Wantage Town	1-2	87		
Sawbridgeworth Town	v	Warboys Town	2-1	63		
Selby Town	v	Yorkshire Amateur	3-2	75		
Shillington	v	Woodford Town	wo			
(Woodford Town withdrawn from competition)						
Somersham Town	v	Ipswich Wanderers	4-0	49		
St Andrews	v	Highfield Rangers	4-1	61		

Home		Away	Res	Att.	Replay	
Sunderland IFG Roker	v	Heaton Stannington	1-0	19		
Sutton Town	v	Shirebrook Colliery	1-3	130		
Tadcaster Albion	v	Pontefract Collieries	2-6	58		
Totternhoe	v	Stotfold	2-1	53		
Truro City	v	Crediton United	0-1	136		
Viking Sports	v	London Colney	1-2	40		
West Bromwich Town	v	Barwell	1-2	28		
Westfields	v	Oadby Town	3-2	61		
Wingate & Finchley	v	Waltham Abbey	5-2	85		
Worsboro Bridge MW	v	Winterton Rangers	2-0	120		
Wotton Rovers	v	Bridgwater Town	0-2	59		

Preliminary Round – 3 October 1992

Home		Away	Res	Att.	Replay	
Abingdon United	v	First Tower United	1-3	50		
AFC Lymington	v	Swanage Town & Herston	3-1†	134		
AFC Totton	v	Banbury United	1-3	75		
Almondsbury Picksons	v	Odd Down	4-2†	42		
Armitage	v	Rothwell Town	1-2†	62		
Armthorpe Welfare	v	Hallam	4-0	41		
Ash United	v	Sheppey United	1-0	48		
Ashford Town (Middx)	v	Havant Town	0-3	47		
Ashton United	v	Skelmersdale United	3-3†	210	3-1	230
Atherton Collieries	v	Merseyside Police	1-0	60		
Backwell United	v	Chard Town	2-1†	56		
Banstead Athletic	v	Whitstable Town	2-2†	69	1-1†	137
(Second replay at Banstead Athletic)			2-1	61		
Barnstaple Town	v	Porthleven	3-1	97		
Barton Rovers	v	Arlesey Town	4-1	118		
Basildon United	v	Lowestoft Town	1-2	67		
Beckenham Town	v	Redhill	3-2	75		
Belper Town	v	Pontefract Collieries	4-3	129		
Berkhamsted Town	v	Bourne Town	1-2	82		
Billingham Town	v	Ryhope CA	3-0	48		
Bilston Town	v	Rushall Olympic	6-0	78		
Blackpool (wren) Rovers	v	Poulton Victoria	5-2	64		
Blakenall	v	Bridgnorth Town	3-4	65		
Blidworth MW	v	Bradford Park Avenue	1-3	110		
Bolehall Swifts	v	Barwell	2-1	60		
Bootle	v	Rossendale United	2-3	47		
Borrowash Victoria	v	Shirebrook Colliery	2-3	52		
Bridgwater Town	v	Cinderford Town	0-4	135		
Brigg Town	v	Sheffield	3-0	54		
Brimsdown Rovers	v	Braintree Town	2-0	60		
Brislington	v	Cirencester Town	2-0	65		
Bristol Manor Farm	v	Frome Town	2-1	60		

Home		Away	Res	Att.	Replay	
Burnham	v	Cobham	4-1	90		
Camberley Town	v	Haywards Heath Town	3-0	71		
Canvey Island	v	Peterborough City	1-0	105		
Chadderton	v	Prescot AFC	1-2	134		
Chatteris Town	v	Boston	2-3	68		
Chichester City	v	Cray Wanderers	0-3	95		
Clapton	v	Hornchurch	3-1	38		
Cleator Moor Celtic	v	Annfield Plain	3-2	69		
Clevedon Town	v	Devizes Town	6-1	267		
Clipstone Welfare	v	Hatfield Main	4-2	104		
Cockfosters	v	Haringey Borough	2-0	65		
Collier Row	v	Potters Bar Town	1-2	86		
Corinthian	v	Slade Green	2-1	42		
Cranleigh	v	Faversham Town	2-1	65		
Crediton United	v	Ottery St Mary	7-0	100		
Croydon Athletic	v	Greenwich Borough	1-3	43		
Darenth Heathside	v	Arundel	2-2†	40	1-3	70
Darlington CB	v	Hebburn	2-1	57		
Darwen	v	Curzon Ashton	2-3	72		
Desborough Town	v	Tiptree United	1-4	60		
Didcot Town	v	Eastleigh	1-2	80		
Downham Town	v	Royston Town	0-3	103		
Dunkirk	v	Ilkeston Town	1-3	181		
Dunstable	v	Long Buckby	5-1	48		
Eastbourne Town	v	Ringmer	2-3	93		
Eastbourne United	v	Hailsham Town	0-8	178		
Ely City	v	Eynesbury Rovers	1-2	69		
Epsom & Ewell	v	Chatham Town	3-1†	57		
Esh Winning	v	Willington	5-1	25		
Eton Manor	v	Hoddesdon Town	1-2	27		
Evenwood Town	v	Crook Town	5-0	25		
Exmouth Town	v	Ilfracombe Town	1-3	110		
Felixstowe Town	v	Mirrless Blackstone	1-2	70		
Flackwell Heath	v	Letchworth Garden City	2-1	30		
Formby	v	Atherton LR	0-2	50		
Friar Lane OB	v	Denaby United	3-3†	179	2-2†	136
(Second replay at Denaby United)			3-0	152		
Garforth Town	v	Eccleshill United	4-3†	102		
Glasshoughton Welfare	v	Selby Town	3-2	75		
Glastonbury	v	Melksham Town	5-3	55		
Glossop North End	v	Rocester	2-3†	210		
Grove United	v	Nantwich Town	1-1†	194	4-1	194
Hadleigh United	v	Witham Town	6-2†	124		
Halesowen Harriers	v	Walsall Wood	3-0	50		
Halstead Town	v	Holbeach United	4-1	106		
Hartley Wintney	v	Portfield	3-0	65		
Heanor Town	v	Arnold Town	0-2	163		

Home		Away	Res	Att.	Replay	
Hemel Hempstead	v	Hanwell Town	4-2	104		
Hertford Town	v	Welwyn Garden City	5-0	80		
Highgate United	v	Pelsall Villa	0-2	25		
Hinckley Town	v	Thackley	2-2†	70	1-3	104
Histon	v	Gorleston	1-0	56		
Horden CW	v	Bedlington Terriers	0-3	22		
Horsham	v	Pagham	2-1†	211		
Kings Heath	v	Stapenhill	1-4	30		
Kingsbury Town	v	Langford	2-1	42		
Lancaster City	v	Flixton	1-3	75		
Lancing	v	Chipstead	0-4	117		
Langley Park	v	Sunderland IFG Roker	0-1	63		
Langney Sports	v	Sittingbourne	0-4	216		
Leatherhead	v	Alma Swanley	2-0	79		
Leverstock Green	v	Brook House	0-1	75		
Louth United	v	Harworth CI	5-4†	72		
Maghull	v	Irlam Town	2-0	32		
Malvern Town	v	Sandwell Borough	1-4	22		
Mangotsfield United	v	Wellington Town	4-1	107		
March Town United	v	Stamford Town	0-1	150		
Meir KA	v	Lye Town	1-1†	56	2-3†	72
Merstham	v	Horsham YMCA	3-1	44		
Mile Oak Rovers	v	Boldmere St Michaels	0-2	55		
Milton Keynes Borough	v	Harpenden Town	5-2	111		
(after abandoned match, 45 mins, waterlogged pitch)						
Minehead	v	Bemerton Heath Harlequins	1-2	103		
Netherfield	v	Oldham Town	5-0	83		
Newbury Town	v	Romsey Town	6-2	144		
Newmarket Town	v	Sawbridgeworth Town	1-2	99		
Newquay	v	Liskeard Athletic	3-2	180		
Newton (WC)	v	Clitheroe	0-6	22		
North Leigh	v	Fairford Town	3-1	74		
Norwich United	v	Somersham Town	5-0	29		
Ossett Town	v	Rainworth MW	2-3†	120		
Oxford City	v	Thame United	3-2	119		
Paget Rangers	v	Raunds Town	4-5	53		
Pegasus Juniors	v	Chasetown	4-2	41		
Pershore Town	v	Stewart & Lloyds	0-1	150		
Priory (Eastwood)	v	Oakham United	3-1	56		
Prudhoe East End	v	Durham City	1-3	102		
Racing Club Warwick	v	Oldbury United	1-2	76		
Ramsgate	v	Egham Town	3-1	82		
Ruislip Manor	v	London Colney	9-0	120		
Rushden & Diamonds	v	Anstey Nomads	3-2	242		
Salford City	v	Douglas High School OB	5-0	100		
Sherborne Town	v	Witney Town	0-4	90		

Home		Away	Res	Att.	Replay	
Shillington	v	Feltham & Hounslow Boro	0-2	62		
Sholing Sports	v	Fleet Town	1-1†	68	1-2	62
Shotton Comrades	v	Norton & Stockton Ancients	3-0	10		
Soham Town Rangers	v	Thetford Town	6-2	82		
South Shields	v	Penrith	2-0	150		
Southall	v	Hampton	0-8	196		
(at Hampton FC)						
St Blazey	v	Torpoint Athletic	3-1	79		
St Helens Town	v	Maine Road	2-4	41		
Steyning Town	v	Corinthian Casuals	1-7	45		
Stocksbridge Park Steels	v	Harrogate Town	4-1	81		
Stowmarket Town	v	Kings Lynn	1-2†	156		
Stratford Town	v	Northfield Town	2-0	82		
Sudbury Wanderers	v	Fakenham Town	4-1†	103		
Thatcham Town	v	Brockenhurst	2-0†	79		
Three Bridges	v	Tunbridge Wells	1-2	110		
Tilbury	v	Cheshunt	2-1†	43		
Tonbridge	v	Southwick	4-1	438		
Torrington	v	Tiverton Town	0-2	145		
Tottenhoe	v	Rainham Town	1-1†	42	1-3	68
Tring Town	v	Bracknell Town	7-0	41		
Tuffley Rovers	v	Chippenham Town	1-0	134		
Tunbridge Wells	v	Three Bridges	1-1	128	2-1	110
Walker	v	Pickering Town	1-1†	85	0-3	137
Washington	v	Ponteland United	0-5	30		
(at Hebburn FC)						
Waterloo Dock	v	Ashville	3-2	42		
Watton United	v	Bury Town	2-0	110		
Wellingborough Town	v	St Andrews	0-4	44		
West Wickham	v	Shoreham	3-4	60		
Westbury United	v	Wantage Town	3-1	102		
Westfields	v	Wednesfield	1-3†	58		
Whitehawk	v	Burgess Hill Town	1-2	66		
Whitstable Town	v	Banstead Athletic	1-1†	137		
Wick	v	Selsey	6-0	74		
Wingate & Finchley	v	Ware	0-2	95		
Wollen Sports	v	Bournemouth	2-3†	25		
Wootton Blue Cross	v	Barkingside	1-1†	55	1-1†	59
(Second replay at Wootton Blue Cross)			2-1	139		
Worsboro Bridge MW	v	Ossett Albion	1-1†	140	1-1	111
(Second replay at Worsboro Bridge MW)			3-3†	182	3-2	171
Worthing United	v	Oakwood	1-2	25		
Worthing	v	Cove	2-0	267		
Wythenshawe Amateurs	v	Burscough	1-3	60		

First Round – 31 October 1992

Home		Away	Res	Att.	Replay	
Alnwick Town	v	Dunston FB	1-1†	74		
Arnold Town	v	Shirebrook Colliery	3-0	121		
Atherton Collieries	v	Blackpool (wren) Rovers	4-1	40		
Atherton LR	v	Grove United	2-0	200		
Backwell United	v	Taunton Town	2-4†	94		
Banbury United	v	Forest Green Rovers	2-2†	144	2-5	84
Banstead Athletic	v	Horsham	4-3	125		
Barnstaple Town	v	Crediton United	2-1	145		
Beckenham Town	v	Ash United	2-3	35		
Bedlington Terriers	v	Eppleton CW	0-2	770		
Belper Town	v	Rainworth MW	4-3	130		
Bemerton Heath H'quins	v	Brislington	2-1†	91		
Bilston Town	v	Pegasus Juniors	2-1	61		
Boston	v	Kings Lynn	1-2†	155		
Bridport	v	AFC Lymington	0-3	240		
Brigg Town	v	Bradford Park Avenue	2-1	156		
Brimsdown Rovers	v	Dunstable	0-1	58		
Burgess Hill Town	v	Tunbridge Wells	2-3	116		
Burnham Ramblers	v	Potters Bar Town	3-1	107		
Burnham	v	Corinthian	5-1	82		
Burscough	v	Netherfield	2-1	128		
Cinderford Town	v	Glastonbury	6-2	110		
Cleator Moor Celtic	v	Ponteland United	2-2†	77	3-6	70
Clevedon Town	v	Mangotsfield United	7-1	434		
Clipstone Welfare	v	Glasshoughton Welfare	6-2	116		
Cockfosters	v	Hertford Town	0-4	106		
Corinthian Casuals	v	Worthing	6-0	90		
Cray Wanderers	v	Oakwood	2-1†	55		
Curzon Ashton	v	Clitheroe	3-3†	72	1-0	135
Durham City	v	Evenwood Town	3-0	110		
East Thurrock United	v	Clapton	2-4†	170		
Eastleigh	v	Oxford City	1-3	106		
Erith & Belvedere	v	Ramsgate	2-1	189		
Eynesbury Rovers	v	Potton United	0-2	285		
Falmouth Town	v	Tiverton Town	0-3	411		
Flackwell Heath	v	Feltham & Hounslow Boro'	2-3†	40		
Fleet Town	v	Witney Town	0-2	85		
Ford United	v	Tilbury	1-0	55		

(Ford United removed from competition, Tilbury reinstated)

Home		Away	Res	Att.	Replay	
Garforth Town	v	Priory (Eastwood)	3-0	110		
Gosport Borough	v	Bournemouth	2-4	145		
Greenwich Borough	v	Cranleigh	1-3	108		
Hadleigh United	v	Histon	1-2	131		
Hailsham Town	v	Wick	3-2	330		
Halstead Town	v	Stamford Town	1-3	149		

Home		Away	Res	Att.	Replay	
Harefield United	v	Brook House	3-1	40		
Harrogate RA	v	Armthorpe Welfare	2-1	66		
Hartley Wintney	v	Arundel	2-0†	105		
Havant Town	v	Epsom & Ewell	1-0	128		
Haverhill Rovers	v	Sawbridgeworth Town	0-1	85		
Hoddesdon Town	v	Hemel Hempstead	1-0	90		
Hucknall Town	v	Louth United	2-1	174		
Ilfracombe Town	v	St Blazey	5-4	110		
Ilkeston Town	v	Lincoln United	2-2†	729	1-2	241
Leatherhead	v	Ringmer	1-0	76		
Leighton Town	v	Tring Town	1-3	417		
Lowestoft Town	v	Sudbury Wanderers	2-1†	190		
Maine Road	v	Maghull	3-1	61		
Mirrless Blackstone	v	Spalding United	2-3†	110		
Newquay	v	Dawlish Town	4-1	152		
North Leigh	v	Bristol Manor Farm	2-1	67		
Northampton Spencer	v	Sandwell Borough	0-3	55		
Norwich United	v	Soham Town Rangers	4-0	40		
Oldbury United	v	Lye Town	3-2	131		
Peacehaven & Telscombe	v	Herne Bay	5-1	211		
Pelsall Villa	v	Raunds Town	4-0	232		
Pickering Town	v	South Shields	3-3†	151	1-1†	285
(Replays at Ryhope CA)			4-3	130		
Prescot AFC	v	Salford City	0-1	104		
Radcliffe Borough	v	Waterloo Dock	1-3	123		
Rainham Town	v	Kingsbury Town	0-2	102		
Rocester	v	Flixton	0-2	217		
Rossendale United	v	Ashton United	2-5	205		
Rothwell Town	v	Bolehall Swifts	4-0	109		
Royston Town	v	Tiptree United	2-2†	74	0-1	59
Ruislip Manor	v	Hampton	1-1†	178	2-1	216
Rushden & Diamonds	v	Halesowen Harriers	3-3†	247	2-0	123
Shoreham	v	Merstham	1-2	80		
Shortwood United	v	Almondsbury Picksons	3-3†	88	0-3	83
Shotton Comrades	v	Darlington CB	1-0	18		
Sittingbourne	v	Camberley Town	7-0	444		
St Andrews	v	Bridgnorth Town	2-2†	87	1-3	85
Stewart & Lloyds	v	Stapenhill	1-2	37		
Stocksbridge Park Steels	v	Friar Lane OB	2-0	101		
Sunderland IFG Roker	v	Esh Winning	0-1	43		
Thackley	v	Worsboro Bridge MW	1-2	149		
Thatcham Town	v	Newbury Town	4-2†	379		
Tonbridge	v	Chipstead	4-0	485		
Ware	v	Milton Keynes Borough	2-3	97		
Watton United	v	Bourne Town	1-3	85		
Wednesfield	v	Boldmere St Michaels	3-0	32		
Welton Rovers	v	Tuffley Rovers	2-0	153		

Home		Away	Res	Att.	Replay	
West Allotment Celtic	v	Chester-le-Street Town	3-3†	170	3-6	97
Westbury United	v	First Tower United	1-2	125		
Whickham	v	Billingham Town	0-2	65		
Willenhall Town	v	Stratford Town	0-0†	75	0-3	75
Wootton Blue Cross	v	Barton Rovers	1-4	112		
Wroxham	v	Canvey Island	0-3	102		

Second Round – 21 November 1992

Home		Away	Res	Att.	Replay	
Ash United	v	Littlehampton Town	0-0	105	0-4	220

(First game abandoned after 90 minutes)

Atherton Collieries	v	Worsboro Bridge MW	2-2	-	3-3†	160

(1st game abandoned after 90 mins, 2nd replay at Worsboro) 1-2† 130

Home		Away	Res	Att.	Replay	
Atherton LR	v	Stocksbridge Park Steels	2-2†	188	2-1	130
Bemerton Heath H'quins	v	Taunton Town	1-0	152		
Bilston Town	v	Wednesfield	6-1	96		
Bridlington Town	v	Eppleton CW	1-0	204		
Burnham Ramblers	v	Banstead Athletic	2-3†	102		
Burnham	v	Sawbridgeworth Town	3-2	90		
Burscough	v	Lincoln United	3-1	141		
Cammell Laird	v	Salford City	6-3	102		
Chester-le-Street Town	v	Esh Winning	5-1	117		
Clevedon Town	v	Barnstaple Town	5-4	324		
Corinthian Casuals	v	Diss Town	1-2	70		
Cranleigh	v	North Leigh	3-0	157		
Cray Wanderers	v	Merstham	1-0	62		
Curzon Ashton	v	Belper Town	3-1	84		
Dunstable	v	Buckingham Town	1-1†	116	1-2	86
Eastwood Hanley	v	North Ferriby United	1-0	47		
Edgware Town	v	Barton Rovers	1-4	184		
Feltham & Hounslow Bor		bye				
First Tower United	v	Havant Town	3-2†	150		
Forest Green Rovers	v	Leatherhead	2-1	123		
Great Harwood Town	v	Bamber Bridge	2-3†	385		
Great Yarmouth Town	v	Lowestoft Town	0-0†	154	0-2	325
Hailsham Town	v	Clapton	4-3	287		
Harefield United	v	Kingsbury Town	2-2	56	3-1†	-

(First game abandoned after 90 minutes)

Home		Away	Res	Att.	Replay	
Harrogate RA	v	Dunston FB	0-6	90		
Hartley Wintney	v	Bournemouth	3-1	95		
Harwich & Parkeston	v	Erith & Belvedere	2-1	198		
Histon	v	Hinckley Athletic	2-3†	76		
Hoddesdon Town	v	Potton United	2-0	130		
Hucknall Town	v	Clipstone Welfare	0-3	289		
Hungerford Town	v	Witney Town	0-3	80		

Home		Away	Res	Att.	Replay	
Kings Lynn	v	Sandwell Borough	2-1	277		
Knowsley United	v	Arnold Town	3-2	88		
Maine Road	v	Flixton	5-5†	107	1-2	188
Malden Vale	v	Hertford Town	3-0	122		
Metropolitan Police	v	Tilbury	0-6	73		
Milton Keynes Borough	v	Tring Town	0-1	102		
Newcastle Town	v	Brigg Town	3-4	86		
Newport (IOW)	v	Thatcham Town	2-1	286		
Newquay	v	AFC Lymington	1-0	225		
Norwich United	v	Stamford Town	3-0	61		
Oldbury United	v	Stratford Town	1-2	83		
Oxford City	v	Evesham United	1-2	150		
Peacehaven & Telscombe	v	Northwood	2-1	201		
Pelsall Villa	v	West Midlands Police	1-1†	206	2-1	127
Pickering Town	v	Billingham Town	2-2†	144	1-5	120
Ponteland United	v	Garforth Town	3-1	72		
Rothwell Town	v	Wisbech Town	5-2	378		
Rushden & Diamonds	v	Gresley Rovers	2-2†	423	1-3	717
Saffron Walden Town	v	Ruislip Manor	3-1	155		
Shotton Comrades	v	Durham City	2-5	62		
Sittingbourne	v	Chertsey Town	4-2	499		
Spalding United	v	Bourne Town	2-2 †	273	1-4	203
Stapenhill	v	Bridgnorth Town	2-2†	135	0-7	105
Sudbury Town	v	Canvey Island	2-3	536		
Tiverton Town	v	Cinderford Town	5-1	355		
Tunbridge Wells	v	Tonbridge	3-1	754		
Walthamstow Pennant	v	Tiptree United	1-0†	30		
(Replay ordered at Walthamstow Pennant)			1-0	15		
Waterloo Dock	v	Ashton United	2-6	88		
Welton Rovers	v	Ilfracombe Town	1-0	131		
Wimborne Town	v	Almondsbury Picksons	1-4	542		
Yate Town	v	Paulton Rovers	1-2	132		

Third Round – 12 December 1992

Home		Away	Res	Att.	Replay	
Atherton LR	v	Ashton United	1-2	300		
Bamber Bridge	v	Cammell Laird	1-2†	437		
Barton Rovers	v	Diss Town	2-1†	192		
Bourne Town	v	Peacehaven & Telscombe	4-4†	213	0-4	304
Bridgnorth Town	v	Atherton Collieries	4-0	130		
Brigg Town	v	Bridlington Town	1-3	254		
Buckingham Town	v	Saffron Walden Town	3-2	209		
Burnham	v	Gresley Rovers	1-2	208		
Burscough	v	Ponteland United	1-0	157		
Canvey Island	v	Kings Lynn	1-0	411		
Clevedon Town	v	Bemerton Heath Harlequins	2-1	437		

Home		Away	Res	Att.	Replay	
Cranleigh	v	Hailsham Town	1-3	285		
Cray Wanderers	v	Tring Town	2-3	77		
Curzon Ashton	v	Chester-le-Street Town	7-1	104		
Dunston FB	v	Billingham Town	5-1	144		
Eastwood Hanley	v	Durham City	2-5	130		
Feltham & Hounslow Bor	v	Tunbridge Wells	1-2	98		
First Tower United	v	Paulton Rovers	0-0†	163	1-5	209
Hartley Wintney	v	Rothwell Town	0-3	195		
Harwich & Parkeston	v	Banstead Athletic	0-3	228		
Hinckley Athletic	v	Clipstone Welfare	1-0	273		
Knowsley United	v	Flixton	5-2†	101		
Littlehampton Town	v	Pelsall Villa	0-1	305		
Newport (IOW)	v	Welton Rovers	2-0	303		
Newquay	v	Evesham United	1-3†	325		
Norwich United	v	Harefield United	1-2†	64		
Sittingbourne	v	Malden Vale	4-2†	761		
Stratford Town	v	Bilston Town	0-2	161		
Tilbury	v	Hoddesdon Town	2-3	86		
Tiverton Town	v	Almondsbury Picksons	2-1	520		
Walthamstow Pennant	v	Lowestoft Town	0-1	51		
Witney Town	v	Forest Green Rovers	1-2	153		

Fourth Round – 16 January 1993

Home		Away	Res	Att.	Replay	
Barton Rovers	v	Tiverton Town	0-4	379		
Bilston Town	v	Ashton United	3-0	184		
Bridlington Town	v	Curzon Ashton	5-3†	252		
Buckingham Town	v	Paulton Rovers	4-0	192		
Burscough	v	Cammell Laird	0-1	457		
Dunston FB	v	Durham City	3-1	329		
Evesham United	v	Clevedon Town	0-2	525		
(Replay ordered at Evesham United)			1-3	502		
Forest Green Rovers	v	Hailsham Town	6-5	251		
Gresley Rovers	v	Bridgnorth Town	3-0	787		
Harefield United	v	Canvey Island	2-2	244	0-1	681
Hinckley Athletic	v	Pelsall Villa	2-2†	369	1-4	433
Hoddesdon Town	v	Tunbridge Wells	3-1	252		
Newport (IOW)	v	Lowestoft Town	4-1	424		
Peacehaven & Telscombe	v	Sittingbourne	4-1	882		
Rothwell Town	v	Knowsley United	1-0	355		
Tring Town	v	Banstead Athletic	0-1	111		

Fifth Round – 6 February 1993

Home		Away	Res	Att.
Banstead Athletic	v	Newport (IOW)	3-0	410
Bilston Town	v	Hoddesdon Town	3-2	241

Home		Away	Res	Att.	Replay
Buckingham Town	v	Pelsall Villa	1-0†	310	
Canvey Island	v	Clevedon Town	1-0†	1123	
Dunston FB	v	Cammell Laird	2-1	532	
Forest Green Rovers	v	Tiverton Town	0-6	671	
Gresley Rovers	v	Peacehaven & Telscombe	1-0	1138	
Rothwell Town	v	Bridlington Town	1-2†	651	

Sixth Round – 27 February 1993

Home		Away	Res	Att.
Bridlington Town	v	Banstead Athletic	1-0	433
Buckingham Town	v	Tiverton Town	1-4	765
Canvey Island	v	Bilston Town	2-0	1854
Gresley Rovers	v	Dunston FB	2-0	1610

Semi-Finals 1st Leg – 20 March 1993

Home		Away	Res	Att.
Bridlington Town	v	Gresley Rovers	2-1	1626
Tiverton Town	v	Canvey Island	2-0	2602

Semi-Finals 2nd Leg – 27 March 1993

Canvey Island	v	Tiverton Town	1-0	3250

Tiverton Town won 2-1 on aggregate

Gresley Rovers	v	Bridlington Town	1-1	2481

Bridlington Town won 3-2 on aggregate

Final – 8 May 1993 at Wembley Stadium

Bridlington Town	v	Tiverton Town	1-0	9061

Radford (64)

The Teams

Bridlington Town: Ian TAYLOR, Steve BRENTANO (Capt), Ian McKENZIE, Lee HARVEY, Paul BOTTOMLEY, David WOODCOCK, Chris CROCOCK, Allan ROBERTS, Graeme JONES, Alan RADFORD (Alan TYRELL), Ged PARKINSON. Sub not used: Chris SWAILS.

Tiverton Town: Ian NOTT, Jason SMITH, Neil SAUNDERS, Mark SAUNDERS, Mark SHORT (Matthew SCOTT), Hedley STEELE (Capt), Lee ANNUNZIATA, Kevin SMITH, Phil EVERETT, Steve DALY, Steve HYNDS (Peter RODGERS).
Referee: RA Hart. Linesman: E Lomas and BD Preist
Editor's Man of the Match: Paul Bottomley (Bridlington Town) – superbly marshalled the unbeaten Bridlington defence.

FA VASE FINALS 1975-1992

1975 *(Att: 9,500)*
HODDESDON TOWN   **2**   (Sedgwick 2)
EPSOM & EWELL   **1**   (Wales)
Hoddesdon Town: Galvin, Green, Hickey, Maybury, Stevenson, Wilson, Bishop, Picking, Sedgwick, Nathan, Schofield
Epsom & Ewell: Page, Bennett, Webb, Wales, Worby, Jones, O'Connell, Walker, Tuite, Eales, Lee

1976 *(Att: 11,858)*
BILLERICAY TOWN   **1**   (Aslett)
STAMFORD   **0**   **aet**
Billericay Town: Griffiths, Payne, Foreman, Pullin, Bone, Coughlan, Geddes, Aslett, Clayden, Scott, Smith
Stamford: Johnson, Kwiatkowski, Marchant, Crawford, Downs, Hird, Barnes, Walpole, Smith, Russell, Broadhurst

1977 *(Att: 14,000)*
BILLERICAY TOWN   **1**   (Clayden)
SHEFFIELD   **1**   (Coughlan og)   **aet**
Billericay Town: Griffiths, Payne, Bone, Coughlan, Pullin, Scott, Wakefield, Aslett, Clayden, Woodhouse, McQueen. Sub: Whettell
Sheffield: Wing, Gilbody, Lodge, Hardisty, Watts, Skelton, Kay, Travis, Pugh, Thornhill, Haynes. Sub: Strutt

Replay at Nottingham Forest (Att: 3,482)
BILLERICAY TOWN   **2**   (Aslett, Woodhouse)
SHEFFIELD   **1**   (Thornhill)
Billericay Town: Griffiths, Payne, Pullin, Whettell, Bone, McQueen, Woodhouse, Aslett, Clayden, Scott, Wakefield
Sheffield: Wing, Gilbody, Lodge, Strutt, Watts, Skelton, Kay, Travis, Pugh, Thornhill, Haynes

1978 *(Att: 16,391)*
BLUE STAR   **2**   (Dunn, Crumplin)
BARTON ROVERS   **1**   (Smith)
Blue Star: Halbert, Feenan, Thompson, Davidson, Dixon S., Beynon, Storey, Dixon P., Crumplin, Callaghan, Dunn. Sub: Diamond
Barton Rovers: Blackwell, Stephens, Crossley, Evans, Harris, Dollimore, Dunn, Harnaman, Fossey, Turner, Smith. Sub: Cox

1979 *(Att: 17,500)*
BILLERICAY TOWN   **4**   (Young 3, Clayden)
ALMONDSBURY GREENWAY   **1**   (Price)
Billericay Town: Norris, Blackaller, Bingham, Whettell, Bone, Reeves, Pullin, Scott, Clayden, Young, Groom. Sub: Carrigan
Almondsbury Greenway: Hamilton, Bowers, Scarrett, Sullivan, Tudor, Wookey, Bowers, Shehean, Kerr, Butt, Price. Sub: Kilbaine

1980 *(Att: 11,500)*
STAMFORD 2 (Alexander, McGowan)
GUISBOROUGH TOWN 0
Stamford: Johnson, Kwiatkowski, Ladd, McGowan, Bliszczak I, Mackin, Broadhurst, Hall, Czarnecki, Potter, Alexander. Sub: Bliszczak S
Guisborough Town: Cutter, Scott, Thornton, Angus, Maltby, Percy, Skelton, Coleman, McElvaney, Sills, Dilworth. Sub: Harrison

1981 *(Att: 12,000)*
WHICKHAM 3 (Scott, Williamson, Peck og)
WILLENHALL TOWN 2 (Smith, Stringer) **aet**
Whickham: Thompson, Scott, Knox, Williamson, Cook, Ward, Carroll, Diamond, Cawthra, Robertson, Turnbull. Sub: Allon
Willenhall Town: Newton, White, Dams, Woodall, Heath, Fox, Peck, Price, Matthews, Smith, Stringer. Sub: Trevor

1982 *(Att: 12,500)*
FOREST GREEN ROVERS 3 (Leitch 2, Norman)
RAINWORTH MINERS WELFARE 0
Forest Green Rovers: Moss, Norman, Day, Turner, Higgins, Jenkins, Burns, Guest, Millard, Leitch, Doughty. Sub: Dangerfield
Rainworth Miners Welfare: Watson, Hallam, Hodgson, Slater, Sterland, Oliver, Knowles, Raine, Radzki, Reah, Comerford. Sub: Robinson

1983 *(Att: 13,700)*
VS RUGBY 1 (Crawley)
HALESOWEN TOWN 0
VS Rugby: Burton, McGinty, Harrison, Preston, Knox, Evans, Ingram, Setchell, Owen, Beecham, Crawley. Sub: Haskins
Halesowen Town: Caldicott, Penn, Edmonds, Lacey, Randall, Shilvock, Hazelwood, Moss, Woodhouse, Joinson E, Joinson L. Sub: Smith

1984 *(Att: 8,125)*
STANSTED 3 (Holt, Gillard, Reading)
STAMFORD 2 (Waddicore, Allen)
Stansted: Coe, Williams, Hilton, Simpson, Cooper, Reading, Callanan, Holt, Reeves, Doyle, Gillard. Sub: Williams
Stamford: Parslow, Smitheringale, Blades, McIlwain, Lyon, Mackin, Genovese, Waddicore, Allen, Robson, Beech. Sub: Chapman

1985 *(Att: 16,715)*
HALESOWEN TOWN 3 (Moss, Joinson L 2)
FLEETWOOD TOWN 1 (Moran)
Halesowen Town: Caldicott, Penn, Sherwood, Warner, Randle, Heath, Hazelwood, Moss (Smith), Woodhouse, Joinson P, Joinson L
Fleetwood Town: Dobson, Moran, Hadgraft, Strachan, Robinson, Milligan, Hall, Trainor, Taylor (Whitehouse), Cain, Kenneley

1986 *(Att: 18,340)*
HALESOWEN TOWN 3 (Moss 2, Joinson L)
SOUTHALL 0
Halesowen Town: Pemberton, Moore, Lacey, Randle (Rhodes), Sherwood, Heath, Penn, Woodhouse, Joinson P, Joinson L, Moss

Southall: MacKenzie, James, McGovern, Croad, Holland, Powell (Richmond), Pierre, Richardson, Sweales, Ferdinand, Rowe

1987	*(Att: 4,254)*
ST HELENS	3 (Lay 2, Rigby)
WARRINGTON	2 (Reid, Cook)

St Helens: Johnston, Benson, Lowe, Bendon, Wilson, McComb, Collins (Gledhill), O'Neill, Cummins, Lay, Rigby. Sub: Deakin
Warrington: O'Brien, Copeland, Hunter, Gratton, Whalley, Reid, Brownville (Woodyer), Cook, Kinsey, Looker (Hill), Hughes

1988	*(Att: 15,000)*
COLNE DYNAMOES	1 (Anderson)
EMLEY	0

Colne Dynamoes: Mason, McFadyen, Westwell, Bentley, Dunn, Roscoe, Rodaway, Whitehead (Burke), Diamond, Anderson, Wood (Coates)
Emley: Dennis, Fielding, Mellor, Codd, Hirst (Burrows), Gartland (Cook), Carmody, Green, Bramald, Devine, Francis

1989	*(Att: 26,487)*
TAMWORTH	1 (Devaney)
SUDBURY	1 (Hubbick) aet

Tamworth: Belford, Lockett, Atkins, Cartwright, McCormack, Myers, Fin, Devaney, Moores, Gordon, Stanton Subs: Rathbone, Heaton
Sudbury: Garnham, Henry, Barker G, Boyland, Thorpe, Klug, Barker D, Barton, Oldfield, Smith, Hubbick. Subs: Money, Hunt

Replay at Peterborough *(Att: 11,201)*

TAMWORTH	3 (Stanton 2, Moores)
SUDBURY	0

Tamworth: Belford, Lockett, Atkins, Cartwright, Finn, Myers, George, Devaney, Moores, Gordon, Stanton. Sub: Heaton
Sudbury: Garnham, Henry, Barker G, Boyland, Thorpe, Klug, Barker D, Barton, Oldfield, Smith, Hubbick. Subs: Money, Hunt

1990	*(Att: 7,932)*
BRIDLINGTON TOWN	0
YEADING	0 aet

Bridlington: Taylor, Pugh, Freeman, McNeil, Warburton, Brentano, Wilkes (Hall), Noteman, Gauden, Whiteman, Brattan (Brown)
Yeading: MacKenzie, Wickens, Turner, Whiskey (McCarthy), Croad, Denton, Mathews, James (Charles), Sweales, Impey, Cordery

Replay at Elland Road *(Att: 5,000)*

BRIDLINGTON TOWN	0
YEADING	1 (Sweales)

Bridlington: Taylor, Pugh, Freeman, McNeil, Warburton, Brentano, Wilkes (Brown), Noteman, Gauden (Downing), Whiteman, Brattan
Yeading: MacKenzie, Wickens, Turner, Whiskey, Croad (McCarthy), Schwartz, Mathews, James, Sweales, Impey (Welsh), Cordery

1991 (Att: 11,313) **aet**
GUISELEY 4 (Tennison 2, Walling, Roberts)
GRESLEY ROVERS 4 (Rathbone, Smith 2, Stokes pen)
Guiseley: Maxted, Bottomley, Hogarth, Tetley, Morgan, McKenzie, Atkinson P (Adams), Tennison, Walling, Roberts A, Roberts B (Annan)
Gresley Rovers: Aston, Barry, Elliott (Adcock), Denby, Land, Astley, Stokes, Smith, Acklam, Rathbone, Lovell (Weston)

Replay at Bramall Lane (Att: 7,885)
GUISELEY 3 (Tennison, Walling, Atkinson I)
GRESLEY ROVERS 1 (Astley)
Guiseley: Maxted, Atkinson I, Hogarth, Tetley, Morgan, McKenzie (Bottomley), Roberts A, Tennison (Noteman), Walling, Atkinson P, Roberts B
Gresley Rovers: Aston, Barry, Elliott, Denby, Land, Astley, Stokes (Weston), Smith, Acklam, Rathbone, Lovell (Adcock)

1992 (Att: 10,772)
GUISELEY 3 (Noteman 2, Colville)
WIMBORNE TOWN 5 (Richardson, Sturgess 2, Killick 2)
Guiseley: Maxted, Atkinson, Hogarth, Tetley (captain) (Wilson), Morgan, Brockie, Roberts, Tennison, Noteman (Colville), Annan, Roberts.
Wimborne Town: Leonard, Langdon (Wilkins), Beacham, Allan, Taplin, Ames, Richardson (captain), Bridle, Killick, Sturgess (Lovell), Lynn.

FA SUNDAY CUP 1992-93

First Round – 11 Oct 1992

AEL v Chequers (Herts) 2-1
Albion Sports v Royal Oak 1-3
Almithak v Blyth Waterloo SC ....1-1 †
    Replay 1-0
(Replay at Blyth Spartans FC)
Altone Steels v FC Coachman 4-0
Bedfont Sunday v Old Wimbledonians 5-1
Berner United v Rolls Royce (Sunday) 2-2 †
    Replay ....3-2 †
Blue Union v Clubmoor Nalgo 0-3
Bolton Woods v Britannia VNC 1-2
Broad Plain House v Caversham Park ..1-2
Chapel North v Inter Volante 2-3
Chesterfield Park v Carnforth 1-4
Clements Hospital v Hundred Acre ..2-0
Coach & Horses v Leyton Argyle ..2-1 †
Collier Row Supprs v Sawston Keys ...0-2 †
Concord Rangers v Blyth Spartans ...1-1 †
    Replay 0-3
Cork & Bottle v Vanaid 0-1
Dereham Hobbies v Priory Sports ..2-1
Dock v Woodlands 84 11-0
E Bowling Unity v Croxteth & G RBL 2-1
Framwellgate M&P v Dudley & W ...7-3
Girton Eagles v Elliott Star (Sunday) ...0-0 †
    Replay 2-3
(Replay at Boreham Wood FC)
Hartlepool Lion Hotel v Nenthead ..1-1 †
    Replay 4-1
Heathfield v Fryerns Community ...2-0
Horn Park v Hove Dynamos 4-0
Iron Bridge v Lobster 1-2
Kenwick Dynamos v Jolly Farmers ..1-2
Leicester City Bus v AD Bulwell ...5-1 †
Littlewoods Athletic v Netherby RBL ..4-1
Luton Way v Brookvale Athletic ....4-3 †

Lynemouth v BRNESCO ....1-1 †
    Replay 0-3
Mayfield United v Baildon Athletic ...wo
(Walkover for Baildon Athletic)
Merton Admiral v Thorn Walk Tavern 6-1
Mitre BS v Star Athletic 7-1
Napoli v Whetley Lane 3-1
North Lynn Sunday v Evergreen ......wo
(Evergreen withdrawn from Competition)
Northwood v Lion Hotel ....3-4 †
Olton Royale v Gamlingay OB 5-1
Olympic Star v Ansells Stockland Star 0-1 †
Oxford Road Social v St Peters 1-3
Phoenix v St Josephs (Sth Oxhey) ...0-1
PooleTown Social v Reading Borough 0-2
Poringland Wanderers v Continental ..4-2
Quested v St Merton 2-1
Renbad Rovers v Manfast Kirkby ...0-3
Sarton United v Santogee 66 0-2
Scaffolding v Railway Hotel 1-0
Seymour v Halewood Labour 4-1
Sheerness Steel Utd v Northfield Rangers 1-3
Somerset Ambury V & E v Hanham S 2-1
Watford Labour Club v Sandwell ...1-0
Wednesfield Albion v Dulwich 1-2
Wirral Boxers v East Levenshulme ...1-3

Second Round – 8 Nov 1992

A3 v Framwellgate M&PM 4-3
AEL v Dereham Hobbies 5-0
Altone Steels v Jolly Farmers 1-3
Ansells Stockland v Poringland Wands 1-0
B&A Scaffolding v Lion hotel 2-1
Bricklayers Sport v Vanaid 1-3
BRNESC v Oakenshaw 1-2
Clubmoor Nalgo v Britannia VNC ...1-1
    Replay 3-4

Coach & Horses v Reading Borough ...1-4
Dock v Napoli ....2-3†
Dulwich v Inter Volante 2-2
   Replay 3-1
E Levenshulme v Baildon Athletic ...3-3
   Replay 2-4
Eagle Knowsley v E Bowling Unity 1-0
Heathfield v Merton Admiral 4-0
Horn Park v Somerset Ambury V&E...1-2
Leicester City bus v St Josephs 0-2
Littlewoods Ath v Manfast Kirkby 0-2
Lobster v Hartlepool Lion Hotel 2-0
Luton Way v Caversham Park...........2-3†
Nicosia v Carnforth 4-0
North Lynn Sunday v Marston Sports..1-2
Olton Royale v St Clements Hospital...4-0
Ouzavich v Ford Basildon 3-1
Quested v Elliott Star (Sunday).........4-1
Ranelagh Sports v Northfield Rangers .4-3
Royal Oak v Mitre BS 2-1
Santogee 66 v Bly Spartans 0-4
Sawston keys v Lodge Cottrell ....1-2†
Seymour v Almithak 2-0
St Josephs (Sth Oxhey) v Berner Utd ..1-2
St Peters v Bedfont Sundays ....2-4†
Watford Labour Club v Theale 0-2

Third Round – 6 Dec 1992

AEL v Caversham Park.....................1-1†
   Replay 3-1
Ansells Stockland v Reading Boro ....1-1†
   Replay 3-1
B&A Scaffolding v Britannia VNC ...1-0
Bedfont Sunday v Somerset A V&E...2-2†
   Replay 2-0
Berner United v Heathfield ....1-3†
Bly Spartans v Quested 2-0
Eagle Knowsley v Manfast Kirkby ....2-3†
Jolly Farmers v Lobster ....1-1†
   Replay 1-2

Lodge Cottrell v Dulwich 0-0
   Replay 3-1
Marston Sports v Royal Oak 2-1
Nicosia v Baildon Athletic 4-0
Oakenshaw v A3 6-2
Ranelagh Sports v Vanaid 2-0
Seymour v Napoli...........................0-0†
   Replay 3-2
St Josephs (Luton) v Olton Royale....0-0
   Replay 1-0
Theale v Ouzavich 5-0

Fourth Round – 17 Jan 1993

AEL v Heathfield ....1-0†
Bly Spartans v Reading Borough 3-4
Lodge Cottrell v Lobster ....3-1†
Manfast Kirkby v B&A Scaffolding 1-0
Martson Sports v Nicosia 1-0
Ranelagh Sports v Theale 2-1
Seymour v Oakenshaw 5-1
St Josephs (Luton) v Bedfont Sunday ..1-2

Fifth Round – 14 Feb 1993

AEL v Marston Sports 3-5
Bedfont Sunday v Ranelagh Sports 2-1
Manfast Kirkby v Reading Borough 0-3
Seymour v Lodge Cottrell 3-1

Semi-Finals – 21 March 1993

Marston Sports v Bedfont Sunday.....0-1
(at Bilston Town FC)
Reading Borough v Seymour 0-2
(at Reading FC)

Final – 2 May 1993

Seymour   1

Bedfont Sunday   0

Att: 606

ENGLAND SEMI-PRO INTERNATIONALS

31 May 1979, Stafford
ENGLAND 5 (Adamson 3 (2 pens), Mutrie, Whitbread)
SCOTLAND 1
Arnold (Stafford), Thompson (Yeovil), Davison (Altrincham), Adamson (Boston), Peake (Nuneaton), Jennings (Enfield), O'Keefe (Mossley), Phillips (Nuneaton), Mutrie (Blyth), Houghton (Blyth), Whitbread (Runcorn). Sub: Simmonite (Boston) for Thompson, Watson (Wealdstone) for Houghton.

3 June 1979, Stafford
ENGLAND 1 (O'Keefe)
HOLLAND 0
Arnold (Stafford), Thompson (Yeovil), Davison (Altrincham), Adamson (Boston), Peake (Nuneaton), Jennings (Enfield), O'Keefe (Mossley), Phillips (Nuneaton), Mutrie (Blyth), Watson (Wealdstone), Whitbread (Runcorn). Sub: Simmonite (Boston) for Thompson.

4 June 1980, Veenendaal, Holland
ENGLAND 2 (Hill, Smith)
ITALY 0
Clarke (Blyth), Simmonite (Boston), Davison (Altrincham), Jennings (Enfield), Adamson (Boston), Mutrie (Blyth), Watson (Wealdstone), Whitbread (Runcorn), Smith I (Mossley), Hill (Maidstone), Mayman (Norwich). Sub: Merrick (Weymouth) for Hill.

6 June 1980, Veenendaal, Holland
SCOTLAND 4
ENGLAND 2 (Mutrie, Hill)
Parker (Yeovil), Simmonite (Boston), Davison (Altrincham), Jennings (Enfield), Merrick (Weymouth), Adamson (Boston), Mutrie (Blyth), Watson (Wealdstone), Smith (Mossley), Hill (Maidstone), Mayman (Northwich). Sub: Clarke (Blyth) for Parker, Whitbread (Runcorn) for Merrick, Phillips (Kettering) for Mayman.

7 June 1980, Veenendaal, Holland
ENGLAND 2 (Whitbread, Watson)
HOLLAND 1
Clarke (Blyth), Stockley (Nuneaton), Hill (Maidstone), Jennings (Enfield), Simmonite (Boston), Phillips (Kettering), Adamson (Boston), Watson (Wealdstone), Denham (Northwich), Mutrie (Blyth), Whitbread (Runcorn). Sub: Smith (Mossley) for Denham.

9 June 1981, Lucca, Italy
ENGLAND 2 (Davison (pen), Williams)
HOLLAND 0
Clarke (Blyth), Thompson (Maidstone), Davison (Altrincham), Barrett (Enfield), Jennings (Enfield), Sellers (Scarborough), Finnegan (Weymouth), Watson (Scarborough), Howard (Altrincham), Williams (Northwich), Rogers (Altrincham). Sub: Ovard (Maidstone) for Rogers.

11 June 1981, Empoli, Italy
ENGLAND   0
SCOTLAND   0
Clarke (Blyth), Thompson (Maidstone), Davison (Altrincham), Barrett (Enfield), Jennings (Enfield), Sellers (Scarborough), Watson (Scarborough), Finnegan (Weymouth), Watson (Scarborough), Howard (Altrincham), Williams (Northwich), Rogers (Altrincham). Sub: Johnson (Altrincham) for Finnegan, Ovard (Maidstone) for Rogers.

13 June 1981, Montecatini, Italy
ITALY   1
ENGLAND   1   (Davison (pen))
Clarke (Blyth), Thompson (Maidstone), Davison (Altrincham), Barrett (Enfield), Jennings (Enfield), Sellers (Scarborough), Johnson (Altrincham), Howard (Altrincham), Whitbread (Altrincham), Rogers (Altrincham). Sub: Ovard (Maidstone) for Whitbread.

27 April 1982, Victoria Stadium, Gibraltar
GIBRALTAR   2
ENGLAND   3   (Ashford, Camillere o.g., Stephens)
Phillips (Barnet), Barrett (Enfield), Jennings (Enfield), Waite (Enfield), Davison (Altrincham), Sellers (Scarborough), Stephens (Sutton United), Johnson (Altrincham), Ashford (Enfield), Rogers (Altrincham), Smith (Alvechurch). Sub: Howard (Altrincham) for Ashford.

1 June 1982, Aberdeen
ENGLAND   0
ITALY   0
Clarke (Blyth), Thompson (Maidstone), Davison (Altrincham), Jennings (Enfield), Barrett (Enfield), Johnson (Altrincham), Stephens (Sutton United), Watson (Scarborough), Howard (Altrincham), Williams (Scarborough), Smith (Alvechurch). Sub: Rogers (Altrincham) for Williams.

3 June 1982, Aberdeen
ENGLAND   1   (Ashford)
HOLLAND   0
Clarke (Blyth), Thompson (Maidstone), Davison (Altrincham), Jennings (Enfield), Barrett (Enfield), Johnson (Altrincham), Stephens (Sutton United), Watson (Scarborough), Howard (Altrincham), Smith (Alvechurch), Ashford (Enfield). Sub: Sellers (Scarborough) for Smith.

5 June 1982, Aberdeen
SCOTLAND   1
ENGLAND   1   (Johnson)
Clarke (Blyth), Thompson (Maidstone), Davison (Altrincham), Jennings (Enfield), Barrett (Enfield), Johnson (Altrincham), Sellers (Scarborough), Watson (Scarborough), Howard (Altrincham), Rogers (Altrincham), Ashford (Enfield). Sub: Stephens (Sutton) for Thompson.

31 May 1983, Scarborough
ENGLAND   2   (Sellers, Cordice)
ITALY   0
Richardson (Maidstone), Thompson (Maidstone), Davison (Altrincham), Robinson (Blyth), Barrett (Enfield), Sellers (Scarborough), Watson (Maidstone), Johnson (Altrincham), Cordice (Wealdstone), Williams (Telford), Ashford (Enfield).

2 June 1983, Scarborough
ENGLAND   6   (Williams, Johnson, Davison (pen), Cordice, Watson, Ashford)
HOLLAND   0
Clarke (Blyth), Thompson (Maidstone), Davison (Altrincham), Robinson (Blyth), Barrett (Enfield), Sellers (Scarborough), Watson (Maidstone), Johnson (Altrincham), Cordice (Wealdstone), Williams (Telford), Ashford (Enfield). Sub: Ironton (Enfield) for Johnson, Derbyshire (Mossley) for Watson.

4 June 1983, Scarborough
ENGLAND   2   (Davison (pen), Williams)
SCOTLAND   1
Clarke (Blyth), Thompson (Maidstone), Davison (Altrincham), Robinson (Blyth), Barrett (Enfield), Sellers (Scarborough), Watson (Maidstone), Johnson (Altrincham), Cordice (Wealdstone), Williams (Telford), Ashford (Enfield). Sub: Derbyshire (Mossley) for Johnson, Ward (Northwich) for Sellers.

27 March 1984, Newtown
WALES   2
ENGLAND   1   (Smith)
Richardson (Maidstone), Thompson (Maidstone), Robinson (Blyth), Newson (Maidstone), Davison (Altrincham), Smith (Runcorn), Morley (Nuneaton), Ironton (Enfield/Maidstone), Cordice (Wealdstone), Culpin (Nuneaton), Ashford (Enfield). Sub: Barrett (Enfield) for Thompson, Watson (Maidstone) for Ironton.

5 June 1984, Palma, Italy
ENGLAND   3   (Johnson, Davison (pen), Barrett)
HOLLAND   3
Clarke (Blyth), Thompson (Maidstone), Newson (Maidstone), Barrett (Enfield), Davison (Altrincham), Watson (Maidstone), Morley (Nuneaton), Taylor (Maidstone), Johnson (Altrincham), Williams (Telford), Ashford (Enfield).

7 June 1984, Modena, Italy
ENGLAND   2   (Williams, Ashford)
SCOTLAND   0
Clarke (Blyth), Thompson (Maidstone), Newson (Maidstone), Barrett (Enfield), Davison (Altrincham), Watson (Maidstone), Morley (Nuneaton), Taylor (Maidstone), Johnson (Altrincham), Williams (Telford), Ashford (Enfield). Sub: Cordice (Wealdstone) for Williams, Joseph (Telford) for Johnson.

9 June 1984, Reggio Emilia, Italy
ITALY   1
ENGLAND   0
Clarke (Blyth), Thompson (Maidstone), Robinson (Blyth), Newson (Maidstone), Davison (Altrincham), Watson (Maidstone), Morley (Nuneaton), Taylor (Maidstone), Johnson (Altrincham), Williams (Telford), Ashford (Enfield). Sub: Cordice (Wealdstone) for Thompson, Pearce (Harrow) for Taylor.

26 March 1985, Telford
ENGLAND   1   (Robinson)
WALES   0
Charlton (Telford), Robinson (Blyth), Glover (Maidstone), Newson (Maidstone), Turner (Telford), Newton (Burton), Joseph (Telford), Morley (Nuneaton), Ashford (Enfield), Mell

(Burton), Hooley (Frickley). Sub: Pape (Harrow) for Charlton, Culpin (Nuneaton) for Hooley, Smithers (Nuneaton) for Mell.

11 June 1985, Houten, Holland
ENGLAND   2   (Culpin, Barrett)
ITALY   2
Charlton (Telford), Constantine (Altrincham), Glover (Maidstone), Barrett (Enfield), Davison (Altrincham), Johnson (Altrincham), Joseph (Telford), Smithers (Nuneaton), Cordice (Wealdstone), Culpin (Nuneaton), Williams (Telford). Sub: Ashford (Enfield) for Williams.

13 June 1985, Utrecht, Holland
ENGLAND   3   (Culpin 3)
HOLLAND   0
Pape (Harrow), Constantine (Altrincham), Glover (Maidstone), Barrett (Enfield), Davison (Altrincham), Johnson (Altrincham), Joseph (Telford), Newton (Burton), Cordice (Wealdstone), Culpin (Nuneaton), Williams (Telford). Sub: Howell (Enfield) for Newton.

15 June 1985, Harderwijk, Holland
ENGLAND   1   (Williams)
SCOTLAND   3
Pape (Harrow), Constantine (Altrincham), Glover (Maidstone), Barrett (Enfield), Davison (Altrincham), Johnson (Altrincham), Joseph (Telford), Newton (Burton), Cordice (Wealdstone), Culpin (Nuneaton), Williams (Telford). Sub: Morley (Nuneaton) for Williams, Howell (Enfield) for Barrett.

18 March 1986, Merthyr Tydfil
WALES   3
ENGLAND   1   (Davies)
Richardson (Maidstone), Constantine (Witton), Davison (Altrincham), Howell (Enfield), Wilcox (Frickley), Stephens (Sutton), Walker (Blyth), Smithers (Nuneaton), Wilson (Frickley), Davies (Kidderminster), Casey (Kidderminster). Sub: Johnson (Altrincham) for Walker, Doherty (Weymouth) for Casey, Joseph (Telford) for Stephens, Pape (Enfield) for Richardson.

24 May 1986, Kidderminster
ENGLAND   2   (Johnson, Casey)
EIRE   1
Pape (Enfield), Shirtliff (Frickley), Davison (Altrincham), Howell (Enfield), Wilcox (Frickley), Stephens (Sutton), Walker (Blyth), Johnson (Altrincham), Ashford (Enfield), Richards (Enfield), Casey (Kidderminster). Sub: Simpson (Stafford) for Stephens, Buchanan (Blyth) for Walker.

26 May 1986, Nuneaton Borough
ENGLAND   2   (Wilcox, Agana)
EIRE   1
Richardson (Maidstone), Shirtliff (Frickley), Davison (Altrincham), Howell (Enfield), Wilcox (Frickley), Johnson (Altrincham), Clayton (Burton), Simpson (Stafford), Ashford (Enfield), Buchanan (Blyth), Agana (Weymouth). Sub: Stephens (Sutton) for Johnson, Walker (Blyth) for Howell, Casey (Kidderminster) for Buchanan.

17 March 1987, Gloucester City
ENGLAND   2   (Casey, Ashford)
WALES   2
Pape (Enfield), Shirtliff (Frickley), Thompson (Scarborough), Brazier (Kidderminster), Howell (Enfield), Jones (Weymouth), Margerrison (Barnet), Joseph (Telford), Casey (Kidderminster), Carter (Runcorn), Davies (Kidderminster). Sub: Ashford (Wycombe) for Margerrison.

18 May 1987, Dunfermline
ENGLAND   1   (Howell)
ITALY   2
Pape (Enfield), Shirtliff (Frickley), Howell (Enfield), Cuddy (Altrincham), Thompson (Scarborough), Ashford (Wycombe), Farrelly (Altrincham), Simpson (Stafford), Casey (Kidderminster), Carter (Runcorn), Davies (Kidderminster). Sub: Abbott (Welling) for Casey, Joseph (Telford) for Shirtliff.

20 May 1987, Kirkcaldy
ENGLAND   4   (Carter 4)
HOLLAND   0
Pape (Enfield), Shirtliff (Frickley), Howell (Enfield), Cuddy (Altrincham), Thompson (Scarborough), Ashford (Wycombe), Farrelly (Altrincham), Simpson (Stafford), Joseph (Telford), Carter (Runcorn), Davies (Kidderminster). Sub: Golley (Sutton) for Ashford, Humphries (Barnet) for Pape.

23 May 1987, Dunfermline
SCOTLAND   1
ENGLAND   2   (Howell, Carter)
Pape (Enfield), Cuddy (Altrincham), Howell (Enfield), Golley (Sutton), Thompson (Scarborough), Ashford (Wycombe), Simpson (Stafford), Farrelly (Altrincham), Joseph (Telford), Carter (Runcorn), Davies (Kidderminster). Sub: Abbott (Welling) for Ashford, Walker (Blyth) for Davies.

15 March 1988, Rhyl
WALES   0
ENGLAND   2   (Carter 2)
Pape (Enfield), Shirtliff (Frickley), Teale (Weymouth), Howell (Enfield), Densmore (Runcorn), Joseph (Telford), Golley (Sutton), Codnor (Barnet), Davies (Kidderminster), Carter (Runcorn), Butler (Maidstone). Sub: Brooks (Cheltenham) for Golley, Norris (Telford) for Carter, McKenna (Boston) for Pape.

29 January 1989, La Spezia, Italy
ITALY   1
ENGLAND   1   (Carter)
Pape (Enfield), Shirtliff (Frickley), Gridlett (Hendon), Howell (Enfield), Densmore (Runcorn), Lake (Macclesfield), Bancroft (Kidderminster), Joseph (Telford), Golley (Maidstone), Carter (Runcorn), Butler (Maidstone). Sub: Davies (Kidderminster) for Butler, Lee (Telford) for Shirtliff, Shearer (Cheltenham) for Lake, Beaney (Maidstone) for Pape.

21 March 1989, Kidderminster
ENGLAND   2   (Rogers, Carter)
WALES   0

Pape (Enfield), Shirtliff (Boston), Gridlett (Hendon), Howell (Enfield), Watts (Leytonstone), Joseph (Telford), Golley (Maidstone), Rogers (Sutton), Bancroft (Kidderminster), Carter (Runcorn), Butler (Maidstone). Sub: Cooke (Kettering) for Bancroft.

25 February 1990, Salerno, Italy
ITALY   2
ENGLAND   0
McKenna (Boston), Shirtliff (Boston), Watts (Redbridge), Howell (Enfield), Skivington (Barrow), Rogers (Sutton), Joseph (Kidderminster), Hessenthaler (Dartford), Furlong (Enfield), Carter (Runcorn), Simpson (Altrincham). Sub: Pape (Enfield) for McKenna, Bancroft (Kidderminster) for Watts, Conner (Dartford) for Hessenthaler, Cooke (Kettering) for Rogers, Hone (Welling) for Shirtliff.

6 March 1990, Merthyr Tydfil
WALES   0
ENGLAND   0
Pape (Enfield), Shirtliff (Boston), Bancroft (Kidderminster), Howell (Enfield), Skivington (Barrow), Gridlet (Barnet), Askey (Macclesfield), Hanlon (Macclesfield), Furlong (Enfield), Ashford (Redbridge), Simpson (Altrincham).

25 May 1990, Dublin
EIRE   1
ENGLAND   2   (Carter 2 (1pen))
McKenna (Boston), Shirtliff (Boston), Bancroft (Kidderminster), Watts (Redbridge), Howell (Enfield), Gridlet (Barnet), Brooks (Cheltenham), Clarke (Barnet), Carter (Runcorn), Ashford (Redbridge), Simpson (Altrincham). Sub: Rodgers (Sutton) for Simpson, Furlong (Enfield) for Ashford, Joseph (Kidderminster) for Clarke.

27 May 1990, Cork
EIRE   0
ENGLAND   3   (Ashford, Furlong, Carter)
Pape (Enfield), Shirtliff (Boston), Rogers (Sutton), Watts (Redbridge), Howell (Enfield), Gridlet (Barnet), Joseph (Kidderminster), Furlong (Enfield), Carter (Runcorn), Ashford (Redbridge), Simpson (Altrincham). Sub: McKenna (Boston) for Pape, Bancroft (Kidderminster) for Simpson, Brooks (Cheltenham) for Watts, Skivington (Barrow) for Ashford.

5 March 1991, Kettering
ENGLAND   0
ITALY   0
Pape (Enfield), Lee (Witton), Watts (Redbridge), Skivington (Barrow), Nicol (Kettering), Conner (Redbridge), Lowe (Barnet), Rogers (Sutton), Carter (Barnet), Furlong (Enfield), Showler (Altrincham). Sub: Willis (Barnet) for Furlong, Ashford (Redbridge) for Showler.

17 May 1991, Stafford
ENGLAND   1   (Carter)
WALES   2
McKenna (Boston), Lee (Witton), Bancroft (Kettering), Skivington (Barrow), Nicol (Kettering), Conner (Redbridge), Lowe (Barnet), Rogers (Sutton), Todd (Berwick), Furlong (Enfield), West (Wycombe). Sub: Carter (Barnet) for West, Showler (Altrincham) for Nicol, Humphries (Kidderminster) for Todd.

3 March 1992, Aberystwyth
WALES   **0**
ENGLAND   **1**   (Mayes)
McKenna (Boston), Shirtliff (Boston), Watts (Redbridge), Nicol (Kettering), Connor (Redbridge), Humphreys (Kidderminster), Richardson (Redbridge), Golley (Welling), Mayes (Redbridge), Robbins (Welling), Cavell (Redbridge). Sub: Price (Stafford) for McKenna, Abbott (Welling) for Humphreys, Read (Farnborough) for Robbins.

2 March 1993, Cheltenham
ENGLAND   **2**   (Robbins (pen), Leworthy)
WALES   **1**
Price (Stafford), Shirtliff (Dagenham & R), Watts (Dagenham & R), Shail (Yeovil), Kerr (Wycombe), Stapleton (Wycombe), Thompson (Wycombe), Richardson (Dagenham & R), Robbins (Welling), Leworthy (Farnborough), Guppy (Wycombe). Ross (Marine) for Robbins.

14 April, Woking
ENGLAND   **1**   (Cavell)
FINLAND UNDER-21   **3**
Price (Stafford), Shirtliff (Dagenham & R), Watts (Dagenham & R), Hone (Welling), Connor (Dagenham & R), Butler (Northwich), Webb (Bromsgrove), Richardson (Dagenham & R), Robbins (Welling), Cavell (Dagenham & R), Hemmings (Northwich). Batty (Woking) for Price, Collins (Enfield) for Butler, Coleman for Robbins, Ross (Marine) for Hemmings.

15th May, Elgin
SCOTLAND   **2**
ENGLAND   **2**   (Richardson, Cavell)
Price (Stafford), Hone (Welling), Watts (Dagenham & R), Richardson (Bromsgrove), Connor (Dagenham & R), Broom (Dagenham & R), Webb (Bromsgrove), Richardson (Dagenham & R), Ross (Marine), Cavell (Dagenham & R), Hemmings (Northwic). Butler (Northwich) for Hemmings, Batty (Woking) for Price, Collins (Enfield) for Webb.

Record Summary by Country

	P	W	D	L	F	A
Eire	4	4	0	0	9	3
Finland	1	0	0	1	1	3
Gibraltar	1	1	0	0	3	2
Holland	8	7	1	0	22	4
Italy	10	2	5	3	9	9
Scotland	9	4	3	2	17	13
Wales	10	5	2	3	13	10
Total	**43**	**23**	**11**	**9**	**74**	**44**

Scorers
Carter 13 (1 pen), Ashford 6, Davison 5 (5 pens), Williams 5, Culpin 4, Johnson 4, Adamson 3 (2 pens), Barrett 2, Casey 2, Cavell 2, Cordice 2, Hill 2, Howell 2, Mutrie 2, Smith I. 2, Watson 2, Whitebread 2, Agana 1, Davies 1, Furlong 1, Leworthy 1, Mayes 1, O'Keefe 1, Richardson 1, Robbins 1, Robinson 1, Rogers 1, Sellers 1, Stephens 1, Wilcox 1, own goals 1.

GM VAUXHALL CONFERENCE

At a stroll...

In the end it all looked a bit of a stroll for Wycombe Wanderers who were confirmed as champions with five games left to play. Their league season was built upon the phenomenal success of the first half of the campaign. They won nine out of their first ten games and went on to amass 48 of their 83 points in the first half of the season with a goal difference of 40 goals. After the disappointments of the preceding season when they missed out on Football League status by the slimmest of margins it was quite an achievement that they could motivate the players so effectively. There were

Final Table 1992-93

		Home					Away					
	P	W	D	L	F	A	W	D	L	F	A	Pts
Wycombe Wanderers	42	13	5	3	46	16	11	6	4	38	21	83
Bromsgrove Rovers	42	9	7	5	35	22	9	7	5	32	27	68
*Dagenham & R'dbridge	42	10	5	6	48	29	9	6	6	27	18	67
Yeovil Town	42	13	5	3	42	21	5	7	9	17	28	66
Slough Town	42	12	3	6	39	28	6	8	7	21	27	65
Stafford Rangers	42	7	6	8	22	24	11	4	6	33	23	64
Bath City	42	9	8	4	29	23	6	6	9	24	23	59
Woking	42	9	2	10	30	33	8	6	7	28	29	59
Kidderminster Harriers	42	9	5	7	26	30	5	11	5	34	30	58
Altrincham	42	7	7	7	21	25	8	6	7	28	27	58
Northwich Victoria	42	5	6	10	24	29	11	2	8	44	26	56
Stalybridge Celtic	42	7	10	4	25	26	6	7	8	23	29	56
Kettering Town	42	10	5	6	36	28	4	8	9	25	35	55
Gateshead	42	9	6	6	27	19	5	4	12	26	37	52
Telford United	42	9	5	7	31	24	5	5	11	24	36	52
Methyr Tydfil	42	4	9	8	26	37	10	1	10	25	42	52
Witton Albion	42	5	9	7	30	34	6	8	7	32	31	50
Macclesfield Town	42	7	9	5	23	20	5	4	12	17	30	49
Runcorn	42	8	3	10	32	36	5	7	9	26	40	49
Welling United	42	8	6	7	34	37	4	6	11	23	35	48
Farnborough Town	42	8	5	8	34	36	4	6	11	34	51	47
Boston United	42	5	6	10	23	31	4	7	10	27	38	40

* One point deducted

occasions in the second half of the season when Wycombe's form looked patchy but it was always matched by similar form amongst the chasing clubs and a challenge for the title never really materialised.

Success in the Vauxhall FA Trophy confirmed their class as they ran out 4-1 winners against Runcorn. The scoreline may have been slightly flattering to Wycombe but there was only ever going to be one name on the Trophy. There was much talk of Martin O'Neill being chosen as Brian Clough's successor at Nottingham Forest but in the end he decided to stay with the Blues on a two year contract.

The last Saturday of the season was played out with four teams contesting second place and no fewer than six facing the prospect of relegation. Once the dust had settled it was Bromsgrove who had clinched second place and Farnborough who were joining Boston on the way out. Bromsgrove Rovers took the transition from the Southern League to Non-League's top flight in their stride. Seventeen points from their last seven games saw them gain the highest placing by a newly promoted club since 1982.

After the financial uncertainties of the preceding seasons this one has been one of consolidation for Yeovil Town. If a third-round FA Cup tie against Arsenal stole the limelight it was the club's highest ever League placing, fourth, which promises the most for the future. Farnborough's relegation came as quite a surprise to most people and as a very unpleasant shock to those at the club itself. They spent most of the season in the lower half of the table but never occupied a relegation place until the final game of the season. Their manager of some 23 years, Ted Pearce, saw his last season at the club. It's a period in which the club has risen from park football to the pinnacle of the semi-pro game. Boston United's season never really got going after a disastrous first half. A spell of reasonable form in the new year raised some hopes but the challenge ultimately proved too great. The magnitude of the task they faced is illustrated by the 40 points they attained the highest of any bottom-placed club in the brief history of the Conference – and yet they were still eight points short of safety.

Northwich Victoria secured their first trophy in ten years of trying. Incoming manager John Williams steered them to Drinkwise Cup triumph in circumstances that few might have predicted. They took a goalless draw from the home leg of the final to Adams Park, home of Wycombe Wanderers, and came back with a 3-2 aggregate win. Their season ended on the brightest of all possible notes with the news that they have raised the money necessary to hold onto their Drill Field ground – the oldest football stadium in the world.

The Alliance Premier League History

The Alliance Premier League was founded in 1979 with 20 clubs drawn from the Southern (13) and Northern Premier (7) Leagues. In 1981 two Isthmian clubs joined to bring the membership up to 22 clubs. The League was known as the Gola League from 1984-85 for two seasons and thereafter under its present title.

Three points for a win was introduced for 1981-82 but modified to apply to away games only for three seasons from 1983-84. Promotion to and relegation from the League has always been a feature of its structure and from 1985-86 representatives of the Southern, Northern Premier and Isthmian Leagues have normally joined at the expense of the three bottom sides.

The promotion of the League's champions to the Football League and the relegation of the 92nd Football League club to the League has been operational since 1986-87, although no club was relegated to the Conference for 1991-92 or 1992-93. With the advent of the FA Premier League, promotion from the Conference to the Football League was to the Third Division from the 1992-93 season.

5-Year One, Two, Three Records

	First....Pts	Second....Pts	Third....Pts
1987-88	Lincoln City 82	Barnet 80	Kettering 75
1988-89	Maidstone United ...84	Kettering Town 76	Boston United 74
1989-90	Darlington............87	Barnet 85	Runcorn 70
1990-91	Barnet 87	Colchester Utd...85	Altrincham 82
1991-92	Colchester Utd 94	Wycombe Wdrs 94	Kettering Town ...73

Leading GMVC Goalscorers 1992-93

Conf	Player (Club)	FAC	VFAT	DC	Total
32	David Leworthy (Farnborough Town)	1	5	1	40
23	Mark Whitehouse (Bromsgrove Rovers)	–	2	1	26
21	Malcolm O'Connor (Northwich Victoria)	2	1	3	27
20	Keith Scott (Wycombe Wanderers)	1	5	2	28
19	Paul Cavell (Dagenham & Redbridge)	8	1	1	29
	Terry Robbins (Welling United)	1	2	1	23
	Andy Sayer (Slough Town)	1	1	–	21
	Karl Thomas (Witton Albion)	–	3	–	22
17	Gary Abbott (Welling United)	–	1	1	19
16	Phil Brown (Kettering Town)	2	–	–	18
	Gary Jones (Boston United)	2	5	1	24
	Mickey Spencer (Yeovil Town)	2	1	2	21
15	Tony Hemmings (Northwich Victoria)	1	–	4	20
	Allan Lamb (Gateshead)	7	1	–	23

Conf=GM Vauxhall Conference, FAC=FA Cup, VFAT=Vauxhall FA Trophy, DC=Drinkwise Cup

ANNUAL AWARDS

Player of the Year: Steve Guppy (Wycombe Wanderers)
Manager of the Year: Martin O'Neill (Wycombe Wanderers)
Goalscorer of the Year: David Leworthy (Farnborough Town)

The *Mail on Sunday* Team of the Year

Position	Player	Club
Goalkeeper	Paul Hyde	Wycombe Wanderers
Right Back	Jason Cousins	Wycombe Wanderers
Left Back	Stewart Brighton	Bromsgrove Rovers
Centre Backs	Andy Kerr	Wycombe Wanderers
	Kevin Richardson	Bromsgrove Rovers
Midfield	Simon Stapleton	Wycombe Wanderers
	Steve Thompson	Wycombe Wanderers
	Paul Webb	Bromsgrove Rovers
Forwards	David Leworthy	Farnborough Town
	Keith Scott	Wycombe Wanderers
	Steve Guppy	Wycombe Wanderers

The *Mail on Sunday* Manager of the Month Awards

Month	Manager	Club
August/September	Martin O'Neill	Wycombe Wanderers
October	Peter Wragg	Macclesfield Town
November	Steve Rutter	Yeovil Town
December	John Williams	Northwich Victoria
January	Gerry Daly	Telford United
February	Ted Pearce	Farnborough Town
March	Steve Rutter	Yeovil Town
April	Graham Allner	Kidderminster Harriers

The *Mail on Sunday* Goalscorer of the Month Awards

Month	Player	Club
August/September	Allan Lamb	Gateshead
October	David Leworthy	Farnborough Town
November	Richard Mitchell	Macclesfield Town
December	Malcolm O'Connor	Northwich Victoria
January	David Leworthy	Farnborough Town
February	Gary Jones	Boston United
March	Karl Thomas	Witton Albion
	Paul Wilson	Yeovil Town
April	Ken McKenna	Runcorn

Leading Goalscorers by Club

Club	Player	Goals
Altrincham	Clive Freeman	8
Bath City	Richard Crowley	11
Boston United	Gary Jones	16
Bromsgrove Rovers	Mark Whitehouse	23
Dagenham & Redbridge	Paul Cavell	19
Farnborough Town	David Leworthy	32
Gateshead	Allan Lamb	15
Kettering Town	Philip Brown	16
Kidderminster Harriers	Paul Davies	11
Macclesfield Town	Colin Lambert	8
	Richard Mitchell	8
Merthyr Tydfil	Ceri Williams	14
Northwich Victoria	Malcolm O'Connor	21
Runcorn	Ken McKenna	12
Slough Town	Andy Sayer	19
Stafford Rangers	Paul Clayton	9
Stalybridge Celtic	Mark Edwards	12
Telford United	Steve Fergusson	8
Welling United	Terry Robbins	19
Witton Albion	Karl Thomas	19
Woking	Trevor Senior	11
Wycombe Wanderers	Keith Scott	20
	Kim Casey	10
Yeovil Town	Michael Spencer	15
	Paul Wilson	13

Championship Shield – 6th October 1992

Wycombe Wanderers   Colchester United 3-0   3309
Scott 39 (pen), Casey 58, 79

Wycombe Wanderers:
Paul Hyde, Jason Cousins, Matt Crossley, Andy Kerr, Glyn Creaser, Simon Hutchinson, Dave Carroll (Dennis Greene), Kim Casey, Simon Stapleton (Keith Ryan), Keith Scott, Steve Guppy.

Colchester United:
Alastair Monk, Paul Abrahams, Paul Roberts, Mark Kinsella, Peter Cawsey, Darren Oxbrow, Jason Cook (Andrew Partner), Gary Bennett, Steve Ball (Warren Donald), Steve McGavin, Nicky Smith.

GMVC RESULTS 1992-93

	Altrincham	Bath City	Boston United	Bromsgrove	Dagenham & R	Farnborough	Gateshead	Kettering Town	Kidderminster	Macclesfield	Merthyr Tydfil
Altrincham	•	1-0	1-1	2-2	1-0	2-2	0-1	3-0	2-2	0-0	0-1
Bath City	3-0	•	2-1	0-3	2-1	5-2	1-1	0-0	2-1	1-0	1-3
Boston United	1-2	1-2	•	1-2	3-1	0-0	0-2	0-1	0-3	3-1	2-0
Bromsgrove Rovers	4-1	1-1	2-1	•	1-2	2-2	3-0	1-1	2-2	3-0	1-2
Dagenham & Redbridge	2-2	2-1	4-0	1-1	•	5-1	3-1	3-2	3-2	1-2	6-1
Farnborough Town	2-5	2-1	2-2	1-1	1-4	•	6-1	1-1	2-2	0-0	2-1
Gateshead	2-0	0-4	2-2	0-0	1-1	1-0	•	1-1	1-0	1-0	4-0
Kettering Town	1-1	0-1	3-3	3-2	1-1	2-1	2-0	•	1-2	1-0	1-3
Kidderminster Harriers	0-1	1-0	0-2	0-1	0-1	1-5	3-3	0-0	•	2-1	1-0
Macclesfield Town	1-1	0-1	1-0	0-2	0-1	1-2	1-0	1-0	1-1	•	0-1
Merthyr Tydfil	2-2	1-1	0-3	1-1	0-2	1-3	0-0	2-1	4-3	1-2	•
Northwich Victoria	1-2	3-1	3-3	0-1	1-1	3-0	4-2	2-2	0-1	1-3	1-2
Runcorn	0-1	1-3	1-2	0-1	0-1	1-4	1-0	3-0	3-1	1-2	2-3
Slough Town	1-4	1-1	3-0	1-3	2-0	3-1	2-1	2-4	0-0	1-0	2-1
Stafford Rangers	0-0	3-2	0-0	3-4	0-1	2-2	1-0	3-0	3-1	2-1	2-1
Stalybridge Celtic	1-0	1-1	2-1	0-1	0-3	6-3	2-1	0-0	2-2	3-1	5-0
Telford United	2-1	0-0	2-2	0-1	0-2	3-1	1-0	3-1	1-1	1-0	5-0
Welling United	2-0	0-3	2-0	4-2	2-2	1-0	2-1	1-1	0-0	2-1	3-1
Witton Albion	1-1	0-0	3-0	1-1	1-1	1-1	1-3	4-2	1-1	4-0	0-2
Woking	0-2	0-1	0-0	0-2	1-1	4-1	1-4	3-2	1-5	1-1	2-2
Wycombe Wanderers	0-2	1-1	3-3	4-0	1-1	1-1	2-1	1-2	1-1	4-0	4-0
Yeovil Town	1-0	2-1	2-1	2-2	0-3	5-2	1-3	2-1	2-2	1-1	0-1

	Northwich Vic	Runcorn	Slough Town	Stafford Rgrs	Stalybridge C	Telford United	Welling United	Witton Albion	Woking	Wycombe	Yeovil Town
Altrincham	0-0	0-2	1-1	1-5	0-0	0-3	2-0	2-1	1-0	0-2	1-2
Bath City	0-5	1-1	0-1	2-1	1-1	4-1	1-1	0-0	2-0	2-0	0-0
Boston United	3-5	0-0	0-0	2-1	1-1	2-2	2-1	2-2	1-2	0-3	1-0
Bromsgrove Rovers	1-2	0-0	0-1	2-3	4-0	0-0	2-2	3-2	1-2	1-0	1-0
Dagenham & Redbridge	4-1	5-1	4-4	0-1	1-2	0-2	1-0	1-1	5-1	1-2	1-1
Farnborough Town	0-3	2-3	1-0	0-1	0-0	0-1	3-2	1-1	0-3	0-2	2-1
Gateshead	0-2	4-1	1-0	0-1	1-2	1-1	1-2	3-1	1-1	0-1	4-1
Kettering Town	2-1	3-3	5-0	2-0	0-0	1-1	2-4	0-0	1-3	0-4	3-0
Kidderminster Harriers	5-3	2-0	1-1	0-2	2-0	2-0	1-1	1-0	1-1	1-4	1-1
Macclesfield Town	1-2	1-1	1-2	4-1	2-1	2-1	1-1	0-2	1-5	1-4	1-1
Merthyr Tydfil	3-0	0-3	1-1	0-0	1-1	4-0	1-1	1-3	1-2	1-4	0-1
Northwich Victoria	•	3-2	0-1	1-2	1-3	1-0	0-1	4-4	2-3	0-0	1-0
Runcorn	0-1	•	0-3	0-2	2-3	3-1	3-0	2-3	0-1	2-1	3-0
Slough Town	0-4	1-1	•	2-1	2-3	2-0	4-2	1-1	3-1	1-1	1-1
Stafford Rangers	1-0	0-1	1-0	•	0-0	2-1	4-3	0-0	0-1	1-0	0-1
Stalybridge Celtic	0-6	0-0	0-0	1-0	•	3-3	0-0	1-2	3-0	2-2	1-1
Telford United	1-0	2-1	1-1	0-0	0-2	•	0-1	0-3	3-3	2-3	1-0
Welling United	1-5	3-2	2-1	1-2	1-4	1-3	•	2-2	1-1	0-1	0-3
Witton Albion	1-3	0-3	1-1	2-5	1-2	2-1	0-1	•	1-2	2-2	1-2
Woking	1-0	4-0	1-2	0-3	2-1	3-2	1-0	1-2	•	0-3	0-0
Wycombe Wanderers	1-0	5-1	1-0	2-2	4-0	4-0	3-0	2-1	0-0	•	5-1
Yeovil Town	1-1	4-0	5-1	2-0	1-1	1-0	1-0	2-0	4-1	3-0	•

ATTENDANCES 1992-93

	Altrincham	Bath City	Boston United	Bromsgrove	Dagenham	Farnborough	Gateshead	Kettering	Kidderminster	Macclesfield	Merthyr Tydfil
Altrincham	•	678	698	1010	517	746	814	527	735	1143	729
Bath City	615	•	508	516	570	617	491	386	870	478	616
Boston United	502	841	•	1037	1137	1103	1040	1481	1228	818	734
Bromsgrove Rovers ...	1117	1030	1235	•	1120	1780	923	1297	3185	1065	1306
Dagenham & Redbridge	823	924	1048	1078	•	1318	1022	1225	1004	1303	805
Farnborough Town ...	738	504	521	533	655	•	637	1007	565	676	602
Gateshead	302	373	362	405	387	346	•	478	321	375	343
Kettering Town	1299	1185	2592	1328	1341	1395	1455	•	1365	1209	1356
Kidderminster Harriers	1225	1134	954	4324	1089	1120	716	1608	•	1032	1158
Macclesfield Town	875	651	429	604	387	574	473	731	593	•	459
Merthyr Tydfil	458	808	606	546	746	402	537	486	657	554	•
Northwich Victoria	774	641	803	508	610	610	672	721	629	785	583
Runcorn	780	504	645	459	475	448	471	492	512	757	483
Slough Town	1101	1021	906	866	1813	1180	862	1095	1069	930	1175
Stafford Rangers	831	921	848	1126	786	947	538	815	1294	1025	618
Stalybridge Celtic	1011	633	484	771	752	378	558	805	702	822	817
Telford United	1063	618	924	935	757	1031	633	1322	1692	1175	703
Welling United	857	862	912	750	1357	842	1049	838	663	959	720
Witton Albion	1084	622	746	912	812	546	771	986	638	1110	614
Woking	2060	1290	1652	1832	1734	2471	1722	1586	1537	1868	2049
Wycombe Wanderers	6284	4085	4560	4282	5106	4141	3290	4430	4353	5748	3716
Yeovil Town	2198	6488	3049	5495	2847	2404	1808	2006	2159	2515	1834

	Northwich Vic	Runcorn	Slough Town	Stafford Rgrs	Stalybridge C	Telford United	Welling United	Witon Albion	Woking	Wycombe W	Yeovil Town
Altrincham	1091	814	832	858	844	504	631	925	839	1512	722
Bath City	535	673	592	573	560	338	506	592	801	1283	1331
Boston United	924	1448	875	985	943	814	1309	939	1135	1460	1118
Bromsgrove Rovers	1125	963	1456	1130	945	1543	957	1145	1808	3675	1196
Dagenham & Redbridge	923	1404	1355	1015	1052	1302	1288	1076	1648	2542	1072
Farnborough Town	702	581	842	741	602	617	513	704	2287	2678	582
Gateshead	349	547	347	297	631	371	517	233	626	815	397
Kettering Town	1221	911	1205	1260	1137	1221	1488	1090	2127	3021	1337
Kidderminster Harriers	1417	1065	1175	1234	1047	1532	1018	1268	1759	3064	1257
Macclesfield Town	1068	631	651	473	844	470	437	762	879	1397	431
Merthyr Tydfil	609	451	589	694	628	380	655	592	380	1408	461
Northwich Victoria	•	772	565	802	691	612	529	1971	984	1860	873
Runcorn	787	•	526	596	700	532	778	753	953	850	421
Slough Town	946	803	•	823	859	914	905	1060	2480	4500	771
Stafford Rangers	953	876	886	•	1133	1007	786	912	1062	1631	854
Stalybridge Celtic	1111	509	786	752	•	1339	705	634	968	1694	753
Telford United	703	947	968	1068	984	•	574	1160	1463	1741	1015
Welling United	633	842	721	712	719	875	•	927	1077	2616	963
Witton Albion	2442	963	742	695	961	756	541	•	930	1272	952
Woking	1992	1890	1948	2044	1713	1317	1647	2041	•	4911	2427
Wycombe Wanderers	4060	6220	7230	4569	4120	3414	3530	4731	5000	•	•
Yeovil Town	2110	1684	2451	1903	1844	2207	2019	2316	2911	2667	•

Attendance Summaries by Club

Club	Psn	(91-92)	Aggregate	(91-92)	Average	(91-92)	% change
Wycombe Wndrs	1	(2)	96,638	(75,726)	4602	(3606)	+28
Yeovil Town	4	(15)	54,915	(44,471)	2615	(2103)	+24
Woking	8	(DLP)	41,731	(30,885)	1987	(1880)	+6
Kettering Town	13	(3)	30,543	(37,917)	1454	(1857)	-22
Kidderminster Hars	9	(19)	30,226	(27,421)	1439	(1302)	+11
Bromsgrove Rovers	2	(BHLP)	30,001	(17,554)	1429	(836)	+71
Slough Town	5	(20)	26,079	(19,425)	1242	(924)	+34
Dagenham & Rbge*	3	(7)	25,227	(15,116)	1201	(719)	+67
Boston United	22	(8)	21,871	(28,820)	1041	(1,173)	-11
Telford United	15	(6)	21,476	(21,826)	1023	(1039)	-1
Welling United	20	(12)	19,894	(17,661)	947	(840)	+13
Stafford Rangers	6	(17)	19,849	(18,342)	945	(873)	+8
Witton Albion	17	(10)	19,095	(19,182)	909	(913)	–
Farnborough Town	21	(5)	17,287	(20,485)	823	(975)	-16
Northwich Victoria	11	(11)	17,120	(17166)	815	(820)	–
Stalybridge Celtic	12	(NPLP)	16,984	(12,195)	809	(581)	+39
Altrincham	10	(18)	16,982	(18,222)	809	(868)	-7
Macclesfield Town	18	(13)	13,819	(15,866)	658	(755)	-13
Bath City	7	(9)	13,481	(14,771)	642	(704)	-8
Runcorn	19	(16)	12,922	(15,316)	615	(629)	-2
Merthyr Tydfil	16	(4)	12,647	(13,658)	602	(650)	-7
Gateshead	14	(14)	8,822	(8,431)	420	(401)	+5
Totals			567,609	(560,742)	1229	(1214)	–

Previous season's records for Redbridge Forest

All Time Top GMVC Attendance

Att	Match			Date
9,432	Lincoln City	v	Wycombe Wanderers	02/05/88
7,542	Lincoln City	v	Boston United	04/04/88
7,230	Wycombe Wanderers	v	Slough Town	23/03/93
7,193	Colchester United	v	Barrow	02/05/92
6,986	Colchester United	v	Altrincham	20/04/91

GMVC – Football League Ups and Downs

Season	Promoted	Relegated
1986-87	Scarborough	Lincoln City
1987-88	Lincoln City	Newport County
1988-89	Maidstone United	Darlington
1989-90	Darlington	Colchester United
1990-91	Barnet	No club relegated
1991-92	Colchester United	No club relegated
1992-93	Wycombe Wanderers	Halifax Town

Hat-trick Heroes

3   Malcolm O'Connor (Northwich Victoria)
1   Boyle (Bath), Cavell (Dagenham), Leworthy (Farnborough), Dobson (Gateshead), Purdie (Kidderminster), Hemmings, (Northwich), McKenna (Runcorn), Robbins (Welling), Wilson (Yeovil)

Highest Aggregate Scores

6-3	Telford United	v	Farnborough Town	12/09/92
5-3	Kidderminster Hrs	v	Northwich Victoria	01/05/93
4-4	D'ham & Redbridge	v	Slough Town	08/02/93
4-4	Runcorn	v	Witton Albion	17/04/93
3-5	Boston United	v	Northwich Victoria	12/12/92

Largest Home Wins

6-1	D'ham & Redbridge	v	Merthyr Tydfil	06/04/93
6-1	Farnborough Town	v	Gateshead	22/08/92
5-0	Kettering Town	v	Slough Town	03/11/92
5-0	Telford United	v	Merthyr Tydfil	12/04/93
5-0	Welling United	v	Merthyr Tydfil	21/11/92

Largest Away Wins

0-6	Stalybridge Celtic	v	Northwich Victoria	02/01/93
0-6	Bath City	v	Northwich Victoria	30/01/93
1-5	Altrincham	v	Stafford Rangers	30/01/93
1-5	Kidderminster Hrs	v	Farnborough Town	27/02/93
1-5	Merthyr Tydfil	v	Woking	24/11/92
1-5	Welling United	v	Northwich Victoria	20/03/93
1-5	Woking	v	Kidderminster Harriers	03/04/93

Matches Without Defeat

10 Wycombe Wanderers (twice), 9 Witton Albion, 8 Altrincham, Bromsgrove Rovers (twice), Kidderminster Harriers, Stafford Rangers, Yeovil Town

Matches Without Victory

13 Witton Albion, 12 Boston United, 10 Macclesfield Town, Stafford Rangers, 9 Merthyr Tydfil, Northwich Victoria

Consecutive Victories

9 Wycombe Wanderers, 5 Bromsgrove Rovers, Northwich Victoria, Stafford Rangers, Yeovil Town

Consecutive Defeats

6 Northwich Victoria, Telford United, 5 Boston United, Macclesfield Town, Welling United, 4 Boston United, Farnborough Town, Runcorn, Stafford Rangers, Telford United, Welling United, Yeovil Town

DRINKWISE CUP

League Cup competition known in previous years as the Bob Lord Trophy.

1st Round 1st Leg

Altrincham Freeman	Macclesfield Town Leicester, Timmons, Farrelly	1-3	821
Northwich Victoria O'Connor, Butler	Gateshead Higgins	2-1	378
Stafford Rangers Simpson, Berry, Hemmings, Wood	Bromsgrove Rovers O'Mearn, Whitehouse	4-2	667
Stalybridge Celtic Priest	Kidderminster Harrs Davies	1-1	554
Woking Puckett	Welling United Abbott, Robbins	1-2	1363
Yeovil Town Spencer, Sanderson	Slough Town	2-0	1319

1st Round 2nd Leg

Bromsgrove Rovers Richardson, og	Stafford Rangers Clayton	2-1	757

Stafford Rangers won 5-4 on aggregate

Gateshead	Northwich Victoria Davies 2	0-2	132

Northwich Victoria won 4-1 on aggregate

Kidderminster Harriers Humphreys, Palmer 2, Davies	Stalybridge Celtic Kirkham 2	4-2	602

Kidderminster Harriers won 5-3 on aggregate

Macclesfield Town	Altrincham	0-0	449

Macclesfield Town won 3-1 on aggregate

Slough Town Hazel 2	Yeovil Town Spencer, Dang	2-2	528

Yeovil Town won 4-2 on aggregate

Welling United Dennis 2	Woking Baron, Senior	2-2	670

Welling United won 4-3 on aggregate

2nd Round

Bath City	Yeovil Town	0-0	520
Boston United Jones	Dagenham & R'dge Butterworth, Pamphlett	1-2	537
Kidderminster Harriers Deakin, Forsyth, Hadley	Kettering Town	3-0	624

Merthyr Tydfil Williams 2, Webley, D'Auria	Farnborough Town Leworthy, Read	4-2	404
Runcorn Shaughnessy, Brabin	Northwich Victoria Hemmings 2, Donnelly	2-3	600
Stafford Rangers	Telford United	0-0	631
Welling United Smith, Dennis	Wycombe Wdrs Scott, West, Greene	2-3	452
Witton Albion	Macclesfield Town Leicester	0-1	763

Replays

Telford United Clarke 3, Cooke, Green	Stafford Rangers Clayton, Berry	5-2	625
Yeovil Town Sanderson	Bath City	1-0	2,090

3rd Round

Northwich Victoria Locke, Hemmings 2	Telford United Bowen	3-1	374
Yeovil Town	Wycombe Wdrs Scott	0-1	2330
Dagenham & Redbridge Conner, Butterworth, Cavell, Nuttell	Merthyr Tydfil Rogers, Coates	4-2	525
Macclesfield Town Lambert, Mitchell 2	Kidderminster Harrs Hadley	3-1	203

Semi-Finals 1st leg

Northwich Victoria O'Connor, Paxton	Macclesfield Town	2-0	821
Wycombe Wanderers Casey, Guppy, Ryan	Dagenham & R'dge Nuttell	3-1	1901

Semi-Finals 2nd leg

Dagenham & Redbridge	Wycombe Wdrs	0-0	1247

Wycombe Wanderers won 3-1 on aggregate

Macclesfield Town McMahon	Northwich Victoria O'Connor	1-1	422

Northwich Victoria won 3-1 on aggregate

Final 1st leg

Northwich Victoria	Wycombe Wdrs	0-0	1005

Final 2nd leg

Wycombe Wanderers Guppy, West	Northwich Victoria Davies 3	2-3 (aet)	3784

Northwich Victoria won 3-2 on aggregate

DIVISION 3

WYCOMBE WANDERERS

Formed in 1884, they were Southern League members from 1896 to 1908. Spells in the Western Suburban and Spartan Leagues before joining the Isthmian League in 1921. They were promoted to the Conference in 1985 and 1987 and won promotion to the Football League in 1992-93 also taking the FA Trophy.

Ground: Adams Park, Hillbottom Rd, Sands, High Wycombe, Bucks, HP12 4HJ
Phone: 0494-472100　　　　　　　　**Info Line:** 0898-446855
Manager: Martin O'Neill **Secretary:** John Goldsworthy **Chairman:** I Beeks
Colours: Light Blue/Dark Blue Quarters, Dark Blue, Light Blue
Change: All Yellow　　　　　　　　**Nickname:** The Blues

5-Year Record		P	W	D	F	A	Pts	Psn	Cup	FAT
88-89	CONF	40	20	11	68	52	71	4	4q	QF
89-90	CONF	42	17	10	64	56	61	10	4q	1
90-91	CONF	42	21	11	75	46	74	5	2	W
91-92	CONF	42	30	4	84	35	94	2	1	QF
92-93	CONF	42	24	11	84	37	83	1	2	W

Major Honours: IL 55/6, 56/7, 70/1, 71/2; IL RU 57/8, 59/60, 69/70; ILD1 73/4, 74/5; ILD1 RU 75/6, 76/7; FAAm 30/1; FAAm RU 56/7; VOLP 82/3, 86/7; ACDC 84/5; ACDC RU 82/3, 83/4; ILCVS 83/4, 85/6, 87/8; FAT 90/1, 92/3; GMVC 92/3; BLT 91/2.

Record Transfer Fee Paid: £32,000 for Nicky Evans (Barnet) 1989

League Appearances and Goalscorers 92-93
(Details listed in the following order: Appearances, substitute appearances, goals)
T.Aylott 3,0,0. P.Barrowcliff 1,1,0. P.Buckle 1,1,0. D.Carroll 34,0,7. K.Casey 20,5,10. G.Cooper 5,0,0. J.Cousins 39,0,0. G.Covington 1,0,0. G.Creaser 20,0,1. M.Crossley 35,0,0. R.Dewhurst 2,0,1. T.Gooden 3,1,0. D.Greene 9,15,1. S.Guppy 38,0,6. H.Hayrettin 5,0,0. S.Hutchinson 21,5,5. P.Hyde 40,0,0. A.Kerr 37,0,6. T. Langford 11,1,5. C.Moussaddik 2,0,0. A.Norman 0,1,0. K.Ryan 14,9,2. K.Scott 36,0,20. T.Sorrell 0,1,0. S.Stapleton 33,0,7. L.Thompson 7,0,0. S.Thompson 30,2,6. A.Vircavs 10,0,0. M.West 5,8,4. 4 own goals. (29 players.)

Biggest Home Win: 5-1 v Runcorn, Yeovil Town
Biggest Home Defeat: 0-2 v Altrincham
Biggest Away Win: 4-0 v Kettering Town
Biggest Away Defeat: 0-3 v Yeovil Town
Ground Capacity: 6,000 (1,300) **Record:** 7,230 v Slough Town Conf 4/93
Rail: High Wycombe (3 miles from ground).
Directions: M40 Junction 4. A4010 towards Aylesbury. Continue across four mini-roundabouts until double mini-roundabout. Turn left into Lane End Road. Hill Bottom Road ¾ mile on right. Ground at end of Industrial Estate.

GMVC CLUBS
ALTRINCHAM

Founded in 1903 and members of the Manchester League until joining the Lancashire Combination Second Division in 1911. Promoted to Division One in 1912 but left to become founder members of the Cheshire County League in 1919. Founder members of the Northern Premier League in 1968 and of the Alliance Premier League in 1979 where they have been ever since.

Ground: Moss Lane, Altrincham, Cheshire, WA15 8AP
Phone: 061-928-1045 **Info Line:** 0898-664845
Manager: Gerry Quinn **Secretary:** Mrs J.Baldwin **Chairman:** Bill King
Colours: Red/White Stripes, Black, White **Change:** Sky Blue **Nickname:** Robins

5-Year Record		P	W	D	L	F	A	Pts	Psn	Cup	FAT
88-89	CONF	40	13	10	17	51	61	49	14	2	QF
89-90	CONF	42	12	13	17	59	48	49	16	4q	1
90-91	CONF	42	23	13	6	87	46	82	3	1	SF
91-92	CONF	42	11	12	19	61	82	45	18	4q	1
92-93	CONF	42	15	13	14	49	52	58	10	2	1

Major Honours: APL 79/80, 90/1; APLC 80/1; APLS 81/2; APLS RU 79/80; FAT 77/8, 85/6; BLT 80/1; BLT RU 79/80; NPLC 69/70; NPLS 79/80.
Record Transfer Fee Received: Paul Edwards (Crewe Alex) – no details
Record Transfer Fee Paid: Gary Simpson (Boston United) – no details
League Appearances and Goalscorers 92-93
(Details listed in the following order: Appearances, substitute appearances, goals)
C. Alcide 2,1,0; W. Baker 2,0,0; C. Bradshaw 9,5,5; M. Carmody 32,2,2; R. Dennis 6,0,0; C. Dyson 16,5,1; D. Emmett 4,0,1; M. Farrat 16,0,0; P. France 38,0,7; C. Freeman 26,6,8; A. Gorton 9,0,0; R. Green 13,1,3; S. Gresty 0,1,0; R. Harris 34,3,4; M. Hayde 20,9,1; C. Shepherd 3,0,0; S. Learoyd 3,0,0; D. Lloyd 1,0,0; A. Newell 6,0,0; M. Ogley 32,1,1; J. Paladino 13,0,0; M. Pollitt 5,0,0; S. Raymond 2,2,2; A. Richards 0,2,0; S. Rudge 6,1,0; S. Saunders 33,1,2; R. Sidderley 38,0,0; P. Sharpe 2,3,0; J. Smith 22,3,3; I. Tunnacliffe 21,0,5; I. Thompson 5,0,1; R. Wilson6,2,0; S. Woodhead 36,3,3. (33 players)
Biggest Home Win: 3-0 v Kettering Town
Biggest Home Defeat: 1-5 v Stafford Rangers
Biggest Away Win: 5-2 v Farnborough Town
Biggest Away Defeat: 1-4 v Bromsgrove Rovers
Ground Capacity: 10,000 (1,000) **Record:** 10,275 v Altrincham Boys, 1925
Rail: Altrincham (½ miles from ground). **Directions:** From South: leave M6 at Junction 19 (Manchester Airport sign) and A556 into Altrincham. From North: leave M6 at Junction 20 on to M56. Leave M56 at Junction 7 for Altrincham and A56 into Altrincham. From town centre the ground is approximately half a mile along Moss Lane from the railway station.

BATH CITY

Formed in 1889. Joined the Western League in 1908 and became Southern League members in 1921. Relegated to Division One in 1965, 1967 and 1972, they were promoted back to the Premier Division in 1966, 1969 and 1974. In 1979 they were founder members of the Alliance Premier League. Relegated to the Beazer Homes League in 1988, they were promoted back to the Conference for a second spell in 1990.

Ground: Twerton Park, Twerton, Bath, Avon, BA2 1DB
Phone: 0225-423087/313247 **Info Line:** 0898-884474
Manager: Tony Ricketts **Secretary:** P.Britton **Chairman:** R.Stock
Colours: Black and White Stripes, Black, Black/White **Change:** All Yellow
Nickname: The Romans

5-Year Record		P	W	D	F	A	Pts	Psn	Cup	FAT
88-89	BHLP	42	15	13	66	51	58	9	2	1
89-90	BHLP	42	30	8	81	28	98	2	1	3
90-91	CONF	42	10	12	55	61	42	20	4q	3
91-92	CONF	42	16	12	54	51	60	9	3q	3
92-93	CONF	42	15	14	53	46	59	7	2	1

Major Honours: SL 58/9, 77/8, 89/90; SL RU 61/2, 89/90; SLD1 RU 68/9; SLC 78/9; SL v NPL 77/8.
Record Transfer Fee Received: £57,000 for Jason Dodds (Southampton) 89
Record Transfer Fee Paid: £10,000 for Tony Ricketts (Yeovil Town)
League Appearances and Goalscorers 92-93
(Details listed in the following order: Appearances, substitute appearances, goals)
P. Bailey 1,0,0; C. Banks 41,0,0; R. Baverstock 2,0,0; M. Boyle 26,5,7; K. Brown 0,2,0; R. Cousins 37,1,4; R. Crowley 40,0,11; G. Dicks 33,1,0; D. Elliott 0,5,0; T. Frankland 1,0,0; J. Gill 39,6; I. Hedges 21,0,0; V. Jones 6,1,0; L. Maddison 4,0,0; A. Mings 19,4,5; D. Mogg 42,0,0; D. Palmer 18,0,0; P. Randall 16,10,1; T. Ricketts 1,2,0; D. Singleton 21,7,1; G. Smart 31,4,5; D. Vernon 12,13,7; I. Weston 33,4,0; G. Withey 30,2,5. (24 Players)
Biggest Home Win: 5-2 v Farnborough Town
Biggest Home Defeat: 0-5 v Northwich Victoria
Biggest Away Win: 4-0 v Gateshead
Biggest Away Defeat: 3-1 v Northwich Victoria
Ground Capacity: 10,300 (730) **Record:** 18,020 v Brighton FAC3 1960
Rail: Bath Spa (2 miles from ground).
Directions: Just off the A36/A4 main Bristol to Bath road – Lower Bristol Road.

BROMSGROVE ROVERS

Formed in 1885. Members of the Birmingham Combination from 1908, they joined the Birmingham & District – later West Midland (Regional) – League in 1953. Moved to the Southern League in 1972 and were promoted to the Premier Division in 1986. Promoted to the Conference for the first time in 1992.
Ground: Victoria Ground, Birmingham Road, Bromsgrove, Worcs
Phone: 0527-78260 **Nickname:** Rovers
Manager: Robert Hope **Secretary:** B.A. Hewings **Chairman:** C. Lloyd
Colours: Red, Black, Red   **Change:** Green, White, Green

5-Year Record		P	W	D	F	A	Pts	Psn	Cup	FAT
88-89	BHLP	42	14	16	68	56	58	10	1	1
89-90	BHLP	42	17	10	56	48	61	10	1	1
90-91	BHLP	42	20	11	68	49	71	5	4q	3q
91-92	BHLP	42	27	9	78	34	90	1	1	1
92-93	CONF	42	18	14	67	49	68	2	4q	3

Major Honours: SLP 91/2: SLP RU 86/7: SLMD 85/6: GMVC RU 92/3.
Record Transfer Fee Received: £10,000 Steve Smith (Walsall)
League Appearances and Goalscorers 92-93
(Details listed in the following order: Appearances, substitute appearances, goals)
Brain 1,0,1; Brighton 35,0,1; Burgher 11,0,2; Byrne 0,1,0; Carty 6,0,1; Cooksey 25,0,0; Cooper 9,6,2; Crisp 28,7,7; Daly 23,10,4; Davis 3,3,0; Gray 29,4,7; Grealish 13,7,0; Green 13,0,0; Hanks 5,4,1; Honeyfield 0,2,0; O'Meara 16,17,1; Oakes 4,0,0; Richardson 34,0,1; Ross 2,1,0; Scandrett 1,3,0; Shilvock 26,10,5; Skelding 36,0,0; Stott 32,1,2; Wardle 28,4,1; Webb 42,0,8; Whitehouse 37,2,23; Williams 5,1,0.
Biggest Home Win: 4-0 v Stalybridge Celtic
Biggest Home Defeat: 2-3 v Stafford Rangers
Biggest Away Win: 3-0 v Bath City
Biggest Away Defeat: 0-4 v Wycombe Wanderers
Ground Capacity: 4,800 (375)
Record: 7,563 v Worcester City, Birmingham Senior Cup 1987/8
Rail: Bromsgrove.
Directions: From M40, exit Bromsgrove, turn left at roundabout and then right onto the A38. The Victoria Ground is situated on the north side of Bromsgrove on the Birmingham Road (A38) opposite petrol station.

DAGENHAM and REDBRIDGE

Formed in the 1992 close season on the amalgamation of Dagenham (founded 1949) and Redbridge Forest. The Forest club was formed by the amalgamation of Leytonstone Ilford and Walthamstow Avenue (1900) in 1988. Leytonstone (1886) and Ilford (1881) joined together in 1979 and the Redbridge Forest name was first used in 1989.

Ground: Victoria Road, Dagenham, Essex, RM10 7XL
Phone: 081-592-1549 **Nickname:** The Stones
Manager: John Still **Secretary:** Ken Mizen **Chairman:** David Andrews
Colours: Red with Blue Trim, Royal Blue, Red **Change:** Yellow and Green

5-Year Records

		P	W	D	F	A	Pts	Psn	Cup	FAT
Leytonstone Ilford/Redbridge Forest										
88-89	VLP	42	26	11	76	37	89	1	2q	3q
89-90	VLP	42	16	11	65	62	59	11	1q	3
90-91	VLP	42	29	6	74	43	93	1	3q	3
91-92	CONF	42	18	9	69	56	63	7	2q	QF
Dagenham										
88-89	VLP	42	11	12	53	68	45	18	1	1
89-90	VLP	42	17	15	54	43	66	6	4q	1
90-91	VLP	42	13	11	62	68	50	14	4q	3q
91-92	DLP	42	15	16	70	59	61	9	1q	1
Dagenham & Redbridge										
92-93	CONF	42	19	11	75	47	67	3	1	2

Major Honours: Leytonstone, Ilford, Walthamstow Avenue, Leytonstone Ilford and Redbridge Forest all Isthmian League champions.
Record Transfer Fee Received: £100,000 for Andy Hessenthaler (Watford) 9/91
Record Transfer Fee Paid: £10,000 for Gary Blackford (Barnet) 1/91
League Appearances and Goalscorers 92-93
(Details listed in the following order: Appearances, substitute appearances, goals)
Allen 1,1,0; Backford 34,2,2; Broom 36,1,6; Butterworth 38,3,7; Cavell 38,0,19; Conner 38,0,4; De Souza 3,0,1; Georgiou 3,2,0; Kimble 10,15,2; Marquis 6,0,0; Mayes 7,2,0; McKenna 40,1,0; Nuttell 29,2,8; Owers 32,1,1; Pamphlett 29,0,6; Porter 1,0,0;; I. Richardson 9,2,3; P. Richardson 9,4,2; Shirtliff 32,1,0; Smart 2,1,0; G. Stebbing 22,3,1; Tomlinson 2,0,0; Walsh 6,6,5; Warner 1,1,0; Watts 41,0,0. (26 Players)

Biggest Home Win: 6-1 v Merthyr Tydfil
Biggest Home Defeat: 0-2 v Telford United
Biggest Away Win: 4-1 v Farnborough Town
Biggest Away Defeat: 3-1 v Boston United
Ground Capacity: 7,500 (450) **Record:** Dagenham: 7,100 v Reading FAC2R 1968. Redbridge Forest: 2,891 v Wycombe CONF 4/92.
Rail: Dagenham East (Underground 500 yards from ground).
Directions: Victoria Road runs off the A1112 between the A12 and A13.

DOVER ATHLETIC

Formed in 1983 on the demise of Dover FC, taking that club's place in the Southern League Southern Division. They were Southern Division champions in 1988 and promoted to the top section. Premier Division champions in 1990 they failed to meet the requirements for promotion to the Conference. They had no such trouble second time around.

Ground: Crabble Athletic Ground, Lewisham Road, Dover CT17 0JB
Phone: 0304 822373 **Nickname:** The Lilywhites
Manager: Chris Kinnear **Secretary:** JF Durrant **Chairman:** JT Husk
Colours: White, Black, Black **Change:** Yellow, Green, Yellow

5-Year Record

		P	W	D	F	A	Pts	Pos	Cup	FAT
88-89	BHLP	42	19	12	65	47	69	6th	4q	2
89-90	BHLP	42	32	6	87	27	102	1st	3q	3
90-91	BHLP	42	21	11	56	37	74	4th	4q	2
91-92	BHLP	42	23	15	66	30	84	2nd	4q	1
92-93	BHLP	40	25	11	65	23	86	1st	3q	2

Major Honours: SL1 87/88; SLP 89/90, 92/93; SLC 90/91; SLC RU 92/93
Record Transfer Fee Received: £11,500 for Tony Rogers (Chelmsford C) 8/92
Record Transfer Fee Paid: £10,000 for Joe Jackson (Yeovil Town) 2/91
Beazer Homes League Appearances and Goalscorers 92-93
(Details listed in the following order: Appearances, substitute appearances, goals)
Barlett 40,0,2; Blewden 39,0,11; Browne 32,1,4; Cuggy 11,22,14; Dent 14,13,9; Tim Dixon 0,3,0; Tony Dixon 40,0,0; R. Donker 0,6,0; Donn 26,2,1; Harrop 2,0,0; Jackson 16,3,2; Little 24,6,1; MacDonald 7,0,1; Milton 39,0,07; Munden 40,0,0; O'Brien 1,0,0; O'Connell 39,0,2; Scott 7,3,1; Smith 14,0,2; Walker 32,1,2; Warner 17,19,4. (21 Players)
Biggest Home Win: 5-0 v Cambridge City
Biggest Home Defeat: 0-1 v Cheltenham Town
Biggest Away Win: 4-0 v Waterlooville
Biggest Away Defeat: 1-2 v Bashley/Crawley Town
Capacity: 4,000 (1,500)
Record: 4,035 v Bromsgrove Rovers, BHP April 1992
Rail: Dover Priory
Directions: Main A2 from London/Canterbury road to first roundabout. Fourth exit down the hill to roundabout, left. Right at first set of traffic lights.

GATESHEAD

Present club formed in 1977 and took the Northern Premier League place of the former Gateshead club. Promoted to the Conference in 1983, they were relegated to the Northern Premier in 1985 only to return to the Conference in 1986. Relegated in 1987, they re-entered the Conference again in 1990.

Ground: The International Stadium, Neilson Road, Gateshead, NE10 0EF
Phone: 091-478-3883   **Info Line:**
Manager: Tommy Cassidy **Secretary:** Clare Tierney **Chairman:** J. Gibson
Colours: White, Black, Black   **Change:** Blue, White, Blue
Nickname: Tynesiders

5-Year Record		P	W	D	F	A	Pts	Psn	Cup	FAT
88-89	HFSP	42	7	13	36	70	34	21	2q	3q
89-90	HFSP	42	22	10	78	58	76	2	3q	2q
90-91	CONF	42	14	6	52	92	48	17	1q	2
91-92	CONF	42	12	12	49	57	48	14	4q	3
92-93	CONF	42	14	10	53	56	52	14	1	4

Major Honours: NPL 82/3, 85/6; NPL RU 89/90; NPLC RU 89/90; NPLS 86/7.
Record Transfer Fee Received: £3,000 for Jimmy McGinley (Sunderland)
Record Transfer Fee Paid: £6,500 for Richard Toone (Boston Utd) 2/91
League Appearances and Goalscorers 92-93
(Details listed in the following order: Appearances, substitute appearances, goals)
B. Askew 26,12,2; D. Bell 32,0,0; R. Bond 2,0,0; T. Chilton 8,1,0; J. Cooke 31,2,3; D. Corner 26,0,3; W. Davidson 5,1,0; P. Dobson 18,0,8; A. Eliot 2,14,0; S. Elliot 28,0,5; C. Farnaby 20,2,5; M. Farret 35,2,6; S.Guthrie 21,6,2; B.Haliday 33,0,0; S. Higgins 25,1,2; B. Johnson 6,4,0; A. Lamb 40,0,11; T. Lowery 3,3,0; P. Mason 1,0,0; G. Nicholson 2,0,0; S.Pyle 0,2,0; D. Roache 4,0,0; S. Smith 42,0,0; G. Stephenson 1,0,0; S. Tupling 13,3,0; J. Wrightson 38,1,0. (26 Players)
Biggest Home Win: 4-0 v Merthyr Tydfil
Biggest Home Defeat: 0-4 v Bath City
Biggest Away Win: 4-1 v Woking
Biggest Away Defeat: 1-6 v Farnborough Town
Ground Capacity: 12,000 (12,000)
Record: 5,012 v Newcastle United, Testimonial 8/84
Rail: Newcastle Central (2 miles from ground).
Directions: Follow A1(M) to the end of motorway, then take first exit to join A6115. Continue on this road for 3 miles passing one roundabout. Stadium is located on the right.

HALIFAX TOWN

Formed in 1911, they were founder members of the Football League Division Three (North) in 1921. Never promoted, they were founder members of the new Division Three in 1958. Relegated in 1963 and promoted again in 1969 achieving their highest ever finishing position of 3rd in 1971. Relegated back to Division Four in 1976 and then to the GM Vauxhall Conference in 1993.

Ground: The Shay, Halifax HX1 2YS
Phone: 0422 353423 **Nickname:** The Shaymen
Manager: Peter Wragg **Secretary:** Bev Fielding **Chairman:** Jim Brown
Colours: Blue/White, Black, Blue/Black
Change: White/Green/Purple, White, White

5-Year Record		P	W	D	F	A	Pts	Pos	Cup	FAT
88-89	FL4	46	13	11	69	75	50	21st	2	(LC1)
89-90	FL4	46	12	13	57	65	49	23rd	2	(LC2)
90-91	FL4	42	12	10	59	79	46	20th	2	(LC2)
91-92	FL4	42	10	8	34	75	38	20th	1	(LC1)
92-93	FL3	42	9	9	45	67	36	22nd	1	(LC1)

Major Honours: None
Record Transfer Fee Received: £250,000 Wayne Allison (Watford) 7/89
Record Transfer Fee Paid: £50,000 Ian Juryeff (Hereford Utd) 9/90
Football League Division Three Appearances and Goalscorers 92-93
Barr 28,0,2; Bracey 41,0,0; Bradley 29,1,1; Brown 1,0,0; Brown 3,0,0; Case 17,3,2; Christie 6,3,0; Circuit 0,1,0; Craven 7,0,0; Edmonds 0,2,0; Everingham 2,0,0; Gayle 2,2,0; German 28,7,1; Greenwood 23,4,6; Griffiths 1,0,0; Hardy 20,1,2; Hildersley 7,6,2; Juryeff 10,0,0; Kamara 0,1,0; Lancashire 2,0,0; Lewis 11,2,0; Lucketti 42,0,3; Matthews 23,0,2; Megson 23,1,2; Obebo 0,4,0; Patterson 18,4,1; Peake 32,1,1; Peel 3,0,0; Ridings 21,0,4; Thomas 10,2,0; Thompstone 30,0,8; Williams 9,0,1; Wilson 22,0,2; Wright 1,0,0
Biggest Home Win: 2-0 v Gillingham
Biggest Home Defeat: 0-4 v Walsall
Biggest Away Win: 5-2 v Northampton
Biggest Away Defeat: 1-4 v Scunthorpe
Ground Capacity: 8,445
Record: 36,885 v Tottenham Hotspur, FA Cup 1953
Rail: Halifax (turn left out of station, ground is 1/2 a mile away)
Directions: From M62 junction 24 follow signs for Halifax town centre. The Shay is on the way into town and is clearly signposted.

KETTERING TOWN

Founded in 1876, Kettering joined the Midland League in 1892. From 1900 the club had intermittent Southern League experience, with periods in the Northants County League (later the UCL), the Central Alliance, the Birmingham & District League and local junior football. Joined the Southern League for the fourth time in 1950. Three times relegated from the top section but promoted back each time, they were Alliance Premier League founder members in 1979.

Ground: Rockingham Road, Kettering, Northants, NN16 9AW
Phone: 0536-83028 **Info Line:** 0898-888639
Manager: Graham Carr **Secretary:** G. Knowles **Chairman:** P. Mallinger
Colours: All Red **Change:** All Blue **Nickname:** Poppies

5-Year Record

		P	W	D	F	A	Pts	Psn	Cup	FAT
88-89	CONF	40	23	7	56	39	76	2	4	2
89-90	CONF	42	18	12	66	53	66	5	1	1
90-91	CONF	42	23	11	67	45	80	4	4q	3
91-92	CONF	42	20	13	72	50	73	3	3	3
92-93	CONF	42	14	13	61	63	55	13	1	1

Major Honours: SLP 78/9; SLC 74/5; GMACC 87; APL RU 78/9; APLC RU 88/9; APLS RU 81; FAT RU 78/9.
Record Transfer Fee Received: £60,000 for Cohen Griffith (Cardiff City)
Record Transfer Fee Paid: £17,500 for Gary Jones (Grantham) 1/90
League Appearances and Goalscorers 92-93
(Details listed in the following order: Appearances, substitute appearances, goals)
Adams 11,0,3; Bancroft 11,0,3; Barber 5,0,0; Beasley 2,0,0; Brown 41,0,4, 16; Clarke 5,0,0; Cunningham 3,1,0; Curtis 6,1,0; Docker 18,0,1; Donald 21,0,2; Donovan 1,2,2; Ellis 2,1,0; Gavin 3,0,1; Gernon 31,0,0; Greenwood 4,0,0; Harris 6,3,3;.Hill 13,3; Hodges 11,1,3; Hope 19,0,3; Howells 1,0,0; Humphries 10,0,0; Lim 6,0,0; Martin 5,0,2; McKernon 9,0,0; Murhpy 11,1,6; Nicol 26,0,0; North 5,0,0; Nuttall 1,0,1; Oxbrow 5,0,0; Price 26,2,1; Radford 4,0,0; Reddish 6,0,0; Reece 6,0,0; Reed 20,1,0; Retallick 2,0,0; Riley 26,1,9; Roderick 17,1,1; Russell 1,1,0; Shearer 9,1,0; Smalley 22,1,0; Smith 1,0,0; Sommer 10,0,0; Sowden 9,1,0; Stebbing 5,0,0; Strinfellow 1,0,0; Swalles 5,0,0; Taylor 3,0,0; Thomlinson 8,0,1; Underwood 3,0,0; Whitehurst 3,1,0; Wood 25,1,1; Wright 18,1,1. (52 Players!)
Biggest Home Win: 5-0 v Slough Town
Biggest Home Defeat: 0-4 v Wycombe Wanderers
Biggest Away Win: 4-2 v Stafford Rangers
Biggest Away Defeat: 0-3 v Altrincham
Ground Capacity: 6,500 (1,250) **Record:** 6,950 v Northampton Town, FAC1 '90. **Rail:** Kettering (1 mile from ground). **Directions:** Located on A6003 Kettering to Oakham road about one mile from town centre.

KIDDERMINSTER HARRIERS

The Athletics Club was formed in 1877, turning to soccer in 1886 and amalgamating with Kidderminster Olympic in 1890. Birmingham League founder members and long-term participants, returning in 1960 after periods in the Birmingham Combination and Southern League. Moved from West Midland League to Southern in 1972, promoted to the Gola League in 1983.

Ground: Aggborough, Hoo Road, Kidderminster, DY10 1NB
Phone: 0562-823931   **Info Line:** 0898-121547
Manager: Graham Allner   **Secretary:** R.Mercer   **Chairman:** D.Reynolds
Colours: Red and White Halves, White, White
Change: Yellow and Blue, Blue, Blue   **Nickname:** The Harriers

5-Year Record

		P	W	D	F	A	Pts	Psn	Cup	FAT
88-89	CONF	40	21	6	68	57	69	5	4q	3
89-90	CONF	42	15	9	64	67	54	13	1	QF
90-91	CONF	42	14	10	56	67	52	13	1	F
91-92	CONF	42	12	9	56	77	45	19	1	3
92-93	CONF	42	14	16	60	60	58	9	1	1

Major Honours: FAT 86/7, RU 90/91; WFAC RU 85/6, 88/9; SLC 79/80; SLP RU 82/3.
Record Transfer Fee Received: £60,000 for Paul Jones (Woves) 6/91
Record Transfer Fee Paid: £17,000 for Antone Joseph, 12/89
League Appearances and Goalscorers 92-93
(Details listed in the following order: Appearances, substitute appearances, goals) P. Bancroft 0,1,0; D. Benton 30,3,1; C. Brindley 42,0,1; N. Cartwright 8,0,3; P. Davis 30,3,11; J. Deakin 30,2,3; R. Forsyth 38,0,7; C. Gillett 6,1,0; C. Gordon 16,0,3; P. Grainger 32,1,6; R. Green 1,0,0; D. Hadley 26,3,7; J Hanson 3,3,0; S. Hodson 6,0,0; P. Howell 6,0,0; D. Humphreys 8,5,1; A. Joseph 1,3,0; J. McGrath 36,0,1; L. Palmer 19,7,6; G. Piggott 3,0,0; J. Purdie 18,1,9; P. Richardson 4,0,0; D. Rogers 1,0,0; D. Steadman 41,0,0; G. Stokes 1,5,0; K. Sullivan 1,0,0; M. Weir 40,0,1; B. Wilcox 4,2,0; W. Williams 8,2,0; M. Wolsey 2,1,0; M. Yates 2,0,0. (31 Players)
Biggest Home Win: 5-3 v Northwich Victoria
Biggest Home Defeat: 1-5 v Farnborough Town
Biggest Away Win: 5-1 v Woking
Biggest Away Defeat: 1-3 v Slough Town
Ground Capacity: 10,000 (400)   **Record:** 9,155 v Hereford Utd, FAC1 48/9
Rail: Kidderminster (½ mile from ground).
Directions: From North and Midlands: A456 turn-off from M5, 10 miles to Kidderminster (mostly dual carriageway), turn left at first set of lights (into Chester Road), turn right at next set of lights, turn into Hoo Road (before ring road). From South: Kidderminster turn-off from M5, 12 miles to Kidderminster (mostly dual carriageway), turn right at first island approaching Kidderminster, first turning left into Hoo Road.

MACCLESFIELD TOWN

Founded in 1874 as Macclesfield, they have occupied their Moss Rose Ground since 1891. Founder members of the Cheshire County League (1919) and participants until being founder members of the Northern Premier League in 1968. Promoted to the Conference in 1987.

Ground: Moss Rose Gd, London Road, Macclesfield, Cheshire, SK11 7SP
Phone: 0625-511545/24324 **Info Line:** 0898-121546
Manager: Sammy McIlroy **Secretary:** B.Lingard
Chairman: A.Brocklehurst
Colours: Blue, White, Blue **Change:** White, Black, Red
Nickname: The Silkmen

5-Year Record		P	W	D	F	A	Pts	Psn	Cup	FAT
88-89	CONF	40	17	10	63	57	61	7	4q	F
89-90	CONF	42	17	15	56	41	66	4	1	2
90-91	CONF	42	17	12	63	52	63	7	4Q	1
91-92	CONF	42	13	13	50	50	52	13	2q	SF
92-93	CONF	42	12	13	40	50	49	18	2	1

Major Honours: FAT 69/70; FAT RU 88/9; NPL 68/9, 69/70, 85/6; NPLC 85/6; NPLPC 86.
Record Transfer Fee Received: £40,000 Mike Lake (Sheffield Utd) 1988
Record Transfer Fee Paid: £6,000 for George Shepherd (Hyde United)
League Appearances and Goalscorers 92-93
(Details listed in the following order: Appearances, substitute appearances, goals)
J. Askey 31,0,7; S. Bimson 32,0,0; C. Blain 12,9,3; S. Bunter 1,0,0; J. Carberry 4,1,0; M. Dempsey 9,2,1; M. Doherty 10,9,0; E. Edwards 39,0,0; M. Farrelly 9,3,1; S. Farrelly 41,0,0; A. Green 5,2,2; R. Green 5,0,0; M. Halliday 1,1,0; M. Hardman 5,7,0; P. Johnson 12,3,0; P. Kendall 33,4,0; C. Lambert 24,1,8; S. Leicester 32,4,2; J. McMahon 21,5,0; R. Mitchell 16,13,8; J. Mulligan 1,0,0; J. O'Neill 4,0,0; S. Pickering 0,1,0; M. Roberts 0,1,0; G. Shepherd 39,0,0; N. Sorvel 35,5,3; S. Sutton 1,0,0; J. Timmons 40,0,3.
Biggest Home Win: 4-1 v Stafford Rangers
Biggest Home Defeat: 0-2 v Bromsgrove Rovers
Biggest Away Win: 3-1 v Northwich Victoria
Biggest Away Defeat: 0-4 v Woking
Ground Capacity: 6,000 (600) **Record:** 8,900 v Stockport, FAC1 12/67
Rail: Macclesfield (1 mile from ground).
Directions: At south end of town on main road to Leek (A523).

MERTHYR TYDFIL

Formed in 1945 and joined the Southern League in the competition's second post-war season. They were re-organised into the First Division in 1959; promoted to the Premier Division in 1961; relegated to the First in 1964; promoted again in 1971; and relegated again in 1972. After the regionalised period they found themselves in the lower section again in 1982. Promoted to the Premier Division in 1988, and promoted to the Conference in 1989.

Ground: Penydarren Park, Merthyr Tydfil, Mid Glam, CF47 8RF
Phone: 0685-384102   **Info Line:** 0898-884533
Manager: Wynford Hopkins **Secretary:** Brian Davies **Chairman:** J. Reddy
Colours: White, Black, Black   **Change:** Red, White, Red
Nickname: The Martyrs

5-Year Record		P	W	D	F	A	Pts	Psn	Cup	FAT
88-89	BHLP	42	26	7	104	58	85	1	1	3
89-90	CONF	42	16	14	67	63	62	9	2	1
90-91	CONF	42	16	9	62	61	57	9	2	2
91-92	CONF	42	18	14	59	56	68	4	4q	2
92-93	CONF	42	14	10	51	79	52	16	1	3

Major Honours: WFAC 48/9, 50/1, 86/7; SL 47/8, 49/50, 50/1, 51/2, 53/4, 88/8, 89/90; SL RU 52/3, 70/71; SLD1 87/8; SLD1 RU 78/; SLC 47/8, 50/1.
Record Transfer Fee Received: £12,000 for Ray Pratt (Exeter City)
Record Transfer Fee Paid: no details
League Appearances and Goalscorers 92-93
(Details listed in the following order: Appearances, substitute appearances, goals)
G. Abrahams 7,0,0; A. Beattie 15,4,1; I. Benbow 14,0,4; T. Boyle 41,0,1; E. Chiverton 1,0,0; M. Coates 31,6,0; D. Cole 11,1,0; D. D'Auria 39,0,1; M. Davies 34,4,0; C. Gill 2,2,0; M. Holtam 12,2,0; T. Hutchison 6,3,0; R. James 39,1,0; S. Morris 12,0,0; A. Needs 4,2,0; K. Rogers 33,4,2; D. Trick 24,2,0; M. Tucker 33,3,5; G. Wager 30,0,0; D. Webley 14,3,5; C. Williams 39,1,15; M. Williams 35,0,3.
Biggest Home Win: 4-0 v Telford United
Biggest Home Defeat: 1-5 v Woking
Biggest Away Win: 3-1 v Bath City, Kettering Town
Biggest Away Defeat: 1-6 v Dagenham & Redbridge
Ground Capacity: 10,000 (1,500)   **Record:** 21,000 v Reading, FAC 1949
Rail: Merthyr Tydfil (½ mile from ground).
Directions: From South (A470): Expressway to Merthyr, through town centre, follow signs to Tregenna Hotel, Park Terrace. From North: Heads of the Valley road to town centre, bear right at traffic lights, follow signs for Tregenna Hotel, Park Terrace.

NORTHWICH VICTORIA

Founded in 1874, the club were Football League Division Two founder members in 1892. After two seasons they left the League and played in the Combination and Manchester League. Cheshire County League founder members in 1919, Northern Premier League founders in 1968 and Alliance Premier League founder members in 1979.
Ground: The Drill Field, Drill Field Road, Northwich, Cheshire, CW9 5HN
Phone: 0606-41450   **Info Line:** 0898-664813
Manager: John Williams **Secretary:** D.R.Nuttall **Chairman:** D.H.Stone
Colours: Green and White, White, White **Change:** Claret, Sky Blue, Claret
Nickname: Vics

5-Year Record		P	W	D	F	A	Pts	Psn	Cup	FAT
88-89	CONF	40	14	11	64	65	53	10	2	2
89-90	CONF	42	15	5	51	67	50	15	1	2
90-91	CONF	42	13	13	65	75	52	12	4q	QF
91-92	CONF	42	16	6	63	48	54	11	1q	3
92-93	CONF	42	16	8	68	55	56	11	2q	1

Major Honours: FAT 83/4; FAT RU 82/3; WFAC RU 1881/2, 1888/9; BLT 79/80, (DCup) 92/3; APLS 80; NPL RU: 76/7; NPLC 72/3; NPLC RU 78/9.
Record Transfer Fee Received: £35,000 for Shaun Teale (Weymouth) 9/87
Record Transfer Fee Paid: £10,000 for Malcolm O'Connor (Hyde) 8/88
League Appearances and Goalscorers 92-93
(Details listed in the following order: Appearances, substitute appearances, goals)
G. Ainsworth 5,0,0; M. Bennett 5,2,0; S. Berryman 3,0,0; J. Bishop 1,1,0; C. Blain 6,2,1; C. Blundell 12,8,0; C. Boyd 28,0,2; T. Bullock 35,0,0; B. Butler 38,0,4; G. Davies 35,1,12; P. Donnelly 8,6,1; G. Easter 1,0,0; M. Hancock 30,0,3; N. Hardy 7,1,1; T. Hemmings 35,0,15; M. Jones 20,5,0; A. Kidd 0,1,0; S. Locke 32,1,0; T. McGee 2,4,0; S. McIlroy 1,0,0; D. Nassari 1,1,0; C. Nixon 2,0,0; M. O'Connor 41,0,21; J. Parker 34,4,2; D. Paxton 4,11,1; B. Siddall 2,0,0; M. Simms 34,0,0; J. Smith 12,0,1; J. Stringer 2,1,0; K. Thelwell 1,1,0; K. Westray 24,1,1; J. Williams.
Biggest Home Win: 3-0 v Farnborough Town
Biggest Home Defeat: 1-3 v Macclesfield, Stalybridge Celtic, Witton Albion
Biggest Away Win: 6-0 v Stalybridge Celtic
Biggest Away Defeat: 1-4 v Dagenham & Redbridge
Ground Capacity: 16,000 (600)   **Record:** 12,000 v Watford, FAC4 1977
Rail: Northwich (1 mile from ground).
Directions: M6 Junction 19. Take Chester road to roundabout and head for Bus Station (6 miles from M6). Ground adjacent to Bus Station.

RUNCORN

Formed in 1918, Runcorn were founder members of the Cheshire League and its first champions in 1919. Left to become founder members of the Northern Premier League in 1968. Joined the Alliance Premier League in its third season, 1981-82, and were champions in their first season.

Ground: Canal Street, Runcorn, Cheshire, WA7 1RZ
Phone: 0928-560076   **Info Line:** 0898-664814
Manager: John Carroll   **Secretary:** D.Bignall   **Chairman:** David Robinson
Colours: Yellow, Green, Yellow   **Change:** Red and White, Red, Red
Nickname: Linnets

5-Year Record

		P	W	D	F	A	Pts	Psn	Cup	FAT
88-89	CONF	40	19	8	77	53	65	6	2	1
89-90	CONF	42	19	13	59	62	70	3	4q	3
90-91	CONF	42	16	10	69	67	58	8	1	2
91-92	CONF	42	11	13	50	63	46	16	1	2
92-93	CONF	42	13	10	58	76	44	19	4q	F

Major Honours: APL 81/2; APLS 82/3, 84/5; BLT 82/3, 84/5; RU 91/2; FAT RU 85/6, 92/3; NPL 75/6, 80/1; NPLS 80/1, 81/2.
Record Transfer Fee Received: £40,000 for Mark Carter (Barnet) 2/91
League Appearances and Goalscorers 92-93
(Details listed in the following order: Appearances, substitute appearances, goals)
G. Anderson 37,0,4; J. Bates 26,12,0; G. Brabin 30,2,5; I. Brady 25,3,1; J. Brown 26,7,6; S. Byrne 5,1,0; J. Carroll 14,0,1; J. Connor 16,3,2; S. Cotton 2,5,1; M. Gallagher 13,0,0; I. Harold 25,0,1; G. Hill 18,0,0; M. Jackson 1,0,0; S. Lundon 10,4,1; Darrell McCarty 16,202; I. McInerny 11,18,2; K. McKenna 15,0,12; P. Mullen 6,4,0; N. Parker 16,20,3; F. Richards 1,1,0; P. Robertson 22,0,0; J. Routledge 16,0,0; N. Sang 5,1,1; S. Shaughnessy 38,0,0; J. Shaw 2,0,0; A. Taylor 9,9,1; J. Wall 29,6,1; A. Williams 26,0,0; D. Wilson 3,1,1.

Biggest Home Win: 3-0 v Welling United
Biggest Home Defeat: 1-4 v Farnborough Town
Biggest Away Win: 3-0 v Merthyr Tydfil, Witton Albion
Biggest Away Defeat: 1-5 v Dagenham & Redbridge, Wycombe Wanderers
Ground Capacity: 8,400 (250)   **Record:** 10,011 v Preston NE, FAC3 1939
Rail: Runcorn (2 miles from ground).
Directions: From South: M56 (Junction 11) follow signs for Warrington for 1 mile, left at roundabout (signposted Widnes, Liverpool). Stay on this road for approx 4 miles, exit at Runcorn Old Town. From North: M62 (Junction 7) follow signs for Widnes/Runcorn. Go over Widnes/Runcorn bridge. Exit for Runcorn Old Town.

SLOUGH TOWN

Slough FC emerged from the amalgamation of several clubs in 1890 and played in the Southern Alliance and Great Western Suburban League. In 1920 they joined the Spartan League. During the Second World War they amalgamated with Slough Centre to become Slough United and in 1945 they became founder members of the Corinthian League. In 1947 Slough Centre reformed and the remaining part of the club became Slough Town. Absorbed into the Athenian League in 1963, they joined the Isthmian set-up in 1973. Promoted into the top section at the first attempt, they stayed there until promoted to the Conference in 1990.

Ground: Wexham Park Stadium, Wexham Road, Slough, SL2 5QR
Phone: 0753-523358 **Info Line:** 0898-446885
Manager: John Docherty **Secretary:** R.B.S.Hayward **Chairman:** T. Abbott
Colours: Amber and Navy broad hoops, Navy Blue, Navy Blue
Change: Royal Blue, White **Nickname:** The Rebels

5-Year Record		P	W	D	F	A	Pts	Psn	Cup	FAT
88-89	VLP	42	24	6	72	42	78	3	4q	1
89-90	VLP	42	27	11	85	38	92	1	1	1
90-91	CONF	42	13	6	51	80	45	19	2q	1
91-92	CONF	42	13	6	56	82	45	20	1	1
92-93	CONF	42	18	11	60	55	65	5	1	2

Major Honours: IPL 81/2, 89/90; ILD2 RU 73/4; ACDC 75/6, 80/1; ILCS RU 81/2.
Record Transfer Fee Received: £20,000 for Eric Young (Brighton)
Record Transfer Fee Paid: £18,000 for Colin Fielder (Farnborough) 8/91
League Appearances and Goalscorers 92-93
(Details listed in the following order: Appearances, substitute appearances, goals)
D. Anderson 37,0,2; L. Briley 37,0,2; T. Bunting 40,0,0; R. Edwards 10,0,0; C. Emberson 2,0,0; C. Fairweather 7,1,1; C. Fielder 1,1,0; M. Fiorre 27,1,7; M. Foran 23,0,2; G. Friel 30,14,3; D. Greene 2,1,0; D. Hancock 1,1,0; I. Hazel 39,2,4; S. Hemsley 8,0,0; B. Lee 8,0,0; P. Maxwell 3,0,0; P. McKinnon 40,3,13; A. Pluckrose 42,0,3; M. Quamina 23,3,0; A. Sayer 42,0,19; S. Scott 17,6,2; N. Stamley 27,6,1; S. Whitby 37,0,0.
Biggest Home Win: 4-2 v Welling United
Biggest Home Defeat: 0-4 v Northwich Victoria
Biggest Away Win: 3-0 v Runcorn
Biggest Away Defeat: 0-5 v Kettering Town
Ground Capacity: 7,000 (395) **Record:** 5,000 v Millwall, FAC1 1982
Rail: Slough (2 miles from ground). **Directions:** From North: M40 Junction 1. Follow A412 for 3 miles, turn right, signposted Wexham Park Hospital. Club ½ mile south of Hospital. From East: M4 Junction 5. Follow A4 for 2 miles, turn right A412, turn left, signposted Hospital. From West: M4 Junction 6. At A4 turn right, follow signs for Wexham Park Hospital.

SOUTHPORT

Founded as Southport Central, they were early Lancashire League members. Changed name, for a season, to Southport Wanderers and then joined the Lancashire Combination. From the Central League they became founder members under their current name of the Football League Division Three (North) in 1921. Lost their Football League place in 1978 and joined the Northern Premier League. Promoted to the Conference for the first time in 1993.

Ground: Haig Avenue, Southport PR8 6JZ **Phone:** 0704 533422
Nickname: The Sandgrounders
Manager: Brian Kettle **Secretary:** Roy Morris **Chairman:** Charles Clapham
Colours: Old Gold/Black, Black, Old Gold/Black **Change:** All White

5-Year Record		P	W	D	F	A	Pts	Pos	Cup	FAT
88-89	HFSP	42	13	12	66	52	51	14	1	1q
89-90	HFSP	42	17	14	54	48	65	7	4q	1q
90-91	HFSP	40	18	14	66	48	68	5	2q	1q
91-92	HFSP	42	16	17	57	48	65	7	2q	1q
92-93	HFSP	42	29	9	103	31	96	1	2	3q

Major Honours: NPLP 92/93, FL4 72/73, FL4RU 66/67, 3DN Cup Winners 37/38, Liverpool Cup 30/31, 31/32, 43/44, 57/58, 63/64, 74/75, 90/91, 92/93
Record Transfer Fee Received: £25,000 for Steve Whitehall (Rochdale) 7/91
Record Transfer Fee Paid: £8,500 for Malcolm Russell (Halifax Town)
HFS Loans League Appearances and Goalscorers 92-93:
(Details listed in the following order: Appearances, substitute appearances, goals)
Baines 23,12,8; Brennan 32,4,8; Dove 23,2,6; Fuller 41,0,0; Gamble 30,7,10; Goulding 26,0,0; Haw 36,0,32; Howard 0,1,0; Jarvis 7,0,4; Joel 0,2,0; McDonald 37,3,1; Mellish 0,6,0; Mooney 42,0,1; Moore 41,0,0; Quinlan 0,2,0; Rigby 1,0,0; Routledge 1,0,0; Schofield 31,2,5; Senior 23,4,6; Walmsley 28,11,4; Withers 40,0,18.
Biggest Home Win: 7-1 v Chorley
Biggest Home Defeat: 1-2 v Emley
Biggest Away Win: 6-1 v Chorley
Biggest Away Defeat: 2-1 v Marine
Capacity: 5,500 (2,000)
Record: 20,010 v Newcastle United, FAC4 Rep. 1/32
Rail: Southport (1½ miles from ground)
Directions: M6 to M58 to Ormskirk, then Southport. Haig Avenue is on right ½ mile before town centre, ground signposted from all entrances to town.

STAFFORD RANGERS

Probably formed around 1876. Members of the North Staffordshire League, then played in the Birmingham League 1900-12, Birmingham Combination 1912-21, and Birmingham League again until the Second World War. Revived by supporters in 1946, they returned to the Birmingham Combination but switched to the Cheshire County League in 1952. Northern Premier League founder members in 1968, they were Alliance Premier League founder members in 1979. Apart from 1983-85 they have been at Conference level ever since.

Ground: Marston Road, Stafford, ST16 3BX
Phone: 0785-42750   **Info Line:** 0898-664839   **Nickname:** Boro
Manager: Brendan Phillips **Secretary:** Mrs A.Meddings **Chairman:** J. Horton
Colours: Black & White, White, White   **Change:** All Yellow with Red Trim

5-Year Record		P	W	D	F	A	Pts	Psn	Cup	FAT
88-89	CONF	42	11	7	49	54	40	19	1	1
89-90	CONF	42	12	12	50	62	48	17	1	SF
90-91	CONF	42	12	14	48	51	50	15	1	1†
91-92	CONF	42	10	16	41	59	46	17	4q	1
92-93	CONF	42	18	10	55	47	64	6	2	1

† Tie awarded to opponents

Major Honours: NPL 71/2, 84/5; FAT 71/2, 78/9; FAT RU 75/6; BLT 85/6; NPLS 84/5.
Record Transfer Fee Received: £100,000 Stan Colleymore (C. Palace) 1990
Record Transfer Fee Paid: £11,000 for Steve Butterworth (VS Rugby) 12/90
League Appearances and Goalscorers 92-93
(Details listed in the following order: Appearances, substitute appearances, goals)
G. Berry 29,3,4; D. Boughey 33,5,7; M. Bradshaw 41,0,3; S. Burr 23,0,6; N. Callaghan 5,0,1; S. Circuit 9,1,0; P. Clayton 22,8,9; J. Dawson 12,2,2; B. Edwards 2,0,0; S. Essex 40,0,3; M. Fisher 7,2,1; T. Griffiths 12,4,1; C. Hemmings 29,3,2; T. Henry 2,0,1; M. Jones 6,1,0; P. Jones 34,2,2; S. Lyons 0,1,0; A. Mettioui 6,0,3; B. Palgrave 29,3,4; J. Pearson 16,0,0; R. Price 42,0,0; W. Simpson 37,0,3; P. Skipper 5,0,0; B. Whitehurst 2,0,0; F. Wood 19,11,2.
Biggest Home Win: 4-3 v Welling United
Biggest Home Defeat: 2-4 v Kettering Town
Biggest Away Win: 5-1 v Altrincham
Biggest Away Defeat: 1-4 v Macclesfield Town
Ground Capacity: 9,500 (426)   **Record:** 8,536 v Rotherham, FAC3 1/75
Rail: Stafford (2 miles from ground).   **Directions:** M6 Junction 14, follow signs for Stafford and Stone, straight over the island, third exit right, signposted Common Road. Ground is straight ahead.

STALYBRIDGE CELTIC

Founded in 1911. In 1921 they moved via the Lancashire Combination and the Central League to be founder members of the Football League Division Three (North). Dropped out after a couple of seasons and joined the Cheshire County League. Became founder members of the North West Counties League in 1982 and, in 1987, founder members of the Northern Premier League First Division. Promoted to the Premier Division in 1988 and to the Conference in 1992.

Ground: Bower Fold, Mottram Road, Stalybridge, Cheshire
Phone: 061-338-2828 **Nickname:** Celtic
Manager: Phil Wilson **Secretary:** Martin Torr **Chairman:** Ray Connor
Colours: All Royal Blue   **Change:** All Red

5-Year Record		P	W	D	F	A	Pts	Psn	Cup	FAT
88-89	HFSP	42	9	13	46	81	40	19	1q	2q
89-90	HFSP	42	12	9	48	61	45	17	1q	1q*
90-91	HFSP	40	22	11	44	26	77	2	1q	2q
91-92	HFSP	42	26	14	84	33	92	1	4q	3
92-93	CONF	42	13	17	48	55	56	12	3q	2

* Tie awarded to opponents
Major Honours: NPL 91/2; NPL RU 90/1; NPL D1 RU 87/8.
Record Transfer Fee Received: £4,000 Eamon O'Keefe (Plymouth Argy)
Record Transfer Fee Paid: £3,000 Martin Pilson (Halifax Town) 7/93
League Appearances and Goalscorers 92-93
(Details listed in the following order: Appearances, substitute appearances, goals)
S. Anderson 12,0,3; J. Aspinall 34,1,0; G. Bauress 30,3,1; P. Bennett 35,1,0; R. Blackman 1,0,0; K. Booth 22,2,0; G. Boyle 19,3,0; J. Brown 36,2,2; F. Bunn 10,2,3; M. Burrell 5,1,0; P. Dixon 33,0,1; N. Edmonds 25,3,0; M. Edwards 33,8,12; M. Filson 34,1,2; P. Higginbotham 5,5,1; J. Hill 12,4,0; R. Hughes 42,0,0; P. King 4,1,0; P. Kirkham 27,5,9; P. Morgan 13,4,2; P. Power 21,4,8; E. Priest 3,3,1; D. Tomlinson 4,1,0; S. Wood 2,2,1.
Biggest Home Win: 3-0 v Woking
Biggest Home Defeat: 0-6 v Northwich Victoria
Biggest Away Win: 4-1 v Welling United
Biggest Away Defeat: 0-4 v Bromsgrove Rovers, Wycombe Wanderers
Capacity: 7,500 (500) **Record:** 9,753 v WBA, FAC1R 1922
Rail: Stalybridge (1 mile from ground).
Directions: M1 or Sheffield: Woodhead Pass to Mottram and Stalybridge. M62: Oldham, Ashton-under-Lyne, Stalybridge. From Manchester, Mancunian Way, Ashton Old Road, Ashton-under-Lyne, Stalybridge.

TELFORD UNITED

Wellington Town were founded in the 1870s and after a period of minor football became Birmingham & District League members in 1898. Moved in 1938 to the Cheshire County League and in 1958 to the Southern League. Apart from the regionalised first season, they spent their Southern League career in the top section, changing their name to Telford United in 1969. Constant members of the Conference since it was founded as the Alliance Premier League in 1979.

Ground: Bucks Head Ground, Watling Street, Wellington, Telford, Shropshire, TF1 2NJ
Phone: 0952-223838   **Info Line:** 0898-121545
Manager: Gerry Daly   **Secretary:** M.J.Ferriday   **Chairman:** Tony Esp
Colours: White, Blue, White   **Change:** Yellow, Red, Red
Nickname: The Lilywhites

5-Year Record	P	W	D	F	A	Pts	Psn	Cup	FAT
88-89	CONF	40	13	9	37	43	48	16	1	W
89-90	CONF	42	15	13	56	63	58	12	1	3
90-91	CONF	42	20	7	62	52	67	6	1	1
91-92	CONF	42	19	7	62	66	64	6	2	QF
92-93	CONF	42	14	10	55	60	52	15	4q	3

Major Honours: WFAC 01/2, 05/6, 39/40; FAT 70/1, 82/3; FAT RU 69/70, 87/8, 88/9; SLC 70/1.
Record Transfer Fee Received: £50,000 for Stephen Norris (Scarborough)
Record Transfer Fee Paid: £10,000 for Paul Mayman (Northwich Victoria)
League Appearances and Goalscorers 92-93
(Details listed in the following order: Appearances, substitute appearances, goals)
D. Acton 39,0,0; N. Beaumont 25,4,1; I. Benbow 24,2,7; M. Bignot 40,0,4; S. Bowen 19,0,1; S. Clarke 14,2,1; A. Cooke 4,4,2; S. Fergusson 29,0,8; S. Francis 22,8,7; T. Garrett 1,4,0; D. Grange 3,0,0; R. Green 16,2,2; C. Hodgin 7,4,1; P. Hunter 2,0,0; T. Langford 22,0,6; A. Lee 32,0,0; L. May 0,4,0; P. McBean 7,1,0; M. Moore 9,1,2; J. Mulligan 7,0,3; M. Myers 33,2,3; S. Nelson 11,0,0; N. Niblett 21,0,1; M. Ogley 0,4,0; S. Parrish 33,0,4; D. Pritchard 39,0,1; L. Rollason 6,2,0; J. Wolverson 0,2,0.

Biggest Home Win: 5-0 v Merthyr Tydfil
Biggest Home Defeat: 0-3 v Witton Albion
Biggest Away Win: 3-0 v Altrincham
Biggest Away Defeat: 4-0 v Merthyr Tydfil, Wycombe Wanderers
Ground Capacity: 8,500 (1,222)   **Record:** 13,000 v Shrewsbury, B'ham Lge 36
Rail: Wellington - Telford West (1 mile from ground).
Directions: M54 Junction 6 to B5061 (Watling Street).

WELLING UNITED

Founded in 1963. Progressed rapidly once they gained senior status, joining the Spartan League in 1976; the Athenian League in 1978; and the Southern League in 1981. They were promoted to the Conference in 1986.
Ground: Park View Road, Welling, Kent
Phone: 081-301-1196 **Info Line:** 0898-800654
Manager: Terry Robbins **Secretary:** B.Hobbins **Chairman:** P.Websdale
Colours: Red, Red, White **Change:** All Sky Blue
Nickname: The Wings

5-Year Record		P	W	D	F	A	Pts	Psn	Cup	FAT
88-89	CONF	40	14	11	45	46	53	11	3	QF
89-90	CONF	42	18	10	62	50	64	6	2	2
90-91	CONF	42	3	15	55	57	54	11	1	3
91-92	CONF	42	14	12	69	79	54	12	1	2
92-93	CONF	42	12	12	57	72	48	20	4q	2

Major Honours: SLP 85/6; SLMC 85/6.
Record Transfer Fee Received: £15,000 for Gary Abbott (Barnet) 1989
Record Transfer Fee Paid: £30,000 for Gary Abbott (Enfield) 1989/90
League Appearances and Goalscorers 92-93
(Details listed in the following order: Appearances, substitute appearances, goals)
G. Abbott 42,0,17; W, Browne 6,0,0; N. Clemence 27,5,1; P. Collins 34,2,0; G. Cooper 5,0,0; L. Dennis 19,16,9; J. Francis 0,1,0; J. Glover 13,0,0; L. Harrison 10,0,0; K. Hoddy 18,7,0; M. Hone 39,2,2; M. Holman 4,0,0; D. Newman 12,2,1; N. Ransom 36,1,1; T. Reynolds 12,0,0; T. Robbins 42,0,19; S. Robinson 30,1,0; A. Salako 18,2,1; G. Smith 22,1,0; N. Sullivan 5,0,0; M. Tivey 7,2,0; L. Turner 1,0,0; S. White 34,3,4; R. Wild 1,0,0; D. Williams 25,0,0.
Biggest Home Win: 5-0 v Merthyr Tydfil
Biggest Home Defeat: 1-5 v Northwich Victoria
Biggest Away Win: 4-2 v Kettering Town
Biggest Away Defeat: 0-3 v Runcorn, Wycombe Wanderers
Ground Capacity: 5,500 (500) **Record:** 3,850 v Blackburn, FAC3 1/89
Rail: Welling SR (¾ mile from ground).
Directions: M25, then A2 towards London taking Welling turn-off. Ground ¾ mile ahead.

WITTON ALBION

Formed in 1890, they joined the Lancashire Combination in 1912. In 1919 they were founder members of the Cheshire County League and they stayed there until joining the Northern Premier League in 1979. They moved to their current ground in 1990 and were promoted to the Conference for the first time in 1991.

Ground: Wincham Pk, Chapel St, Windham, Northwich, Cheshire, CW9 6DA
Phone: 0606 43008   **Nickname:** Albion
Manager: Mike McKenzie **Secretary:** D. Leather **Chairman:** D. Shirley
Colours: Red and White Stripes, Black, Red   **Change:** All Blue

5-Year Record		P	W	D	F	A	Pts	Psn	Cup	FAT
88-89	HFSP	42	22	13	67	39	79	3	3q	1
89-90	HFSP	42	22	7	67	39	73	3	4q	2
90-91	HFSP	42	28	9	81	31	93	1	1	SF
91-92	CONF	42	16	10	63	60	58	10	2	F
92-93	CONF	42	11	17	62	65	50	17	1	SF

Major Honours: HFSP 90/1; PRC 90/1; FAT RU 91/2.
Record Transfer Fee Received: £11,500 Paul Henderson (Chester City). £35,000 Mike Whitlow and Neil Parsley (Leeds United)
League Appearances and Goalscorers 92-93
(Details listed in the following order: Appearances, substitute appearances, goals)
S. Adams 23,1,0; C. Alford 24,12,14; S. Anderson 1,2,0; D. Bancroft 5,10,0; A. Bondswell 3,0,1; S. Bullock 1,0,0; B. Burke 32,1,12; L. Coathup 38,0,0; Jim Connor 38,0,3; Joe Connor 8,5,1; J. Gallagher 25,6,0; S. Gardner 5,1,0; B. Grant 4,5,0; J. Healey 1,1,0; M. Holt 6,3,0; M. Hughes 7,0,3; P. Kelly 3,0,0; A. Kilner 4,1,1; M. Lambert 4,0,0; M. Lillis 33,3,2; M. Lutkevitch 1,2,0; K. Mason 29,0,0; D. McCarty 5,0,2; J. McCluskie 0,2,0; S. McNeilis 33,0,0; A. Murphy 2,2,2; K. Paladino 13,0,0; I. Redman 9,1,0; C. Rose 23,3,2; S. Senior 39,0,0; J. Smart 1,0,0; G. Stewart 5,2,2; K. Thomas 37,2,20; D. Tomlinson 0,3,0.
Biggest Home Win: 4-2 v Kettering Town
Biggest Home Defeat: 2-5 v Stafford Rangers
Biggest Away Win: 3-0 v Telford United
Biggest Away Defeat: 1-3 v Gateshead
Capacity: 5,000 (650) **Record:** 10,000 v Northwich, Ches. Cty Lge 1947/8
Rail: Northwich (1½ miles from ground).
Directions: M6 Junction 19. A556 towards Northwich for 3 miles. Turn right at beginning of dual carriageway on to A559. Turn right at cross-roads (A559 Warrington and Wincham). After another ¾ mile turn left opposite Black Greyhound Inn into Wincham Lane, ground ¾ mile on left immediately after crossing Canal Bridge.

WOKING

Founded in 1889. Played in the West Surrey League from 1895. They joined the Isthmian League in 1911 and had been there ever since. They were relegated in 1983 and again in 1985, but were promoted to Division One in 1987, to the Premier Division in 1990 and to the Conference in 1992.
Ground: Kingfield Sports Ground, Kingfield, Woking, Surrey, GU22 9AA
Phone: 0483-772740   **Nickname:** Cards
Manager: Geoff Chapple **Secretary:** Philip Ledger **Chairman:** Ted Hills
Colours: Red with White Trim, White with Red Trim, White with Red Trim
Change: All Yellow with Blue trim

5-Year Record		P	W	D	F	A	Pts	Psn	Cup	FAT
88-89	VL1	40	24	10	72	30	82	3	1	3
89-90	VL1	42	30	8	102	39	98	2	2	3
90-91	VLP	42	24	10	84	39	82	4	3	1
91-92	DLP	42	30	7	96	25	97	1	3	2
92-93	CONF	42	17	8	58	62	59	8	2	1

Major Honours: ILP 91/2; ILD1 RU 89/90; ILD1 81/2.
Record Transfer Fee Received: £25,000 Mark Harris (Crystal Palace)
Record Transfer Fee Paid: £5,000 Fred Hyatt (Burnham)
League Appearances and Goalscorers 92-93
(Details listed in the following order: Appearances, substitute appearances, goals)
T. Alexander 24,0,0; T. Baron 11,0,1; L. Batty 39,0,0; M. Biggins 26,0,5; D. Broderick 3,0,0; D. Brown 29,3,2; K. Brown 38,0,0; A. Bushay 12,0,2; T. Buzaglo 7,7,2; R. Buzaglo 3,1,1; R. Carroll 11,5,2; A. Clement 23,1,2; D. Coleman 6,0,1; C. Fielder 27,1,1; J. Finch 1,0,0; M. Fleming 28,1,5; D. Greene 4,2,1; D. Honey 1,0,0; B. Horne 1,0,0; T. Joyce 7,0,0; P. Kelly 1,0,0; S. Milton 4,3,2; A. Murphy 2,0,0; R. Nugent 32,0,2; R. Peters 7,0,0; A. Pape 1,0,0; D. Puckett 25,9,9; G. Roffe 2,0,0; Z. Rowe 1,0,0; T. Senior 26,5,11; S. Steele 22,7,5; L. Wye 17,0,0; S. Wye 18,0,1.
Biggest Home Win: 4-0 v Macclesfield Town , Runcorn
Biggest Home Defeat: 1-5 v Kidderminster Harriers
Biggest Away Win: 5-1 v Merthyr Tydfil
Biggest Away Defeat: 1-5 v Dagenham & Redbridge
Capacity: 6,000 (650)   **Record:** 6,000 v Swansea, FAC2R 1978
Rail: Woking (1½ miles from ground).
Directions: M25 Junction 10. Follow towards Woking, and then towards Kingfield.

YEOVIL TOWN

Formed in 1895 as Yeovil Casuals, they became simply Yeovil in 1908 and, on joining the Western League in 1919, became Yeovil and Petters United. Joined the Southern League in 1922. Changed their name to Yeovil Town just after the Second World War. They were founder members of the Alliance Premier League in 1979. Relegated to the Isthmian arm of the Pyramid in 1985, they were promoted back in 1988.

Ground: Huish Park, Boundary Road, Yeovil, Somerset, BA22 8YF
Phone: 0935-23662 **Info Line:** 0898-333092
Manager: Steve Rutter **Secretary:** R.L.Brinsford **Chairman:** Bryan Moore
Colours: White, Green, White **Change:** All Sky Blue
Nickname: The Glovers

5-Year Record		P	W	D	F	A	Pts	Psn	Cup	FAT
88-89	CONF	40	15	11	68	67	56	9	2	2
89-90	CONF	42	17	12	62	54	63	7	1	3
90-91	CONF	42	13	11	58	58	50	14	1	1
91-92	CONF	42	11	14	40	49	47	15	2	QF
92-93	CONF	42	18	12	59	49	66	4	3	1

Major Honours: SL 54/5, 64/5, 70/1; SL RU 23/4, 31/2, 34/5, 69/70, 72/3; SLC 48/9, 54/5, 60/1, 65/6; VOL 87/8; VOL RU 85/6, 86/7; ACDC 67/8; BLT 89/90; ILCS 86/7.
Record Transfer Fee Received: £45,000 for Mark Shail (Bristol City) 5/93
Record Transfer Fee Paid: £15,000 for Joe Jackson (Worcester) 9/90
League Appearances and Goalscorers 92-93
(Details listed in the following order: Appearances, substitute appearances, goals)
P. Batty 33,2,6; N. Coates 27,5,1; D. Coles 42,0,0; R. Cooper 29,3,3; H.Dang 1,6,1; W. Dobbins 17,0,0; P. Ferns 24,1,0; N. Flory 2,1,0; S. Harrower 39,0,3; M. Hughes 1,2,0; D. Leonard 2,0,0; M. McPherson 1,3,0; P. Nevin 12,14,3; S. Rutter 17,2,0; P. Sanderson 37,4,4; M. Shail 33,0,4; J. Sherwood 41,0,2; S. Sivell 0,1,0; M. Spencer 38,1,15; T. Tayor 2,0,0; A. Wallace 10,6,2; J. Williams 7,0,0; P. Wilson 35,1,13.
Biggest Home Win: 5-1 v Slough Town
Biggest Home Defeat: 0-3 v Dagenham & Redbridge
Biggest Away Win: 3-0 v Welling United
Biggest Away Defeat: 1-5 v Wycombe Wanderers
Ground Capacity: 9,000 (5,000)
Record: 8,612 v Arsenal, FAC3 1/93
Rail: Yeovil Pen Mill – Bristol/Westbury to Weymouth Line (2½ miles from ground). Yeovil Junction – Waterloo/Salisbury to Exeter Line (4 miles from ground).   **Directions:** Leave A303 at Cargate roundabout and take B3088 signposted Yeovil. Take first exit at next roundabout and first exit again at next roundabout into Boundary Road.

RELEGATED CLUBS
BOSTON UNITED

League Appearances and Goalscorers 92-93
(Details listed in the following order: Appearances, substitute appearances, goals)
T. Allpress 4,0,0; P. Bastock 42,0,0; P. Casey 26,0,1; S. Chambers 34,3,0; D. Cork 6,0,0; D. Coverdale 2,5,1; A. Curtis 6,2,1; H. Curtis 37,0,0; R. Curtis 18,3,0; D. Davis 25,0,0; R. Futcher 2,0,0; P. Gavin 1,0,0; J. Graham 12,13,7; N. Grayson 34,2,4; M. Hallam 4,2,0; M. Hardy 36,0,2; L. Howarth 7,0,1; G. Jones 31,1,16; I. Knight 9,1,0; G. Lee 25,0,0; S. Lister 7,0,0; L. McJannet 5,0,0; R. McKenzie 1,0,0; J. Miller 2,1,1; D. Moss 17,0,10; D. Munton 4,1,1; K. Oakes 1,0,0; T. Slack 10,0,0; T. Sorrell 1,0,0; S. Stout 15,8,1; R. Toone 1,1,0; D. Trott 0,5,0; G. West 10,0,0; C. White 9,0,0.

FARNBOROUGH TOWN

League Appearances and Goalscorers 92-93
(Details listed in the following order: Appearances, substitute appearances, goals)
S. Baker 30,0,1; P. Batey 18,2,1; P. Bell 3,5,0; B. Broome 7,2,0; A. Bye 36,0,2; D. Coleman 29,3,3; A. Coles 1,1,0; E. Collins 11,2,2; D. Coney 23,0,6; M. Danzey 1,0,0; B. Goodsell 1,0,0; M. Holland 21,0,0; D. Holmes 16,0,0; J. Horton 42,0,9; G Howells 9,0; M. Jones 7,2,0; D. Leworthy 42,0,32; P. Manning 14, 0; D. Morris 3,0,0; R. Newbery 11,7,1; J. Power 26,0,0; B. Pratt 8,3,0; S Read 10,8,3; A. Rogers 11,2 1; I. Savage 12,8,0; M. Taylor 6,0,0; M. Turkington 5,3,0; J. Wigmore 41,0,3; D. Williamson 4,0,0; R. Wilson 14,2,4.

Ever Present Players

Boston United	P. Bastock
Farnborough Town	D. Leworthy
Gateshead	S. Smith
Slough Town	A. Pluckrose, A. Sayer
Stafford Rangers	R. Price
Stalybridge Celtic	R. Hughes
Welling United	G. Abbott, T. Robbins
Bromsgrove Rovers	P. Webb
Promoted Clubs	
Southport	Mooney
Dover Athletic	Barlett, Tony Dixon, M. Munden

DIADORA LEAGUE

Of trees and things

Two big issues in the Diadora League attracted much outside interest this season. The first was the arrival of Aldershot Town, hot from the ashes of former Football League club, Aldershot. The new club was admitted to Diadora Division Three where they swept all before them, setting attendance records galore. Their season's average of over 2,000 was only topped in Non-League circles by three Conference teams.

The second of the season's talking points was the rather negative issue of no club being promoted from the league. One club is normally accepted into the GMVC provided its facilities meet with approval. With Chesham United deciding that they had too much to do and too little time to do it in, the stage was set for St Albans City to take their place. Unhappily they were rebuffed. St Albans' attractive Clarence Park ground includes two old oak trees which the Conference ground grading committee took a dislike to. With the trees protected by a preservation order, there was no way the club could comply with the Conference's demands.

On the field the situation was much brighter with sparkling performances by the leading clubs. Chesham had a terrific season leading throughout, losing only four league games and having a sequence of 23 games without defeat including a remarkable 14 straight wins. They also notched up a century of goals. St Albans spent all season chasing them never quite getting within reach and also scored over a hundred league goals.

For Enfield it was a frustrating season. Having just missed out on promotion the two previous seasons coming second to sides who were promoted, they came third this year to two teams who weren't. In Jimmy Bolton, Carshalton Athletic had the League's top scorer with a total of 37 goals - just one short of the all-time record. The club finished fourth in the table ahead of their bigger club neighbours Sutton United. Sutton's inconsistency in the league stopped them from mounting a significant challenge for the title but they demonstrated their potential with cup wins in the FA Trophy over Chesham and Wycombe Wanderers. Sutton's 3-2 win at Adams Park set them up for the home leg but they failed to capitalise, crashing 4-0 as the Conference front-runners turned on the style.

In Division One Hitchin started off the season with a 7-0 thumping of Heybridge Swifts and always looked like being one of the teams to beat. They topped the table at the end of October and were never caught – at one stage establishing a lead of 13 points, although they still needed a win from their final game, Gary Williams scoring with just four minutes remaining to save Hitchin's season.

For Molesey it was the first full season with manager Tony Dunne in charge. Highlights included an unbeaten sequence of 18 games to bring in the New Year and a League Cup final show-down with Premier Division Marlow. One-one at half-time, Molesey had the better of the second half but failed to score and suffered the sucker punch of a goal in the 90th minute.

Dorking completed the clutch of clubs going up and went on to reach the final of the Full Members competition but lost by the only goal to Tooting & Mitcham. Only two clubs demoted this season – Lewes and Aveley.

Gerry Armstrong's Worthing side completed their turn-around in fortunes. They went on to take the Division Two title with a strong run of form just two seasons after their relegation from the First Division. With Ruislip Manor in second place Berkhamsted clinched third ahead of local rivals Hemel Hempstead.

Aldershot won the Third Division title, losing only two league games all season playing in front of an average home gate of 2,100. They also helped out one or two other clubs thanks to their travelling army of 900 fans – the 1900 who watched the derby game at Camberley was around the same figure as their neighbours' total gates for the preceding season.

Not yet eligible for either FA Vase or FA Cup, the club performed well in their remaining competitions only being knocked out by clubs from higher leagues. It wasn't all Aldershot though. With three promotion places to contest, Thame United and Collier Row finally came out ahead of Leighton Town, Cove and Northwood. The bottom clubs were all spared relegation as the League still lacks members.

Diadora Ups, Downs, Ins and Outs

Club	Division	Position	Movement
Staines Town	Premier	20th	Relegated to Division One
Windsor & Eton	Premier	21st	Relegated to Division One
Bognor Regis	Premier	22nd	Relegated to Division One
Hitchin Town	One	1st	Promoted to Premier
Molesey	One	2nd	Promoted to Premier
Dorking	One	3rd	Promoted to Premier
Lewes	One	20th	Relegated to Division Two
Aveley	One	21st	Relegated to Division Two
Harlow Town	One	Resigned	Readmitted to Division Three
Worthing	Two	1st	Promoted to Division One
Ruislip Manor	Two	2nd	Promoted to Division One
Berkhamsted Town	Two	3rd	Promoted to Division One
Harefield United	Two	21st	Relegated to Division Three
Southall	Two	22nd	Relegated to Division Three
Aldershot Town	Three	1st	Promoted to Division Two
Thame United	Three	2nd	Promoted to Division Two
Collier Row	Three	3rd	Promoted to Division Two
Farnham Town	Three	–	Resigned
Petersfield United	Three	19th	Resigned – to Wessex League
Cheshunt	SpL	3rd	Elected to Division Three
Oxford City	SML	1st	Elected to Division Three

Diadora Charity Shield

Grays Athletic ....1 Woking 5
Durant 59 Buzaglo 3, 19 Puckett 5, 20 Nugent 49
Attendance: 550

The Isthmian League History

The Isthmian League was founded in 1905 with just six clubs. It gradually increased in size to 16 in 1963, when four prominent Athenian Leaguers joined, to total 20 clubs. Membership reached 22 for the first time in 1972.

In 1973 a 16-club Division Two was added, which grew to 22 clubs in 1975. These divisions were renamed as the Premier and First Divisions in 1977 when a new Division Two of 17 clubs was added. In 1983-84 all three divisions comprised 22 clubs. For the 1984-85 season Division Two was split into North and South Divisions, but for 1991-92 a single Division Two returned, with the clubs finishing in the bottom half of the regionalised tables in 1990-91 forming a new Division Three. While feeder leagues serve the lowest division, the League champions are normally promoted to the Conference, replacing a relegated club.

Diadora took over sponsorship in 1991. Former sponsors have been Rothmans, Berger, Servowarm and Vauxhall.

5-Year One, Two, Three Records

Premier Division

	1st	Pts	2nd	Pts	3rd	Pts
1987-88	Yeovil Town	81	Bromley	76	Slough Town	72
1988-89	Ley'stone Ilf	89	Farnborough T	81	Slough Town	78
1989-90	Slough Town	92	Wokingham T	89	Aylesbury Utd	84
1990-91	Redbridge For	93	Enfield	89	Aylesbury Utd	83
1991-92	Woking	97	Enfield	79	Sutton Utd	70

Division One

	1st	Pts	2nd	Pts	3rd	Pts
1987-88	Marlow	101	Grays Ath	100	Woking	82
1988-89	Staines Town	87	Basingstoke T	83	Woking	82
1989-90	Wivenhoe T	100	Woking	98	Southwick	84
1990-91	Chesham Utd	89	Bromley	80	Yeading	77
1991-92	Stevenage Boro'	96	Yeading	82	Dulwich Hamlet	75

Division Two (North)

	1st	Pts	2nd	Pts	3rd	Pts
1987-88	Wivenhoe Town	88	Collier Row	79	Tilbury	69
1988-89	Harlow Town	90	Purfleet	78	Tring Town	76
1989-90	Heybridge Sw	87	Aveley	85	Hertford Town	83
1990-91	Stevenage Bor	107	Vauxhall Motors	82	Billericay Town	74

Division Two (South)

	1st	Pts	2nd	Pts	3rd	Pts
1987-88	Chalfont St P	87	Met Police	86	Dorking	86
1988-89	Dorking	100	Whyteleafe	84	Finchley	72
1989-90	Yeading	91	Molesey	83	Abingdon Town	75
1990-91	Abingdon Town	94	Maidenhead Utd	92	Egham Town	87

Division Two

	1st	Pts	2nd	Pts	3rd	Pts
1991-92	Purfleet	89	Lewes	83	Billericay Tn	80

Division Three

	1st	Pts	2nd	Pts	3rd	Pts
1991-92	Edgware Town	93	Chertsey Town	91	Tilbury	87

LEAGUE CUP

A last minute goal secured the Diadora League Cup for Marlow and put paid to a quite remarkable performance by First Division Molesey in reaching the final of the competition with a series of outstanding displays – not least a marvellous two leg semi-final victory over Enfield.

5-Year Finals List

Year	Teams	Score	Venue
1987-88	Yeovil Town v Hayes	3-1	Basingstoke
1988-89	B. Stortford v Farnborough Town	1-0	Hayes
1989-90	Aveley v St Albans City	3-0	Dagenham
1990-91	Woking v Carshalton Athletic	2-1	Kingstonian
1991-92	Grays Athletic v Enfield	3-1	Dagenham

The 'Isthmian League Cup' was first competed for during the 1974-75 season when Tilbury beat Croydon 3-1 over two legs. It was known as the 'AC Delco Cup' from 1985-86 until 1990-91.

Preliminary Round

Billericay Town v East Thurrock Utd 2-0
Bracknell Town v Banstead Ath 0-3
Camberley Town v Edgware Town ...1-0
Cove v Berkhampstead Town 3-2
Feltham & HB v Barton Rovers 2-1
Flackwell Heath v Chertsey Town ...1-3
Hemel Hempstead v Lewes 3-1
Hertford Town v Southall 3-1
Hungerford Town v Met. Police 1-5
Kingsbury Town v Harefield United ...2-0
Leatherhead v Altershot Town ......† 1-1
Replay 2-3
Leighton Town v Farnham Tn ... walk over
Farnham resigned
Northwood v Collier Row 4-1
Petersfield United v Horsham 2-3
Purfleet v Royston Town 3-1
Rainham Town v Hampton 1-5
Saffron Walden Town v Newbury Tn 2-0
Thame United v Epsom & Ewell 3-0
Tilbury v Ruislip Manor ....† 2-4
Tring Town v Egham Town 1-2
Ware v Malden Vale 1-2
Witham Town v Clapton 1-0
Worthing v Hornchurch 2-0

1st Round

Abingdon Town v Camberley Town ...3-1
Aylesbury United v Aveley 4-2
barking v Wivenhoe Town..............1-6
Basingstoke Tn v Walton & Hersham 3-0
Bognor Regis Town v Met. Police 1-3
Boreham Wood v Feltham & HB ..† 4-1
Chalfont St. Peter v Saffron Walden ...2-1
Chertsey Town v Egham Town ......† 2-3
Cove v Hayes 0-5
Croydon v Carshalton Athletic ......† 3-3
Replay 1-0
Dulwich Hamlet v St Albans City ...† 1-0
Enfield v Whyteleafe 7-0
Grays Athletic v Windsor & Eton 2-3
Hampston v Dorking ....† 1-0
Harrow Borough v Bromley 3-0
Hemel Hempstead v Marlow 1-4
Hendon v Hertford Town 7-0
Horsham v Staines Town 2-4
Kingstonian v Malden Vale 3-2
Kingsbury Town v Aldershot Town 0-1
Leighton Tn v Tooting & Mitcham Utd 2-3
Leyton v Chesham United 2-1
Maidenhead United v Yeading .....† 1-1
Replay 1-4

103

Molesey v Bishops's Stortford 2-1
Purfleet v Harlow Town .... walk over
   Harlow Town resigned
Ruislip Manor v Heybridge Swifts......3-0
Stevenage Borough v Billericay Town 1-2
Sutton United v Hitchin Town 2-0
Thame United v Wembley 3-1
Uxbridge v Northwood 0-1
Wokingham Town v Witham Town ...2-0
Worthing v Banstead Athletic ....† 3-1

2nd Round

Abingdon Town v Molesey ....† 3-3
   Replay ....† 1-0
Aldershot Town v Hampton ....† 5-2
Aylesbury United v Thame United ...† 3-3
   Replay ....† 3-2
Basingstoke Town v Met. Police 0-1
Boreham Wood v Purfleet 2-0
Dulwich Hamlet v Worthing 1-3
Hayes v Croydon 1-2
Hendon v Ruislip Manor 2-1
Kingstonian v Billericay Town ......† 1-0
Leyton v Tooting & Mitcham United...2-3
Marlow v Egham Town 5-1
Northwood v Windsor & Eton 2-3
Staines Town v Yeading 0-1
Sutton United v Chalfont St Peter 4-1
Wivenhoe Town v Harrow Borough ...2-1
Wokingham Town v Enfield 0-1

3rd Round

Aylesbury United v Enfield 1-2
Hendon v Aldershot Town 2-1
Marlow v Yeading 3-1

Met. Police v Wivenhoe Town 1-2
Molesey v Tooting & Mitcham United 3-0
Sutton United v Boreham Wood 3-0
Windsor & Eton v Hayes 0-1
Worthing v Kingstonian 1-2

4th Round

Hendon v Enfield........................† 1-1
   Replay 0-2
Kingstonian v Marlow 0-4
Molesey v Hayes 2-0
Wivenhoe Town v Sutton United 1-2

Semi-Finals 1st Leg

Enfield v Molesey 1-0
Sutton United v Marlow 0-2

Semi-Finals 2nd Leg

Marlow v Sutton United 2-1
Marlow won 4-1 on agg
Molesey v Enfield 5-0
Molesey won 5-1 on agg

Final

at Aldershot Town FC
Marlow 2
   Blackman 7, Watkins 90
Molesey 1
   Rose 16 (pen)
Att: 944

League Cup Attendance Summaries 1992-93

Round	Matches	Total	Average
Preliminary	23	4,352	189
First	33	6,448	195
Second	18	5,274	293
Third	8	2,161	270
Fourth	5	1,193	239
Semi-Finals	4	1,425	356
Final	1	944	
Total	**92**	**21,797**	**237**

FULL MEMBERS CUP

Club captain Micky Stephens scored a 69th minute goal to give Tooting & Mitcham United a 1-0 win over Dorking at Kingsmeadow Stadium.

Preliminary Round

Abingdon Town v Basingstoke Town....1-2
Aveley v Bromley 2-5
Aylesbury United v Marlow 2-5
Bishop's Stortford v Billericay Town....5-0
Chesham United v Stevenage Borough..1-3
Hayes v Wembley 1-0
Heybridge Swifts v Wivenhoe Town.....0-1
Molesey v Dulwich Hamlet 2-0
Sutton United v Lewes 3-1
Uxbridge v Harrow Borough 0-1
Wokingham Tn v Chalfont St. Peter......2-0

1st Round

Barking v Leyton 0-2
Bishop's Stortford v Hayes 1-2
Bromley v Maidenhead United 3-0
Carlshalton Ath v Bognor Regis Town..1-0
Croydon v Wokingham Town................1-2
Dorking v Walton & Hersham 1-0
Grays Athletic v Wivenhoe Town..........2-0
Hendon v Boreham Wood ....† 0-0
  Boreham Wood won 4-2 on pens
Marlow v St Albans City........................3-2
Molesey v Staines Town 2-0
Purfleet v Harrow Borough 2-1
Stevenage Borough v Enfield 0-2
Sutton United v Kingstonian 2-1
Tooting & Mitcham v Basingstoke Tn...3-1
Windsor & Eton v Whyteleafe 3-0
Yeading v Hitchin Town.........................1-2

2nd Round

Boreham Wood v Hayes 2-4
Bromley v Dorking 2-4
Enfield v Grays Athletic.........................1-2
Hitchin Town v Leyton ....† 1-1
  Hitchin won 4-1 on pens
Marlow v Purfleet 2-3
Sutton United v Tooting & Mitcham Utd 2-3
Windsor & Eton v Molesey 2-1
Wokingham Town v Carshalton Ath ..† 2-2
  Carshalton won 4-3 on pens

3rd Round

Carshalton Athletic v Windsor & Eton ..6-1
Dorking v Hitchin Town ....† 2-1
Hayes v Grays Athletic 2-1
Tooting & Mitcham v Purfleet..............† 1-1
  Tooting won 4-3 on pens

Semi-Finals

Carshalton Ath v Dorking 1-2
Hayes v Tooting & Mitcham United......0-2

Final

at Kingstonian FC
Dorking...0
Tooting & Mitcham United......................1
  Stephens 69
Att: 673

ASSOCIATE TROPHY

Northwood crowended their first season in the Diadora League by defeating Barton Rovers 3-1 to clinch the Associate memebers Trophy for the first time. Vic Schwartz's 72nd minute goal looked to have won the Trophy in normal time but iGraham Golds equalised for Rovers in stoppage time. Within a minute of extra time Rob Holland restored Northwoods advantage and Frank Omere clinched the tie with a goal on 107 minutes.

Preliminary Round

Aldershot Town v Chertsey 4-1
Banstead Ath v Egham Town .... † 1-1
Banstead won 5-4 on pens
Barton Rovers v Clapton 3-0
Bracknell Town v Newbury Town......0-2
East Thurrock United v Collier Row ...1-0
Hemel Hemstead v Tring Town ....† 2-2
Hungerford Town v Hampton 0-1
Leighton Town v Flackwell Heath......2-1
Royston Town v Hornchurch 3-0
Saffron Walden Town v Ware 1-0

1st Round

Berkhampstead Town v Tring Town ...2-1
Cove v Banstead Athletic 2-3
Adandoned in extra time – fog
Replay 0-2
Edgware Town v Hertford Town 4-1
Horsham v Aldershot Town 0-1
Leatherhead v Camberley Town ...... † 1-1
Leatherhead won 4-1 on pens
Leighton Town v Barton Rovers 1-2
Met. Police v Feltham & HB 4-0
Newbury Town v Hampton ....† 1-1
Newbury won 6-5 on pens
Northwood v East Thurrock United ...3-1
Petersfield United v Malden Vale 1-3
Royston Town v Saffron Walden Tn ...1-2
Ruislip Manor v Rainham Town 3-1
Southall v Epsom & Ewell 3-2
Tilbury v Kingsbury Town 1-4
Thame United v Witham Town 2-1
Worthing v Harefield United 4-0

2nd Round

Barton Rovers v Ruislip Manor 3-0
Berkhampstead Town v Edgware Tn † 0-2
Cove v Thame United......................0-2
Kingsbury Tn v Saffron Walden Tn ...4-3
Met. Police v Leatherhead .... † 2-3
Newbury Town v Malden Vale 3-1
Southall v Northwood 1-2
Worthing v Aldershot Town .... † 4-4
Worthing won 5-3 on pens

3rd Round

Kingsbury Town v Barton Rovers ... † 0-1
Newbury Town v Met. Police 3-7
Northwood v Edgware Town 3-2
Thame United v Worthing 0-1

Semi-Finals

Barton Rovers v Met. Police .... † 2-2
Northwood v Worthing .... † 3-1
Replay
Met. Police v Barton Rovers 1-2

Final

at Barton Rovers FC
Barton Rovers 1
    Golds 90
Northwood 3
    Schwartz 62, Holland 92, Omere 107
Att: 241
After Extra Time

PREMIER DIVISION

Final Table 1992-93

	P	W	D	L	F	A	Pts
Chesham United	42	30	8	4	104	34	98
St Albans	42	28	9	5	103	50	93
Enfield	42	25	6	11	94	48	81
Carshalton Ath	42	22	10	10	96	56	76
Sutton United	42	18	14	10	74	57	68
Grays Athletic	42	18	11	13	61	64	65
Stevenage Boro	42	18	8	16	62	60	62
Harrow Borough	42	16	14	12	59	60	62
Hayes	42	16	13	13	64	59	61
Aylesbury United	42	18	6	18	70	77	60
Hendon	42	12	18	12	52	54	54
Basingstoke	42	12	17	13	49	45	53
Kingstonian	42	14	10	18	59	58	52
Dulwich Hamlet	42	12	14	16	52	66	50
Marlow	42	12	11	19	72	73	47
Wokingham	42	11	13	18	62	81	46
Bromley	42	11	13	18	51	72	46
Wivenhoe Town	42	13	7	22	41	75	46
Yeading	42	11	12	19	58	66	45
Staines Town	42	10	13	19	59	77	43
Windsor & Eton	42	8	7	27	40	90	31
Bognor Regis	42	5	10	27	46	106	25

Leading Premier League Goalscorers
J. Bolton (Carshalton) 36 goals, S. Clark (St Albans) 35 goals, C. Townsend (Chesham) 24 goals, T. Langley (Wokingham) 21 goals, J. Warden (Carshalton) 20 goals, M. Gittings (Stevenage Borough)

Promotions and Relegations

Club	Position	Movement
Staines Town	20th	Relegated to Division One
Windsor & Eton	21st	Relegated to Division One
Bognor Regis	22nd	Relegated to Division One

Clubs Joining Premier Division

Club	Position	From
Hitchin Town	1st	Division One
Molesey	2nd	Division One
Dorking	3rd	Division One

PREMIER DIVISION RESULTS 1992-93

	Aylesbury Utd	Basingstoke	Bognor Regis	Bromley	Carshalton	Chesham Utd	Dulwich	Enfield	Grays Athletic	Harrow Boro'	Hayes
Aylesbury United	•	1-0	2-0	6-1	3-2	1-4	0-2	1-1	1-2	0-1	1-1
Basingstoke Town	1-2	•	0-0	1-1	0-1	0-0	2-1	4-0	4-0	0-0	1-0
Bognor Regis Town	4-5	1-3	•	3-2	0-6	0-4	2-2	0-6	4-1	1-3	1-2
Bromley	1-2	1-0	3-0	•	0-4	2-2	2-2	0-5	2-3	1-1	1-1
Carshalton Athletic	1-0	0-0	2-0	0-2	•	1-1	2-0	1-2	2-1	1-1	1-3
Chesham United	2-1	2-1	6-1	0-0	5-1	•	4-0	0-1	3-2	2-2	2-0
Dulwich Hamlet	0-1	0-0	2-2	1-1	1-7	1-4	•	0-1	2-0	1-2	1-0
Enfield	3-1	4-1	6-2	2-0	2-1	0-1	1-2	•	2-1	0-1	1-1
Grays Athletic	2-1	3-2	2-1	4-1	2-2	2-0	0-0	3-2	•	2-1	2-3
Harrow Borough	2-3	0-0	2-0	0-2	2-4	0-3	1-1	1-0	0-0	•	1-0
Hayes	4-0	1-3	1-0	3-3	0-4	1-3	0-0	0-1	0-1	2-2	•
Hendon	1-1	0-0	0-0	1-1	1-2	0-0	2-1	0-0	1-0	1-2	2-0
Kingstonian	7-1	1-1	1-2	2-2	0-5	2-1	2-2	2-3	2-1	2-2	1-1
Marlow	3-4	0-0	3-0	2-2	3-2	0-1	0-1	1-1	1-1	1-2	1-2
St Albans City	1-0	4-1	2-1	4-0	0-3	1-4	3-1	0-0	6-0	1-0	1-0
Staines Town	1-4	0-1	4-1	2-3	3-2	1-1	1-1	2-2	6-1	0-0	0-1
Stevenage Borough	1-3	0-2	0-0	0-1	3-1	0-2	2-4	0-3	1-1	2-1	1-2
Sutton United	4-0	1-0	2-2	3-1	1-4	1-0	2-0	3-2	3-3	0-1	2-3
Windsor & Eton	2-3	1-0	0-0	0-1	0-4	2-5	0-0	1-3	0-2	3-0	3-1
Wivenhoe Town	2-1	3-2	4-1	1-0	2-2	0-0	0-1	0-4	2-0	1-1	5-0
Wokingham Town	0-2	3-1	1-3	1-1	2-2	0-0	3-1	0-3	2-0	4-0	1-2
Yeading	2-1	1-2	2-1	0-0	1-1	1-2	0-2	3-5	2-3	—	—

	Hendon	Kingstonian	Marlow	St Albans City	Staines Town	Stevenage	Sutton United	Windsor & Eton	Wivenhoe Town	Wokingham	Yeading
Aylesbury United	1-1	2-0	0-3	3-2	5-3	1-2	0-4	3-0	1-2	1-0	1-1
Basingstoke Town	1-1	0-0	2-1	1-2	1-1	0-0	1-1	3-0	1-1	5-0	0-6
Bognor Regis Town	0-2	3-4	1-5	2-6	0-0	2-6	1-1	0-1	2-0	2-2	1-4
Bromley	1-0	0-2	0-1	1-3	4-1	1-2	1-1	1-2	3-0	0-2	1-0
Carshalton Athletic	3-1	3-0	3-2	3-5	2-1	3-1	2-1	1-3	3-1	3-1	1-1
Chesham United	4-0	2-1	4-3	2-2	1-0	7-1	7-0	1-0	5-0	1-1	3-0
Dulwich Hamlet	2-1	4-1	1-0	0-5	2-0	1-1	0-2	0-0	4-0	2-1	0-1
Enfield	0-2	2-2	1-4	0-2	4-1	2-1	1-0	6-0	2-1	3-0	4-1
Grays Athletic	0-0	1-1	2-5	3-0	1-1	1-0	1-3	0-0	1-1	4-1	3-0
Harrow Borough	1-1	2-0	2-1	3-6	2-2	2-1	4-3	7-1	2-1	4-2	3-0
Hayes	1-1	2-3	0-0	0-0	4-0	0-1	2-2	0-0	1-1	1-1	0-0
Hendon	•	1-0	2-0	2-2	1-1	1-2	0-1	2-0	0-1	3-1	3-3
Kingstonian	2-4	•	5-1	1-1	3-1	2-3	0-1	3-0	5-1	3-2	1-2
Marlow	3-0	1-1	•	1-1	5-2	2-1	0-1	2-1	1-2	7-2	1-1
St Albans City	3-3	2-0	1-4	•	2-2	2-1	0-1	3-0	1-0	0-1	2-0
Staines Town	4-1	1-0	2-0	2-1	•	2-2	1-1	0-1	1-0	1-1	1-1
Stevenage Borough	0-2	2-0	2-1	1-2	1-2	•	1-0	1-1	3-0	2-0	2-2
Sutton United	1-2	1-1	2-1	3-1	2-4	1-1	•	1-1	1-0	1-2	0-2
Windsor & Eton	2-0	1-0	1-2	0-3	3-1	2-4	0-3	•	1-1	1-2	1-3
Wivenhoe Town	2-2	2-3	2-1	0-2	1-1	0-0	1-3	2-0	•	1-0	0-2
Wokingham Town	2-2	0-4	2-2	1-3	2-2	3-0	3-3	1-3	2-0	•	2-2
Yeading	1-3	1-2	0-0	1-2	0-1	2-2	4-0	1-0	0-0	2-4	•

ATTENDANCES 1992-93

	Aylesbury Utd	Basingstoke	Bognor Regis	Bromley	Carshalton	Chesham Utd	Dulwich	Enfield	Grays Athletic	Harrow Boro'	Hayes
Aylesbury United	•	467	500	506	673	1134	303	903	503	549	403
Basingstoke Town	337	•	299	229	424	544	361	492	195	371	331
Bognor Regis Town	230	220	•	320	240	417	280	250	140	360	268
Bromley	210	246	369	•	510	342	588	412	439	205	192
Carshalton Athletic	508	393	336	406	•	601	447	502	465	381	328
Chesham United	1266	694	769	905	805	•	1106	1064	809	1512	1044
Dulwich Hamlet	272	227	124	431	390	416	•	724	152	366	301
Enfield	1070	671	574	727	742	1220	555	•	385	476	732
Grays Athletic	373	301	231	238	265	468	346	485	•	347	302
Harrow Borough	300	257	230	307	304	434	302	412	236	•	292
Hayes	333	305	206	369	284	513	249	465	204	351	•
Hendon	204	253	201	257	237	476	238	759	174	263	357
Kingstonian	693	560	483	638	503	703	398	773	403	735	505
Marlow	410	229	232	258	301	829	270	619	278	357	255
St Albans City	1302	837	619	597	814	3120	955	1643	617	903	610
Staines Town	554	255	328	237	330	682	328	490	275	384	326
Stevenage Borough	605	501	613	656	704	871	862	785	665	525	563
Sutton United	678	709	821	682	807	672	630	714	583	408	574
Windsor & Eton	248	196	168	263	163	415	1687	386	148	200	255
Wivenhoe Town	282	166	262	291	172	284	206	502	347	258	303
Wokingham Town	299	345	305	285	219	561	271	396	299	289	440
Yeading	258	189	110	262	221	383	251	370	208	262	544

	Hendon	Kingstonian	Marlow	St Albans City	Staines Town	Stevenage	Sutton Utd	Windsor & Eton	Wivenhoe	Wokingham	Yeading
Aylesbury United	346	410	768	748	542	977	602	555	409	477	753
Basingstoke Town	334	402	333	555	363	449	605	297	314	302	345
Bognor Regis Town	330	300	210	240	210	285	425	210	160	230	170
Bromley	380	456	228	403	452	270	339	400	391	283	322
Carshalton Athletic	365	551	328	566	345	463	1288	402	271	409	331
Chesham United	910	910	1107	1456	871	710	806	675	785	643	844
Dulwich Hamlet	752	374	263	263	314	292	401	502	230	507	330
Enfield	851	715	843	1116	465	952	809	624	690	665	406
Grays Athletic	417	367	289	382	351	320	402	277	346	245	310
Harrow Borough	420	345	276	386	294	356	263	249	289	325	281
Hayes	380	419	295	469	301	311	448	313	278	270	596
Hendon	•	357	303	403	216	374	504	247	227	211	186
Kingstonian	625	•	458	695	574	503	897	540	443	742	405
Marlow	287	361	•	580	260	266	308	290	242	386	210
St Albans City	865	742	722	•	809	910	867	526	472	647	727
Staines Town	416	506	287	356	•	508	564	447	274	393	279
Stevenage Borough	619	459	531	1107	454	•	583	637	481	414	683
Sutton United	674	1173	479	728	625	597	•	382	580	501	584
Windsor & Eton	153	266	265	369	221	269	440	•	185	265	190
Wivenhoe Town	273	258	216	242	196	323	393	241	•	462	166
Wokingham Town	245	530	317	446	258	348	435	457	233	•	286
Yeading	297	306	206	386	191	286	282	320	307	233	•

111

Attendance Summaries by Club

	Pos	(91-92)	Att	(91-92)	Ave	(91-92)	% change
Chesham United	1	(4)	19,733	(11,889)	940	(566)	+66.0
St Albans City	2	(13)	19,304	(10,438)	919	(497)	+84.9
Enfield	3	(2)	15,235	(12,207)	581	(581)	+24.7
Sutton United	5	(3)	13,601	(15,285)	648	(728)	-10.9
Stevenage Borough	7	(1st Div)	13,318	(12,859)	633	(643)	-1.3
Aylesbury United	10	(7)	12,528	(15,128)	597	(720)	-17.0
Kingstonian	13	(10)	12,276	(14,410)	585	(686)	-14.9
Carshalton Athletic	4	(8)	9,686	(8,963)	461	(427)	+7.9
Staines Town	20	(20)	8,199	(8,464)	390	(403)	-3.2
Basingstoke Town	12	(14)	7,882	(10,753)	375	(512)	-26.7
Dulwich Hamlet	14	(1st Div)	7,631	(2,970)	363	(149)	+143.6
Bromley	17	(12)	7,437	(10,843)	354	(516)	-31.3
Hayes	9	(19)	7,358	(6,369)	350	(303)	+15.5
Wokingham Town	16	(5)	7,258	(8,034)	346	(383)	-9.6
Marlow	15	(6)	7,228	(7,474)	344	(356)	-3.3
Grays Athletic	6	(15)	7,012	(7,720)	334	(368)	-10.2
Harrow Borough	8	(18)	6,558	(9,234)	312	(440)	-9.8
Hendon	11	(17)	6,447	(6,200)	307	(295)	+4.0
Bognor Regis Town	22	(21)	5,495	(5,608)	262	(267)	-1.8
Wivenhoe Town	18	(16)	5,843	(5,109)	278	(243)	+14.4
Yeading	19	(1st Div)	5,272	(2,883)	251	(144)	+74.3
Windsor & Eton	21	(11)	5,232	(6,626)	249	(316)	-21.2
Total			203,305	(236,638)	440	(512)	-14.0

Best League Attendances at 10 Grounds 1992-93

3120	St Albans City	v	Chesham United	13/02/93
1512	Chesham United	v	Harrow Borough	28/12/92
1288	Carshalton Athletic	v	Sutton United	28/12/92
1220	Enfield	v	Chesham United	17/10/92
1173	Sutton United	v	Kingstonian	28/12/92
1134	Aylesbury United	v	Chesham United	24/04/93
1107	Stevenage Borough	v	St Albans City	23/01/93
897	Kingstonian	v	Sutton United	19/09/92
829	Marlow	v	Chesham United	26/12/92
759	Hendon	v	Enfield	28/12/92

Premier League Top Scorers By Club

Club	Player	Tot	Lg	IC	LC
Aylesbury United	Graham Westley	27	16	4	–
(includes 5 league & 4 league cup goals for Enfield)					
Basingstoke Town	Pat Coombs	12	12	–	–
Bognor Regis Town	Jonathan Lockhart	5	5	–	–
Bromley	Sean Devine	18	16	–	2
Carshalton Athletic	Jimmy Bolton	40	37	–	3
Chesham United	Chris Townsend	24	24	–	–
Dulwich Hamlet	Robert Wilson	13	12	1	–
(includes 8 league & 1 league cup goals for Croydon)					
Enfield	Darren Collins	26	18	3	–
(includes 8 league & 3 league cup goals for Aylesbury United)					
Grays Athletic	Winston Whittingham	22	19	1	2
Harrow Borough	Steve Conroy	13	11	2	–
Hayes	David Pearce	18	15	3	–
Hendon	Barry Blackman	13	11	2	–
Kingstonian	David Pearce	31	27	3	1
(includes 15 league & 3 league cup goals for Hayes)					
Marlow	David Lay	21	13	6	2
St Albans City	Steve Clark	36	36	–	–
Staines Town	Gary Crawshaw	19	18	1	–
Stevenage Borough	Martin Gittings	20	20	–	–
Sutton United	Dominic Feltham	17	15	1	1
Windsor & Eton	Michael Creighton	11	9	1	1
Wivenhoe Town	Mitchell Springett	10	8	1	1
Wokingham Town	Tommy Langley	21	21	–	–
Yeading	Les Charles	15	15	–	–

DLC = Diadora League Cup   FMC = Full Members' Cup

William Hill Manager of Month Awards

Month	Manager	Club
September	John Mitchell	St Albans City
October	Gerald Aplin	Chesham United
November	Gerald Aplin	Chesham United
December	Billy Smith	Carshalton Athletic
January	John Mitchell	St Albans City
February	Billy Smith	Carshalton Athletic
March	Gerald Aplin	Chesham United
April	John Mitchell	St Albans City
Manager of the Season	Gerald Aplin	Chesham United

PREMIER DIVISION CLUBS

AYLESBURY UNITED

Founded by an amalgamation of the Printing Works and Night Schools Clubs. Once a Spartan League side, they were Delphian League founder members in 1951, moving on to the Athenian on the absorption of that League in 1963. The club joined the Southern League in 1976 and moved to a new out-of-town ground in 1986. Promoted to the Conference in 1988 but relegated to the Vauxhall League after one season.

Ground: The Stadium, Buckingham Road, Aylesbury, Bucks, HP19 3QL
Phone: 0296-436350 **Nickname:** The Ducks **Founded:** 1897
Manager: Alan Davies **Secretary:** Tony Graham **Chairman:** N. Stonell
Colours: Green and White Hoops, White, Green **Change:** All Red

5-Year Record	P	W	D	F	A	Pts	Psn	Cup	FAT
88-89	CONF	40	9	9	43	71	36	20	2	2
89-90	VLP	42	25	9	86	30	84	3	2	2
90-91	VLP	42	24	11	90	47	83	3	1	2
91-92	DLP	42	16	17	69	46	65	7	2	2
92-93	DLP	42	18	6	70	77	60	10	1	1

Ground Capacity: 7,800 (400) **Record:** 6,000 v England, friendly 6/88
Rail: Aylesbury (1 mile from ground).
Directions: Opposite Horse & Jockey PH on A413 Buckingham Rd.

BASINGSTOKE TOWN

The club were Hampshire League members from 1900 until 1971 when they joined the Southern League. In 1947 they moved to an out-of-town site – the Camrose Ground. They were in the Southern League's top section from 1985 until 1987 when they moved to the Isthmian League set-up. Spent one season in the Premier Division before relegation but were promoted back from Division One at the first attempt.

Ground: The Camrose Grd, Western Way, Basingstoke, Hants, RG24 6HW
Phone: 0256-461465 **Nickname:** Stoke **Founded:** 1896
Manager: Alan Humphries **Secretary:** David Knight **Chairman:** G. Hill
Colours: Blue with Gold Trim, Blue, Blue **Change:** Gold, Black, Black

5-Year Record	P	W	D	F	A	Pts	Psn	Cup	FAT
88-89	VL1	40	25	8	85	36	83	2	2q	1
89-90	VLP	42	18	9	65	55	63	8	2	1q
90-91	VLP	42	12	7	57	95	43	18	4q	1q

| 91-92 | DLP | 42 | 14 | 11 | 56 | 65 | 53 | 14 | 2q | 1q |
| 92-93 | DLP | 42 | 12 | 17 | 49 | 45 | 53 | 12 | 1q | 1 |

Ground Capacity: 6,000 (840)   **Record:** 4,091 v Northampton Tn, FAC1
Rail: Basingstoke (1½ miles from ground).
Directions: M3 Junction 6, then follow A30. Ground off Winchester Rd.

BROMLEY

Initially played in the South London League. Founder members of the Southern League Second Division in 1894 but after two seasons switched to the London League. Movement saw Kent and more London League action before being Spartan League founder members in 1907. Isthmian Leaguers from 1908 to 1911, they then returned to the Kent League. After the First World War they joined the Athenian League. In 1938 their Hayes Lane ground was opened and in 1952 they returned to the Isthmian League. Relegated from the top division in 1975, 1984 and again in 1990, they returned to the Premier Division in 1991.

Ground: Hayes Lane, Bromley, Kent, BR2 9EF
Phone: 081-460-5291   **Nickname:** Lillywhites   **Founded:** 1892
Manager: George Wakeling **Secretary:** J.Cooper **Chairman:** G.Beverly
Colours: White, Black, White   **Change:** Red, Black

5-Year Record	P	W	D	F	A	Pts	Psn	Cup	FAT
88-89	VLP	42	13	15	61	48	54	14	3q	1
89-90	VLP	42	7	11	32	69	32	21	4q	3q
90-91	VL1	42	15	14	62	37	80	2	2q	2q
91-92	DLP	42	14	12	51	57	54	12	3q	2
92-93	DLP	42	11	13	51	72	46	17	2q	3q

Ground Capacity: 8,500 (2,000)   **Record:** 12,000 v Nigeria, Friendly, 9/49
Rail: Bromley South (1 mile from ground).
Directions: M25, Junction 4. A21 to Bromley.

CARSHALTON ATHLETIC

Formed in 1905 by the amalgamation of Mill Lane Mission (1903) and Carshalton St Andrews (1897). Originally in the Southern Suburban League, they were founder members of the Surrey Senior League in 1922 and of the Corinthian League in 1946. They switched to the Athenian League in 1956 and in 1973 were founder members of the Isthmian League Division Two. Promoted to the top section in 1977, they have stayed there ever since.

Ground: War Memorial SG, Colston Avenue, Carshalton, Surrey, SM5 2EX
Phone: 081-642-8425   **Nickname:** Robins   **Founded:** 1903
Manager: Billy Smith **Secretary:** Ron McLean **Chairman:** Trevor Cripps

Colours: White with Maroon Trim, Maroon with White Trim, White
Change: Maroon, White, White

5-Year Record		P	W	D	F	A	Pts	Psn	Cup	FAT
88-89	VLP	42	19	15	59	36	72	4	2q	2
89-90	VLP	42	19	5	63	59	59*	10	2q	3q
90-91	VLP	42	17	7	80	67	64	9	2q	1
91-92	DLP	42	18	8	64	67	62	8	1q	3q
92-93	DLP	42	22	10	96	56	76	4	1q	1q

* Three points deducted

Ground Capacity: 8,000 (200)   **Record:** 8,200 v Tooting & Mitcham 1951
Rail: Carshalton (300 yards from ground).
Directions: From station turn left into North Street and then first right into Camden Road. At end cross over West Street into Colston Avenue.

CHESHAM UNITED

Formed by the amalgamation of Chesham Town (1879) and Chesham Generals (1887), the club were members of the Spartan League until 1947 when they joined the Corinthian League. They became Athenian Leaguers in 1963 and were Isthmian League Division Two founder members in 1973. They were relegated in 1986 but promoted back to Division One in 1987. Promoted to the top division for the first time in 1991.

Ground: The Meadow, Amy Lane, Amersham Rd, Chesham, Bucks, HP5 1NE
Phone: 0494-783964   **Nickname:** United   **Founded:** 1919
Manager: Gerald Aplin **Secretary:** D. Stanley **Chairman:** Tony Aplin
Colours: Claret and Blue Stripes, Claret, Blue **Change:** no details

5-Year Record		P	W	D	F	A	Pts	Psn	Cup	FAT
88-89	VL1	42	12	9	54	67	45	14	1q	2q
89-90	VL1	42	15	12	46	49	57	10	Pr	1q
90-91	VL1	42	27	8	102	37	89	1	2q	1
91-92	DLP	42	20	10	67	48	70	4	4q	1
92-93	DLP	42	30	8	104	34	98	1	4q	3

Ground Capacity: 5,000 (150)   **Record:** 5,000 v Camb. Utd, FAC3 12/79
Rail: Chesham (¼ mile from ground).
Directions: Located on the A416 – follow Amersham signs from Chesham.

DORKING

Formed around 1880, they were Surrey Senior League founder members in 1922. Moved to their present ground in 1953 and joined the Corinthian League in 1956 and the Athenian in 1963. In 1974 amalgamated with Guildford City to become Guildford and Dorking United in the Southern

League. Further spells in County and Athenian leagues before joining the Isthmian League in 1981 adopting their present name in 1982. Reached Division One in 1989, the Premier in 1993.
Ground: Meadowbank, Mill Lane, Dorking, Surrey, RH4 1DX
Phone: 0306-884112   **Nickname:** The Chicks **Founded:** 1977
Manager: John Rains **Secretary:** Brian Stone **Chairman:** Tom Howes
Colours: Green and White Hoops, White, White **Change:** Blue, White, Red

5-Year Record	P	W	D	F	A	Pts	Psn	Cup	FAT
88-89	VL2S	40	32	4	109	35	100	1	1q	(V1)
89-90	VL1	42	19	12	66	41	69	6	1q	1q
90-91	VL1	42	20	5	78	67	65	10	4q	1
91-92	DL1	40	16	7	68	65	55	11	2q	2
92-93	DL1	40	23	9	73	40	78	3	1	3q

Ground Capacity: 600 (150)   **Record:** 4,500 v Folkestone, 1954/5
Rail: Dorking (½ mile from ground).
Directions: From town centre turn right at Woolworth's into Mill Lane.

DULWICH HAMLET

Founded in 1893, they competed in local leagues, joining the Isthmian League from the Southern Suburban League in 1907. Isthmian Leaguers since that time, they were relegated in 1977, promoted to the top section in 1978, relegated for a second time in 1990, but promoted again last season.
Ground: Champion Hill Stadium, Dog Kennel Hill, Dulwich
Phone: 071-274-8707   **Nickname:** The Hamlet **Founded:** 1893
Manager: Jim Cannon **Secretary:** Terry Stephens **Chairman:** Steve Dye
Colours: Blue and Pink Stripes, Blue, Blue   **Change:** All Yellow

5-Year Record	P	W	D	F	A	Pts	Psn	Cup	FAT
88-89	VLP	42	12	12	58	57	48	17	4q	2q
89-90	VLP	42	6	8	32	80	26	22	4q	1q
90-91	VL1	42	16	11	67	54	59	12	1q	1q
91-92	DL1	40	22	9	71	40	75	3	2q	2q
92-93	DLP	42	12	14	52	56	50	14	1q	3q

Ground Capacity: **Record:** 752 v Hendon DLP, 3/10/92
Rail: East Dulwich.
Directions: Located 200 yards from East Dulwich Station.

ENFIELD

Founded as Enfield Spartans, adopting their current name on joining the North Middlesex League in 1900. London League members from 1905, they were Athenian League founder members in 1912. In 1936 they moved to their current home and in 1963 joined the Isthmian League. Joined the Alliance Premier League for the 1981-82 season, being relegated in 1990.

Ground: The Stadium, Southbury Road, Enfield, Middx, EN1 1YQ
Phone: 081-363-2858 **Nickname:** The E's **Founded:** 1893
Manager: Graham Roberts **Secretary:** Alan Diment **Chairman:** T. Unwin
Colours: White, Blue, Blue   **Change:** All Yellow

5-Year Record		P	W	D	F	A	Pts	Psn	Cup	FAT
88-89	CONF	40	14	8	62	67	50	13	2	2
89-90	CONF	42	10	6	52	89	36	22	4q	2
90-91	VLP	42	26	11	83	30	89	2	3q	2
91-92	DLP	42	24	7	59	45	79	2	2	2
92-93	DLP	42	25	6	94	48	81	3	4q	2

Ground Capacity: 8,500 (820)   **Record:** 10,000 v Tottenham, f.o., 1963
Rail: Southbury Road (½ mile from ground). **Directions:** Located at junction of A10 and A110 (Enfield). Five minutes from M25/A10 junction.

GRAYS ATHLETIC

Founded in 1890 and took occupation of their Bridge Road ground in 1894. Athenian League founder members in 1912, they reappeared after the First World War in the London League. After the Second World War they were Corinthian League founder members and first champions. Moved to the Athenian again in 1958 and in 1983 joined the Isthmian League set-up. They were the first champions of Division Two (South) in 1985 and promoted to the Premier Division in 1988.

Ground: The Recreation Ground, Bridge Road, Grays, Essex, RM17 6BZ
Phone: 0375-377753 **Nickname:** The Blues **Founded:** 1890
Managers: Jeff & Fred Saxton **Secretary:** Jeff Saxton **Chairman:** F. Harris
Colours: Royal Blue, White, Royal Blue   **Change:** Silver, Grey, Black

5-Year Record		P	W	D	F	A	Pts	Psn	Cup	FAT
88-89	VLP	42	19	13	62	47	70	5	1	2q
89-90	VLP	42	19	13	59	44	70	5	1q	1q
90-91	VLP	42	20	8	66	53	68	6	3q	2q
91-92	DLP	42	14	11	53	68	53	15	4q	1q
92-93	DLP	42	18	11	61	64	65	6	3q	3

Ground Capacity: 5,500 (350) **Record:** 9,500 v Chelmsford FAC 1959
Rail: Grays (1 mile from ground).

Directions: A13 towards Southend, turn right at traffic lights towards Grays. Bridge Road after ½ mile on left.

HARROW BOROUGH

Formed as Roxonian. Moved to their Earlsmead Ground and joined the Spartan League in 1934 adopting the name Harrow Town in 1938. In 1958 they joined the Delphian League and were absorbed into the Athenian League in 1963. In 1967 their name was changed to Harrow Borough and in 1975 they were elected to the Isthmian League. Promoted to the top section in 1979, they have stayed there ever since.

Ground: Earlsmead, Carlyon Avenue, South Harrow, Middx, HA2 8SS
Phone: 081-422-5221   **Nickname:** The Boro   **Founded:** 1933
Manager: George Borg **Secretary:** Peter Rogers **Chairman:** Martin Murphy
Colours: All Red   **Change:** All Light Blue

5-Year Record		P	W	D	F	A	Pts	Psn	Cup	FAT
88-89	VLP	42	9	13	53	75	40	19	1q	3q
89-90	VLP	42	11	10	51	79	43	18	1q	2
90-91	VLP	42	10	8	57	84	38	20	1q	3q
91-92	DLP	42	11	13	58	78	46	18	1q	2
92-93	DLP	42	16	14	59	60	62	8	1q	3q

Ground Capacity: 4,750 (200)   **Record:** 3,000 v Wealdstone, FAC 46
Rail: Northolt Park (½ mile from the ground).
Directions: Take A40 and exit in direction of South Harrow. Left at lights; right at roundabout; fifth right.

HAYES

Originally founded as a boys' team – Botwell Mission. Played in the Great Western Suburban League 1919-24, moving to their Church Road ground in 1921. Spartan League members from 1924, changing their name to Hayes in 1929 and being elected to the Athenian League in 1930. Moved to the Isthmian League in 1971 and have stayed in the top section since then.

Ground: Townfield House, Church Road, Hayes, Middx, UB3 2LE
Phone: 081-573-4598   **Nickname:** The Missioners   **Founded:** 1909
Manager: Clive Griffiths **Secretary:** John Price **Chairman:** Derek Goodall
Colours: Red and White Stripes, Black, Black **Change:** Blue and White

5-Year Record		P	W	D	F	A	Pts	Psn	Cup	FAT
88-89	VLP	42	18	12	61	47	66	8	1	3q
89-90	VLP	42	14	11	61	59	53	14	1	1q
90-91	VLP	42	20	5	60	57	65	8	2	1
91-92	DLP	42	10	14	52	63	44	19	2	2q

| 92-93 | DLP | 42 | 16 | 13 | 64 | 59 | 61 | 9 | 1 | 2q |

Ground Capacity: 9,500 (450)   **Record:** 15,370 v Bromley, FAAmC 2/51
Rail: Hayes and Harlington (1 mile from ground).   **Directions:** M4, exit A312.

HENDON

Founded in 1908 as Hampstead Town. Reached the Athenian League in 1919 via the Finchley, Middlesex and London Leagues. In 1933 they changed their name to Golders Green Town and in 1946 changed again to their present title. Moved to the Isthmian League in 1963 and have stayed in the top section since that time.

Ground: Claremont Road, Cricklewood, London, NW2 1AE
Phone: 081-458-3093   **Nickname:** Dons   **Founded:** 1908
Manager: Peter Taylor **Secretary:** Michael Cox **Chairman:** Victor Green
Colours: Green, White, Green   **Change:** All Yellow

5-Year Record	P	W	D	F	A	Pts	Psn	Cup	FAT
88-89	VLP	42	13	17	51	68	56	12	1	1
89-90	VLP	42	15	10	54	63	55	12	4q	1
90-91	VLP	42	12	10	48	62	46	15	2q	3q
91-92	DLP	42	13	9	59	73	48	17	2q	3q
92-93	DLP	42	12	18	52	54	54	11	3q	2q

Ground Capacity: 8,000 (500)   **Record:** 9,000 v Northampton, FAC 52
Rail: Brent Cross (Underground ½ mile from ground).
Directions: M1/A406 roundabout. Take minor exit towards Refuge Centre. At second mini roundabout turn right into Claremont Rd. Continue for about 1 mile – ground on left.

HITCHIN TOWN

While Hitchin Town were in existence from 1865 to 1914, the club reformed in1928 and joined the Spartan League Western Division. They joined the Athenian League for season 1939-40, becoming Isthmian Leaguers in 1963. They were relegated from the top section for the first time in 1988.

Ground: Top Field, Fishponds Road, Hitchin, Herts, SG5 1NU
Phone: 0462-434483   **Nickname:** The Canaries   **Founded:** 1865
Manager: Andy Melvin **Secretary:** Alan Sexton **Chairman:** T. Barratt
Colours: Yellow, Green, Yellow   **Change:** All Red

5-Year Record	P	W	D	F	A	Pts	Psn	Cup	FAT
88-89	VL1	40	21	11	60	32	74	4	1q	1q
89-90	VL1	42	22	13	60	30	79	4	3q	3q
90-91	VL1	42	21	9	78	50	72	5	1q	2q
91-92	DL1	40	17	10	55	45	61	8	Pr	2q
92-93	DL1	40	25	7	67	29	82	1	2q	2q

Ground Capacity: 4,000 (400) **Record:** 7,878 v Wycombe W, FAAmC3 2/56
Rail: Hitchin (1 mile from ground).
Directions: On A505 a mile from town centre.

KINGSTONIAN

Formed on the amalgamation of Old Kingstonians and Kingston Town, themselves the two parts of a "split" Kingston and Surbiton YMCA formed in 1885. Joined the Athenian League in 1919, then the Isthmian in 1929. Relegated from the Premier Division in 1979, they were promoted back in 1985 and have been there ever since.
Ground: Kingsmeadow Stadium, 422A Kingston Road, Kingston-Upon-Thames, Surrey, KT1 2HL
Phone: 081-547-3336 **Nickname:** The K's **Founded:** 1885
Manager: Chris Kelly **Secretary:** William McNully **Chairman:** no details
Colours: Red and White Hoops, Black, Black **Change:** All White

5-Year Record		P	W	D	F	A	Pts	Psn	Cup	FAT
88-89	VLP	42	19	11	54	37	68	6	3q	1
89-90	VLP	42	24	9	87	51	81	4	1q	QF
90-91	VLP	42	21	12	86	57	75	5	4q	3q
91-92	DLP	42	17	8	71	59	59	10	4q	1
92-93	DLP	42	14	10	59	58	52	13	1	2

Ground Capacity: 6,500 (1,200) **Record:** 1,930 v Barrow, FAT4 3/90
Rail: Kingston (1 mile from ground).
Directions: On A307 Kingston to Richmond road. Kingsmeadow is signposted.

MARLOW

Known in their early days as Great Marlow. Joined the Spartan League in 1908 but for 1911-12 moved to the Great Western Suburban League. In 1924 they moved to the Reading & District League, returning to the Spartan in 1928. In 1965 they became Athenians, joining the top division in 1973. Joined the Isthmian League Division Two (North) in 1984, transferred to the South Section in 1985, then promoted twice in consecutive seasons.
Ground: Alfred Davis Memorial Gd, Oak Tree Rd, Marlow, Bucks, SL7 3ED
Phone: 0628-483970 **Nickname:** The Blues **Founded:** 1870
Manager: David Russell **Secretary:** Paul Burdell **Chairman:** M. Eagleton
Colours: Royal Blue with White Trim, Royal Blue, Royal Blue
Change: All Gold and Black

5-Year Record		P	W	D	F	A	Pts	Psn	Cup	FAT
88-89	VLP	42	9	11	48	83	38	20	2q	3q
89-90	VLP	42	11	13	42	59	46	17	4q	2q
90-91	VLP	42	18	13	72	49	67	7	4q	3q
91-92	DLP	42	20	7	56	50	67	6	1	1
92-93	DLP	42	12	11	72	73	47	15	3	2q

Ground Capacity: 8,000 (500)   **Record:** no details

Rail: Marlow (1 mile from ground).

Directions: M4 or M40 take A404 to Marlow. Follow A4135 towards town centre. At Esso Garage turn right into Maple Rise. Ground in opposite road.

MOLESEY

Formerly Molesey St Pauls United, in 1953 Molesey joined the Surrey Senior League moving to the Spartan Leaguein 1959. They joined the Athenian League in 1973 and were founders of the Isthmian League Division Two in 1977. They were later members of the Division Two (South) being promoted for the first time in 1990.

Ground: 412 Walton Road, West Molesey, Surrey, KT8 0JG

Phone: 081-979-4823   **Nickname:** Moles   **Founded:** 1950

Manager: Tony Dunne   **Secretary:** John Chambers   **Chairman:** Gary Mayne

Colours: White, Black, Black   **Change:** Yellow, Blue, Yellow

5-Year Record		P	W	D	F	A	Pts	Psn	Cup	FAT
88-89	VL2S	40	19	13	58	42	70	4	2q	(VPr)
89-90	VL2S	40	24	11	76	30	83	2	2q	(V4)
90-91	VL1	42	22	5	65	46	71	8	2q	1
91-92	DL1	40	16	9	55	61	57	10	1q	1q
92-93	DL1	40	23	11	81	38	80	2	2q	1q

Ground Capacity: 4,800 (400)   **Record:** 1,255 v Sutton, Surrey Snr Cup sf 1966

Rail: Hampton Court (1 mile from ground).

Directions: A3, take A309 at Hook. Turn right at Marquis of Grandby PH to Hampton Court Station. Left through Molesey. Ground on left after 1 mile.

ST ALBANS CITY

Formed in 1908 and immediately joined the Spartan League. They became Athenians in 1920 and moved to the Isthmian League three seasons later. They were relegated in 1974 and again in 1983, but were promoted to Division One in 1984 and to the Premier Division in 1986.

Ground: Clarence Park, Hatfield Road, St Albans, Herts, AL1 4NF

Phone: 0727-64296   **Nickname:** Saints   **Founded:** 1908

Manager: Steve Ketteridge   **Secretary:** S. Trulock   **Chairman:** B. Tominey

Colours: Blue with Yellow sleeves, Blue, Yellow Change: Yellow & Green

5-Year Record		P	W	D	F	A	Pts	Psn	Cup	FAT
88-89	VLP	42	12	9	51	59	45	17	2q	1q
89-90	VLP	42	13	10	49	59	49	15	1q	1q
90-91	VLP	42	11	12	60	74	45	16	1q	1q
91-92	DLP	42	14	11	66	70	53	13	2q	3q
92-93	DLP	42	28	9	103	50	98	2	1	2

Ground Capacity: 7,000 (1,000)   **Record:** 9,757 v Ferryhill Ath., FAAmC 1926
Rail: St Albans City (300 yards from ground).
Directions: M25 Junction 22. Across two roundabouts towards city. At first lights turn right. Left at next lights. Right at second lights into Clarence Road. Ground located inside Clarence Park.

STEVENAGE BOROUGH

Founded in 1976, they joined the United Counties League in 1980 and were promoted to the top section after their first season. Moved to the Vauxhall Opel League in 1984 and promoted to the First Division in 1986. Relegated in 1988, they have been promoted twice since then.

Ground: Stevenage Stadium, Broadhall Way, Stevenage, Herts, SG2 8RH
Phone: 0438-367059   **Nickname:** The Boro   **Founded:** 1976
Manager: Paul Fairclough   **Secretary:** Ron Berners   **Chairman:** Ken Vale
Colours: Red and White Stripes, White, White **Change:** All Yellow with Red Trim

5-Year Record		P	W	D	F	A	Pts	Psn	Cup	FAT
88-89	VL2N	42	20	13	84	55	73	4	2q*	(VPr)
89-90	VL2N	42	22	6	60	45	72	4	1q	(V3)
90-91	VL2N	42	34	5	122	28	107	1	1q	(V1)
91-92	DL1	40	30	6	95	37	96	1	1q	1q
92-93	DLP	42	18	8	62	60	62	7	3q	2

* Tie awarded to opponents
Ground Capacity: 5,000 (480)   **Record:** 3,000, Charity, 5/80
Rail: Stevenage (1 mile from ground).
Directions: A1(M) Junction 7. On B197 from 2nd roundabout.

SUTTON UNITED

Sutton gained senior status and a South Suburban League place in 1910. Joined the Athenian League in 1921, moving to an expanded Isthmian League in 1963. Always in the top division, they declined promotion to the Conference in 1985 but accepted it the following season. Relegated in 1991.

Ground: Boro Sports Ground, Gander Green Lane, Sutton, Surrey, SM1 2EY
Phone: 081-644-5120   **Nickname:** U's   **Founded:** 1898
Manager: Alan Gane   **Secretary:** B. Williams   **Chairman:** D. Hermitage

Colours: All Amber   Change: All White

5-Year Record		P	W	D	F	A	Pts	Psn	Cup	FAT
88-89	CONF	40	12	15	64	54	51	12	4	2
89-90	CONF	42	19	6	68	64	63	8	1	1
90-91	CONF	42	10	9	62	82	39	21	1	1
91-92	DLP	42	19	13	88	51	70	3	1	1
92-93	DLP	42	18	14	74	57	68	5	1	SF

Ground Capacity: 8,000 (1,000) **Record:** 14,000 v Leeds Utd, FAC3 1/70
Rail: West Sutton (adjacent to ground).
Directions: M25 Junction 8. Take A217 to Sutton. Follow A217 signs towards London. Right at second set of lights into Gander Green Lane.

WIVENHOE TOWN

Formed as Wivenhoe Rangers. Played locally, moving from the Colchester & East Essex League to the Essex & Suffolk Border League in 1971 and to the Essex Senior League in 1979. Joined the Isthmian League set-up in 1986. Promoted to Division One in 1988 and to the Premier Division in 1990.

Ground: Broad Lane Ground, Elmstead Road, Wivenhoe, Essex, CO7 7HA
Phone: 0206-225380   **Nickname:** The Dragons   **Founded:** 1925
Manager: Mick Loughton   **Secretary:** R. Adler   **Chairman:** D. Whymark
Colours: Blue, White, White   **Change:** no details

5-Year Record		P	W	D	F	A	Pts	Psn	Cup	FAT
88-89	VL1	40	22	6	62	44	72	5	1q	3q
89-90	VL1	42	31	7	94	36	100	1	4q	2
90-91	VLP	42	16	11	69	66	59	10	2q	3
91-92	DLP	42	16	4	56	81	52	16	1q	2
92-93	DLP	42	13	7	41	75	46	18	2q	1

Ground Capacity: 3,000 (200)   **Record:** 1,912 v Runcorn, FAT2 1990
Rail: Wivenhoe (1 mile from ground).
Directions: Leave Colchester in direction of Clacton. Take Wivenhoe exit and ground is visible.

WOKINGHAM TOWN

Played in local soccer, moving to their Finchampstead Road ground in 1906. Joined the Metropolitan & District League in 1954, the Delphian in 1957 and the Corinthian in 1959. They were absorbed into the Athenian League in 1963, switching to the Isthmian in 1973. They were promoted to the top section in 1982 and have stayed there ever since.

Ground: Finchampstead Road, Wokingham, Berks, RG11 2NR
Phone: 0734-780253   **Nickname:** The Town   **Founded:** 1875
Manager: Roy Merryweather **Secretary:** J. Aulsberry **Chairman:** P.Walsh

Colours: Amber, Black, Black   **Change:** Red, White, Red

5-Year Record		P	W	D	F	A	Pts	Psn	Cup	FAT
88-89	VLP	42	15	11	60	54	56	11	3q	1
89-90	VLP	42	26	11	67	34	89	2	4q	2
90-91	VLP	42	15	13	58	54	58	11	3q	1
91-92	DLP	42	19	10	73	58	67	5	2q	3q
92-93	DLP	42	11	13	62	81	46	16	1q	3q

Ground Capacity: 4,000 (200)
Record: 3,475 v Norton Woodseats, FAAmCup 57/8
Rail: Wokingham (½ mile from ground).
Directions: From town centre turn left into Denmark Street. Follow to Finchampstead Road.

YEADING

Formed in 1965. From local leagues and the Middlesex League they joined the Spartan League in 1984 and were promoted to the Premier Division in 1985. Joined Division 2 (South) of the Vauxhall League in 1987 and have been promoted twice since.

Ground: The Warren, Beaconsfield Road, Hayes, Middx
Phone: 081-848-7362   **Nickname:** The Dinc   **Founded:** 1965
Manager: Gordon Bartlett **Secretary:** Peter Bickers **Chairman:** P. Spurden
Colours: Red and Black Stripes, Black, Black   **Change:** All Yellow

5-Year Record		P	W	D	F	A	Pts	Psn	Cup	FAT
88-89	VL2S	40	13	9	47	63	46*	15	Pr	(V2)
89-90	VL2S	40	29	4	86	37	91	1	2q	(VW)
90-91	VL1	42	23	8	75	45	77	3	1q	3q
91-92	DL1	40	24	10	83	34	82	2	2q	2q
92-93	DLP	42	11	12	58	66	45	19	3q	1

* Two points deducted
Ground Capacity: 5,000 (100)   **Record:** 1,546 v Hythe, FAVsf 1990
Rail: Hayes (2 miles from ground).
Directions: A4020 Uxbridge Road. Turn right towards Southall, right into Springfield Road and left into Beaconsfield Road.

DIVISION ONE

Final Table 1992-93

	P	W	D	L	F	A	Pts
Hitchin Town	40	25	7	8	67	29	82
Molesey	40	23	11	6	81	38	80
Dorking	40	23	9	8	73	40	78
Purfleet	40	19	12	9	67	42	69
Bishops Stortford	40	19	10	11	63	42	67
Abingdon Town	40	17	13	10	65	47	64
Tooting & Mitcham	40	17	12	11	68	46	63
Billericay Town	40	18	6	16	67	61	60
Wembley	40	14	15	11	44	34	57
Walton & Hersh	40	14	12	14	58	54	54
Boreham Wood	40	12	14	14	44	43	50
Maidenhead United	40	10	18	12	45	50	48
Leyton	40	11	14	15	56	61	47
Whyteleafe	40	12	10	18	63	71	46
Uxbridge	40	11	13	16	50	59	46
Heybridge Swifts	40	11	9	20	47	65	42
Croydon	40	11	9	20	54	82	42
Chalfont St Peter	40	7	17	16	48	70	38
Barking	40	10	8	22	42	80	38
Lewes	40	9	10	21	34	80	37
Aveley	40	9	7	24	45	87	34

Leading Division One Goalscorers

Hynes (Whyteleafe) 30 goals, Lunn (Dorking) 22, Pearson (Molesey) 22, Collins (Tooting & Mitcham) 21, Rose (Molesey) 18, Jones (Billericay) 18, Das (Bishops Stortford) 17, Tompkins (Tooting & Mitcham) 15

William Hill Manager of Month Awards

Month	*Manager*	*Club*
September	John Rains	Dorking
October	Chris Wainwright	Walton & Hersham
November	Tony Dunne	Molesey
December	John Radford	Bishops Stortford
January	Trevor Ford	Tooting & Mitcham
February	John Rains	Dorking
March	Tony Dunne	Molesey
April	Gary Calder	Purfleet
Manager of the Season	Andy Melvin	Hitchin Town

Division One Top Scorers By Club

Club	Player	Total	League	DLC	FMC
Abingdon Town	Liam Herbert	18	16	2	–
Aveley	Toney Macklin	8	8	–	–
Barking	Jeff Wood	12	12	–	–
Billericay Town	Steve Jones	20	18	2	–
Bishop's Stortford	Marc Das	18	17	–	1
Boreham Wood	Andy Weddell	10	9	1	–
Calfont St Peter	lance Cadogan	12	10	2	–
Croydon	Robert Wilson	9	8	1	–
Dorking	Steve Lunn	28	22	–	6
Heybridge Swifts	David Matthews	12	12	–	–
Hitchin Town	Gary Williams	11	11	–	–
Lewes	Mark Rice	9	9	–	–
Leyton	Anthony Samuels	15	15	–	–
Maidenhead United	Paul Mulvaney	11	11	–	–
Molesey	Neil Pearson	26	22	2	2
Purfleet	George Georgiou	12	11	–	1
Tooting & Mitcham Utd	John Collins	23	21	1	1
Uxbridge	Nicky Ryder	12	12	–	–
Walton & Hersham	Alan Gregory	12	12	–	–
Wembley	Robert Hutchinson	10	9	1	–
Whyteleafe	Mark Hynes	30	30	–	–

DLC=Diadora League Cup, FMC=Full Members' Cup

Promotions and Relegations from Division One

Club	Position	Movement
Hitchin Town	1st	Promoted to Premier Division
Molesey	2nd	Promoted to Premier Division
Dorking	3rd	Promoted to Premier Division
Lewes	20th	Relegated to Division Two
Aveley	21st	Relegated to Division Two

Clubs Joining Division One

Club	Position	From
Staines Town	20th	Relegated from Premier Division
Windsor & Eton	21st	Relegated from Premier Division
Bognor Regis	22nd	Relegated from Premier Division
Worthing	1st	Promoted from Division Two
Ruislip Manor	2nd	Promoted from Division Two
Berkhamsted Town	3rd	Promoted from Division Two

DIVISION ONE RESULTS 1992-93

	Abingdon Tn	Aveley	Barking	Billericay	Bishop's S	Boreham Wd	Chalfont St P	Croydon	Dorking	Heybridge	Hitchin Tn
Abingdon Town	•	4-1	1-2	4-1	1-1	2-1	5-1	1-1	1-1	2-5	0-1
Aveley	5-1	•	2-2	0-2	1-0	0-2	2-1	1-3	1-3	2-2	1-1
Barking	1-0	2-1	•	1-1	1-2	1-0	2-1	1-2	0-2	1-2	0-0
Billericay Town	0-1	2-0	3-2	•	4-0	2-2	4-0	3-2	1-3	2-1	0-2
Bishop's Stortford	0-1	3-0	5-1	4-1	•	1-0	1-1	2-0	1-2	2-1	0-1
Boreham Wood	2-1	3-0	5-1	2-1	0-1	•	2-2	0-1	0-0	1-1	0-1
Chalfont St. Peter	2-2	2-2	3-0	2-0	2-2	1-1	•	1-1	2-2	0-1	0-3
Croydon	0-1	0-1	1-0	0-4	3-2	4-3	2-4	•	1-1	5-0	1-0
Dorking	0-1	4-2	7-0	2-1	1-0	0-2	4-1	2-1	•	2-1	0-7
Heybridge Swifts	1-2	1-2	2-1	1-2	2-3	1-1	0-2	3-0	0-2	•	•
Hitchin Town	1-1	3-0	3-2	2-0	2-1	1-0	6-0	2-0	1-2	1-0	•
Lewes	0-3	0-1	1-2	0-1	1-0	0-0	1-0	3-0	0-1	1-3	0-2
Leyton	0-0	1-2	2-1	3-1	2-2	1-1	2-2	1-0	0-1	0-0	2-0
Maidenhead United	0-0	1-0	3-4	4-1	0-0	1-2	4-0	4-2	1-1	0-0	2-3
Molesey	2-1	1-2	2-0	2-2	2-0	1-2	0-0	3-1	1-1	3-1	0-2
Purfleet	0-1	2-1	0-0	2-0	2-0	1-0	1-0	6-0	3-0	3-0	1-2
Tooting&Mitcham Utd	5-0	1-0	6-1	3-2	0-1	0-0	0-0	3-1	1-0	1-1	2-0
Uxbridge	0-1	4-1	2-0	3-2	1-1	1-4	3-2	6-0	1-2	2-1	1-2
Walton & Hersham	2-2	6-0	1-2	0-2	0-0	3-0	1-1	0-1	3-0	2-2	2-1
Wembley	3-2	3-1	1-1	3-0	1-1	0-1	2-0	1-0	1-1	0-2	1-1
Whyteleafe	0-2	3-1	2-2	0-1	1-2	1-2	3-0	3-3	2-2	1-1	1-0

	Lewes	Leyton	Maidenhead	Molesey	Purfleet	Tooting & M	Uxbridge	Walton & H	Wembley	Whyteleafe
Abingdon Town	4-0	2-2	0-0	0-2	3-3	1-1	0-1	2-1	2-0	4-2
Aveley	4-0	1-3	3-3	2-3	0-2	2-2	0-0	1-4	0-1	2-1
Barking	1-2	3-1	1-0	0-5	0-2	0-1	1-1	1-1	1-0	0-1
Billericay Town	1-1	1-3	3-0	2-2	2-0	3-0	2-1	4-2	1-1	3-1
Bishop's Stortford	6-0	3-3	0-0	1-2	1-0	2-1	4-1	2-0	0-1	3-2
Boreham Wood	2-0	1-1	2-2	0-0	0-0	0-4	0-1	0-2	0-2	1-1
Chalfont St Peter	4-1	1-1	1-1	1-1	2-2	2-1	0-1	0-2	0-1	4-2
Croydon	2-2	2-2	3-3	0-3	0-5	3-1	1-1	1-2	1-3	2-3
Dorking	5-0	2-1	1-0	1-2	0-1	1-2	1-0	4-0	1-0	2-1
Heybridge Swifts	1-2	2-3	0-1	3-5	0-1	0-2	2-0	3-3	0-3	5-0
Lewes	•	1-0	1-1	2-4	4-1	2-0	4-4	2-2	0-3	3-0
Leyton	0-0	•	1-1	0-0	2-2	1-1	1-0	1-1	0-0	5-1
Maidenhead United	4-0	1-0	•	•	•	2-2	4-0	3-1	1-1	2-6
Molesey	0-1	2-0	2-0	•	2-1	1-1	3-3	0-0	2-1	2-0
Purfleet	3-1	3-0	3-0	3-2	•	1-1	3-2	2-1	1-1	3-2
Tooting&Mitcham U	6-1	1-1	1-1	1-1	0-4	•	•	0-0	2-3	0-0
Uxbridge	1-1	1-1	1-1	1-1	1-1	0-2	•	1-1	1-0	3-2
Walton & Hersham	1-2	4-1	2-1	1-1	1-3	0-0	1-0	•	•	0-0
Wembley	1-1	0-2	1-2	0-1	2-1	0-0	0-0	1-1	•	0-0
Whyteleafe	4-0	4-2	5-1	1-2	1-0	1-1	1-3	2-0	0-0	•

DIVISION ONE CLUBS

ABINGDON TOWN

Ground: Culham Road, Abingdon, Oxon, OX14 3BT
Phone: 0235-21684　　**Nickname:** Over The Bridge　　**Founded:** 1889
Manager: Trevor Butler **Secretary:** Dave Sharp **Chairman:** Brian Tonkin
Colours: Yellow with Green Trim, Green with Yellow Trim, Yellow
Change: All Blue
Ground Capacity: 2,000 (80)　　**Record:** 1,400 v Oxford City, FAC 9/60
Rail: Culham (2 miles from ground).
Directions: On A415 ½ mile south of the town centre.

BARKING

Ground: Mayesbrook Park, Lodge Avenue, Dagenham, Essex, IG3 9EG
Phone: 081-595-6511　　**Nickname:** The Blues　　**Founded:** 1880
Manager: vacant **Secretary:** Mike Roberts **Chairman:** John Knight
Colours: Blue, White, Blue　　**Change:** All White with Blue Trim
Ground Capacity: 4,200 (200)　　**Record:** 1,900 v Aldershot FAC2 1988
Rail: Upney (Underground 1½ miles from ground).
Directions: Mayesbrook Park is about a mile along the A1153 from the A13 Thatched Cottage roundabout.

BERKHAMSTED TOWN

Ground: Broadwater, Lower Kings Road, Berkhamsted, Herts, HP4 2AA
Phone: 0442-826815　　**Nickname:** Lilywhites　　**Founded:** 1895
Manager:　　**Secretary:** A Dumpleton **Chairman:** Bob Sear
Colours: White, Black, Black　　**Change:** All Sky Blue
Rail: Berkhamsted (ground next to station).
Directions: A41 to Berkhamsted. Ground next to station.

BILLERICAY TOWN

Ground: New Lodge, Blunts Wall Road, Billericay, Essex, CM12 9SA
Phone: 0277-652188　　**Nickname:** Town　　**Founded:** 1880
Manager: John Kendall **Secretary:** Len Dewson **Chairman:** Brian Cornes
Colours: Royal Blue with White Trim, White, Royal Blue with White Trim
Change: Yellow, Black, Black　　**Rail:** Billericay (¾ mile from ground).
Ground Capacity: 2,500 (250)
Record: 3,841 v West Ham Utd, Floodlight opening 28/9/77.

Directions: M25 Junction 28 and via Shenfield (A129), right at first lights. M25 Junction 29 and via Basildon (A129), left at second set of lights.

BISHOP'S STORTFORD

Ground: George Wilson Stadium, Rhodes Av, B. Stortford, Herts, CM23 3JN
Phone: 0279-654140/656538 **Nickname:** Bishops   **Founded:** 1874
Manager: John Radford **Secretary:** Jim Gill   **Chairman:** Jim Gill
Colours: Blue and White Stripes, Blue, Blue   **Change:** All Red
Ground Capacity: 6,000 (228)
Record: 6,000: v Middlesbrough FAC3 1/83 v Peterborough FAC2 12/72
Rail: Bishop's Stortford (½ mile from ground).
Directions: M11 Junction 8. A120 towards Bishop's Stortford. Take South Street to South Road and Rhodes Avenue. About ½ mile on left.

BOGNOR REGIS TOWN

Ground: Nyewood Lane, Bognor Regis, West Sussex, PO21 2TY
Phone: 0243-828683   **Nickname:** The Rocks   **Founded:** 1883
Manager: Mick Pullen **Secretary:** M Jones **Chairman:** Stanley Rowlands
Colours: White/Green, Green, White **Change:** All Yellow/ Red Trim
Ground Capacity: 6,000 (243)   **Record:** 3,642 v Swansea, FAC1R 1984
Rail: Bognor Regis (1 mile from ground).
Directions: Follow seafront westward from the pier. Continue past Aldwich Shopping Centre and turn right into Nyewood Lane. Entrance on left.

BOREHAM WOOD

Ground: Broughinge Road, Borehamwood, Herts, WD6 5AL
Phone: 081-953-5097   **Nickname:** The Wood   **Founded:** 1948
Manager: Bobby Makin **Secretary:** Tony Perkins **Chairman:** Phil Wallace
Colours: White, Black, Red   **Change:** Red, Red, Black
Ground Capacity: 5,000 (220)   **Record:** 2,500 v St. Albans, FAAmC 1970/1
Rail: Elstree & Borehamwood (1 mile from ground).
Directions: M25, A1 south towards London. Exit at first turn-off towards Borehamwood. Located off roundabout near BBC studios.

CHALFONT ST PETER

Ground: The Playing Fields, Amersham Rd, Chalfont St Peter, Bucks, SL9 7BQ
Phone: 0753-885797   **Nickname:** The Saints   **Founded:** 1926
Manager: Tony O'Driscoll **Secretary:** Mal Keenan **Chairman:** David Ward
Colours: White, Green, Green   **Change:** All Yellow
Ground Capacity: 2,500 (200)   **Record:** 2,500 v Watford, benefit 4/85
Rail: Gerrards Cross (2 miles from ground).

Directions: West side of A413 by Ambulance Station and Community Centre, north of town.

CROYDON

Ground: Croydon Sports Arena, Albert Road, S. Norwood, London, SE25 4QL
Phone: 081-654-3462   **Nickname:** Blues   **Founded:** 1953
Manager: Dave Mehmet **Secretary:** Geoff Beeson **Chairman:** N. Moran
Colours: All Blue   **Change:** All Red
Ground Capacity: 8,000 (450)   **Record:** 1,450 v Wycombe W, FAC4q 1975
Rail: Norwood Junction (200 yards).
Directions: Albert Rd is just off the junction of the A215 and A213.

HEYBRIDGE SWIFTS

Ground: Scraley Road, Heybridge, Maldon, Essex
Phone: 0621-852978   **Nickname:** Swifts   **Founded:** 1880
Manager: Gary Hill **Secretary:** Dennis Fenn **Chairman:** Michael Gibson
Colours: Black and White Stripes, Black, Red **Change:** Orange, White, White
Ground Capacity: 5,000 (200)   **Record:** 2,500, Charity 1990
Rail: Witham (6 miles from ground).
Directions: North of Maldon and Heybridge village. Then right off B1022 in direction of Tolleshunt D'Arcy (Scraley Road). Ground on right-hand side.

LEYTON

Ground: 282 Lea Bridge Road, Leyton, London, E10 7LD
Phone: 081-539-5405   **Nickname:** not known   **Founded:** 1975
Manager: Peter McGillicuddy **Secretary:** M. Roberts **Chairman:** G. Gross
Colours: Blue, White, Blue   **Change:** White, Blue, White
Ground Capacity: 3,000 (200)   **Record:** 500 v Wickham, FAV6 1984
Rail: Leyton or Blackhorse Road Underground (1½ miles from ground).
Directions: Located on the Lea Bridge Road behind the Hare and Hounds PH.

MAIDENHEAD UNITED

Ground: 1 York Road, Maidenhead, Berks, SL6 1SQ
Phone: 0628-24739   **Nickname:** Tanners   **Founded:** 1869
Manager: John Watt **Secretary:** Stan Payne **Chairman:** Jim Parsons
Colours: White, Black, White   **Change:** All Red
Ground Capacity: 1,500 (100)   **Record:** 9,401 v Southall, FAAm C 1936
Rail: Maidenhead (400 yards from ground).
Directions: In town centre. Two minutes walk from cark parks.

PURFLEET

Ground: Essex Hotel & L.C., Ship Lane, Grays, Essex, RM15 4HB
Phone: 0708-868901   **Nickname:** None   **Founded:** 1985
Manager: Gary Calder   **Secretary:** N. Posner   **Chairman:** H. South
Colours: Green, Green, Yellow   **Change:** All Yellow
Ground Capacity: 2,500 (300)   **Record:** 980 v West Ham 1989
Rail: Purfleet (2 miles from ground).
Directions: M25 or A13 to Dartford Tunnel roundabout. Take Ship Lane – signposted ground located on right.

RUISLIP MANOR

Ground: Grosvenor Vale, off West End Road, Ruislip, Middx, HA4 6JQ
Phone: 0895-637487   **Nickname:** The Manor   **Founded:** 1938
Colours: White, Black, Black   **Change:** All Yellow
Ground Capacity: 3,000 (200)
Record: 2,000 v Tooting & M, FAC 1962
Rail: Ruislip Manor Underground (Metropolitan line – ½ mile from ground)
Directions: From station turn left and then first right (Shenley Ave). Third left (Cranley Drive).

STAINES TOWN

Ground: Wheatsheaf Park, Wheatsheaf Lane, Staines, Middx, TW18 2PD
Phone: 0784-455988   **Nickname:** Swans   **Founded:** 1892
Manager: Wayne Wanklyn **Secretary:** Len Gregory **Chairman:** Alan Boon
Colours: Old Gold with Royal Blue Trim, Blue, Blue
Change: Blue and White Stripes, White, White
Ground Capacity: 2,000 (700)
Record: 2,500 v Banco di Roma, Anglo-Italian Cup, 10/75
Rail: Staines (¾ mile from ground).
Directions: Off Laleham Road (B376) from town centre.

TOOTING AND MITCHAM UNITED

Ground: Sandy Lane, Mitcham, Surrey, CR4 2HD
Phone: 081-648-3248   **Nickname:** Terrors   **Founded:** 1932
Manager: Trevor Ford **Secretary:** Chris Jackson **Chairman:** Jack Payne
Colours: White, Black, Red   **Change:** All Light Blue
Ground Capacity: 7,500 (1,900)   **Record:** 15,000 v Wimbledon 1951
Rail: Tooting (¼ mile from ground).
Directions: Off Streatham Road near the Swan Hotel, to the north of Mitcham Town centre.

UXBRIDGE

Ground: Honeycroft, Horton Road, West Drayton, Middx, UB7 8HX
Phone: 0895-443557 **Nickname:** Reds **Founded:** 1871
Manager: George Talbot **Secretary:** Alan Brown **Chairman:** A. Holloway
Colours: Red, White, Red **Change:** All Sky Blue
Ground Capacity: 5,000 (200) **Record:** 1,000 v Arsenal, f.o. 1981
Rail: West Drayton (1 mile from ground).
Directions: From West Drayton Station: Turn right, first right into Horton Road. Ground signposted a mile on left.

WALTON AND HERSHAM

Ground: Sports Ground, Stompond Lane, Walton-on-Thames, Surrey
Phone: 0932-245263 **Nickname:** Swans **Founded:** 1896
Manager: Chris Wainwright **Secretary:** Gerry Place **Chairman:** Nick Swindley
Colours: Red and White, White, Red **Change:** All Blue
Ground Capacity: 6,500 (500) **Record:** 6,500 v Brighton, FAC 1973/4
Rail: Walton-on-Thames (½ mile from ground).
Directions: ¼ mile south of Walton-on-Thames town centre on A244 to Esher.

WEMBLEY

Ground: Vale Farm, Watford Road, Sudbury, Wembley, Middx, HA0 4UR
Phone: 081-904-8169 **Nickname:** The Lions **Founded:** 1946
Manager: Alan Dafforn **Secretary:** Mrs J. Gumm **Chairman:** Brian Gumm
Colours: Red, White, Red **Change:** All Sky Blue
Ground Capacity: 3,000 (250) **Record:** 2,000 v Hendon, Mid Snr Cup, 59/60
Rail: Sudbury (400 yards from ground).
Directions: Watford Road is part of the A404 and runs on from Harrow Road when driving north from High Road, Wembley.

WHYTELEAFE

Ground: 15 Church Road, Whyteleafe, Surrey, CR3 0AR
Phone: 081-660-5491 **Nickname:** Leafe **Founded:** 1946
Manager: Paul Hinshelwood **Secretary:** Syd Maddex **Chairman:** A. Lidbury
Colours: Green and White, Green, White **Change:** Yellow, Black, Black
Ground Capacity: 5,000 (200) **Record:** not known
Rail: Whyteleafe (600 yards from ground).
Directions: Off A22 three miles north of M25 Junction 6

WINDSOR AND ETON

Ground: Stag Meadow, St. Leonards Road, Windsor, Berks, SL4 3DR
Phone: 0753-860656   **Nickname:** The Royals   **Founded:** 1891
Manager: Alf Coulton   **Secretary:** C. Cherry   **Chairman:** M. Broadley
Colours: Red with Green Piping, Red, White   **Change:** White, Black, White
Ground Capacity: 5,000 (350)   **Record:** 8,500
Rail: Windsor & Eton Central (1½ miles from ground).
Directions: M4 Junction 6. Follow A332 towards Windsor. Left at lights. Opposite Stag & Hounds public house.

WORTHING

Ground: Woodside Road, Worthing, West Sussex, BN14 7HQ
Phone: 0903-39575   **Nickname:** The Rebels   **Founded:** 1886
Manager: Gerry Armstrong   **Secretary:** Barry Lindfield
Chairman: Beau Reynolds
Colours: All Red   **Change:** All White
Ground Capacity: 4,500 (430)   **Record:** 5,000 FAAMCup 1908
Rail: Worthing.   **Directions:** To the north of the sea-front and town centre.

Division One Home Attendances By Club

Club	Pos	(91-92)	Att	(91-92)	Ave	(91-92)	% change
Hitchin Town	1	(8)	8497	(6599)	425	(330)	+28.7
Bishop's Stortford	5	(Prem Div)	6164	(7096)	308	(338)	-8.8
Billericay Town	8	(Div Two)	5995	(5313)	300	(253)	+18.5
Dorking	3	(11)	4796	(3430)	240	(172)	+39.5
Maidenhead United	12	(16)	3373	(4335)	169	(217)	-22.1
Abingdon Town	6	(6)	3165	(4962)	181	(248)	-27.0
Heybridge Swifts	16	(19)	2991	(3147)	150	(157)	-4.4
Purfleet	4	(Div Two)	2945	(1932)	147	(92)	+59.7
Tooting & Mitcham	7	(7)	2820	(2973)	141	(149)	-5.3
Walton & Hersham	10	(9)	2745	(2975)	137	(149)	-8.0
Chalfont St Peter	18	(13)	2490	(2509)	125	(125)	–
Uxbridge	15	(15)	2463	(2344)	123	(117)	+5.1
Molesey	2	(10)	2458	(1958)	123	(98)	+25.5
Lewes	20	(Div Two)	2433	(3780)	122	(180)	-32.2
Leyton	13	(14)	2415	(2310)	121	(116)	+4.3
Whyteleafe	14	(20)	2415	(2153)	121	(108)	+12.0
Aveley	21	(21)	2293	(1970)	115	(99)	+16.1
Boreham Wood	11	(4)	2213	(2845)	111	(142)	-21.8
Wembley	9	(5)	1884	(2383)	94	(119)	-21.0
Barking	19	(12)	1849	(2143)	92	(107)	-14.0
Croydon	17	(18)	1293	(2117)	65	(106)	-38.6
Total			68,147	(71,775)	162	(171)	-5.2

DIVISION TWO

Final Table 1992-93

	P	W	D	L	F	A	Pts
Worthing	42	28	7	7	105	50	91
Ruislip Manor	42	25	12	5	78	33	87
Berkhamsted Town	42	24	8	10	77	55	80
Hem Hempstead	42	22	12	8	84	52	78
Metropolitan Police	42	22	6	14	84	51	72
Malden Vale	42	20	9	13	77	54	69
Chertsey Town	42	20	7	15	84	60	67
Saffron Walden	42	19	10	13	63	49	67
Newbury Town	42	14	18	10	53	51	60
Hampton	42	16	11	15	59	59	59
Edgware Town	42	16	10	16	84	75	58
Egham Town	42	16	9	17	60	71	57
Banstead Athletic	42	14	13	15	67	51	55
Leatherhead	42	14	11	17	66	61	53
Ware	42	12	11	19	68	76	47
Witham Town	42	10	16	16	54	65	46
Tilbury	42	12	8	22	55	101	44
Barton Rovers	42	9	14	19	40	66	41
Hungerford Town	42	11	8	23	37	93	41
Rainham Town	42	9	10	23	56	80	37
Harefield United	42	10	7	25	37	72	37
Southall	42	7	7	28	43	106	28

Leading Scorers Division Two
Newing (Hemel Hempstead – includes 23 for Edgware Town) 27 goals, Skerrit (Egham Town) 23, Linsell (Hemel Hempstead) 20, Freeman (Worthing) 19, Tiltman (Worthing) 18, Blair (Malden Vale) 17.

Promotions and Relegations

Club	Position	Movement
Worthing	1st	Promoted to Division One
Ruislip Manor	2nd	Promoted to Division One
Berkhamsted Town	3rd	Promoted to Division One
Rainham Town	20th	Relegated to Division Three
Harefield United	21st	Relegated to Division Three
Southall	22nd	Relegated to Division Three

Division Two Top Scorers By Club

Club	Player	Tot	Lg	DLC	AMC
Banstead Athletic	Gary Grabban	19	18	1	–
Barton Rovers	Graham Golds	6	4	–	2
Berkhamsted Town	Gary Harthill	17	16	–	1
Chertsey Town	Sean West	11	11	–	–
	Tony Argrave	11	8	3	–
Edgware Town	Steve Newing	25	23	–	2
Egham Town	Derek Tryalen	19	18	1	–
Hampton	Michael Beadle	12	9	2	1
Harefield United	Andy McShannon	9	–	–	–
Hemel Hempstead	Steve Newing	29	27	–	2
(includes 23 for Edgware Town)					
	Andy Linsell	20	20	–	–
Hungerford Town	Steven Tucker	7	7	–	–
Leatherhead	Raymond Arnett	16	15	1	–
Malden Vale	Stan Blair	20	17	3	–
Metropolitan Police	Mario Russo	18	12	1	5
Newbury Town	Matthew McDonnell	18	13	–	5
Rainham Town	Michael Waite	11	11	–	–
Ruislip Manor	David Lenstock	18	17	1	–
Saffron Walden Town	Wayne Mitchall	17	15	1	1
Southall	Eric Jones	8	6	2	–
	Abdul Harrak	8	8	–	–
Tilbury	Mark Phillips	11	11	–	–
Ware	Damon Miles	20	20	–	–
Witham Town	Jason Thompson	16	16	–	–
Worthing	Daren Freeman	21	19	2	–

DLC=Diadora League Cup AMC=Associate Members' Cup

William Hill Manager of Month Awards

Month	Manager	Club
September	Eric Howard	Egham Town
October	Tony Mercer	Saffron Walden Town
November	Colin Rose	Metropolitan Police
December	Gordon Taylor	Hemel Hempstead
January	Jim Kelman	Chertsey Town
February	Gerry Armstrong	Worthing
March	Roy Butler	Berkhamsted Town
April	Roy Butler	Berkhamsted Town
Manager of the Season	Gerry Armstrong	Worthing

DIVISION TWO RESULTS 1992-93

	Banstead Ath	Barton Rovers	Berkhamsted	Chertsey Town	Edgware Town	Egham Town	Hampton	Harefield Utd	Hemel Hemp	Hungerford Tn	Leatherhead
Banstead Athletic	•	2-2	0-1	0-1	1-2	1-2	1-1	5-2	1-1	8-0	4-2
Barton Rovers	1-0	•	1-1	1-1	3-0	0-0	1-0	0-0	0-3	3-0	0-0
Berkhamsted Town	1-1	2-0	•	4-0	3-3	1-2	6-1	1-0	1-3	2-2	2-1
Chertsey Town	1-2	0-1	5-1	•	5-1	0-3	2-1	3-0	1-0	7-2	2-1
Edgware Town	1-1	2-1	0-3	4-0	•	1-0	4-1	6-1	2-2	4-1	1-1
Egham Town	0-2	0-0	1-1	0-1	2-5	•	1-2	1-3	6-4	1-1	3-2
Hampton	0-0	2-0	0-0	1-3	3-3	2-3	•	2-2	1-0	1-0	0-1
Harefield United	3-2	0-2	0-0	2-1	1-2	1-0	0-1	•	1-1	0-1	1-1
Hemel Hempstead	1-1	3-0	0-0	1-0	2-0	2-0	0-3	1-0	•	3-0	2-1
Hungerford Town	0-5	2-0	0-1	2-1	1-1	0-2	3-3	1-3	1-6	•	•
Leatherhead	0-0	3-1	5-0	0-1	5-3	4-0	3-3	0-1	1-1	3-0	1-2
Malden Vale	2-0	2-2	3-4	0-0	2-1	1-0	4-0	0-1	3-2	45-1	1-1
Met Police	4-1	4-2	3-0	0-1	0-2	5-0	3-1	2-1	3-1	4-1	2-2
Newbury Town	1-1	3-0	0-2	2-2	1-0	0-0	1-2	3-0	2-2	0-0	0-1
Rainham Town	2-0	3-0	2-4	2-2	0-2	1-3	3-0	3-0	3-0	3-0	5-0
Ruislip Manor	1-1	4-0	4-0	1-0	3-1	0-0	1-0	2-1	1-0	1-0	1-3
Saffron Walden Town	0-2	2-0	2-1	2-2	1-0	2-0	0-1	0-3	1-1	1-2	1-1
Southall	0-3	0-3	0-3	0-5	1-0	0-2	0-1	0-3	0-7	0-3	3-2
Tilbury	3-2	2-1	2-1	1-3	0-4	1-1	1-1	0-3	4-4	3-4	1-1
Ware	2-1	2-0	0-3	0-3	4-1	2-3	2-2	2-2	2-3	2-3	2-1
Witham Town	2-2	2-2	1-1	1-3	1-2	1-4	0-1	0-2	0-0	2-0	3-1
Worthing	2-1	4-0	2-2	2-1	2-2	4-0	3-0	6-0	2-3	3-1	3-1

	Malden Vale	Met Police	Newbury Town	Rainham Town	Ruislip Manor	Saffron Walden	Southall	Tilbury	Ware	Witham	Worthing
Banstead Athletic	2-0	1-0	0-1	4-1	1-2	1-0	1-0	4-1	2-2	0-0	0-3
Barton Rovers	0-3	0-1	0-1	1-1	2-1	2-2	1-1	0-2	3-2	1-1	0-2
Berkhamsted Town	1-0	1-2	1-1	2-1	1-0	3-1	6-3	3-0	2-0	0-3	1-2
Chertsey Town	1-3	1-3	1-1	2-4	2-1	2-3	5-0	6-1	2-3	1-1	1-2
Edgware Town	1-1	3-1	1-2	2-2	0-1	1-2	4-4	2-3	5-2	4-2	1-2
Egham Town	0-2	2-0	1-1	2-0	1-3	2-0	3-2	2-1	1-3	3-3	2-5
Hampton	0-1	1-3	0-0	2-0	0-1	1-1	0-2	7-0	3-1	3-0	3-0
Harefield United	0-3	0-2	2-2	2-0	0-1	0-1	0-0	3-0	1-4	1-2	0-4
Hemel Hempstead	2-1	1-0	3-2	4-2	1-4	3-0	4-3	2-1	1-0	0-0	0-0
Hungerford Town	0-0	1-0	1-0	1-4	0-0	0-1	1-0	1-4	2-1	1-3	1-1
Leatherhead	2-2	1-1	1-2	0-1	1-2	1-2	2-3	3-0	0-2	3-0	0-2
Malden Vale	•	3-1	4-1	1-2	1-1	2-0	3-1	3-1	4-3	0-1	2-1
Met Police	3-1	•	•	4-0	•	1-3	2-3	3-1	5-1	3-0	0-1
Newbury Town	2-1	3-0	•	3-2	0-2	0-4	3-2	1-1	1-1	0-1	3-1
Rainham Town	0-0	2-4	1-2	•	•	•	1-0	1-3	0-4	1-1	1-3
Ruislip Manor	2-2	0-0	2-1	2-1	•	3-2	2-2	8-0	0-4	2-2	3-2
Saffron Walden Town	2-2	1-0	2-3	0-0	1-1	•	4-0	0-1	0-3	3-0	3-2
Southall	0-3	3-6	3-0	0-4	1-2	1-2	•	1-0	2-4	2-1	1-2
Tilbury	3-3	0-1	4-2	2-1	1-2	2-2	0-0	•	1-0	2-2	1-3
Ware	0-3	1-1	2-1	1-1	1-1	1-1	2-1	2-0	•	•	3-4
Witham Town	2-3	2-0	1-0	0-0	1-3	0-2	7-0	1-1	1-0	•	1-5
Worthing	2-3	2-2	1-1	5-2	2-0	3-1	5-1	3-0	1-0	3-2	•

DIVISION TWO CLUBS

ALDERSHOT TOWN
Ground: Recreation Ground, High Street, Aldershot, Hants, GU11 1TW
Phone: 0252-20211 **Nickname:** The Shots **Founded:** 1992
Colours: Red with Blue trim, Blue, Blue **Change:** White, Blue, Red
Rail: Aldershot (½ mile from ground)
Directions: M3, J4. A325 to Aldershot. Follow signs for Town Centre (A323). Follow A323 for two miles, ground on left.

AVELEY
Ground: Mill Field, Mill Road, Aveley, Essex, RM15 4TR
Phone: 0708-865940 **Nickname:** The Millers **Founded:** 1927
Colours: Royal Blue, White, White **Change:** Red, White, White
Rail: Rainham/Purfleet (1/2 mile from ground).
Directions: South of Sandy Lane (B1335) off the A13.

BANSTEAD ATHLETIC
Ground: Merland Rise, Tadworth, Surrey, KT20 5JG
Phone: 0737-350982 **Nickname:** The A's **Founded:** 1944
Colours: Amber with Black Trim, Black, Black **Change:** Red and White
Rail: Tattenham Corner.
Directions: M25, A217 to Tadworth. Follow signs towards swimming pool, the ground is located nearby.

BARTON ROVERS
Ground: Sharpenhoe Road, Barton-le-Cley, Bedford, MK45 4SD
Phone: 0582-882607 **Nickname:** Rovers **Founded:** 1898
Colours: White, Royal Blue, Royal Blue **Change:** Yellow, Royal Blue, Royal Blue
Rail: Harlington (4½ miles from ground).
Directions: M1 Junction 12. Right at top of slip road. Continue through Harlington and Sharpenhoe until you reach Barton. Ground visible on right.

CHERTSEY TOWN
Ground: Alwyns Lane, Chertsey, Surrey KT19 9DW
Phone: 0932-561744 **Nickname:** The Curlews **Founded:** 1890
Colours: Blue and White Stripes, White, Blue **Change:** All Yellow
Rail: Chertsey (half mile from ground)
Directions: Off Windsor St. at the north end of the town's shopping centre.

COLLIER ROW
Ground: Sungate, Collier Row Road, Romford, Essex, RM5 2BH
Phone: 0708-722766 **Nickname:** **Founded:** 1929
Colours: Red, Black, Black **Change:** All Silver Grey
Rail: Romford (4 miles from ground).
Directions: A12 from London. Left at Moby Dick pub (signposted Collier Row) lights. Right at next roundabout. Ground set back 200 yards on right.

EDGWARE TOWN
Ground: White Lion Ground, High Street, Edgware, Middx HA8 5AQ
Phone: 081-952-64799 **Nickname:** Town **Founded:** 1939
Colours: All Green **Change:** not known
Rail: Edgware (underground).
Directions: From station turn left and left again at lights. Ground on right.

EGHAM TOWN
Ground: Tempest Road, Egham, Surrey, TW20 8BB
Phone: 0784-435226 **Nickname:** Town **Founded:** 1963
Colours: Blue with Yellow sleeves, Blue, Blue with Amber tops
Change: All White with Blue and Gold trim
Rail: Egham (1½ miles from ground).
Directions: M25 Staines exit. Left at Police Station, left at next junction, first left after Prince Alfred public house.

HAMPTON
Ground: Beveree Stadium, Beaver Close, off Station Road, Hampton, Middx, TW12 2BX
Phone: 081-979-2456 **Nickname:** Beavers **Founded:** 1920
Colours: Blue and Red Stripes, Red, Blue **Change:** Yellow and Red
Rail: Hampton (500 yards from ground).
Directions: M3 Junction 1. A308 to High Street.

HEMEL HEMPSTEAD
Ground: Vauxhall Road, Adeyfield, Hemel Hempstead, Herts, HP2 4HW
Phone: 0442-42081 **Nickname:** Hemel **Founded:** 1885
Colours: All Red **Change:** All Blue
Rail: Hemel Hempstead (1½ miles from ground).
Directions: M1 Junction 8. Across two roundabouts and right into Leverstock Green Road. Vauxhall Road first on left.

HUNGERFORD TOWN
Ground: Bulpit Lane, Hungerford, Berks, RG17 0AY
Phone: 0488-682939 **Nickname:** Crusaders **Founded:** 1886
Colours: White, Navy Blue, White **Change:** All Red
Rail: Hungerford (¾ miles from ground).
Directions: M4 Junction 14. A4, turn right. Turn left at Bear Hotel. Left into Priory Road after town centre (A338), second left into Bulpit Lane.

LEATHERHEAD
Ground: Fetcham Grove, Guildford Road, Leatherhead, Surrey, KT22 9AS
Phone: 0372-372634 **Nickname:** Tanners **Founded:** 1946
Colours: Green, White, Green **Change:** White, Black, Black
Rail: Leatherhead (½ mile from ground).
Directions: M25 Junction 9. Follow signs to Leisure Centre.

LEWES
Ground: The Dripping Pan, Mountfield Road, Lewes, Sussex, BN7 1XN
Phone: 0273-472100 **Nickname:** The Rooks **Founded:** 1885
Colours: Red and Black Hoops, Black, Red **Change:** Yellow, Blue
Rail: Lewes.
Directions: From station turn left. Left into Mountfield Road. Ground about 100 yards on left hand side.

MALDEN VALE
Ground: Grand Drive, Raynes Park, London, SW20 9NB
Phone: 081-542-2193 **Nickname:** The Vale **Founded:** 1967
Colours: Royal Blue with White Trim, Navy Blue, Red **Change:** All Red
Rail: Raynes Park (500 yards from ground).
Directions: Grand Drive (B279) is off of Bushey Road by Bushey Mead Park driving towards Raynes Park along from Kingston Road.

METROPOLITAN POLICE
Ground: Metropolitan Police (Imber Court) Sports Club, Ember Lane, East Molesey, Surrey, KT8 0BT
Phone: 081-398-1267 **Nickname:** The Blues **Founded:** 1919
Colours: All Blue **Change:** All Red
Rail: Thames Ditton (½ mile from ground).
Directions: A3, A308 to Scilly Isles roundabout. Turn right into Hampton Court Way. Left at roundabout into Imber Court Road.

NEWBURY TOWN
Ground: Town Ground, Faraday Road, Newbury, Berks, RG13 2AD
Phone: 0635-40048 **Nickname:** The Town **Founded:** 1887
Colours: Amber, Black, Black **Change:** Red and White
Rail: Newbury (½ mile from ground).
Directions: A34 Robin Hood roundabout. Take A4 towards Reading. Right at lights into Faraday Road.

RAINHAM TOWN
Ground: Purfleet FC, Ship Lane, Grays, Essex, RM15 4HB
Phone: 0708-868901 **Nickname:** The Reds **Founded:** 1945
Colours: Red and White, Red, Red **Change:** All Blue
Rail: Purfleet (2 miles from ground).
Directions: M25 or A13 to Dartford Tunnel roundabout. Take Ship Lane – signposted ground located on right.

SAFFRON WALDEN TOWN
Ground: Catons Lane, Saffron Walden, Essex, CB10 2DU
Phone: 0799-22789 **Nickname:** The Bloods **Founded:** 1872
Colours: Red and Black Stripes, Black with Red Trim, Black with Red Trim
Change: All Yellow with Red Trim
Rail: Audley End (ground 3 miles from station).
Directions: M11 Junction 9. Take third exit at roundabout (B184). Follow signs to town. Left at Museum Street and left into Catons Lane. (Beware the one-way system! *Ed.*)

THAME UNITED
Ground: Windmill Road, Thame, Oxon, OX9 3NR
Phone: 0844-213017 **Nickname:** **Founded:** 1883
Colours: All Red and Black **Change:** All Blue
Rail: Haddenham & Thame Parkway (BR) (1HALF miles from ground).
Directions: Turn into Nelson Street from Market Square.

TILBURY
Ground: Chadfields, St Chad's Road, Tilbury, Essex RM18 8NL
Phone: 03752-3093 **Nickname:** Dockers **Founded:** 1900
Colours: Black and White Stripes, Black, White **Change:** All Red
Rail: Tilbury Town (1½ miles from ground).
Directions: M25 Junction 30/31. Take Tilbury Docks turn. Follow turn off to Chadwell St Mary. Ground on right.

WARE
Ground: Buryfield, Park Road, Ware, Herts, SG12 0AJ
Phone: 0920-463247   **Nickname:** Blues   **Founded:** 1892
Colours: Blue and White Stripes, Blue, Red   **Change:** All Amber and Black
Rail: Ware (1 mile from ground).
Directions: A10 and B1001. South side of Watton Road.

WITHAM TOWN
Ground: Spa Road, Witham, Essex, CM8 1UN
Phone: 0376-500146   **Nickname:** The Town   **Founded:** 1947
Colours: Red and Black Stripes, Black, Black   **Change:** All Blue
Rail: Witham (¾ mile from ground).
Directions: A12 to Witham. Left at lights. Ground on left just beyond railway bridge.

DIVISION THREE

Final Table 1992-93

	P	W	D	L	F	A	Pts
Aldershot Town	38	28	8	2	90	35	92
Thame United	38	21	11	6	84	38	74
Collier Row	38	21	11	6	68	30	74
Leighton Town	38	21	10	7	89	47	73
Cove	38	21	8	9	69	42	71
Northwood	38	19	11	8	84	68	68
Royston Town	38	17	8	13	59	42	59
East Thurrock United	38	17	7	14	69	58	58
Kingsbury Town	38	15	9	14	62	59	54
Hertford Town	38	14	10	14	61	64	52
Flackwell Heath	38	15	6	17	82	76	51
Tring Town	38	12	11	15	59	63	47
Hornchurch	38	11	13	14	53	52	46
Horsham	38	12	7	19	63	72	43
Epsom & Ewell	38	10	11	17	52	67	41
Bracknell Town	38	7	13	18	52	94	34
Clapton	38	8	7	23	46	74	31
Camberley Town	38	8	7	23	37	72	31
Petersfield United	38	6	12	20	36	90	30
Feltham & Hounslow	38	5	4	29	47	119	19

Promotion and Relgation

Club	Position	Movement
Aldershot Town	1st	Promoted to Division Two
Thame United	2nd	Promoted to Division Two
Collier Row	3rd	Promoted to Division Two
Petersfield United	20th	Resigned – to Wessex League
Farnham Town	–	Resigned – Club folded

Clubs Joining Division Three

Club	Position	Movement
Harefield United	21st	Relegated form Division Two
Southall	22nd	Relegated from Division Two
Harlow Town	–	Resigned from Division One
Oxford City	1st	Campri South Midlands
Cheshunt	3rd	London Spartan League

DIVISION THREE RESULTS 1992-93

	Aldershot	Bracknell	Camberley	Clapton	Collier Row	Cove	E Thurrock	Epsom & E	Feltham & H	Flackwell
Aldershot Town	*	2-2	6-1	4-2	1-1	1-1	1-0	1-1	2-0	3-1
Bracknell	3-3	*	3-3	1-3	1-1	0-1	2-3	2-0	2-1	0-4
Camberley	1-3	0-0	*	1-0	0-1	1-2	0-3	0-1	2-1	0-2
Clapton	2-1	1-2	1-4	*	0-3	2-1	1-2	1-3	1-1	0-6
Collier Row	1-2	5-1	1-0	0-0	*	1-1	3-1	5-1	2-0	3-1
Cove	1-3	3-2	2-0	1-0	3-1	*	3-1	4-3	6-0	1-0
East Thurrock Utd	0-1	2-2	4-2	2-0	0-2	1-1	*	3-0	4-2	1-4
Epsom & Ewell	1-2	2-2	0-3	1-1	1-0	2-2	1-1	*	1-1	1-4
Feltham & Hounslow	1-3	3-5	1-3	4-1	0-4	0-1	0-1	1-3	*	1-1
Flackwell Heath	3-6	0-4	4-0	4-2	43-4	3-1	3-1	0-0	4-1	*
Hertford Town	2-3	3-2	3-1	0-2	0-0	1-2	1-2	0-1	4-0	4-6
Hornchurch	1-3	2-0	0-1	3-0	1-2	0-0	1-0	2-1	3-0	5-2
Horsham	0-1	2-2	1-3	3-1	0-2	1-3	0-4	0-1	6-0	2-1
Kingsbury Town	0-1	4-0	0-0	2-0	0-0	4-2	3-2	2-1	3-2	2-1
Leighton Town	1-0	6-0	4-2	1-1	1-3	0-1	2-3	0-3	4-1	3-1
Northwood	1-1	4-3	3-1	2-1	0-2	0-0	0-4	3-3	2-2	5-4
Petersfield United	0-3	0-1	1-0	1-0	0-3	1-0	0-0	1-0	3-0	0-6
Royston Town	0-1	9-0	1-0	2-1	0-3	3-0	0-0	1-1	2-0	6-0
Thame United	2-2	9-0	1-1	1-1	2-0	1-0	2-0	2-0	3-3	1-0
Tring Town	0-2	4-1	0-1	1-1	2-3	1-6	2-2	1-2	3-1	2-0

	Hertford Town	Hornchurch	Horsham	Kingsbury Tn	Leighton Town	Northwood	Petersfield Utd	Royston Town	Thame United	Tring Town
Aldershot Town	0-0	5-2	3-2	4-0	2-1	4-0	3-0	1-0	2-1	4-0
Bracknell	5-2	0-0	1-1	0-2	0-4	0-0	0-0	1-1	2-4	2-2
Camberley	0-2	1-2	2-2	0-1	0-3	1-4	1-1	1-1	0-2	0-4
Clapton	2-3	2-1	1-3	1-1	0-3	0-1	4-0	3-4	5-1	1-0
Collier Row	0-0	0-0	1-0	2-2	1-2	5-0	3-0	2-2	0-0	0-0
Cove	3-1	1-5	3-0	2-1	2-4	0-0	1-1	1-3	2-3	3-0
East Thurrock Utd	3-0	1-3	3-2	2-2	0-1	4-1	1-1	2-1	1-4	3-1
Epsom & Ewell	2-3	2-2	3-0	5-3	2-3	2-5	2-4	1-1	0-1	0-1
Fletham & Hounslow	2-3	2-2	0-5	1-5	2-7	3-5	3-2	3-2	1-1	2-3
Flackwell Heath	3-3	1-2	2-1	1-0	2-1	2-2	2-2	1-0	0-3	1-1
Hertford Town	•	3-1	2-1	3-1	0-0	1-1	0-0	1-2	1-2	2-0
Hornchurch	0-2	•	3-1	5-3	1-1	2-3	0-1	1-0	1-1	2-4
Horsham	4-1	2-1	•	3-0	1-0	3-1	3-1	2-0	1-1	1-3
Kingsbury Town	1-2	1-1	2-3	•	1-0	4-1	4-1	•	1-1	2-2
Leighton Town	2-1	4-3	5-1	3-2	•	1-3	5-0	3-2	2-1	3-2
Northwood	2-5	3-3	2-3	2-5	1-2	1-3	•	0-4	0-5	1-1
Petersfield United	1-2	3-0	1-1	1-0	2-2	3-2	1-2	•	1-2	1-0
Royston town	1-1	1-0	4-1	1-1	3-2	0-2	8-0	0-0	•	0-1
Thame United	0-0	1-0	4-1	2-3	1-1	3-3	0-2	3-1	3-1	•
Tring Town										

Leading Scorers Division Three

Drewe (Leighton Town) 30 goals, Whitehead (Hertford) 29, Read (Collier Row) 28, Stairs (Aldershot Town) 27, Mott (Thame United) 26, Wallace (East Thurrock Utd) 25, Wood (Flackwell Heath) 23.

Division Three Top Scorers By Club

Club	Player	Total	League	DLC	AMC
Aldershot Town	Steve Stairs	31	27	4	—
Bracknell Town	Jason Day	11	11	—	—
Bamberley Town	Stephen Russell	6	6	—	—
Clapton	Peter Mason	16	16	—	—
Collier Row	Tony Read	28	28	—	—
Cove	Nigel Thompson	19	18	1	—
East Thurrock United	Daniel Wallace	25	25	—	—
Epsom & Ewell	Marcus Alcindor	13	11	—	2
Feltham & Hounslow B.	Mark Lester	18	18	—	—
Flackwell Heath	Tony Wood	25	23	1	1
Hertford Town	David Whitehead	30	29	1	—
Hornchurch	Brian Weekes	22	22	—	—
Horsham	Paul Harris	18	15	3	—
Kingsbury Town	Mark Ivers	12	10	1	1
	Ian Brown-Peterside	12	8	—	4
Leighton Town	Steve Drewe	33	30	1	2
Northwood	Victor Schwartz	22	19	2	1
Petersfield United	Phillip Vaughan	9	8	—	1
Royston Town	Paddy Butcher	19	17	—	2
Thame United	Nigel Mott	30	26	3	1
Tring Town	Chris Campbell	8	6	—	2
	Enzo Mecili	8	7	—	1

William Hill Manager of Month Awards

Month	Manager	Club
September	Steve Wignall	Aldershot Town
October	Steve Wignall	Aldershot Town
November	Bill Harrison	Leighton Town
December	Steve Wignall	Aldershot Town
January	Chick Botley	Cove
February	Chick Botley	Cove
March	Bill Harrison	Leighton Town
April	Alan Merison	Northwood
Manager of the Season	Steve Wignall	Aldershot Town

DIVISION THREE CLUBS

BRACKNELL TOWN
Ground: Larges Lane, Bracknell, Berks, RG12 3AN
Phone: 0344-423255 **Nickname:** The Robins **Founded:** 1894
Colours: All Red **Change:** All Sky Blue
Rail: Bracknell (400 yards from ground).
Directions: Turn left at Tyre Co. at the Met Office Roundabout (A329). Ground next to Cricket Club.

CAMBERLEY TOWN
Ground: Krooner Park, Krooner Road, off Frimley Road, Camberley, Surrey, GU15 2QP
Phone: 0276-65392 **Nickname:** Town **Founded:** 1969
Colours: All Red **Change:** All Sky Blue
Rail: Camberley or Frimley (both 1 mile from ground).
Directions: M3 Junction 4. Keep left take and A321 to shops. Krooner Road on left past mini-roundabout.

CHESHUNT
Ground: The Stadium, Theobalds Lane, Cheshunt.
Phone: 0992-26752 **Nickname:** **Founded:** 1946
Colours: All Amber
Rail: Theobalds Grove (½ mile from ground)
Directions: M25, J5. A10 towards Hertford. Ground on right.

CLAPTON
Ground: Old Spotted Dog Ground, Upton Lane, Forest Gate, London, E7 9NP
Phone: 081-552-4729 **Nickname:** The Tons **Founded:** 1878
Colours: Red and White Stripes, Black, Black **Change:** All Dark Green
Rail: Forest Gate (BR) or Plaistow (District Line).
Directions: Upton Lane runs adjacent to West Ham Park and off of the Portway-Plashett Road junction (B165).

COVE
Ground: Oak Farm Field, off Romayne Close, Cove, Farnborough, Hants
Phone: 0252-543615 **Nickname:** **Founded:** 1897
Colours: Amber, Black with Amber Stripe, Amber **Change:** not known
Rail: Farnborough Main (2 miles from ground).
Directions: M3 (Junction 4) take A325, then Prospect Avenue (signed Farnborough Town) to bottom, left at roundabout follow signs to Cove FC.

EAST THURROCK UNITED
Ground: Rookery Hill, Corringham, Essex
Phone: 0375-644166 **Nickname:** Rocks **Founded:** 1969
Colours: Amber and Black **Change:** All Blue
Rail: Basildon or Stanford le Hope (Both 1 mile from ground).
Directions: A1014 (from A13 London-Southend road) at Stanford le Hope. Proceed for just over 2 miles. Ground located on left.

EPSOM AND EWELL
Ground: Banstead Athletic FC (Merland Rise)
Phone: 0737-3509482 **Nickname:** E's **Founded:** 1917
Colours: All Royal Blue **Change:** not known
Rail: Tattenham Corner
Directions: As for Banstead Athletic.

FELTHAM & HOUNSLOW BOROUGH
Ground: Feltham Sports Arena, Shakespeare Ave, Feltham, Middx, TW13 4RQ
Phone: 081-890-6119/6905 **Nickname:** Borough **Founded:** 1991
Colours: Blue and White Hoops, Blue, White **Change:** All Red
Rail: Feltham (400 yards from ground).
Directions: M3/M4 – A316 Hanworth Road. Turn left into Burns Avenue and then second left into Shakespeare Avenue.

FLACKWELL HEATH
Ground: Wilks Park, Heath End Road, Flackwell Heath, High Wycombe, Bucks, HP10 9EA
Phone: 06285-23892 **Nickname:** Heathens **Founded:** 1907
Colours: Red, White, Red **Change:** Yellow and Black
Rail: High Wycombe (4½ miles from ground).
Directions: M40 Junction 3. Follow signs to Flackwell Heath. Ground situated at rear of Magpie public house at Heath End.

HAREFIELD UNITED
Ground: Preston Park, Breakspear Road North, Harefield, Middx, UB9 6DG
Phone: 0895-823474 **Nickname:** The Hare **Founded:** 1868
Colours: Red and White Stripes, Black, Black and Red
Change: All Sky and Navy Blue **Rail:** Denham (2 miles from ground).
Directions: M25 Junction 17. Follow signs for Swakeleys roundabout on A40 and turn off on B467 following signs to Harefield.

HARLOW TOWN
Ground: Harlow SC, Hammarskjold Road, Harlow, Essex, CM20 2JF

Phone: 0279-444183　　**Nickname:** The Owls　　**Founded:** 1879
Manager: Dave Edwards　**Secretary:** G. Auger　**Chairman:** Alan Howick
Colours: Black & Blue stripes, Black, Blue　　**Change:** White, White, Blue
Ground Capacity: 10,000 (450)　**Record:** 9,723 v Leicester C., FAC4 1/80
Rail: Harlow Town (½ mile from ground).
Directions: West of Fifth Avenue off A414/A1169 roundabout.

HERTFORD TOWN
Ground: Hertingfordbury Park, West Street, Hertford, Herts, SG13 8EZ
Phone: 0992-583716　　**Nickname:** The Blues　**Founded:** 1927
Colours: All Blue　　　　**Change:** All Yellow
Rail: Hertford North (Moorgate) or Hertford East (Liverpool St) (ground about 1 mile from both). **Directions:** A1M Junction 4. Follow signs to Hertford. Look out for Trimco Garage on right of dual carriageway. Go around next roundabout and come back. West Street on left (club signposted).

HORNCHURCH
Ground: The Stadium, Bridge Avenue, Upminster, Essex, RM14 2LX
Phone: 04022-20080　　**Nickname:** Urchins　　**Founded:** 1923
Colours: All White with Red Trim　　**Change:** All Yellow
Rail: Upminster Bridge (BR) (½ mile from ground).
Directions: 1 mile east of town centre on A124. Bridge Avenue on right after railway bridge.

HORSHAM
Ground: Queen Street, Horsham, West Sussex, RH13 5AD
Phone: 0403-52310　　**Nickname:** The Hornets　**Founded:** 1885
Colours: Lincoln Green and Amber, Green, Amber　　**Change:** All White
Rail: Horsham (1 mile from ground).
Directions: Opposite Queen's Head pub in town centre.

KINGSBURY TOWN
Ground: Silver Jubilee Park, Townsend Lane, Kingsbury, London, NW9 0DE
Phone: 081-205-1645　**Nickname:** Town　　**Founded:** 1927
Colours: All Blue　　　　**Change:** All White
Rail: Kingsbury (Underground – 1 mile from ground).
Directions: Take Kingsbury Road from Edgware Road. At top of hill turn left into Townsend Lane.

LEIGHTON TOWN
Ground: Bell Close, Lake Street, Leighton Buzzard, Beds
Phone: 00525-373311　　**Nickname:** Town　　**Founded:** 1885

Colours: All Red   **Change:** All Blue
Rail: Leighton Buzzard.
Directions: Leighton by-pass. Second right – continue to mini-roundabout. Entrance to ground on roundabout by Camden Motors.

NORTHWOOD
Ground: Chestnut Avenue, Northwood, Middx
Phone: 0927-427148   **Nickname:** Woods   **Founded:** 1900
Colours: All Red   **Change:** All Blue
Rail: Northwood Hills (½ mile from ground).
Directions: A404 Pinner-Rickmansworth Road. Chestnut Avenue is located on left before a large bridge, ½ mile past Northwood Hills roundabout.

OXFORD CITY
Ground: Court Place Farm, Marsh Lane, Marston, Oxford, OX3 0NQ
Phone: 0862-744493   **Nickname:** City   **Founded:** 1882
Colours: Blue & White, White, White   **Change:** All Red
Rail: Oxford (4 Miles) **Directions:** Oxford Northern bypass. Follow signs for John Radcliffe Hospital. Ground lies off slip road. Floodlights are visible from bypass.

ROYSTON TOWN
Ground: Garden Walk, Royston, Herts, SG8 7HP
Phone: 0763-241204   **Nickname:** The Crows   **Founded:** 1875
Colours: White shirts, Black shorts   **Change:** Red, Black
Rail: Royston **Directions:** A1 to A505, Royston and on to by-pass. At second roundabout turn right and then second left.

SOUTHALL
Ground: Western Road, Southall, Middx, UB2 5HX
Phone: 081-574-1084   **Nickname:** The Fowlers   **Founded:** 1871
Colours: All Red and White   **Change:** Grey and White
Rail: Southall (½ mile from ground).
Directions: From A4020 Uxbridge Road turn into South Road (A3005). Follow on through into The Green and then King Street. Western Road is first major right-hand turn.

TRING TOWN
Ground: Pendley Sports Centre, Cow Lane, Tring, Herts, HP23 5NS
Phone: 044282-3075   **Nickname:** Ts   **Founded:** 1904
Colours: Red and White, White, Red **Change:** All Blue
Rail: Tring (1½ miles from ground).
Directions: A41 – Cow Lane is to the east of town.

BEAZER HOMES LEAGUE

Dover at a canter

It was Dover's season all the way and they won the Premier League by a comfortable margin to claim the Conference place they had so narrowly missed the year before. All eyes will be on them next season to see if they can emulate Bromsgrove Rovers' exploits in the Vauxhall Conference. 1992's Beazer Homes League champions finished second in their first season at the higher level – the best performance by a newcomer at that level since Runcorn in 1982.

Not everything went Dover's way, though. Midlands Division Stourbridge spoilt the party by gaining a 3-2 aggregate victory in the league's cup competition. In their first season down from the Vauxhall Conference, Cheltenham put forward a good case for a speedy return eventually finishing second ahead of Corby and newly promoted Hednesford. Of the other new clubs Weymouth found the challenge too stiff and were relegated alongside one of the previous season's contenders VS Rugby. The Warwickshire club suffered with major upheavals off the pitch being matched by disarray on it. Dartford managed four games at the start of the season before going out of business, leaving the division one club short.

In the Southern Division Sittingbourne looked good all season and their fine ground and the large crowds it attracts will be a welcome asset to the Premier Division. Gravesend & Northfleet led for much of the season and in Steve Portway they had the goal-getter *par excellence* – he scored 58 in league and league cup competitions – but the club's form fell away badly towards the end of the season and they ended in fourth place. Salisbury City's story is quite the reverse. The turn of the year saw them with just 26 points from 18 games but they then had a phenomenal second half to their season capturing 62 out of a possible 72 points to storm up from 11th place and snatch a well-deserved second place. However promotion to the top bracket was not forthcoming. The club's current facilities are not up to par and the league took the difficult decision not to allow them to groundshare their way around the regulations. Salisbury can perhaps consider themselves unlucky – they have been looking to improve their set-up for some time but have been continually thwarted by events beyond their control. Andover gave their notice to quit midway through the season saving Bury Town from the trauma of relegation.

In the Midlands Division Gresley Rovers had a fine first season finishing up in second place. Like Salisbury they had suffered from a lack of facilities but now they can take their place in the Premier Division with a ground to suit. They also reached the semi-finals of the FA Vase. Nuneaton, the one-time giants of the Non-League game, have been in the doldrums for many a year but they will be hoping that their recent progress may signal a return to their days of former glory. They return to the Premier Division as champions. After a year in exile Barri have decided to return to their Welsh home and throw in their lot with the Konica League of Wales. How long, one wonders, before Newport AFC, also of the Midlands Division, and Colwyn Bay and Caernarfon Town of the Northern Premier League, also follow suit. It cannot be easy playing *home* games at such a remove.

The 1993-94 season is the Southern League's centenary year. Celebrations are to include representative matches against an FA XI, one against the first ever Southern League champions and one against the most recent ex-Southern League club to gain football League status. The two clubs in question are Millwall and Wimbledon.

Sportique Managers of the Season

Premier Division	Chris Kinnear	Dover Athletic
Midlands Division	John Barton	Nuneaton Borough
Southern Division	John Ryan	Sittingbourne

Beazer Homes League Honours

Premier Division Champions	Dover Athletic
Midland Division Champions	Nuneaton Borough
Southern Division Champions	Sittingbourne
Championship Match Winners	Bromsgrove Rovers
Barclays Commercial Service Cup Winners	Stourbridge

1992-93 Championship Match

Bromsgrove Rovers 2   Dover Athletic 0
Shilvock 83, Webb 88 (pen)

The Southern League History

A two-division Southern League was formed for the 1893-94 season, consisting of nine and seven clubs respectively. The format has changed considerably over the years consequent upon the withdrawal of amateur clubs; the participation of reserve sides; and the creation of a Third Division of the Football League formed by the members of the Southern League's Division One in 1920.

Predominantly a competition for Football League reserve sides between the Wars, the League emerged from the Second World War as a single division of mainly first teams. The League expanded, 13 clubs joining in 1958 and, following a regionalised season, a Premier and a First Division were introduced for 1959-60.

The First Division was regionalised in 1971 (South and North) but between 1979-80 and 1982-83 the whole competition was regionalised, with Midland and South Divisions. In 1983 it returned to the Premier Division and regionalised Division One (Midland and South) format.

While feeder Leagues serve Division One, the League champions are normally promoted to the Conference, with a club relegated from the Conference joining the Premier Division. Prior to 1983 two Southern Leaguers were normally promoted. Beazer Homes have been sponsors of the League since 1987-88.

5-Year One, Two, Three Records

Premier Division

	1st	Pts	2nd	Pts	3rd	Pts
1987-88	Aylesbury Utd	89	Dartford	89	Cambridge City	80
1988-89	Merthyr Tydfil	85	Dartford	82	VS Rugby	79
1989-90	Dover Athletic	102	Bath City	98	Dartford	87
1990-91	Farnborough T	85	Gloucester City	83	Cambridge City	77
1991-92	Bromsgrove R	90	Dover Athletic	84	VS Rugby	80

Southern Division

	1st	Pts	2nd	Pts	3rd	Pts
1987-88	Dover Athletic	94	Waterlooville	91	Salisbury	83
1988-89	Chelmsford C	95	Gravesend	87	Poole Town	83
1989-90	Bashley	82	Poole Town	77	Buckingham Tn	76
1990-91	Buckingham T	83	Trowbridge T	78	Salisbury	77
1991-92	Hastings Town	91	Weymouth	78	Havant Town	75

Midland Division

	1st	Pts	2nd	Pts	3rd	Pts
1987-88	Merthyr Tydfil	94	Moor Green	86	Grantham Town	85
1988-89	Gloucester City	92	Atherstone Utd	87	Tamworth	87
1989-90	Halesowen Tn	92	Rushden Town	89	Nuneaton Boro	85
1990-91	Stourbridge	90	Corby Town	85	Hednesford Tn	82
1991-92	Solihull Boro	97	Hednesford Tn	91	Sutton Coldf'ld	74

BARCLAYS COMMERCIAL SERVICES CUP

Preliminary Round

			1st Leg	2nd Leg	Agg
Sudbury Town	v	Baldock Town	1-0	7-0	8-0
Worcester City	v	Cheltenham Town	0-2	1-6	1-8

1st Round

			1st Leg	2nd Leg	Agg
Ashford Town	v	Gravesend & N'fleet	0-4	0-3	0-7
Barri	v	Witney Town	1-2	1-2	2-4
Burnham	v	Braintree Town	2-2	1-2	3-4
Burton Albion	v	Gresley Rovers	0-1	2-3	2-4
Bury Town	v	Dunstable	2-4	2-2	4-6
Cambridge City	v	Sudbury Town	1-3	3-3	4-6
Canterbury City	v	Sittingbourne	1-0	3-3	3-4
Corby Town	v	Hinckley Town	7-1	6-0	13-1
Dorchester Town	v	Bashley	1-1	0-2	1-3
Erith & Belvedere	bye				
Evesham United	v	Cheltenham Town	1-1	2-1	3-2
Fareham Town	v	Weymouth	2-2	3-0	5-2
Fisher Athletic	v	Crawley Town	1-4	2-5	3-9
Forest Green Rovers	v	Dudley Town	0-0	2-2	2-2
(Forest Green Rovers won on away goals rule)					
Halesowen Town	v	Solihull Borough	3-1	4-3	7-4
Hastings Town	v	Chelmsford City	1-4	1-0	2-4
Hednesford Town	v	King's Lynn	4-0	1-0	5-0
Margate	v	Dover Athletic	2-1	1-3†	3-4
Moor Green	v	Gloucester City	1-0	0-3	1-3
Newport IOW	v	Waterlooville	0-1	2-3	2-4
Nuneaton Borough	v	VS Rugby	0-0	1-0	1-0
Poole Town	v	Andover	0-0	1-0	1-0
Racing Club Warwick	v	Leicester Utd	2-2	0-4	2-6
Redditch United	v	Bridgnorth Town	3-0	1-0	4-0
Rushden & Diamonds	v	Atherstone Utd	4-0	3-2	7-2
Salisbury	v	Havant Town	3-1	2-0	5-1
Sutton Coldfield	v	Grantham Town	2-1	2-0	4-1
Tamworth	v	Bedworth United	0-0	3-2	3-2
Trowbridge Town	v	Stourbridge	2-1	2-6	4-7
Wealdstone	v	Buckingham Town	2-5	0-1	2-6
Weston-super-Mare	v	Newport AFC	4-4	1-4	5-8
Yate Town	v	Bilston Town	1-1	1-2†	2-3

2nd Round

			Result	Replay
Bilston Town	v	Stourbridge	1-1	0-2
Canterbury City	v	Dover Athletic	1-3	
Chelmsford City	v	Dunstable	2-2	3-1
Forest Green Rovers	v	Witney Town	0-1	
Gravesend & N'fleet	v	Erith & Bel'dere	3-2	
Halesowen Town	v	Evesham United	2-1	
Hednesford Town	v	Redditch United	4-0	
Leicester United	v	Nuneaton Borough	0-3	
Newport AFC	v	Gloucester City	1-1	2-3
Poole Town	v	Bashley	1-4	
Rushden & Diamonds	v	Buckingham	6-2	
Salisbury	v	Fareham Town	1-0	
Sudbury Town	v	Braintree Town	3-1	
Sutton Coldfield	v	Gresley Rovers	0-0	1-3
Tamworth	v	Corby Town	2-0	
Waterlooville	v	Crawley Town	2-3	

3rd Round

			Result	Replay
Bashley	v	Crawley Town	1-2	
Chelmsford Town	v	Sudbury Town	2-2	1-1
(Sudbury Town won on away goals rule)				
Dover Athletic	v	Gravesnd & Northfleet	3-0	
Gloucester City	v	Halesowen Town	2-2	1-2
Nuneaton Borough	v	Tamworth	2-1	
Rushden & Diamonds	v	Gresley Rovers	2-1	
Salisbury City	v	Witney Town	1-2	
Stourbridge	v	Hednesford	2-1	

4th Round

			Result	Replay
Crawley Town	v	Dover Athletic	1-2	
Nuneaton Borough	v	Halesowen Town	0-5	
Stourbridge	v	Rushden & Diamonds	2-2	4-2†
Sudbury Town	v	Witney Town	4-1	

Semi-Finals

			1st Leg	2nd Leg	Agg
Dover Athletic	v	Sudbury Town	1-0	1-2	2-2
(Dover Athletic won on away goals rule)					
Stourbridge	v	Halesowen Town	2-0	2-3	4-3

Final

			1st Leg	2nd Leg	Agg
Stourbridge	v	Dover Athletic	2-0	1-2	3-2

† *after extra time*

PREMIER DIVISION

Final Table 1991-92

	P	W	D	L	F	A	Pts
Dover Athletic	40	25	11	4	65	23	86
Cheltenham Town	40	21	10	9	76	40	73
Corby Town	40	20	12	8	68	43	72
Hednesford Town	40	21	7	12	72	52	70
Trowbridge Town	40	18	8	14	70	66	62
Crawley Town	40	16	12	12	68	59	60
Solihull Borough	40	17	9	14	68	59	60
Burton Albion	40	16	11	13	53	50	59
*Bashley	40	18	8	14	60	60	59
Halesowen Town	40	15	11	14	67	54	56
Waterlooville	40	15	9	16	59	62	54
Chelmsford City	40	15	9	16	59	69	54
Gloucester City	40	14	11	15	66	68	53
Cambridge City	40	14	10	16	62	73	52
*Atherstone	40	13	14	13	56	60	50
Hastings Town	40	13	11	16	50	55	50
Worcester City	40	12	9	19	45	62	45
Dorchester Town	40	12	6	22	52	74	42
Moor Green	40	10	6	24	58	79	36
VS Rugby	40	10	6	24	40	63	36
†Weymouth	40	5	10	25	39	82	23

Dartford resigned from league – record expunged

* 3 points deducted, † 2 points deducted

Promotions and Relegations

Club	Position	Movement
Dover Athletic	Champions	Promoted to GMVC
VS Rugby	20th	Relegated to Midlands Division
Weymouth	21st	Relegated to Southern Division
Dartford	Resigned from league – record expunged	

Clubs Joining Premier Division

Club	From
Farnborough Town	GMVC
Sittingbourne	Southern Division
Nuneaton Borough	Midlands Division
Gresley Rovers	Midlands Division

Leading Premier Division Goalscorers by Club

Club	Top Scorers	Goals
Atherstone United	Judd	13
	Donovan	12
Bashley	Patmore	12
	Whale	11
Burton Albion	Redfern	10
Cambridge City	Ryan	20
Chelmsford City	Restarick	15
	Brown	13
	Rogers	11
Cheltenham Town	Smith	27
	Eaton	11
	Howells	11
Corby Town	Hofbauer	14
	Murphy	14
Crawley Town	Fishenden	16
	Whittington	15
Dorchester Town	Manson	19
Dover Athletic	Cuggy	14
	Blewden	11
	Dent	10
Gloucester City	Bayliss	19
Halesowen Town	Hazlewood	13
	Massey	11
Hastings Town	Giles	8
Hednesford	O'Connor	20
	Hallam	13
Moor Green	Fearon	11
Solihull Borough	Burton	23
	Carter	22
Trowbridge Town	Knight	17
	Webb	10
VS Rugby	Hardwick	10
Waterlooville	Cormack	19
	Boyce	13
Weymouth	Drewitt	8
Worcester City	Phillips	13

PREMIER DIVISION RESULTS 1992-93

	Atherstone Utd	Bashley	Burton Albion	Cambridge C	Chelmsford C	Cheltenham	Corby Town	Crawley Town	Dorchester	Dover Athletic	Gloucester C
Atherstone United	•	0-1	1-1	2-4	3-1	1-1	0-2	2-1	0-1	0-0	2-1
Bashley	2-1	•	0-1	2-0	5-3	1-3	1-1	1-3	2-1	2-1	0-3
Burton Albion	1-1	2-0	•	2-0	2-0	0-3	1-2	3-1	4-0	0-0	0-3
Cambridge City	0-3	1-1	1-0	•	3-1	0-3	1-2	6-4	3-1	1-2	6-3
Chelmsford City	2-1	2-3	1-3	1-1	•	1-1	3-4	2-1	4-2	1-1	3-1
Cheltenham Town	2-2	1-2	0-0	2-0	5-1	•	0-1	3-0	3-1	1-1	4-0
Corby Town	2-3	5-2	1-1	1-0	2-0	3-0	•	3-0	2-2	1-0	1-1
Crawley Town	1-1	3-0	2-2	0-0	3-0	0-0	2-3	•	5-1	2-1	2-1
Dorchester Town	0-1	1-0	2-1	5-0	3-0	2-0	1-1	2-3	•	0-1	1-1
Dover Athletic	2-0	3-2	3-0	5-0	3-0	0-1	2-0	0-0	3-0	•	2-0
Gloucester City	4-0	1-1	1-3	2-3	1-2	1-5	0-1	1-1	1-0	1-1	•
Halesowen Town	2-2	3-1	1-2	1-0	1-2	2-1	1-2	4-1	2-2	1-1	2-2
Hastings Town	0-0	0-0	3-0	1-1	1-1	1-0	1-0	2-0	3-2	0-1	0-1
Hednesford Town	1-1	4-1	3-0	1-1	3-2	0-2	1-2	4-2	3-1	1-1	6-0
Moor Green	1-1	1-2	1-4	3-5	3-1	1-0	3-3	1-0	1-0	0-1	1-3
Solihull Borough	5-0	1-2	2-2	0-0	1-2	0-5	1-0	2-2	3-1	0-2	1-2
Trowbridge Town	1-1	3-3	1-4	1-4	1-0	3-3	1-1	1-2	4-1	0-1	3-1
VS Rugby	1-1	1-2	2-2	2-1	1-2	0-5	1-1	3-0	6-1	0-4	1-2
Waterlooville	1-0	0-2	0-1	2-1	1-2	1-2	1-1	1-1	1-2	0-1	1-1
Weymouth	1-3	0-0	1-0	2-0	2-3	0-1	0-3	1-1	2-3	2-3	1-5
Worcester City	2-1	3-0	0-0	2-1	2-2	2-4	2-1	1-2	1-4	1-2	2-0

Wycombe Wanderers v Altrincham. Wycombe's Steve Guppy gets up high to shield the ball during a GM Vauxhall Conference tie. Photo: Philip Brown.

Bridlington Town celebrate with the FA Vase after defeating Tiverton Town in the final. Photo: Dennis Nicholson.

Wycombe Wanderers celebrate with the FA Trophy after beating Runcorn in the final to complete the Non-League double.

The Non-League game isn't all glamour you know. Chatham hope to replace their entrance in the near future. Photo: Mike Floate.

Tony 'Rambo' Reynolds heads clear for Welling United during a Conference game against Witton Albion. Photo: Mike Floate.

Steve Portway of Gravesend & Northfleet fires in a shot against Fisher Athletic. Portway banged in 58 for 'The Fleet'. Photo: Mike Floate.

Bognor's Mick Pullen gets in a timely tackle on Carshalton's David Cooper. Photo: Dennis Nicholson.

Hasting Town's Paul Giles attempts to control the ball as Dover's Jason Bartlett and Tony Dixon wait to challenge. Photo: Roger Turner.

Epsom's Dean Meyer prepares to clear with Aldershot's Shaun May looking on. Photo: Dennis Nicholson.

Tiverton 'keeper Ian Nott collects before Canvey Island's Kevin Newbury can connect during the FA Vase semi final. Photo: Bruce Smith.

Andy Kerr scores Wycombe Wanderers' second goal against Runcorn in the FA Trophy final at Wembley. Photo: Ian Morsman.

Horsham's Andy Wright controls the ball ahead of Epsom's Marcus Alindor. Photo: Mike Floate.

	Halesowen	Hastings Town	Hednesford	Moor Green	Solihull Boro	Trowbridge	VS Rugby	Waterlooville	Weymouth	Worcester City
Atherstone United	1-1	2-3	4-2	4-3	4-2	0-1	1-0	4-4	1-0	1-0
Bashley	4-3	2-1	0-1	6-1	2-0	1-1	2-0	3-0	2-0	1-0
Burton Albion	1-1	0-0	1-5	1-2	0-2	4-2	1-2	0-2	2-0	1-0
Cambridge City	0-3	0-0	3-1	4-4	1-3	3-2	2-1	2-1	3-2	0-0
Chelmsford City	1-0	2-0	0-2	2-0	0-0	2-2	2-0	2-2	2-2	2-0
Cheltenham Town	2-1	0-1	1-1	1-0	1-3	1-0	1-3	5-0	2-2	4-1
Corby Town	1-1	1-1	2-2	2-0	2-2	0-0	0-1	3-1	4-0	1-2
Crawley Town	3-0	2-1	2-1	1-1	2-1	2-0	0-1	1-1	2-2	4-0
Dorchester Town	1-0	0-1	2-1	0-0	1-4	1-3	1-0	2-3	0-1	2-1
Dover Athletic	1-1	2-1	1-1	1-1	1-0	4-0	1-0	2-0	2-0	1-1
Gloucester City	3-1	6-2	1-3	2-2	1-1	2-4	4-0	1-1	1-1	4-0
Halesowen Town	•	0-2	0-1	5-1	3-1	0-1	2-1	2-2	2-1	3-2
Hastings Town	1-4	•	1-2	1-0	5-1	2-1	1-2	0-2	5-2	1-1
Hednesford Town	0-3	3-2	•	5-1	1-1	2-1	2-0	3-1	1-1	2-3
Moor Green	2-0	3-0	1-2	•	0-1	4-0	1-2	0-2	3-1	2-1
Solihull Borough	2-3	1-1	3-0	3-2	•	4-0	1-0	3-2	4-2	2-1
Trowbridge Town	1-1	4-1	3-2	3-2	1-3	•	4-2	1-0	3-0	2-1
VS Rugby	1-3	1-1	1-1	2-1	3-3	2-3	•	3-1	1-1	4-0
Waterlooville	1-1	0-2	1-0	2-1	4-2	1-0	1-3	•	2-1	0-0
Weymouth	2-1	1-0	0-3	0-1	1-2	0-3	1-3	2-1	•	2-2
Worcester City	1-0	2-0	0-0	0-2	3-0	0-5	0-0	1-3	2-0	•

PREMIER ATTENDANCES 1992-93

	Atherstone Utd	Bashley	Burton Albion	Cambridge Cty	Chelmsford	Cheltenham	Corby Town	Crawley Town	Dorchester	Dover Athletic	Gloucester
Atherstone United	*	256	377	303	275	290	227	302	304	326	321
Bashley	302	*	468	310	202	478	335	484	745	457	241
Burton Albion	689	478	*	498	564	656	324	574	323	725	495
Cambridge City	253	202	281	*	319	404	224	306	224	379	251
Chelmsford City	619	512	768	704	*	804	640	567	628	1058	737
CheltenhamTown	681	1010	1099	812	474	*	715	886	701	1159	2200
Corby Town	309	344	497	456	351	341	*	419	266	452	321
Crawley Town	479	613	536	578	960	769	804	*	421	1273	705
Dorchester Town	581	462	442	405	403	586	431	643	*	716	433
Dover Athletic	1160	1265	1022	1169	1344	2093	1914	1429	1276	*	1540
Gloucester City	427	385	486	485	379	1072	380	370	359	568	*
Halesowen Town	946	709	572	618	581	590	547	720	582	988	558
Hasting Town	439	339	444	368	374	367	401	736	368	1774	1442
Hednesford Town	671	547	573	467	415	610	533	454	428	667	522
Moor Green	395	251	307	256	281	465	312	265	272	439	276
Solihull Borough	208	248	244	234	197	287	161	214	206	257	251
Trowbridge Town	384	546	559	413	339	512	441	347	374	626	363
V.S. Rugby	467	421	387	482	330	407	352	365	264	383	358
Waterlooville	296	310	284	300	214	317	284	342	425	265	323
Weymouth	830	1206	823	887	568	683	713	651	1615	831	690
Worcester City	681	672	648	659	705	1037	709	669	681	636	771

	Halesowen	Hastings Town	Hednesford	Moor Green	Solihull Boro	Trowbridge	VS Rugby	Waterlooville	Weymouth	Worcester City
Atherstone United	301	288	279	381	286	342	520	312	262	308
Bashley	325	125	302	265	253	297	325	337	884	341
Burton Albion	729	433	605	606	413	356	451	578	355	382
Cambridge City	273	286	288	318	176	225	276	254	162	263
Chelmsford City	566	583	803	576	605	637	622	563	586	565
Cheltenham Town	650	666	801	739	1069	707	723	643	801	895
Corby Town	490	410	290	490	370	447	446	315	384	249
Crawley Town	637	753	666	502	627	646	764	729	560	519
Dorchester Town	458	441	547	405	508	642	550	708	3027	460
Dover Athletic	1127	2014	1234	1245	1276	1470	1303	1476	1197	1947
Gloucester City	469	387	551	330	408	472	487	352	557	598
Halesowen Town	•	632	630	772	742	414	962	795	893	874
Hastings Town	442	•	517	462	405	414	435	418	447	450
Hednesford Town	866	420	•	619	490	489	827	343	386	364
Moor Green	504	287	466	•	599	280	320	211	351	362
Solihull Borough	246	214	410	527	•	198	201	208	221	258
Trowbridge Town	410	322	325	302	514	•	368	362	390	393
VS Rugby	501	239	263	436	430	416	•	260	269	456
Waterlooville	415	212	256	384	305	403	374	•	312	382
Weymouth	774	607	719	1163	836	1034	775	1291	•	909
Worcester	1002	550	863	731	614	633	806	484	585	•

Sportique Manager of the Month Awards

Month	Manager	Club
August	John Murphy	Trowbridge Town
September	Brian Godfrey	Gloucester City
October	Vince Hilaire/Billy Gilbert	Waterlooville
November	John Morris	Halesowen Town
December	Chris Kinnear	Dover Athletic
January	Lindsay Parsons	Cheltenham Town
February	Chris Kinnear	Dover Athletic
March	John Morris	Halesowen Town
April/May	Trevor Parker	Bashley
Season	Chris Kinnear	Dover Athletic

Attendance Summaries by Club

Club	Pos	(91-92)	Att	(91-92)	Ave	(91-92)	% change
Dover Athletic	1	(2)	28,500	(28,697)	1425	(1367)	+4.2
Weymouth	21	(Sth Div)	17,640	(n/a)	882	(n/a)	n/a
Cheltenham Town	2	(GMVC)	17,440	(18,593)	872	(885)	-1.5
Halesowen Town	10	(8)	14,360	(17,985)	718	(856)	-16.1
Worcester City	17	(16)	14,180	(17,780)	709	(847)	-16.3
Crawley Town	6	(17)	13,540	(10,468)	677	(498)	+35.9
Chelmsford City	12	(18)	13,140	(13,501)	657	(643)	+2.2
Dorchester Town	18	(11)	12,840	(13,586)	642	(647)	-0.8
Hednesford Town	4	(Mid Div)	10,680	(n/a)	534	(n/a)	n/a
Burton Albion	8	(10)	10,240	(13,245)	512	(631)	-18.9
Hastings Town	16	(Sth Div)	10,080	(n/a)	504	(n/a)	n/a
Gloucester City	13	(12)	9,540	(12,343)	477	(588)	-18.9
Trowbridge Town	5	(7)	8,300	(11,256)	415	(536)	-22.6
Corby Town	3	(14)	7,640	(6,690)	382	(319)	+19.7
VS Rugby	20	(3)	7,580	(13,189)	379	(628)	-39.6
Bashley	9	(4)	7,480	(8,114)	374	(386)	-3.1
Moor Green	19	(9)	6,860	(11,095)	343	(528)	-35.0
Waterlooville	11	(15)	6,400	(4,901)	320	(233)	+37.3
Atherstone Utd	15	(13)	6,260	(7,078)	313	(337)	-7.12
Cambridge City	14	(5)	5,360	(6,983)	268	(333)	-19.5
Solihull Borough	7	(Mid Div)	5,080	(n/a)	254	(n/a)	n/a
Totals			225,960	(257,836)	538	(558)	-3.6

PREMIER DIVISION CLUBS

ATHERSTONE UNITED

Formed in 1979 and joined Division One of the West Midlands (Regional) League. Promoted to the top section in 1982. Moved to the Beazer Homes League in 1987 and promoted to the Premier Division in 1989.
Ground: Sheepy Road, Atherstone, Warwickshire, CV9 3AD
Phone: 0827-717929 **Nickname:** The Adders **Founded:** 1979
Manager: Joe Gallagher **Secretary:** K.J. Allen **Chairman:** Alan Bates
Colours: Red and White, Red, Red **Change:** Yellow, Blue, Blue

5-Year Record		P	W	D	F	A	Pts	Psn	Cup	FAT
88-89	BHLM	42	26	9	85	38	87	2	2q	1
89-90	BHLP	42	19	10	60	52	67	6	1q	1q
90-91	BHLP	42	14	10	55	58	53	15	2	3q
91-92	BHLP	42	15	8	54	66	53	13	1	1
92-93	BHLP	40	13	14	56	60	50*	15	4q	3q

* Three points deducted

Ground Capacity: 7,500 (400) **Record:** 2,816 v VS Rugby, FAC1 1987
Rail: Atherstone (1 mile from ground). **Directions:** Ground ½ mile north of town centre on the B4116 Twycross/Ashby road.

BASHLEY

Founded in 1947. Gained senior status and a Hampshire County League place in 1983. Promoted to Division Two of the League after two seasons, they were Wessex League founder members in 1986. In 1989 they joined the BHL Southern Section and were champions and promoted at the first attempt.
Ground: Bashley Rec., Bashley Road, New Milton, Hants, BH25 5RY
Phone: 0425-620280 **Nickname:** The Bash **Founded:** 1947
Manager: Trevor Parker **Secretary:** S.G. Hynds **Chairman:** T.R. Adams
Colours: Yellow and Black Stripes, Black, Black
Change: Blue and White Stripes, White, White

5-Year Record		P	W	D	F	A	Pts	Psn	Cup	FAT
88-89	WSX	32	26	4	87	24	82	1	3q	(VQF)
89-90	BHLS	42	25	7	80	47	82	1	1q	(V5)
90-91	BHLP	42	15	12	56	52	57	10	4q	1q
91-92	BHLP	42	22	8	70	44	74	4	2q	2
92-93	BHLP	40	18	8	60	60	59	9	3q	2

Ground Capacity: 4,000 (200) **Record:** 3,500 v Emley, FAVsf, 3/88
Rail: New Milton. **Directions:** M27 turn-off to New Forest, Lyndhurst A35 to Bournemouth, take B3058, follow road to Rising Sun, Wootton, keep on to Bashley.

BURTON ALBION

Formed in 1950 and joined the Birmingham & District League. Moved to the Southern League in 1958. Promoted to the top section in 1966, 1972 and 1974, they were relegated in 1970, 1973 and 1977. In 1979 became Northern Premier League founder members. Moved to the Beazer Homes League Premier Division in 1987.

Ground: Eton Park, Princess Way, Burton-on-Trent, DE14 2RU
Phone: 0283-44303   **Nickname:** Brewers   **Founded:** 1950
Manager: Eric Avins   **Secretary:** David Twigg   **Chairman:** S. Brassington
Colours: All Yellow   **Change:** All Red

5-Year Record		P	W	D	F	A	Pts	Psn	Cup	FAT
88-89	BHLP	42	18	10	79	68	64	8	4q	2
89-90	BHLP	42	20	12	64	40	72	4	4q	1
90-91	BHLP	42	15	15	59	48	60	7	4q	2
91-92	BHLP	42	15	10	59	61	55	10	4q	3q
92-93	BHLP	40	16	11	53	50	59	8	1q	3q

Ground Capacity: 8,000 (300)   **Record:** 5,860 v Weymouth, SLC Final 64
Rail: Burton-on-Trent.
Directions: M1-A50, turn right at mini roundabout (Derby), left at next island. M42/A38, take second turn for Burton, right at island.

CAMBRIDGE CITY

Founded as Cambridge Town in 1908 from a split from Cambridge St Mary's FC. Were an Amateur Football Alliance Club in the Southern Amateur League, but joined the Spartan League in 1935. Became Athenian Leaguers and changed to their current name in 1950 but adopted professionalism and moved to the Southern League in 1958. Relegated from the top section twice, they were last promoted in 1986.

Ground: City Ground, Milton Road, Cambridge, CB4 1UY
Phone: 0223-357973   **Nickname:** City Devils   **Founded:** 1908
Manager: Stephen Fallon   **Secretary:** Martin Carter   **Chairman:** D. Rolph
Colours: White, Black, White   **Change:** All Sky Blue

5-Year Record		P	W	D	F	A	Pts	Psn	Cup	FAT
88-89	BHLP	42	20	10	72	51	70	5	2q	3q
89-90	BHLP	42	17	11	76	46	62	8	3q	3q
90-91	BHLP	42	21	14	63	43	77	3	3q	2q
91-92	BHLP	42	18	14	71	53	68	5	1q	3q
92-93	BHLP	40	14	10	62	73	52	14	3q	1q

Ground Capacity: 5000 (400)   **Record:** 12,500 v Leytonstone, FAAmC 1956
Rail: Cambridge.   **Directions:** 50 yards on left from beginning of the A1134 Cambridge to Ely road.

CHELMSFORD CITY

Formed in 1938 as a professional club on the demise of the city's amateur club. Immediately joined the Southern League where they have been ever since. Relegated from the top section in 1977 and 1988 they were promoted back in 1979 and 1989.
Ground: The Stadium, New Writtle Street, Chelmsford, Essex, CM2 0RP
Phone: 0245-353052 **Nickname:** City **Founded:** 1938
Manager: Joe Sullivan **Secretary:** Mrs Y. Fawcett **Chairman:** D. Wakeling
Colours: Claret and White, Claret, Claret **Change:** Sky Blue

5-Year Record		P	W	D	F	A	Pts	Psn	Cup	FAT
88-89	BHLS	42	30	5	106	38	95	1	4q	1q
89-90	BHLP	42	11	10	52	72	43	18	4q	1q
90-91	BHLP	42	11	15	57	68	48	18	1	1q
91-92	BHLP	42	12	12	49	56	48	18	2q	1q
92-93	BHLP	40	15	9	59	69	54	12	1q	1q

Ground Capacity: 2,500 (300) **Record:** 16,480 v Colchester U, SLge 9/49
Rail: Chelmsford.
Directions: From London A12, A1016 to Chelmsford. New Writtle Street is off New London Road. Follow signs to the Essex County Ground which is next to the football ground.

CHELTENHAM TOWN

Formed in 1892, joined the Birmingham Combination in 1932 and moved to the Southern League in 1935. Relegated in 1962 and 1969, they were promoted to the Premier Division in 1964, 1977 and, a season after regionalisation, 1983. They joined the Vauxhall Conference in 1985 but were relegated last season.
Ground: Whaddon Road, Cheltenham, Glos, GL52 5NA
Phone: 0242-513397 **Info Line:** 0898-333-96 **Nickname:** The Robins
Manager: Lindsay Parsons **Secretary:** **Chairman:** David Courtney
Colours: Red and White, Black, Red **Change:** White with Red Trim

5-Year Record		P	W	D	F	A	Pts	Psn	Cup	FAT
88-89	CONF	40	12	12	55	58	48	15	2q	2
89-90	CONF	42	16	11	58	60	59	11	3q	2
90-91	CONF	42	12	12	54	72	48	16	1	3
91-92	CONF	42	10	13	56	82	43	21	3q	2
92-93	BHLP	40	21	10	76	40	73	2	2	1

Ground Capacity: 7,000 (1,200) **Record:** 8,326 v Reading FAC
Rail: Cheltenham – Lansdown (2 miles from ground)
Directions: From North: M5 Junction 10; From South: M5 Junction 11 – follow signs to Cheltenham, then take A46 (Winchcombe and Broadway). Ground situated off Prestbury Road.

CORBY TOWN

United Counties Leaguers until moving to the Midland League in 1952. Joined the Southern League in 1958. Promoted to the Premier Division in 1965, they were relegated in 1968 but, after the period of regionalisation, were re-organised back into the top division in 1982. Relegated in 1990 but promoted to the Premier again after just one season.
Ground: Rockingham Triangle Stadium, Rockingham Rd, Corby, NN17 2AE
Phone: 0536-401007 **Nickname:** The Steelmen **Founded:** 1948
Manager: Elwyn Roberts **Secretary:** J. Wiseman **Chairman:** T. McConnachie
Colours: White, Black, Black **Change:** All Yellow

5-Year Record		P	W	D	F	A	Pts	Psn	Cup	FAT
88-89	BHLP	42	14	11	55	59	53	16	1q	3q
89-90	BHLP	42	10	6	57	77	36	20	1q	1q
90-91	BHLM	42	27	4	99	48	85	2	3q	1q
91-92	BHLP	42	13	12	66	81	51	14	3q	1q
92-93	BHLP	40	20	12	86	43	72	3	4q	1q

Ground Capacity: 3,000 (1,150) **Record:** 2,240 v Watford, Pre-season, 1986
Rail: Kettering (8 miles from ground).
Directions: Northern outskirts of town at junction of A6003 and A6116 above village of Rockingham. Ground opposite entrance to Rockingham Castle grounds.

CRAWLEY TOWN

After many seasons of local football the club joined the Sussex County League in 1951. In 1956 they moved to the Metropolitan & District League and in 1963 joined the Southern League. Promoted in 1969, they were relegated in 1970 but returned to the Premier Division in 1984.
Ground: Town Mead, Ifield Avenue, West Green, Crawley, Sussex
Phone: 0293-21800 **Nickname:** The Reds **Founded:** 1896
Manager: Steve Wicks **Secretary:** Stan Markham **Chairman:** John Maggs
Colours: Red, Red, White **Change:** Blue, Blue, White or Blue

5-Year Record		P	W	D	F	A	Pts	Psn	Cup	FAT
88-89	BHLP	42	14	16	61	56	58	12	4q	3q
89-90	BHLP	42	13	12	53	57	51	15	1q	3q
90-91	BHLP	42	12	12	45	67	48	19	2q	2q
91-92	BHLP	42	12	12	62	67	48	17	3	1q
92-93	BHLP	40	16	12	68	59	60	=6	4q	2q

Ground Capacity: 2,500 (250) **Record:** 3,256 v Wimbledon, FAC4Q 11/69
Rail: Crawley.
Directions: M23 Junction 10. Turn right on to A264 for Horsham, turn left at second roundabout, over mini-roundabout, turn right at next roundabout into Ifield Avenue. Ground 150 yards on the right behind the fire station.

DORCHESTER TOWN

After many seasons of local football, joined the Western League in 1947. In 1972 they joined the Southern League First Division. They were promoted in 1978, relegated in 1984, but returned to the top division in 1987.
Ground: The Avenue Stadium, Dorchester, Dorset, DT1 2RY
Phone: 0305-262451 **Nickname:** The Magpies **Founded:** 1880
Manager: Paul Arnold **Secretary:** A.E. Miller **Chairman:** P.J. Aiken
Colours: Black and White Stripes, Black, Black **Change:** All Sky Blue

5-Year Record		P	W	D	F	A	Pts	Psn	Cup	FAT
88-89	BHLP	42	14	16	56	61	58	13	3q	1
89-90	BHLP	42	16	7	52	67	55	13	1	1q
90-91	BHLP	42	15	12	47	54	57	11	2q	3q
91-92	BHLP	42	14	13	66	73	55	11	4q	3q
92-93	BHLP	40	12	6	52	74	42	18	2q	2q

Ground Capacity: 7,210 (710) **Record:** 1,860 v Weymouth, League 1990/1
Rail: Dorchester South.
Directions: Half mile to south side of town centre, ground immediately on junction of town by-pass with A354.

FARNBOROUGH TOWN

Founded in 1967, first playing in the Surrey Senior League Division One in 1968. Promoted to Premier Division in 1971, moved to the London Spartan League in 1972. Moved to a new ground at Cherrywood Road changed leagues, becoming Athenians in 1976-77 and Isthmians the next season. Promoted to the Premier Division in 1985. Promoted to the Conference in 1989 but relegated after only one season, being allocated to the Southern League. Returned to the Conference a season later only to be relegated two years later at which point life-time manager Ted Pearce resigned.
Ground: John Roberts Ground, Cherrywood Road, Farnborough, Hants, GU14 8UD **Phone:** 0252-541469/541171 **Nickname:** Boro
Manager: Alan Taylor **Secretary:** T. Parr **Chairman:** Charlie Mortimore
Colours: All Yellow with Blue Trim **Change:** White with Red Trim, White, Red

5-Year Record		P	W	D	F	A	Pts	Psn	Cup	FAT
88-89	VLP	42	24	9	85	61	81	2	4q	2q
89-90	CONF	42	10	12	60	73	42	21	1	3
90-91	BHLP	42	26	7	79	43	85	1	1	2
91-92	CONF	42	18	12	68	543	66	5	3	3
92-93	CONF	42	12	11	68	87	47	21	4q	4

Ground Capacity: 4,000 (300) **Record:** 3,069 v Colchester, CONF 11/91
Rail: Farnborough (Main) or Farnborough North. **Directions:** M3, J4. A325, turn into Prospect Ave (signnposted ground). Second right (Cherrywood Rd).

GLOUCESTER CITY

Played in several Gloucestershire Leagues before joining the Birmingham Combination in 1932. In 1939 they joined the Southern League. They were re-organised into the lower division in 1959; promoted in 1969; relegated in 1971; re-organised into the top division on the end of regionalisation in 1982; relegated in 1985 and promoted again in 1989.
Ground: Meadow Park, Sudmeadow Road, Hempsted, Gloucester, GL2 6HS
Phone: 0452-23883 **Nickname:** The Tigers **Founded:** 1883
Manager: Brian Godfrey **Secretary:** Ken Turner **Chairman:** George Irvine
Colours: All Yellow **Change:** White, Black, Black

5-Year Record		P	W	D	F	A	Pts	Psn	Cup	FAT
88-89	BHLM	42	28	8	95	37	92	1	3q	3q
89-90	BHLP	42	17	11	80	68	62	9	2	3q
90-91	BHLP	42	23	14	86	49	82	2	4q	3
91-92	BHLP	42	15	9	67	70	54	12	2q	1
92-93	BHLP	40	14	11	66	68	53	13	1q	2

Ground Capacity: 5,000 (600) **Record:** 3,877 v Cardiff, FAC2R 12/90
Rail: Gloucester.
Directions: Take A40 into city centre towards the historic docks area, then Severn Road, then right into Hempsted Lane and right into Sudmeadow Road. Ground is on the left 50 yards up the road.

GRESLEY ROVERS

Formed in 1882 and played in many leagues including the Derbyshire Senior, Leicestershire Senior, Central Alliance and Birmingham Combnination. They joined the West Midlands (Regional) League from the East Midlands League in 1975 and moved to the Beazer Homes League in 1992.
Ground: Moat Street, Church Gresley, Burton on Trent
Phone: 0283-216315 **Nickname:** Rovers **Founded:** 1882
Manager: Steve Dolby **Secretary:** Rodney Summers **Chairman:** Peter Hall
Colours: White, Red, Red **Change:** All Blue

5-Year Record		P	W	D	F	A	Pts	Psn	Cup	FAT
88-89	WML	40	24	13	100	30	85	2	2q	(V3)
89-90	WML	40	24	8	89	42	80	3	1q	(V2)
90-91	WML	42	32	5	104	36	101	1	1q	(VF)
91-92	WML	36	24	7	83	37	79	1	2q	(V4)
92-93	BHLM	42	27	6	94	55	87	2	2q	(VSF)

Ground Capacity: 3,500 (250) **Record:** 3,950 Birmingham Lg 1957/8
Rail: Burton on Trent (5 miles from ground).
Directions: Take A444 south from Burton on Trent . After approx four miles turn left onto A514. Ground just off A514.

HALESOWEN TOWN

Early members of the Birmingham & District League, but members of the Birmingham Combination for the period between the Wars. Re-joined the Birmingham & District – later the West Midlands (Regional) – League in 1946, moving on to the Southern League in 1986. Promoted to the Premier Division in 1990.

Ground: Grove Recreation Ground, Stourbridge Rd/Old Hawne La, Halesowen
Phone: 021-550-2179   **Nickname:** Yeltz   **Founded:** 1873
Manager: John Morris   **Secretary:** Stuart Tildsley   **Chairman:** Ron Moseley
Colours: Blue, White, Blue   **Change:** Red, White or Black, Red

5-Year Record		P	W	D	F	A	Pts	Psn	Cup	FAT
88-89	BHLM	42	25	10	85	42	85	4	1	1q
89-90	BHLM	42	28	8	100	49	92	1	1	1q
90-91	BHLP	42	17	9	73	67	60	8	1	1q
91-92	BHLP	42	15	15	61	49	60	8	1	1q
92-93	BHLP	40	15	11	67	54	56	10	4q	3q

Ground Capacity: 4,500 (420)   **Record:** 5,000 v Hendon, FAC1 11/54
Rail: Old Hill Birmingham/Stourbridge.
Directions: M5 Junction 3. A456 to first roundabout (turn right), at second roundabout take second left into Old Hawne Lane ground 400 yards on left.

HASTINGS TOWN

Formed around 1895 as Hastings and St. Leonards, they joined the Sussex County League in 1921. Were in local football between 1927 and 1952 when they rejoined the County League. Success in the League came after changing their name, and in 1985 they took Hastings United's place in the Southern League and took up occupation too of their ground.

Ground: The Pilot Field, Elphinstone Road, Hastings, East Sussex, TN34 2AX
Phone: 0424-444635   **Nickname:** Town   **Founded:** 1898
Manager: Peter Sillett   **Secretary:** Richard Cosens   **Chairman:** David Nessling
Colours: All White   **Change:** All Yellow

5-Year Record		P	W	D	F	A	Pts	Psn	Cup	FAT
88-89	BHLS	42	21	11	75	48	74	7	2q	(V1)
89-90	BHLS	42	20	9	64	54	69	8	1q	(V4)
90-91	BHLS	40	18	11	66	46	65	7	Pr	(V5)
91-92	BHLS	42	28	7	80	37	91	11	1q	(V4)
92-93	BHLP	40	13	11	55	50	50	16	2q	1

Ground Capacity: 10,000 (500)   **Record:** 1,200 v Weymouth, BHL, 1991/2
Rail: Hastings.   **Directions:** From A21 turn left into St Helen's Road. Turn left into St. Helen's Park Road (about 1 mile) which leads into Downs Road. Go to the end of this road and at T-junction turn left. Ground is immediately on the right.

HEDNESFORD TOWN

Formed in 1880. Early members of the Birmingham Combination and Birmingham District League. Rejoined the Combination in 1945, they returned to the Birmingham & District (later the West Midlands (Regional)) and, apart from two seasons in the 1970s in the Midland Counties League, stayed there until joining the Southern League in 1984.

Ground: Cross Keys Ground, Hill Street, Hednesford, Staffs
Phone: 05438-2870 **Nickname:** The Pitmen **Founded:** 1880
Manager: John Baldwin **Secretary:** Bob Cooper **Chairman:** Mike Smith
Colours: White, Black, Black **Change:** All Yellow

5-Year Record		P	W	D	F	A	Pts	Psn	Cup	FAT
88-89	BHLM	42	12	15	49	57	51	15	Pr	2q
89-90	BHLM	42	11	14	50	62	47	17	Pr	1q
90-91	BHLM	42	25	7	79	47	82	3	2q	1q
91-92	BHLM	42	26	13	81	37	91	2	1q	2q
92-93	BHLP	40	21	7	72	52	70	4	4q	2q

Ground Capacity: 3,500 (500) **Record:** 10,000 v Walsall, FAC5Q 1919/20
Rail: Hednesford.
Directions: M6 Junction 11. Continue to Cannock, take A460 to Hednesford, after 2 miles turn right opposite Shell garage; ground at the bottom of the hill on the right.

MOOR GREEN

Formed in 1901 by members of the Ashfield CC, they had three pre-Second World War seasons in the Central Amateur League. After the War they competed in the Birmingham Combination and when that was disbanded joined the Birmingham & District League. In 1965 they moved to the Worcestershire (later Midland) Combination and in 1983 joined the Southern League. Promoted to the Premier Division in 1988 for the first time.

Ground: Sherwood Road, Hall Green, Birmingham, B28 0EX
Phone: 021-777-2757 **Nickname:** The Moors **Founded:** 1901
Manager: Bob Faulkner **Secretary:** Brian Smith **Chairman:** Brian Smith
Colours: Light Blue, Dark Blue, Light Blue **Change:** All Green

5-Year Record		P	W	D	F	A	Pts	Psn	Cup	FAT
88-89	BHLP	42	14	13	58	70	55	15	4q	1q
89-90	BHLP	42	18	7	62	59	61	11	1q	2q
90-91	BHLP	42	15	6	64	75	51	16	1q	1
91-92	BHLP	42	15	11	61	59	6	9	1q	3q
92-93	BHLP	40	10	6	58	79	36	19		

Ground Capacity: 2,500 (250) **Record:** 5,000 v Romford, FAAmC11951
Rail: Hall Green and Yardley Wood.
Directions: Off Highfield Road, which is off the main A34 Birmingham to Stratford Road, at Hall Green, South Birmingham, 4 miles from M42.

NUNEATON BOROUGH

In the Central Alliance before joining the Birmingham Combination in 1938. Moved to the Birmingham & District League in 1952 and the Southern league in 1958. Relegated in 1960 but promoted again in 1963. Founder members of the Alliance Premier League – relegated in 1981 only to return in 1982. Relegated to the Southern in 1987 and to the Midlands Division the following season.

Ground: Manor Park, Beaumont Road, Nuneaton, Warwickshire, CV10 0SY
Phone: 0203-342690   **Nickname:** Boro   **Founded:** 1937
Manager: Paul Sugrue **Secretary:** Keith Parker **Chairman:** Joe Shooter
Colours: Blue and White, White, Blue   **Change:** Yellow, Black, Black

5-Year Record		P	W	D	F	A	Pts	Psn	Cup	FAT
88-89	BHLM	42	19	9	71	58	66	6	2q	3q
89-90	BHLM	42	26	7	81	47	85	3	Pr	2
90-91	BHLM	42	21	11	74	51	70*	5	3q	3q
91-92	BHLM	42	17	11	68	53	62	6	2q	1q
92-93	BHLM	42	29	5	102	45	92	1	1	2

(* Four points deducted)
Ground Capacity: 2,800 (600)   **Record:** 22,114 v Rotherham, FAC3 1967
Rail: Nuneaton.   **Directions:** M6 Junction 3. A444 to Nuneaton, first exit at first island, at second island turn left then second left into Greenmoor Road. At end of road turn right, ground on left.

SITTINGBOURNE

Founded as Sittingbourne United, dropping the United in 1886. Spent periods in the Kent and SE Leagues and three seasons in the Southern League before returning to the Kent League in 1930. Members again in 1959-1967 when they dropped back to the Kent League. Promoted back in 1991.

Ground: Central Park, Eurolink, Sittingbourne, Kent.
Phone: 0795-475547   **Nickname:** Bourne   **Founded:** 1881
Manager: John Ryan **Secretary:** I. Kingsnorth **Chairman:** M. Fletcher
Colours: Red with Black Trim, White, Red   **Change:** White and Green

5-Year Record		P	W	D	F	A	Pts	Psn	Cup	FAT
88-89	KL	38	18	12	59	43	66	5	Pr	(VPr)
89-90	KL	38	27	5	85	39	86	1	1q	(V2)
90-91	KL	40	32	8	87	19	104	1	2q	(V1)
91-92	BHLS	42	19	10	63	41	61*	9	2q	(V4)
92-93	BHLS	42	26	12	102	43	90	1	4q	(V4)

(* Six points deducted)
Ground Capacity: 2,800 (200)   **Record:** not known
Rail: Sittingbourne (½ mile from ground).
Directions: A2 to Sittingbourne. Well signposted from all directions.

SOLIHULL BOROUGH

Formed in 1951, they joined the Midland Combination from local football in 1969. Recently left their Widney Lane ground to share at Moor Green pending occupation of a new stadium. Elected to Beazer Homes League for 1990-91 season and won promotion to Premier Division in first season.
Ground: Moor Green FC, Sherwood Road, Hall Green, Birmingham, B28 0EX
Phone: 021-777-2757 **Nickname:** The Borough **Founded:** 1951
Manager: Ralph Punsheon **Secretary:** J. France **Chairman:** J. Hewitson
Colours: All Red **Change:** Yellow and Blue

5-Year Record		P	W	D	F	A	Pts	Psn	Cup	FAT
88-89	MC	34	7	6	41	72	20	17	-	(V1)
89-90	MC	38	16	3	53	52	51	10	-	(V1)
90-91	MC	40	24	6	74	35	78	2	1q	(VPr)
91-92	BHLM	42	29	10	92	40	97	1	2q	(V3)
92-93	BHLP	40	17	9	68	59	60	=6	1	3q

Ground Capacity: 2,500 (300) **Record:** not known
Rail: Hall Green and Yardley Wood.
Directions: Off Highfield Road, which is off the main A34 Birmingham to Stratford road at Hall Green, South Birmingham, 4 miles from M42.

TROWBRIDGE TOWN

Founder members of the Western League in 1892, they moved into an expanded Southern League in 1958 and were promoted to the Alliance Premier League from third place in the Midland Division in 1981. They were relegated after three seasons and fell further, into the Southern's Division One, in 1985. Promoted back into the BHL Premier Division in 1991.
Ground: Frome Road, Trowbridge, Wilts, BA14 0DB
Phone: 0225-752076 **Nickname:** The Bees **Founded:** 1880
Manager: John Murphy **Secretary:** Jeff Hooper **Chairman:** John Fitchin
Colours: Old Gold, Black, Black **Change:** All White

5-Year Record		P	W	D	F	A	Pts	Psn	Cup	FAT
88-89	BHLS	42	19	7	59	52	64	10	1q	1q
89-90	BHLS	42	20	9	79	64	69	7	2q	(VPr)
90-91	BHLS	40	22	12	67	31	78	2	2q	(VSF)
91-92	BHLP	42	17	10	69	51	61	7	3q	1q
92-93	BHLP	40	18	8	70	66	62	5	1q	2q

Ground Capacity: 5,000 (200) **Record:** 9,009 v Weymouth, FAC4Q 49
Rail: Trowbridge.
Directions: Follow inner relief-road signs to Frome. Ground is on left past Ship Inn.

WATERLOOVILLE

They were Hampshire League members from 1953 to 1971, when they moved to the Southern League. Promoted to the top section in 1972, they were relegated in 1973. On the ending of the League's regionalisation they found themselves in the top section again, only to be relegated after one year in 1983. They moved back into the top section in 1988.

Ground: Jubilee Park, Aston Park, Waterlooville, PO7 7XG
Phone: 0705-263423   **Nickname:** The Ville   **Founded:** 1910
Manager: Gilbert/Hilaire   **Secretary:** M. Richards   **Chairman:** F. Faulkner
Colours: White, White, Blue   **Change:** All Yellow

5-Year Record		P	W	D	F	A	Pts	Psn	Cup	FAT
88-89	BHLP	42	13	13	61	63	52	17	1	1q
89-90	BHLP	42	13	10	63	81	49	16	1q	1q
90-91	BHLP	42	11	13	51	70	46	20	1q	1q
91-92	BHLP	42	13	11	43	56	50	15	2q	2q
92-93	BHLP	40	15	9	59	62	54	11	1q	1q

Ground Capacity: 4,000 (500)   **Record:** 4,500 v Wycombe W, FAC1 1976
Rail: Havant (4 miles from ground).   **Directions:** Take town by-pass road (B2150), turn right at Asda roundabout, along dual carriageway to next roundabout and return back towards town. Aston Park Road is the first left.

WORCESTER CITY

Early members of the Birmingham & District League, City joined the Southern League in 1938. Relegated in 1967 and 1974, they were promoted to the top division in 1968 and 1977, becoming Alliance Premier League founder members in 1979. They lost their place in 1985 and returned to the Southern League.

Ground: St George's Lane, Barbourne, Worcester, WR1 1QT
Phone: 0905-23003   **Nickname:** City   **Founded:** 1908
Manager: Martin Bennett   **Secretary:** G. Jukes   **Chairman:** B. Connally
Colours: Blue and White, Blue, Blue   **Change:** All Red

5-Year Record		P	W	D	F	A	Pts	Psn	Cup	FAT
88-89	BHLP	42	20	13	72	49	73	4	4q	1
89-90	BHLP	42	15	10	62	63	54 †	14	3q	1
90-91	BHLP	42	18	12	55	42	66	6	3q	3q
91-92	BHLP	42	12	13	56	59	49	16	4q	1
92-93	BHLP	40	12	9	45	62	45	17	2q	1

Ground Capacity: 10,000 (1,500)   **Record:** 17,042 v Sheff. Utd, FAC4 1959
Rail: Foregate Street.   **Directions:** M1 Junction 6. Take Kidderminster road to roundabout. Turn left into Worcester, at first set of lights turn right and then third left.

†*One point deducted*

MIDLAND DIVISION

Final Table 1992-93

	P	W	D	L	F	A	Pts
Nuneaton Borough	42	29	5	8	102	45	92
Gresley Rovers	42	27	6	9	94	55	87
Rushden & Diamonds	42	25	10	7	85	41	85
Barri	42	26	5	11	82	49	83
Newport AFC	42	23	8	11	73	58	77
Bedworth Utd	42	22	8	12	72	55	74
Stourbridge	42	17	9	16	93	79	60
Sutton Coldfield Town	42	17	9	16	82	78	60
Redditch Utd	42	18	6	18	75	79	60
Tamworth	42	16	11	15	65	51	59
Weston-super-Mare	42	17	7	18	79	86	58
Leicester Utd	42	16	9	17	67	67	57
Grantham Town	42	16	9	17	60	73	57
Bilston Town	42	15	10	17	74	69	55
Evesham United	42	15	8	19	67	83	53
Bridgnorth Town	42	15	7	20	61	68	52
Dudley Town	42	14	8	20	60	75	50
Yate Town	42	15	5	22	63	81	50
Forest Green Rovers	42	12	6	24	61	97	42
*Hinckley Town	42	9	11	22	56	89	37
King's Lynn	42	10	6	26	45	90	36
RC Warwick	42	3	7	32	40	88	16

* 1 point deducted

Promotions and Relegations

Club	Position	Movement
Nuneaton Borough	1st	Promoted to Premier Division
Gresley Rovers	2nd	Promoted to Premier Division
Barri	4th	Resigned – moved to Konica League of Wales

Clubs Joining Midland Division

Club	Position	Movement
VS Rugby	20th	Premier Division
Armitage '90 AFC	1st	Ansells Midlands Combination
Clevedon Town	1st	Great Mills Western League

Leading Midland League Goalscorers

Player	Club	Goals
Wright	Stourbridge	46
Culpin	Nuneaton Borough	39
Draper	Bedworth United	25
Withers	Barri	24
Bake	Bilston	23
Hall	Stourbridge	23
Watkins	Rushden & Diamonds	23

Sportique Manager of the Month Awards

Month	Manager	Club
August	Paul Hendrie	Redditch United
September	George Rooney	Nuneaton Borough
October	Steve Dolby	Gresley Rovers
November	Sammy Chung	Tamworth
December	Roy Chisholm	Barri
January	Roger Ashby	Rushden & Diamonds
February	John Barton	Nuneaton Borough
March	Steve Dolby	Gresley Rovers
April/May	Roger Ashby	Rushden & Diamonds
Season	John Barton	Nuneaton Borough

MIDLAND DIVISION RESULTS 1992-93

	Barri	Bedworth Utd	Bilston Town	Bridgnorth Tn	Dudley Tow'n	Evesham Utd	Forest Green	Grantham Tn	Gresley Rov	Hinckley Town	King's Lynn
Barri	•	1-2	2-1	1-2	3-1	3-1	2-0	0-1	1-2	1-0	2-0
Bedworth United	0-1	•	2-1	3-2	2-0	0-1	3-2	3-0	2-2	1-1	0-1
Bilston Town	1-1	1-2	•	0-3	6-2	1-0	5-0	3-1	1-0	2-2	5-2
Bridgnorth Town	2-4	0-2	0-0	•	0-0	1-0	4-1	1-0	1-4	0-1	3-0
Dudley Town	1-3	0-3	2-2	2-1	•	0-2	1-0	0-2	2-5	1-0	2-0
Evesham United	3-4	1-0	3-2	2-3	0-0	•	1-2	0-2	2-5	5-2	2-0
Forest Green Rovers	1-6	1-2	4-1	3-2	1-2	0-3	•	2-2	0-2	1-1	7-1
Grantham Town	1-2	4-1	1-0	1-3	2-0	2-2	2-2	•	0-1	1-1	0-0
Gresley Rovers	3-1	2-2	2-0	1-2	6-3	5-0	2-3	2-3	2-0	2-1	1-2
Hinckley Town	1-2	2-2	3-1	1-0	2-2	1-5	1-1	2-0	•	1-0	2-1
King's Lynn	0-2	1-3	0-3	0-0	1-3	5-2	3-1	1-3	1-2	2-2	0-2
Leicester United	2-2	0-1	0-1	2-1	1-0	2-3	5-0	3-1	1-4	0-1	•
Newport AFC	0-0	1-3	3-1	2-0	3-0	5-1	5-0	6-1	3-2	3-1	0-0
Nuneaton Borough	1-3	1-1	2-1	2-1	1-0	2-3	3-1	1-2	0-1	3-1	4-1
Racing ClubWarwick	1-0	1-3	2-3	0-2	3-0	5-1	1-2	2-0	0-2	2-2	3-0
Redditch United	2-4	3-1	3-1	1-2	3-3	2-5	2-1	4-1	3-1	3-0	0-1
Rushden&Diamonds	1-1	3-2	3-1	4-1	3-2	5-0	6-1	1-2	6-0	2-2	4-2
Stourbridge	1-0	1-1	0-2	2-3	0-0	4-1	4-2	2-0	2-5	3-0	3-1
Sutton Coldfield Town	0-3	2-1	1-2	4-1	2-1	4-1	1-1	0-1	1-1	2-7	1-0
Tamworth	0-1	0-1	1-1	2-3	1-2	1-2	1-3	0-0	1-1	2-1	4-1
Weston-super-Mare	3-1	1-4	3-1	3-2	3-0	1-2	1-3	2-2	4-4	5-0	3-0
Yate Town	0-1	0-3	3-2	1-0	2-5	1-0	0-2	2-2	2-3	5-0	1-0

	Leicester Utd	Newport AFC	Nuneaton Boro	RC Warwick	Redditch Utd	Rushden & D	Stourbridge	Sutton C'ldfield	Tamworth	Weston-s-Mare	Yate Town
Barri Town	3-1	4-1	1-4	3-1	0-1	2-1	0-2	3-3	2-0	3-0	3-1
Bedworth United	2-2	0-1	2-1	1-0	2-1	0-3	4-1	2-2	0-3	2-1	0-3
Bilston Town	4-2	1-1	3-4	2-1	0-2	0-1	1-0	1-1	1-1	3-1	6-3
Bridgnorth Town	3-0	0-1	1-2	4-2	2-1	2-2	0-6	2-3	2-3	1-2	1-1
Dudley Town	0-1	0-1	1-3	3-2	1-2	1-2	1-0	0-0	0-0	5-1	1-1
Evesham United	0-4	2-2	0-2	2-2	1-1	1-4	2-2	4-2	4-1	3-1	0-3
Forest Green Rovers	3-1	1-2	2-3	4-1	1-4	1-1	1-4	0-3	1-1	4-0	1-1
Grantham Town	2-1	1-0	2-3	1-0	0-5	2-1	3-3	4-1	1-3	3-1	3-0
Gresley Rovers	2-3	3-5	0-1	3-2	4-0	1-0	1-1	1-3	3-2	4-2	3-1
Hinckley Town	1-2	3-4	1-5	2-0	1-0	1-1	1-5	1-0	0-0	1-2	3-1
King's Lynn	2-0	1-1	0-2	0-3	0-2	1-0	3-1	1-1	4-1	0-2	4-2
Leicester United	•	1-2	1-2	2-2	4-1	1-3	2-1	3-2	1-0	3-1	4-0
Newport AFC	1-1	•	0-3	2-1	2-3	1-2	1-2	2-2	3-2	0-1	3-1
Nuneaton Borough	2-0	1-1	•	3-1	2-1		2-3	1-2	1-3	1-2	4-1
Racing Club Warwick	0-0	1-2	0-2	•	8-1	2-2	1-1	1-1	0-1	2-2	3-1
Redditch United	2-2	1-3	2-3	2-1	•	2-0	5-2	1-1	1-2	2-3	2-1
Rushden & Diamonds	3-0	1-0	0-2	3-0	0-0	•		2-0	0-0	3-0	0-3
Stourbridge	4-0	1-3	2-3	6-3	0-0	4-1	•	5-1	0-3	1-0	2-1
Sutton Coldfield Town	2-1	2-4	1-3	1-0	4-2	0-2	4-3	•	0-1	3-3	2-2
Tamworth	3-4	4-3	0-0	1-0	2-1	0-3	5-2	2-1	•	0-1	5-2
Weston-super-Mare	1-1	3-0	2-1	6-1	3-4		1-5	3-3	2-1	•	3-0
Yate Town	1-0	0-2	3-1	3-0	4-0		3-2	0-3	1-1	2-0	•

MIDLAND DIVISION CLUBS

ARMITAGE '90
Ground: Kings Bromley, Handsacre, Rugeley, Staffs.
Phone: **Founded:** 1990
Managers: Gary Haynes and Danny McMullen
Colours: Blue, Blue, Blue
Ground Capacity: 1500 (300) **Record:** not known
Rail: Rugeley **Directions:** A38 to Alrewas. Head towards Kings Bromley. At end of KNB turn left, first right, ground one mile on right.

BEDWORTH UNITED
Ground: The Oval, Miners' Welfare Park, Bedworth, Warwicks, CV12 8NN
Phone: 0203-314302 **Nickname:** The Greenbacks **Founded:** 1947
Manager: Brendon Phillips **Secretary:** B. Jacques **Chairman:** Alan Robinson
Colours: Green, White, Green **Change:** Yellow, Green, Yellow
Ground Capacity: 4,000 (300) **Record:** 5,127 v Nuneaton B, 2/82
Rail: Bedworth. **Directions:** M6 Junction 3. B4113 to Bedworth, 1½ miles from Junction 3, adjacent to leisure centre.

BILSTON TOWN
Ground: Queen Street, Bilston, West Midlands, WV14 7EX
Phone: 0902-744653 **Nickname:** not known **Founded:** 1895
Manager: Steve Bowater **Secretary:** Morris Baker **Chairman:** A. Hickman
Colours: Tangerine, Black, Tangerine **Change:** All White
Ground Capacity: 7,000 (350) **Record:** v Wolverhampton, 1953/4, f.o.
Rail: Wolverhampton. **Directions:** M6 Junction 10. A454 Wolverhampton, pick up A563 Bilston, and after approx 1¼ miles turn left at Beckett Street.

BRIDGNORTH TOWN
Ground: Crown Meadow, Innage Lane, Bridgnorth, Shropshire, WV16 6PZ
Phone: 0746-762747/766064 **Nickname:** Town **Founded:** 1946
Manager: Billy Ball **Secretary:** Gordon Thomas **Chairman:** J. Heseltine
Colours: Blue, White, Blue **Change:** All Red
Ground Capacity: 1,600 (400) **Record:** 1,600 v South Shields, FAVase
Rail: Wolverhampton. **Directions:** Through High Street, fork left into Innage Lane, ground 200 yards on left.

CLEVEDON TOWN

Ground: The Hand Stadium, Davis Lane, Clevedon, Avon, BS21 6TG
Phone: 0275-341641　　**Founded:** 1880
Manager: Steve Fey　　**Secretary:** Mike Williams　**Chairman:** Brian Baker
Colours: Blue, White, White　　**Change:** Yellow, Blue, Yellow
Ground Capacity: 3,650 (350)　　**Record:** 1,295 v Tiverton, GMWL '93
Rail: Yatton　　**Directions:** M5, J20 the Hand Stadium is both visible and sign-posted.

DUDLEY TOWN

Ground: The Round Oak Stadium, John Street, Brierly Hill, West Midlands
Phone: 0384-263478　　**Nickname:** The Robins　　**Founded:** 1893
Manager: Paddy Page　**Secretary:** Tony Turpin　**Chairman:** N.D. Jeynes
Colours: Red, White, Black　　**Change:** All Yellow
Ground Capacity: 3,000 (204)　　**Record:** 1,000 v Tamworth, 1989
Rail: Stourbridge. **Directions:** From Dudley take the A461 towards Stourbridge for about two miles. On entering Brierly Hill turn right on to the B4180 and into John Street. Stadium entrance is 200 yards on right.

EVESHAM UNITED

Ground: Common Road, Evesham, Worcs
Phone: 0386-2303　　**Nickname:** not known　　**Founded:** 1945
Manager: not known　**Secretary:** not known　**Chairman:** not known
Colours: Red and White Stripes, Red, Red　**Change:** White with Black Stripe, Black, Black
Ground Capacity: 2,000 (350)　　**Record:** 1,400 v Aston Villa, Friendly
Rail: Evesham. **Directions:** From Birmingham, on entering Evesham turn left into Swan Lane. Common Road off Swan Lane.

FOREST GREEN ROVERS

Ground: The Lawn, Nympsfield Road, Forest Green, Nailsworth, Glos
Phone: 045-383-4860　　**Nickname:** Rovers　　**Founded:** 1898
Manager: Bobby Jones　**Secretary:** D. Roberts　**Chairman:** A. Coburn/T. Horsley
Colours: White, Navy, Red or White　**Change:** Red, White, Red or White
Ground Capacity: 4,000 (142)　　**Record:** 2,000 v Wolves, f.o. 2/81
Rail: Stroud.
Directions: Approx 4 miles from Stroud on A46 to Bath. On entering Nailsworth turn right into Spring Hill, ground is 1 mile at top of hill on left.

GRANTHAM TOWN

Ground: South Kestevan Sports Stadium, Trent Road, Grantham, Lincs
Phone: 0476-62011   **Nickname:** The Gingerbreads   **Founded:** 1874
Manager: Bob Duncan   **Secretary:** P.S. Nixon   **Chairman:** A. Balfe
Colours: White, Black, Black   **Change:** Yellow, Blue, Blue
Ground Capacity: 4,000 (700)   **Record:** 1,402 v Ilkeston Town, FAC, 8/91
Rail: Grantham.

HINCKLEY TOWN

Ground: Leicester Road, Hinckley, Leics
Phone: 0455-615062   **Nickname:** The Eagles   **Founded:** 1958
Manager: Dave Grundy   **Secretary:** Julie Barnes   **Chairman:** David Needham
Colours: White, Claret, Sky Blue   **Change:** Yellow, Navy, Yellow
Ground Capacity: 3,000 (250)   **Record:** 1,500 v Real Sociedad, f.o. 8/87
Rail: Hinckley.
Directions: M69 Junction 1. Take A447 then A47 towards Leicester. Ground is on A47 about 2 miles from town centre on left.

KING'S LYNN

Ground: The Walks Stadium, Tennyson Road, King's Lynn, Norfolk, PE30 5PB
Phone: 0553-760060   **Nickname:** The Linnets   **Founded:** 1876
Manager: Alan Day   **Secretary:** M. Saddleton   **Chairman:** M.Saddleton
Colours: Yellow, Blue, Blue   **Change:** All Red
Ground Capacity: 8,200 (1,200)   **Record:** 13,500 v Exeter C, FAC1 1951
Rail: King's Lynn.
Directions: A10-A47. At mini-roundabout take Vancouse Avenue. Follow Vancouse Avenue for about 400 yards, ground on left.

LEICESTER UNITED

Ground: United Park, Winchester Road, Blaby, Leicester, LE43 3HN
Phone: 0533-778998   **Nickname:** United   **Founded:** 1900
Manager: Andy Potter   **Secretary:** J. Goodman   **Chairman:** Gary Glover
Colours: Red and White Stripes, Black with Red and White Flash, Black with Two Red Hoops   **Change:** All White
Ground Capacity: 6,000 (450)   **Record:** not known
Rail: Narborough.
Directions: M69/M1 Junction. 2½ miles along the Blaby to Countesthorpe road.

NEWPORT AFC

Ground: Meadow Park, Sudmeadow Road, Hempsted, Gloucester, GL2 6HS
Phone: not known **Nickname:** The Exiles **Founded:** 1989
Manager: John Relish **Secretary:** Marc Williams **Chairman:** David Hando
Colours: Amber, Black, Black **Change:** All White
Ground Capacity: 5,000 (600) **Record:** 2,400
Directions: Take A40 into city centre towards the historic docks area, then Severn Road, then right into Hempsted Lane and right into Sudmeadow Road. Ground is on the left 50 yards up the road.

RACING CLUB WARWICK

Ground: Townsend Meadow, Hampton Road, Warwick
Phone: 0926-495786/493622 **Nickname:** Racing **Founded:** 1919
Manager: Stuart Dixon **Secretary:** Patrick Murphy **Chairman:** Jim Wright
Colours: Red, White, Black **Change:** Yellow, Black, Black
Ground Capacity: 1,000 (300) **Record:** 1,000 v Halesowen, FAC 87/8
Rail: Warwick. **Directions:** The ground is situated on the B4095 Warwick to Redditch road (Henley in Arden) next to the Owners' and Trainers' Car Park on Warwick Racecourse.

REDDITCH UNITED

Ground: Valley Stadium, Bromsgrove Road, Redditch, Worcs, B97 4RN
Phone: 0527-67450 **Nickname:** The Reds **Founded:** 1900
Manager: Paul Hendrie **Secretary:** M. Langfield **Chairman:** R. Berry
Colours: All Red **Change:** Yellow, Blue, Blue
Ground Capacity: 7,500 (200) **Record:** 5,500 v Bromsgrove, Lge 1954/5
Rail: Redditch. **Directions:** M42 to town centre take ring road and come off on access 7. This takes you into Bromsgrove Road. Also first exit off dual carriageway from Bromsgrove on the Batchley side of Redditch. Ground 400 yards from main line station and town centre.

RUSHDEN & DIAMONDS

Ground: Nene Park, Irthlingborough, Northants
Phone: 0933-650345 **Nickname:** not known **Founded:** 1992 (amalgamation)
Manager: Roger Ashby **Secretary:** David Joyce **Chairman:** Max Griggs
Ground Capacity: 3,500 (350) **Record:** (new club)
Rail: Wellingborough.
Directions: On A6 on outskirts of Irthlingborough.

STOURBRIDGE

Ground: War Memorial Athletic Ground, High Street, Amblecote, Stourbridge, DY8 4EB
Phone: 0384-394040 **Nickname:** The Glassboys **Founded:** 1876
Manager: John Chambers **Secretary:** Hugh Clark **Chairman:** J.C. Driscoll
Colours: Red and White, White, Red **Change:** White, Black, White
Ground Capacity: 2,000 (320) **Record:** 10,000 v WBA, 1902
Rail: Stourbridge Town.
Directions: On left-hand side of road 250 yards from Stourbridge ring road on A491 to Wolverhampton and opposite Royal Oak public house.

SUTTON COLDFIELD TOWN

Ground: Central Ground, Coles Lane, Sutton Coldfield, W. Midlands, B72 1NL
Phone: 021-354-2997 **Nickname:** The Royals **Founded:** 1897
Manager: Phil Sharpe **Secretary:** Gerry Shanahan **Chairman:** C. Holt
Colours: Royal Blue, White, Royal Blue **Change:** White, Royal Blue, White
Ground Capacity: 4,500 (250) **Record:** 2,029 v Doncaster, FAC1 10/80
Rail: Sutton Coldfield. **Directions:** A5127 into Sutton Coldfield, turn right at Odeon Cinema (Holland Road) and then first right into Coles Lane ground is 150 yards on the left.

TAMWORTH

Ground: The Lamb Ground, Kettlebrook, Tamworth, B77 1AA
Phone: 0827-65798 **Nickname:** The Lambs **Founded:** 1933
Manager: Sammy Chung **Secretary:** Rod Hadley **Chairman:** Malcolm Jones
Colours: Red, Black, Black or Red **Change:** All Yellow
Ground Capacity: 2,500 (400) **Record:** 4,920 v Atherstone, 4/48
Rail: Tamworth.
Directions: A5 Watling Street to Two Gates, turn into Tamworth Road; ground 1½ miles on left-hand side at Kettlebrook.

VS RUGBY

Ground: Butlin Road, Rugby, Warwickshire, CV21 3ST
Phone: 0788-543692 **Nickname:** The Valley **Founded:** 1956
Manager: Jimmy Knox **Secretary:** Kevin Horrigan **Chairman:** R.Gallimore
Colours: Sky Blue, Navy Blue, Sky Blue **Change:** All White with Red Trim
Ground Capacity: 5,000 (400) **Record:** 3,961 v Northampton, FAC1R 1984
Rail: Rugby.
Directions: Butlin Road is off the B5414 on the east side of Rugby close to Junction 1 of M6, the A5, and Junctions 18 and 20 of M1.

WESTON-SUPER-MARE

Ground: Woodspring Park, Winterstoke Road, Weston-super-Mare, BS22 8JP
Phone: 0934-21618 **Nickname:** not known **Founded:** 1948
Manager: John Ellenor **Secretary:** GD Milson **Chairman:** Paul Bliss
Colours: White, Blue, Blue **Change:** Yellow, Black, Yellow
Ground Capacity: 4,000 (500) **Record:** 692 v Cheltenham 1987
Rail: Weston-super-Mare (1 mile from ground).
Directions: M5 Junction 21. Follow Town Centre for three miles. Left at traffic lights (Herluin Way) opposite Mac's Garage. Follow to roundabout. Turn left, ground on right.

YATE TOWN

Ground: Lodge Road, Yate, Bristol, BS17 5LE
Phone: 0454-228103 **Nickname:** Bluebells **Founded:** 1946
Manager: Peter Jackson **Secretary:** Terry Tansley **Chairman:** R. Hawkins
Colours: White, Navy, White **Change:** All Red
Ground Capacity: 2,000 (200) **Record:** 2,000 v Bristol Rvrs, Test. 1990
Rail: Parkway Bristol (5 miles from ground).
Directions: M4 Junction 18. Take A46 signposted Stroud, filter left on to A432 at first set of lights towards Yate. Ground is signposted from Yate Ring Road.

SOUTHERN DIVISION

Final Table 1992-93

	P	W	D	L	F	A	Pts
Sittingbourne	42	26	12	4	102	43	90
Salisbury City	42	27	7	8	87	50	88
Witney Town	42	25	9	8	77	37	84
Gravesend & Northfleet	42	25	4	13	99	63	79
Havant Town	42	23	6	13	78	55	75
Sudbury Town	42	20	11	11	89	54	71
Erith & Belvedere	42	22	5	15	73	66	71
Ashford Town	42	20	8	14	91	66	68
Braintree Town	42	20	6	16	95	65	66
Margate	42	19	7	16	65	58	64
Wealdstone	42	18	7	17	75	69	61
Buckingham Town	42	16	11	15	61	58	59
Baldock Town	42	15	9	18	59	63	54
Poole Town	42	15	7	20	61	69	52
Fareham Town	42	14	8	20	67	65	50
Burnham	42	14	8	20	53	77	50
Canterbury City	42	12	10	20	54	76	46
Newport IOW	42	9	16	17	44	56	43
Fisher Athletic	42	8	9	25	38	98	33
Andover	42	7	9	26	42	99	30
Dunstable	42	5	14	23	42	92	29
Bury Town	42	8	5	29	46	119	29

Promotions and Relegations

Club	Position	Movement
Sittingbourne	1st	Promoted to Premier Division
Andover	20th	Resigned - to Wessex League

Clubs Joining Southern Division

Club	Position	Movement
Weymouth	21st	Premier Division
Tonbridge AFC	1st	Winstonlead Kent League

Leading Southern League Goalscorers

Player	Team	Goals
S. Portway	Gravesend	58
P. Smith	Sudbury	34
M. Buglione	Margate	31
S. Parnel	Sudbury	27
L. McRobert	Ashford	26
K. Clarke	Witney	25
D. Arter	Sittingbourne	23
J. Lillis	Sittingbourne	18
R. Taylor	Fareham Town	18

Sportique Manager of the Month Awards

Month	Manager	Club
August	Keith Miller	Fareham Town
September	Gary Aldous	Gravesend & Northfleet
October	Keith Baker	Buckingham Town
November	Richie Powling	Sudbury Town
December	Dennis Byatt	Wealdstone
January	Gary Aldous	Gravesend & Northfleet
February	Geoff Butler	Salisbury
March	Rob Eagles	Baldock Town
April/May	Geoff Butler	Salisbury
Season	John Ryan	Sittingbourne

SOUTHERN DIVISION RESULTS 1992-93

	Andover	Ashford Tn	Baldock Tn	Braintree Tn	Buckingham	Burnham	Bury Town	Canterbury C	Dunstable	Erith & Belv	Fareham Town
Andover	•	1-1	2-1	0-5	0-2	1-2	2-0	3-3	2-2	1-1	1-4
Ashford Town	4-3	•	1-0	7-4	2-2	1-3	7-0	2-1	4-0	0-2	3-0
Baldock Town	3-2	3-3	•	1-1	2-1	1-2	2-1	5-1	1-1	3-0	0-2
Braintree Town......	5-0	2-2	4-0	•	2-0	3-0	4-1	4-0	1-0	0-2	3-2
Buckingham Town ..	2-0	2-0	0-2	2-0	•	0-2	1-1	23-1	1-1	0-1	2-1
Burnham	1-1	2-0	2-0	1-2	0-3	•	1-2	1-1	1-1	0-1	2-0
Bury Town	1-2	1-4	3-2	0-4	2-0	2-2	•	•	2-1	2-7	1-4
Canterbury	2-3	3-2	0-2	2-1	0-4	0-2	1-0	0-5	2-2	1-2	3-0
Dunstable	1-3	1-2	0-0	1-7	2-3	2-0	5-1	6-1	•	1-3	2-0
Erith & Belvedere ..	4-0	2-6	0-3	1-3	1-0	4-1	3-2	1-2	2-0	•	3-2
Fareham Town	3-0	1-2	1-2	2-2	0-0	1-0	2-0	1-0	1-1	8-0	•
Fisher Athletic	1-3	2-1	2-0	2-0	1-3	1-0	3-0	0-0	4-0	1-0	1-6
Gravesend & Northfleet	5-0	3-1	0-1	4-0	3-4	1-2	4-1	4-0	3-0	3-5	0-1
Havant Town	1-0	0-3	0-2	3-2	1-0	4-1	0-1	1-0	4-1	0-0	2-1
Margate	1-0	0-4	0-2	2-5	1-0	1-1	0-2	0-0	2-2	1-2	0-0
Newport IOW	1-1	2-1	0-0	0-0	0-0	0-1	2-2	1-0	0-0	0-2	3-1
Poole Town	2-1	0-0	1-3	0-1	1-3	4-0	1-2	4-0	4-1	1-2	0-0
Salisbury	3-3	2-0	0-0	1-2	2-1	2-1	5-3	0-0	1-0	0-2	2-0
Sittingbourne	4-0	4-0	4-1	3-1	1-4	4-0	3-0	4-0	2-2	4-1	3-1
Sudbury Town	2-1	1-1	4-1	4-1	5-2	1-1	4-1	3-1	5-0	2-0	2-2
Wealdstone	5-0	2-3	0-3	2-1	3-4	1-2	3-1	1-0	2-2	3-1	4-1
Witney Town	1-0	2-2	1-0	3-1	2-1	2-0	0-0	1-0	2-2	2-1	1-0

188

	Fisher Athletic	Gravesend &	Havant Town	Margate	Newport IOW	Poole Town	Salisbury	Sittingbourne	Sudbury Town	Wealdstone	Witney Town
Andover	3-0	2-2	0-1	0-0	1-4	0-1	0-5	0-3	0-3	0-2	0-5
Ashford Town	4-0	1-0	2-2	1-4	1-2	5-1	0-1	2-2	0-2	2-1	1-0
Baldock Town	0-0	2-2	2-4	0-3	1-0	4-3	0-0	1-1	0-3	3-4	1-2
Braintree Town	6-1	0-1	0-2	0-1	1-0	3-1	5-1	3-3	1-1	4-1	2-3
Buckingham Town	0-0	2-0	2-4	0-0	0-0	0-0	2-4	3-1	1-1	0-4	0-0
Burnham	1-2	0-5	2-1	1-3	1-1	3-0	0-0	2-3	3-2	1-3	2-6
Bury Town	2-3	2-7	0-4	0-5	0-2	1-4	0-3	1-5	3-1	0-4	3-2
Canterbury City	2-0	2-3	0-0	5-1	1-0	1-0	1-2	1-1	3-1	3-1	1-1
Dunstable	0-0	2-3	1-2	1-1	1-0	0-3	1-0	1-1	1-6	2-1	0-1
Erith & Belvedere	1-0	1-4	0-2	1-0	2-1	2-0	2-3	1-0	1-1	5-1	2-0
Fareham Town	1-1	3-3	1-2	1-0	2-1	1-3	1-2	1-2	1-0	0-1	2-5
Fisher Athletic	•	0-4	1-4	0-5	2-2	2-0	2-0	1-1	0-4	3-0	0-1
Gravesend & Northfl	2-1	•	4-3	1-2	1-1	3-1	0-2	3-3	2-0	4-2	2-1
Havant Town	6-0	3-2	•	•	1-1	3-1	3-5	2-1	0-2	1-2	1-3
Margate	1-3	2-0	2-0	•	1-1	3-1	0-2	0-0	0-0	1-2	1-2
Newport IOW	6-0	1-2	1-2	2-1	•	0-0	4-0	0-4	1-2	1-3	0-2
Poole Town	1-1	2-3	3-2	4-0	2-3	•	•	0-4	3-1	1-0	1-0
Salisbury	4-1	3-0	2-1	3-0	2-1	2-1	•	1-2	3-1	1-3	1-1
Sittingbourne	6-0	1-0	3-2	3-0	4-2	0-0	0-1	•	2-2	1-0	4-0
Sudbury Town	3-1	1-3	1-1	2-3	4-1	5-1	1-1	1-3	•	2-1	0-2
Wealdstone	2-0	3-0	1-2	1-4	0-0	2-1	4-3	2-2	0-0	•	1-1
Witney Town	3-0	7-0	1-0	1-2	5-0	2-0	1-1	0-1	1-1	1-1	•

SOUTHERN DIVISION CLUBS

ASHFORD TOWN

Ground: The Homelands, Ashford Road, Kingsnorth, Ashford, Kent, TN26 1NJ
Phone: 0233-61183 **Nickname:** Nuts & Bolts **Founded:** 1930
Manager: Neil Cugley **Secretary:** A. Lancaster **Chairman:** K. Cunningham
Colours: White with Green Trim, Green, Green and White **Change:** All Yellow
Ground Capacity: 5,000 (500) **Record:** not known
Rail: Ashford (3 miles from ground).
Directions: Off A2070 4 miles south of Ashford town centre. Approach Ashford A20 from Maidstone, at second roundabout take Tenterden A28 – after 1 mile turn left at Tesco roundabout into Brookfield Road (B2229) to traffic lights and turn right into Kingsnorth Road (A2070). Continue for 2 miles through Kingsnort, ground is on left at illuminated bollards.

BALDOCK TOWN

Ground: Norton Road, Baldock, Herts
Phone: 0462-89544 **Nickname:** Reds **Founded:** 1889
Manager: **Secretary:** Don Swain **Chairman:** Mr Challis
Colours: Red, White, Red **Change:** All Yellow
Ground Capacity: 2,900 (200) **Record:** 1,200 v Arsenal, f.o. 1983
Rail: Baldock.
Directions: On main A505 Hitchin to Baldock road. Turn left into Norton Road, left after Orange Tree public house, ground on right after railway bridge.

BRAINTREE TOWN

Ground: Cressing Road Stadium, Clockhouse Way, Braintree, Essex
Phone: 0376-345617 **Nickname:** The Iron **Founded:** 1894
Manager: Peter Collins/Brian Honeywood **Secretary:** T. Woodley
Chairman: G. Rosling
Colours: Yellow and Blue **Change:** All Blue or All White
Ground Capacity: 4,000 (292) **Record:** 4,000 v Spurs, Charity, 5/52
Rail: Braintree & Bocking (1 mile from ground).
Directions: A12 to Witham; follow B1018 to Braintree. Take first left after The Sportsman Snooker Club, then left again. Entrance on left.

BUCKINGHAM TOWN

Ground: Ford Meadow, Ford Street, Buckingham, Bucks
Phone: 0280-816257   **Nickname:** The Robins   **Founded:** 1883
Manager: Keith Barber **Secretary:** E.J. Seaton **Chairman:** C.D. Lawrence
Colours: All Red   **Change:** All White
Ground Capacity: 2,000 (150)   **Record:** 2,500 v Orient, FAC1 1984
Rail: Milton Keynes.
Directions: From town centre take Aylesbury A413 out of town. Turn right at Phillips garage (about 400 yards).

BURNHAM

Ground: Wymers Wood Road, Burnham, Slough, Bucks, SL1 8JG
Phone: 0628-602567   **Nickname:** The Blues   **Founded:** 1876
Manager: Colin Barnes **Secretary:** David Eavis **Chairman:** Malcolm Higton
Colours: Blue and White, Blue, White **Change:** Red and White, Red, Red
Ground Capacity: 4,000 (100)   **Record:** 2,451 v Orient, FAC 1984/5
Rail: Burnham.
Directions: North-west of village centre, 2 miles from M4, Junction 7.

BURY TOWN

Ground: Ram Meadow, Cotton Lane, Bury St. Edmunds
Phone: 0284-754721/754820   **Nickname:** The Blues   **Founded:** 1872
Manager: Chris Symes **Secretary:** Mike Parker **Chairman:** Vic Clark
Colours: Blue and White   **Change:** Red, Black, Red
Ground Capacity: 3,500 (200)   **Record:** 2,500 v Enfield, FAC4Q 86
Rail: Bury St Edmunds.   **Directions:** Leave A45 by second exit towards central Bury St Edmunds and take third exit at roundabout. Take first exit at next roundabout into Northgate Street. At second set of traffic lights turn left into Mustow Street and immediately left again into Cotton Lane. Ground is 300 yards on right through coach/car park.

CANTERBURY CITY

Ground: Kingsmead Stadium, Kingsmead Road, Canterbury, Kent, CT2 7PH
Phone: 0227-464732   **Nickname:** City   **Founded:** 1947
Manager: Les Hall **Secretary:** Richard Tolson **Chairman:** Derek Owen
Colours: Royal Blue and White, Royal Blue and two White Hoops.
Change: Green and White, Green, Green.
Ground Capacity: 5,000 (500)   **Record:** 3,001 v Torquay, FAC1 1964
Rail: Canterbury East or West.
Directions: From London just off M2 and A2, follow signs for A28 into Kingsmead Road. Ground opposite swimming pool.

DUNSTABLE

Ground: Creasey Park, Brewers Hill Road, Dunstable, Beds.
Phone: 0582-606691　　**Nickname:** The Blues　　**Founded:** 1895
Manager: John Wortley　**Secretary:** Doug Simpson　**Chairman:** A. Fieldhouse
Colours: Blue and White Quarters, Blue, White　　**Change:** All Red
Ground Capacity: 5,000 (200)　　**Record:** 6,000 v Man. Utd, 1974
Rail: Luton.
Directions: Brewers Hill Road runs west from A505 at the north end of Dunstable, at large traffic island turn right.

ERITH & BELVEDERE

Ground: Park View, Lower Road, Belvedere, Kent, DA17 6DF
Phone: 081-311-4444　　**Nickname:** The Deres　　**Founded:** 1922
Manager: Harry Richardson　**Secretary:** David Joy　**Chairman:** E. Powell
Colours: Blue and White, Blue, White　　**Change:** All Red
Ground Capacity: 6,000 (250)　　**Record:** 8,000 v Coventry City, FAC 1932
Rail: Belvedere.
Directions: Entrance in Station Road, off Lower Road, adjacent to Belvedere (BR) Station.

FAREHAM TOWN

Ground: Cams Allders, Highfield Avenue, Fareham, Hants, PO14 1JA
Phone: 0329-231512　　**Nickname:** Town　　**Founded:** 1947
Manager: Harry Miller　**Secretary:** K.F. Atkins　**Chairman:** R.A. Grant
Colours: Red, White, Red　　**Change:** White, Black, White
Ground Capacity: 5,500 (300)
Record (Club): 6,035 v Kidderminster, FATsf 1987 (at The Dell, Soton)
Rail: Fareham.　**Directions:** From Fareham railway station take A27 towards Southampton. Second turning left into Redlands Lane, turn right at Redlands Inn into St Michaels Grove, and then first left into Highfield Avenue.

FISHER '93

Ground: Surrey Docks Stadium, Salter Road, London, SE16 1LQ
Phone: 071-237-1432　　**Nickname:** The Fish　　**Founded:** 1908
Manager: Jimmy Quinn　**Secretary:** M. Vigus　　**Chairman:** P. Woolf
Colours: Black and White Stripes, White, Black & White **Change:** All Red
Ground Capacity: 5,300 (400)　　**Record:** 4,283 v Barnet, GMVC 5/91
Rail: 400yds from Rotherhithe Underground Station.
Directions: Near south-side entrance to Rotherhithe Tunnel.

GRAVESEND & NORTHFLEET

Ground: Stonebridge Road, Northfleet, Gravesend, Kent, DA11 9BA
Phone: 0474-533796   **Nickname:** The Fleet   **Founded:** 1946
Manager: Gary Aldous   **Secretary:** Stephen Jones   **Chairman:** L. Ball
Colours: Red, White, Red   **Change:** White, Black, White
Ground Capacity: 9,750 (4,000)   **Record:** 12,036 v Sunderland, FAC4 1963
Rail: Northfleet.
Directions: From Dartford Tunnel follow A226 to Northfleet or A2 (Northfleet turn-off B262). Pick up B2175 to junction with A226, turn left, ground about 1 mile on right-hand side at bottom of hill.

HAVANT TOWN

Ground: Westleigh Park, Martin Road, Havant, Hants
Phone: 0705-455465   **Nickname:** not known   **Founded:** 1958
Manager: Tony Mount   **Secretary:** T. Brock   **Chairman:** R. Jones
Colours: Yellow, Black, Yellow and Black   **Change:** Green, White, White
Ground Capacity: 3,000 (214)   **Record:** 3,000 v Wisbech, FA Vase 1985/6
Rail: Havant (1 mile from ground).
Directions: M27, A27 B2149 to Havant. Right into Bartons Road, then first right into Martin Road.

MARGATE

Ground: Hartsdown Park, Hartsdown Road, Margate, Kent, CT9 5QZ
Phone: 0843-221769   **Nickname:** Gat   **Founded:** 1880
Manager: Mark Waetherley **Secretary:** K. Tomlinson **Chairman:** G. Wallis
Colours: Royal Blue and White, Royal Blue, Royal Blue **Change:** All White
Ground Capacity: 8,500 (400)   **Record:** 8,500 v Spurs, FAC3 1/73
Rail: Margate.
Directions: Follow A28 to Margate, turn right opposite hospital at pedestrian lights into Hartsdown Road, proceed over crossroads and the ground is on the left.

NEWPORT IoW

Ground: St. Georges Pk, St. Georges Way, Newport, Isle of Wight, PO30 4BA
Phone: 0983-525027   **Nickname:** not known   **Founded:** 1888
Manager: J. Horne **Secretary:** C.R. Cheverton **Chairman:** K. Newbery
Colours: Gold, Royal Blue, Gold   **Change:** White, Red, White
Ground Capacity: 5,000 (300)   **Record:** 2,500 v Fulham, g.o. 1988
Rail: Ryde Esplanade.

Directions: Roads from all ferry ports lead to Coppins Bridge roundabout at eastern extremity of town. Take Sandown/Ventnor exit, continue to next roundabout and take first exit for St Georges Way.

POOLE TOWN

Ground: Poole Stadium, Wimborne Road, Poole, Dorset, BH15 2BP
Phone: 0202-674747   **Nickname:** The Dolphins   **Founded:** 1880
Manager: Brian Chambers **Secretary:** Barry Hughes **Chairman:** Derek Block
Colours: All Blue   **Change:** Yellow, Blue, Yellow
Ground Capacity: 6,000 (1,250)   **Record:** 11,155 v Watford, FAC 1962/3
Rail: Poole.
Directions: Close to the centre of Poole and near railway station

SALISBURY

Ground: Victoria Park, Castle Road, Salisbury, Wiltshire, SP1 3ER
Phone: 0722-336689   **Nickname:** The Whites   **Founded:** 1947
Manager: Geoff Butler   **Secretary:** S. Gallagher **Chairman:** P. McEnhill
Colours: White, Black, Black   **Change:** All Blue
Ground Capacity: 4,600 (200)   **Record:** 8,900 v Weymouth, Western Lge 48
Rail: Salisbury.
Directions: From city centre take A345 towards Amesbury. Victoria Park is located on the left as you leave the city.

SUDBURY TOWN

Ground: Priory Stadium, Priory Walk, Sudbury, Suffolk
Phone: 0787-79095   **Nickname:** not known   **Founded:** 1898
Managers: Richie Powling **Secretary:** David Webb **Chairman:** not known
Colours: All Yellow   **Change:** All Red
Ground Capacity: 5,000 (200)   **Record:** 4,700 v Ipswich, Test. 1978
Rail: Sudbury.   **Directions:** From town centre proceed along Friars Street, passing the cricket ground, until the Ship and Star public house. Turn left into Priory Walk and follow this road down to the ground.

TONBRIDGE AFC

Ground: Longmead Stadium, Darenth Ave, Tonbridge, Kent.
Phone: 0732-352417   **Nickname:** The Angels   **Founded:** 1948
Manager: Phil Emblen **Secretary:** Steve Wadhaugh
Chairman: Ken Shellito
Colours: Blue/While, Blue, Blue

Ground Capacity: 5,000 (200)
Record: 8,236 v Aldershot, FAC 1st Rd 1951
Rail: Tonbridge (2 miles).
Directions: From Tonbridge High Street, north on A227 sign-posted Gravesend. Left at second mini-roundabout. Pinnacles PH. Ground and large car park at end of road.

WEALDSTONE

Ground: The Warren, Beaconsfield Rd, Hayes, Middx. (Share with Yeading)
Phone: 081-848-7362 **Nickname:** Stones **Founded:** 1906
Manager: Brian Hall **Secretary:** Peter Braxton **Chairman:** David Pollock
Colours: White / Blue Trim, White, Blue **Change:** Yellow, Royal Blue, Yellow
Ground Capacity: 3,000 (496) **Record:** 13,504 v Leytonstone, FAAmC 1949
Rail: Harrow-on-the-Hill (Underground – Metropolitan line).
Directions: From M1 leave at Junction 5 and follow North Watford signs and then signs to football ground.

WEYMOUTH

Ground: Wessex Stadium, Radipole Road, Weymouth, Dorset, DT4 0TJ
Phone: 0305-785558 **Nickname:** The Terras **Founded:** 1889
Manager: Len Drake **Secretary:** S.Charlton **Chairman:** A. Caswell
Colours: Maroon, Sky Blue, Sky Blue **Change:** All White
Ground Capacity: 10,000 (900) **Record:** 5,500 v Man Utd 1987 grd opening
Rail: Weymouth. **Directions:** Approach Weymouth on Dorchester road (A354), turn right at first roundabout to town centre, turn right at next roundabout (signposted) and ground is straight on.

WITNEY TOWN

Ground: Marriot's Close, Welch Way, Witney, Oxon, OX8 7AE
Phone: 0993-702549/705930 **Nickname:** not known **Founded:** 1885
Manager: Malcolm McIntosh **Secretary:** C. Miles **Chairman:** A. Oakey
Colours: Yellow, Royal Blue, Royal Blue **Change:** Blue, White, White
Ground Capacity: 2,000 (200) **Record:** 800 v Billericay, 5/76
Rail: Oxford.
Directions: Situated off the A40 (12 miles west of Oxford), the ground is sited near the town centre and adjacent to a public car park.

NORTHERN PREMIER LEAGUE

Southport the team to beat

Southport dominated the title chase from a long way out – the "Sandgrounders" were simply the best and most consistent team throughout the campaign, playing a brand of football that was admired wherever they went. The fact that they won the title whilst also having the best Premier Division disciplinary record speaks volumes for the style and skill that the management team of Brian Kettle and Steve Joel brought to Haig Avenue. Nobody gave them a chance of meeting the stringent ground-grading criteria laid down by the GMVC but Charlie and his co-directors worked ceaselessly to prove the sceptics wrong and match the brilliance out on the pitch. Kettle's side will surely hold their own at the higher level.

Southport's nearest challengers were Winsford United who had a marvellous season. In addition to finishing runners-up at their first assault on the Premier Division title, they appeared in no fewer than four Cup Finals, winning all of them! They took the HFS Loans Cup, beating Warrington Town on penalties at Maine Road, and completed the HFS Cup double by taking the President's Cup, getting the better of Southport 5-4 on aggregate. United also completed the double in the Cheshire County FA competitions, defeating GM Vauxhall opposition on both occasions. The Mid-Cheshire FA Cup went their way when Northwich Victoria fell victim to Mike McKenzie's incredible cup fighters. A row also ensued about the unfairness of Winsford having to play the Final of the Cheshire Senior Cup on their opponent's ground at Witton Albion. The argument, in the end, proved irrelevant as United brushed Albion aside to win 3-0 in their 70th and last game of the campaign. Amazingly, captain Cec Edey played in all seventy matches!

The tribute paid to Southport for their success in winning the league is measured by the fact that no team has ever got as many points as United without taking the title! The "nearly men" of the Premier Division were Morecambe. Arguably the best side on paper, they had a tendency to lose games they should have at least drawn and to draw games they should have won.

During the season Morecambe set all sorts of club records for their time in the NPL, including scoring seven in a game for the first time (a 7-4 goal avalanche against Emley watched by their smallest crowd of the season) which was quickly followed by eight away at Goole Town!

Most pundits' idea of Champions in August last year were Barrow. On the back of their regular 1,000 plus gates, and the income thereby generated, how could they fail to dominate the HFS scene and bounce straight back to Conference football? In the end, seven clubs proved to be better than the "Bluebirds" but, for the first month, things went reasonably well and, in September, there was even a brief flirtation with the Premier Division leadership.

Joining the top flight are Bridlington Town and Knowsley United. The Yorkshire side, in particular, had a brilliant campaign culminating in their fine FA Vase triumph over Tiverton Town. Since installing Colin Richardson as manager just three games into the season, Bridlington went from strength to strength. After hitting top spot on 3rd October they were never headed. Strangely, despite their success, they play in front of about 200 when at home, a poor effort from the townspeople which begs the question of what happens to the 2,000 who travelled to Wembley for the Vase final on a normal Saturday afternoon? The club are also experiencing difficulty with the local Council for permission to improve their Queensgate ground. It's a state of affairs that is difficult to comprehend with the club having brought so much credit to the town. In the light of these difficulties it is possible that Bridlington may begin the new season ground-sharing with Doncaster Rovers, some sixty miles away.

Knowsley United gained admission to the big league on the very last day of the season when they grabbed the runners-up spot with an away victory at Shepshed Albion. Ashton United had finished their fixtures the previous midweek to leave the Merseyside club needing just one point to take second place. Rossendale United finished bottom and will swap places with Bamber Bridge of the Bass North West Counties while Shepshed Albion resigned from the League. *Phil Bradley*

The Northern Premier League History

The Northern Premier League was formed in 1968 with 20 clubs drawn from the Cheshire County League (7), Lancashire Combination (5), Midland League (4), North Regional League (3) and the West Midlands (Regional) League (1). In 1970-71 the League comprised 22 clubs, later increasing to 24 but returning to 22 by the end of the 1970s. A second division of 19 clubs was added in 1987-88, which increased to 22 the following season.

Promotion to and relegation from the League has always been a feature of its structure, while, since the formation of the Alliance Premier League, a team is normally promoted to that League in exchange for a relegated club.

Previously the Multipart League, it was known as the HFS Loans League from 1987 until the end of the 1992-93 season when, with the unfortunate demise of the sponsors, it reverted to its Northern Premier League moniker.

5-Year One, Two, Three Records

Premier Division

	1st	Pts	2nd	Pts	3rd	Pts
1987-88	Chorley	88	Hyde United	85	Caernarfon Town	76
1988-89	Barrow	87	Hyde United	80	Witton Albion	79
1989-90	Colne Dynamoes	102	Gateshead	76	Witton Albion	73
1990-91	Witton Albion	93	Stalybridge C	77	Morecambe	73
1991-92	Stalybridge Celtic	92	Marine	78	Morecambe	76

First Division

	1st	Pts	2nd	Pts	3rd	Pts
1987-88	Fleetwood Town	73	Stalybridge C	72	Leek Town	70
1988-89	Colne Dynamoes	98	Bishop Auckland	89	Leek Town	85
1989-90	Leek Town	86	Droylsden	80	Accrington St	76
1990-91	Whitley Bay	85	Emley	84	Worksop Town	82
1991-92	Colwyn Bay	94	Winsford United	93	Worksop Town	80

LEAGUE CUP

Preliminary Round
Curzon Ashton v Eastwood Town 5-2
Radcliffe Borough v Shepshed Albion ..2-1

1st Round
Alfreton Town v Ashton United 2-3
Bridlington Town v Guiseley 2-1
Harrogate Town ....wo
Knowsley Utd v Great Harwood Town .2-1
Lancaster City v Farsley Celtic 1-2
Netherfield v Congleton Town..............2-0
Radcliffe Borough v Caernarfon Town..2-3
Rossendale Utd v Gretna......................1-1
   Replay 0-3
Workington v Curzon Ashton 1-0
Worksop Town v Warrington Town 1-3

2nd Round
Accrington Stanley v Gainsborough 1-1
   Replay 0-1
Bridlington Town v Knowsley United...0-1
Caernarfon Town v Ashton United 3-2
Colwyn Bay v Harrogate Town..............6-0
Farsley Celtic v Winsford United 1-2
Fleetwood Town v Workington 2-2
   Replay 0-1
Goole Town v Barrow...........................1-3
Gretna v Frickley Athletic....................3-2
Hyde United v Droylsden.....................3-2
Marine v Morecambe 1-0
Matlock Town v Horwich 3-1
Mossley v Emley..................................1-6
Netherfield v Leek Town 2-0
Southport v Buxton..............................4-1
Warrington Town v Bishop Auckland ...1-0
Whitley Bay v Chorley 2-2
   Replay 3-1

3rd Round
Emley v Colwyn Bay............................1-1
   Replay 2-3
Gainsborough Trinity v Barrow.............2-1
Knowsley United v Gretna....................1-2

Marine v Caernarfon Town....................1-0
Matlock Town v Netherfield.................2-2
   Replay 3-0
Whitley Bay v Warrington Town...........1-3
Winsford United v Hyde United 4-0
Workington v Southport.......................2-1

4th Round
Gainsborough Trinity v Workington......2-4
Marine v Gretna 1-1
   Replay ....2-3†
Matlock Town v Warrington Town 1-2
Winsford United v Colwyn Bay.............3-0

Semi-Final 1st Leg
Warrington Town v Gretna 3-2
Workington v Winsford United 0-1

Semi-Final 2nd Leg
Gretna v Warrington Town...................1-1
(Warrington Town won 4-3 on aggregate)
Winsford United v Workington 1-0
(Winsford United won 2-0 on aggregate)

Final
at Manchester City FC
Warrington Town 1
Winsford United 1
after extra time
Winsford United won 6-5 on penalties

† after extra time

PRESIDENT'S CUP

1st Round
Buxton v Netherfield 3-1
Caernarfon Town v Morecambe 1-3
Emley v Worksop Town 1-2
Guiseley v Accrington Stanley 0-4
Hyde United v Colwyn Bay 0-1
Knowsley United v Southport 1-4
Warrington Town v Marine 2-3
Winsford United v Leek Town 2-1

2nd Round
Accrington Stanley v Southport 3-5
Buxton v Morecambe 0-3
Marine v Worksop Town 3-0
Winsford United v Colwyn Bay 5-3

Semi-Final 1st Leg
Marine v Winsford United 1-1
Southport v Morecambe 2-0

Semi-Final 2nd Leg
Winsford United v Marine 3-1
(Winsford United won 4-2 on aggregate)
Morecambe v Southport 1-0
(Southport won 2-1 on aggregate)

Final 1st Leg
Winsford United 2
Maynard, Sheridan
Southport 0
Att: 587

Final 2nd Leg
Southport 4
Haw 3, Mooney
Winsford United 3
Sheridan 2, Blackwood   Att: 1137
(Winsford United won 5-4 on aggregate)

FIRST DIVISION CUP

1st Round
Bridlington Town v Curzon Ashton ...2-1
Caernarfon Town v Netherfield 2-1
Congleton Town v Knowsley United 1-2
Great Harwood Town v Gretna........2-0
Lancaster City v Eastwood Town 1-0
Shepshed Albion v Ashton United ...1-1
   Replay 1-2

2nd Round
Ashton United v Rossendale United ...3-1
Bridlington Town v Alfreton Town ...3-2
Caernarfon Town v Farsley Celtic 0-1
Great Harwood Town ....wo
Guiseley v Warrington Town 1-0
Lancaster City v Knowsley United ...2-1
Workington v Harrogate Town 0-2
Worksop Town v Radcliffe Borough 1-1
   Replay 0-1

3rd Round
Ashton United v Bridlington Town ...0-3

Farsley Celtic v Lancaster City 4-4
   Replay 2-3
Great Harwood Tn v Radcliffe Boro' 1-1
   Replay 3-1
Guiseley v Harrogate Town 1-1
   Replay 4-0

Semi-Final 1st Leg
Bridlington Tn v Great Harwood Tn 2-2
Lancaster City v Guiseley 1-5

Semi-Final 2nd Leg
Great Harwood Tn v Bridlington Tn 0-3
(Bridlington Town won 5-2 on aggregate)
Guiseley v Lancaster City 1-1
(Guiseley won 6-2 on aggregate)

Final 1st Leg
Guiseley v Bridlington Town 1-1

Final 2nd Leg
Bridlington Town v Guiseley 2-3
(Guiseley won 4-3 on aggregate)

PREMIER DIVISION

Final Table 1992-93

	P	W	D	L	F	A	Pts
Southport	42	29	9	4	103	31	96
Winsford United	42	27	9	6	91	43	90
Morecambe	42	25	11	6	93	51	86
Marine	42	26	8	8	83	47	86
Leek Town	42	21	11	10	86	51	74
Accrington Stanley	42	20	13	9	79	45	73
Frickley Athletic	42	21	6	15	62	52	69
Barrow	42	18	11	13	71	55	65
Hyde United	42	17	13	12	87	71	64
Bishop Auckland	42	17	11	14	63	52	62
Gainsborough Trinity	42	17	8	17	63	66	59
Colwyn Bay	42	16	6	20	80	79	54
Horwich	42	14	10	18	72	79	52
Buxton	42	13	10	19	60	75	49
* Matlock Town	42	13	11	18	56	79	47
Emley	42	13	6	23	62	91	45
Whitley Bay	42	11	8	23	57	96	41
Chorley	42	10	10	22	52	93	40
Fleetwood Town	42	10	7	25	50	77	37
Droylesden	42	10	7	25	47	84	37
Mossley	42	7	8	27	53	95	29
Goole Town	42	6	9	27	47	105	27

Three points deducted

Leading Premier Division Goalscorers

Goals	Player	Club
33	John Coleman	Morecambe
32	Steve Haw	Southport
26	Paul Beck	Accrington Stanley
	Chris Camden	Marine
	Andy Graham	Hyde United
25	Brian Ross	Marine
24	Bevan Blackwood	Winsford United
	Phil Chadwick	Hyde United
23	Peter Donnelly	Colwyn Bay
22	John Brady	Barrow
21	Tony McDonald	Horwich
	Stuart Lowe	Buxton

Annual Awards 1992-93
Premier Division
Manager of the Year	Mike McKenzie	Winsford United
Player of the Year	Brian Ross	Marine
Goalscorer of the Year	Steve Haw	Southport
	John Coleman	Morecambe

First Division
Manager of the Year	Colin Richardson	Bridlington Town
Player of the Year	Mark Place	Eastwood Town
Goalscorer of the Year	Liam Watson	Warrington Town

Premier Division Awards
Mail On Sunday Manager of the Month Awards
Month	Manager	Club
September	Brian Kettle	Southport
October	Brian Kettle	Southport
November	Neil Baker	Leek Town
December	Roly Howard	Marine
January	Mike McKenzie	Winsford United
February	Brian Kettle	Southport
March	Gary Simpson	Gainsborough
April	Mike McKenzie	Winsford United

Mail On Sunday Player of the Month Awards
Month	Player	Club
September	Dave Sutton	Leek Town
October	Russell Payne	Chorley
November	Brian Ross	Marine
December	Nicky Bramald	Emley
January	Phil Chadwick	Hyde United
February	Ashley Hoskin	Accrington Stanley
March	John Brady	Barrow
April	Danny Sheridan	Winsford United

PREMIER DIVISION RESULTS 1992-93

	Accrington St	Barrow	Bishop Auck	Buxton	Chorley	Colwyn Bay	Droylesden	Emley	Fleetwood	Frickley Ath	Gainsborough
Accrington Stanley	*	2-0	0-0	2-2	3-1	3-1	4-1	6-1	1-0	1-1	0-1
Barrow	2-0	*	4-3	3-2	2-1	5-0	3-0	0-1	2-0	1-2	2-2
Bishop Auckland	0-0	2-1	*	0-0	5-0	1-1	2-0	2-1	0-1	0-3	2-2
Buxton	0-1	0-4	0-3	*	2-3	1-0	1-2	3-0	0-3	2-0	2-3
Chorley	0-1	1-1	0-0	1-1	*	4-2	2-0	1-3	2-1	1-2	1-0
Colwyn Bay	1-0	2-3	1-2	7-3	1-0	*	3-0	2-1	3-1	0-1	3-0
Droylesden	3-3	1-3	1-1	0-0	2-2	1-1	*	1-2	1-1	2-1	0-2
Emley	0-3	1-3	2-3	0-1	2-1	1-1	1-3	*	4-3	1-2	1-2
Fleetwood Town	0-2	2-2	0-1	0-2	2-1	1-2	1-6	3-1	*	2-0	1-2
Frickley Athletic	3-2	2-1	3-0	2-0	1-1	1-0	2-1	3-1	1-2	*	4-0
Gainsborough Trinity	0-2	1-0	1-1	0-2	2-1	2-1	0-1	1-0	1-0	1-1	*
Goole Town	0-5	1-0	2-1	0-2	0-2	3-1	1-2	1-3	0-0	0-1	1-4
Horwich RMI	2-2	0-2	3-1	3-0	2-1	0-2	2-1	1-0	2-1	1-3	2-0
Hyde United	2-6	2-2	2-3	2-2	4-0	3-1	2-1	2-0	3-1	0-0	7-2
Leek Town	3-1	2-2	1-0	5-1	3-0	1-4	2-1	2-1	4-1	4-0	1-2
Marine	2-0	2-2	1-5	1-3	1-0	2-1	1-2	2-0	2-0	1-2	1-2
Matlock Town	1-2	0-1	2-1	1-0	3-1	1-1	2-2	2-1	0-1	2-1	2-1
Morecambe	2-0	3-1	3-1	2-1	2-0	3-1	0-1	7-4	4-2	3-0	3-4
Mossley	0-5	1-2	1-0	2-3	1-4	1-4	3-0	1-2	2-0	1-2	2-1
Southport	2-2	2-3	1-0	2-1	7-1	2-0	3-0	2-0	5-0	2-1	1-2
Whitley Bay	1-1	1-1	1-4	2-0	2-2	2-4	5-0	2-0	0-1	3-2	3-0
Winsford United	2-0	1-4	2-0	1-1	0-1	3-2	5-2	5-1	2-0	1-1	1-0

	Goole Town	Horwich RMI	Hyde United	Leek Town	Marine	Matlock Town	Morecambe	Mossley	Southport	Whitley Bay	Winsford Utd
Accrington Stanley	3-0	2-1	1-1	2-0	1-1	2-0	1-1	2-2	2-2	2-0	1-3
Barrow	4-1	1-1	2-1	1-2	3-1	1-0	0-3	2-2	0-2	0-1	0-0
Bishop Auckland	1-1	1-0	3-0	1-0	1-0	0-1	2-2	4-0	1-3	3-2	2-2
Buxton	2-1	2-2	2-1	2-1	1-5	1-1	4-1	6-1	0-2	0-0	2-3
Chorley	1-5	2-2	3-3	2-1	0-6	1-1	1-2	4-2	1-6	1-4	0-4
Colwyn Bay	4-2	4-2	2-4	2-3	2-2	3-1	0-1	2-1	2-4	4-4	2-3
Droylesden	1-0	1-3	1-0	0-1	1-3	2-0	1-2	1-4	2-5	1-2	0-4
Emley	1-2	5-3	1-5	5-5	4-1	2-3	1-2	2-0	0-4	2-1	1-2
Fleetwood Town	3-1	-	1-2	3-0	3-1	2-3	1-2	3-2	1-2	2-2	1-2
Frickley Athletic	3-0	2-1	1-1	1-2	0-0	1-0	2-0	2-1	2-5	3-0	1-2
Gainsborough Trinity	3-0	2-2	1-1	1-4	2-3	2-4	2-3	1-1	1-1	7-1	3-1
Goole Town	•	1-2	2-0	0-1	0-3	0-4	2-8	1-1	0-5	5-1	2-4
Horwich RMI	3-1	•	1-1	1-1	1-2	2-4	0-1	5-2	1-1	3-3	2-0
Hyde United	3-3	4-1	3-5	2-4	3-3	2-0	2-2	4-2	1-0	2-1	3-3
Leek Town	6-1	0-0	•	•	1-2	6-0	0-0	3-3	1-0	3-0	0-0
Marine	3-3	3-0	3-3	1-1	•	2-2	0-6	1-0	2-1	3-1	2-0
Matlock Town	3-3	3-2	0-1	1-2	1-0	2-2	•	0-3	1-5	1-2	3-3
Morecambe	1-1	3-2	3-3	0-4	1-1	•	0-6	3-1	0-2	4-2	0-0
Mossley	0-0	1-4	1-2	0-4	0-3	0-0	•	•	•	5-0	2-4
Southport	3-0	3-2	1-0	0-2	0-0	3-0	1-0	3-0	•	1-0	0-1
Whitley Bay	2-0	0-1	1-0	0-2	1-5	2-3	0-3	1-1	1-5	•	0-3
Winsford United	3-0	3-1	1-0	2-0	5-1	0-0	2-0	1-0	1-2	6-0	•

PREMIER ATTENDANCES 1992-93

	Accrington St	Barrow	Bishop Auck	Buxton	Chorley	Colwyn Bay	Droylsden	Emley	Fleetwood	Frickley Ath	Gainsborough
Accrington Stanley	•	801	513	471	459	392	407	1049	703	671	513
Barrow	1558	•	1165	1278	1094	1126	1534	1502	1711	1080	1127
Bishop Auckland	313	297	•	238	261	217	273	241	241	249	271
Buxton	325	393	325	•	351	343	273	275	291	351	236
Chorley	376	330	101	183	•	150	224	200	214	276	155
Colwyn Bay	140	298	215	128	187	•	150	186	118	92	110
Droylsden	323	404	148	216	351	347	•	301	149	225	161
Emley	369	290	377	249	254	283	216	•	229	512	546
Fleetwood Town	266	498	206	72	159	242	115	124	•	136	133
Frickley Athletic	257	225	209	286	222	231	178	325	200	•	278
Gainsborough Trinity	398	481	401	446	283	326	349	407	313	419	•
Goole Town	211	305	212	183	188	210	243	302	190	305	235
Horwich	255	303	186	174	410	173	183	225	208	196	189
Hyde United	444	414	284	403	334	280	440	349	249	278	307
Leek Town	525	516	359	565	408	360	407	319	402	366	253
Marine	355	611	349	362	681	418	331	335	311	325	334
Matlock Town	377	516	365	476	274	256	308	347	297	425	397
Morecombe	680	1075	369	350	450	350	409	292	525	350	320
Mossley	401	455	215	300	343	238	644	395	219	187	308
Southport	1328	1723	678	752	526	765	1185	419	1207	2230	1007
Whitley Bay	173	359	453	267	203	227	315	219	207	308	109
Winsford United	380	420	450	390	304	401	457	546	556	486	280

	Goole Town	Horwich RMI	Hyde united	Leek Town	Marine	Matlock Town	Morecambe	Mossley	Southport	Whitley Bay	Winsford Utd
Accrington Stanley	545	508	604	465	458	495	1288	463	641	288	467
Barrow	848	941	1006	971	1510	1047	1194	1421	1510	1252	1193
Bishop Auckland	380	215	221	302	221	213	332	240	426	401	302
Buxton	227	243	323	810	280	497	348	320	327	311	412
Chorley	176	328	210	144	247	212	418	195	501	187	287
Colwyn Bay	102	131	149	188	186	120	253	126	350	136	551
Droylsden	153	203	247	263	156	209	166	342	593	186	311
Emley	372	250	196	365	389	497	311	447	504	346	342
Fleetwood Town	117	146	181	168	150	199	430	103	334	113	185
Frickley Athletic	274	148	191	265	234	178	174	170	393	104	223
Gainsborough Trinity	449	338	334	348	474	479	351	410	520	380	454
Goole Town	•	188	260	222	185	223	190	190	298	220	210
Horwich	173	•	172	210	201	186	265	158	339	189	207
Hyde United	253	251	•	242	343	305	307	812	576	261	653
Leek Town	369	346	414	•	470	457	544	368	732	324	660
Marine	306	344	384	481	•	323	602	345	1611	326	533
Matlock	269	288	356	570	372	•	304	370	367	341	360
Morecambe	367	362	356	407	440	388	•	395	680	529	395
Mossley	244	208	509	202	279	270	401	•	567	225	350
Southport	382	883	534	1157	2078	913	904	544	•	1128	1177
Whitley Bay	180	156	253	188	131	238	201	149	205	•	235
Winsford United	403	242	412	406	460	429	541	526	801	401	•

Attendance Summaries by Club

Club	Position (91-92)	Att	(91-92)	Ave	(91-92)	%change
Barrow	8 (GMVC)	26,068	(26,225)	1,241	(1259)	-1.4
Southport	1 (7)	21,520	(7,677)	1025	(366)	+180.0
Accrington Stanley	6 (8)	12,201	(10,601)	581	(505)	+15.0
Marine	4 (2)	9,667	(8,690)	460	(414)	+11.2
Morecambe	3 (3)	9,489	(7,824)	452	(373)	+21.1
Winsford United	2 (1st Div)	9,291	(8,409)	442	(400)	+10.6
Leek Town	5 (4)	9,164	(10,550)	436	(502)	-13.1
Gainsborough Trin	11 (18)	8,405	(6,553)	400	(312)	+28.3
Hyde United	9 (9)	7,785	(9,324)	371	(444)	-16.5
Matlock Town	15 (19)	7,635	(8,545)	364	(407)	-10.7
Buxton	14 (5)	7,361	(8,757)	351	(417)	-15.9
Emley	16 (6)	7,344	(8,207)	350	(391)	-10.6
Mossley	21 (16)	6,960	(6,760)	331	(322)	+2.9
Bishop Auckland	10 (11)	5,854	(5,332)	279	(254)	+9.7
Droylsden	20 (15)	5,454	(6,045)	260	(288)	-9.8
Chorley	18 (21)	5,114	(6,020)	244	(287)	-15.1
Whitley Bay	17 (17)	4,776	(5,809)	227	(277)	-17.9
Goole Town	22 (12)	4,770	(6,472)	227	(308)	-26.3
Frickley Athletic	7 (14)	4,765	(5,477)	227	(261)	-13.1
Horwich RMI	13 (13)	4,602	(5,425)	219	(258)	-15.1
Fleetwood Town	19 (10)	4,081	(4,102)	194	(195)	-0.3
Colwyn Bay	12 (1st Div)	3,916	(10,180)	186	(485)	-61.6
Total		186,222	(161,033)	403	(349)	+15.5

Best Attendances at 10 Grounds 1992-93

2,230	Southport	v	Frickley Athletic	24/04/93
1,711	Barrow	v	Fleetwood Town	26/12/92
1,611	Marine	v	Southport	12/04/93
1,288	Accrington Stanley	v	Morecambe	02/01/93
1,075	Morecambe	v	Barrow	31/8/92
812	Hyde United	v	Mossley	01/01/93
810	Buxton	v	Leek Town	28/12/92
801	Winsford United	v	Southport	19/12/92
732	Leek Town	v	Southport	07/11/92
644	Mossley	v	Droylesden	26/12/92

Biggest Wins

Goole Town	v	Morecambe	2-8	24/04/93
Southport	v	Chorley	7-1	31/08/92
Gainsborough Trinity	v	Whitley Bay	7-1	12/04/92
Leek Town	v	Matlock Town	6-0	06/10/92
Winsford United	v	Whitley Bay	6-0	24/04/93
Chorley	v	Marine	0-6	07/10/92
Matlock Town	v	Morecambe	0-6	27/03/93

Biggest Aggregates

Morecambe	v	Emley	7-4	30/03/93
Goole Town	v	Morecambe	2-8	24/04/93

Top League Goalscorers by Club

Club *Scorers and goals*

Club	Scorers and goals
Accrington Stanley	Paul Beck 26, Bernie Hughes 8, Mike Lutkevich 8
Barrow	John Brady 22, Neil Dohety 10, Ken McKenna 6
Bishop Auckland	Gary Hyde 14, Lee Howey 10, Lobb 6
Buxton	Stuart Lowe 23, Mark Hopkins 10, Carl Holmes 5
Chorley	Peter McCrae 19, Carle Dyson 6
Colwyn Bay	Peter Donnelly 23, Jones 16, Roberts 13
Droylsden	Steve Bunter 11, Wardle 7
Emley	Bob Clarke 15, Ian Tunnacliffe 13, Graham Cooper 7
Fleetwood Town	Stuart Diggle 10, Mark Hilditch 6, Steve Curley 5
Frickley Athletic	Gary Brook 17, Gary Hatto 14, Simon Fuller 7
Gainsborough Trinity	Gary Bishop 9, Gratson 9, Richard Toone 8
Goole Town	Dave Warmesley 9, Ian Dunn 7, Hotte 6
Horwich	Tony McDonald 21, Ray Redshaw 19, Paul Moss 8
Hyde United	Andy Graham 25, Phil Chadwick 24, David Nolan 9
Leek Town	Darren Twigg 18, Wheaton 18, Dave Sutton 11
Marine	Chris Camden 26, Brian Ross 26, Andrew Draper 6
Matlock Town	Tilly 13, Marsh and Sheppard 6
Morecambe	John Coleman 30, Steve Holden 18, Ian Cain 14
Mossley	Reed 10, Graham Hoyland 9, Colin Heywood 4
Southport	Steve Haw 32, Peter Withers 18, Gamble 10
Whitley Bay	Ian Chandler 16, John Kiddie 7, Colin McCloed 7
Winsford United	Bevan Blackwood 22, Bryne 12, Maynard 9

PREMIER DIVISION CLUBS

ACCRINGTON STANLEY

Reformed in 1968 as successors to the Football League side, they joined the Lancashire Combination in 1970. Moved to the Cheshire County League in 1978 and then on to the North West Counties League in 1982. They were founder members of the Northern Premier League First Division in 1987.
Ground: Crown Ground, Livingstone Road, Accrington
Phone: 0254-383235 **Nickname:** Reds **Founded:** 1968
Manager: Phil Staley **Secretary:** Philip Terry **Chairman:** John Alty
Colours: All Red   **Change:** Yellow, Green, Green

5-Year Record		P	W	D	F	A	Pts	Psn	Cup	FAT
88-89	HFS1	42	21	10	81	60	73	6	2q	1q
89-90	HFS1	42	22	10	80	53	76	5	2q	1q
90-91	HFS1	42	21	13	83	57	76	4	4q	3q
91-92	HFSP	42	17	12	78	62	63	8	2q	3q
92-93	HFSP	42	20	13	79	45	73	6	2	1

Capacity: 2,460 (150)   **Record:** 1,110 v Fleetwood, NPL 1988
Rail: Accrington (1½ miles from ground).
Directions: M6: A677 to Blackburn, A6119 Ring Road, take M65 and leave at first exit A678 to Clayton-le-Moors, then A680 to Accrington. Livingstone Road approx 50 yards past Crown Hotel on left.

BARROW

Formed in 1901 and Lancashire Combination members from 1903-1921 when they joined the Football League. The club lost their League place in 1972, dropping into the Northern Premier League and becoming founder members of the Alliance Premier League in 1979. Subsequently relegated from the Alliance three times and promoted twice.
Ground: Holker Street, Barrow in Furness, Cumbria
Phone: 0229-820346/823061   **Info Line:** 0898-888620
Manager: Richard Dinnis   **Secretary:** Cyril Whiteside
Chairman: John Barker
Colours: White, Navy, White   **Change:** All Red
Nickname: Bluebirds

5-Year Record		P	W	D	F	A	Pts	Psn	Cup	FAT
88-89	HFSP	42	26	9	69	35	87	1	1	3
89-90	CONF	42	12	16	51	67	52	14	3q	W

90-91	CONF	42	15	12	59	65	57	10	3	2
91-92	CONF	42	8	14	52	72	38	22	4q	2
92-93	HFSP	42	18	11	71	55	65	8	4q	1

Ground Capacity: 7,000 (1,500) **Record:** 16,840 v Swansea Tn, FAC 1/54
Non-Lg: 6,002 v Enfield, FAT 4/88
Rail: Barrow in Furness (½ miles from ground).
Directions: M6 Junction 36. Follow A590 to Barrow. Turn right at fourth set of lights, and continue for ½ mile.

BISHOP AUCKLAND

Formed as Auckland Town by theology undergraduates from Auckland Castle. Early Northern League and Northern Alliance members, after changing to their current name they rejoined the Northern League in 1893. In 1988 they joined the HFS Loans League and were promoted in 1989.
Ground: Kingsway, Bishop Auckland, Co. Durham
Phone: 0388-603686 **Nickname:** Bishops **Founded:** 1886
Manager: Harry Dunn **Secretary:** Nicky Postma
Chairman: Steve Newcomb
Colours: All Light and Dark Blue **Change:** Red and White

5-Year Record		P	W	D	F	A	Pts	Psn	Cup	FAT
88-89	HFS1	42	28	5	78	28	89	2	2q	3
89-90	HFSP	42	17	8	72	64	59	11	2	1
90-91	HFSP	40	17	10	62	56	61	7	1	1
91-92	HFSP	42	16	9	48	58	57	11	4q	1
92-39	HFSP	42	17	11	63	53	62	10	3q	2

Capacity: 4,500 (300) **Record:** 17,000 v Coventry C, FAC2 1952
Rail: Bishop Auckland (½ mile from ground).
Directions: A1 to Scotch Corner. Follow signs to Bishop Auckland; ground behind town centre.

BOSTON UNITED

Formed in 1934 when they joined the Midland League. Moved to the Southern League in 1958 but transferred to the Central Alliance League in 1960 and then to the reformed Midland in 1961. Resigned in 1964, and in 1966 re-emerged as United Counties Leaguers, moving on to the West Midlands (Regional) League after one season. Northern Premier League founders in 1968 and Alliance Premier League founder members in 1979.
Ground: York Street Ground, York Street, Boston, Lincolnshire
Phone: 0205-365524/5 **Info Line:** 0898-121539
Manager: Peter Morris **Secretary:** J.Blackwell **Chairman:** P.Malkinson

Colours: Off Gold, Black, Off Gold **Change:** White with Red/Blue Trim
Nickname: Pilgrims

5-Year Record		P	W	D	F	A	Pts	Psn	Cup	FAT
88-89	CONF	40	22	8	61	51	74	3	3q	3
89-90	CONF	42	13	8	48	67	47	18	3q	1
90-91	CONF	42	12	11	55	69	47	18	1	1
91-92	CONF	42	18	9	71	66	63	8	2q	1
92-93	CONF	42	9	13	50	69	40	22	2q	4

Ground Capacity: 14,000 (2,000)
Record: 10,086 v Corby Town, Floodlight opening 1955
Rail: Boston (10 minutes from ground), also Peterborough or Grantham.
Directions: From North: A17 from Sleaford to Boston. Over railway crossing bear right to lights over bridge. Through lights to York Street. From South: A16 from Spalding to Boston. Turn right at first set of traffic lights over bridge. Through lights to York Street.

BRIDLINGTON TOWN

Founded by school leavers in 1925 as Bridlington Centrals, the club joined the Yorkshire League from the East Riding Amateur League in 1959 when they also changed to their present name. Founder members of the Northern Counties (East) League First Division in 1982 and promoted to the HFS League in 1990.

Ground: Queensgate, Bridlington, YO16 5LN
Phone: 0262-606879/670391 **Nickname:** Seasiders **Founded:** 1926
Manager: Colin Richardson **Secretary:** Alan Proudlock
Chairman: Charles Dunn
Colours: All Red **Change:** All Blue

5-Year Record		P	W	D	F	A	Pts	Psn	Cup	FAT
88-89	NCEP	32	21	5	67	26	68	3	3q	(V3)
89-90	NCEP	34	22	9	72	23	75	1	3q	(VF)
90-91	HFS1	42	15	15	72	52	60	9	1q	(V5)
91-92	HFS1	42	22	9	86	46	75	6	1	(V3)
92-93	HFS1	40	25	11	84	35	86	1	1q	(VW)

Capacity: 3,000 (750) **Record:** 3,000 v Scarborough
Rail: Bridlington (¾ mile from ground).
Directions: M62 Junction 37. Howden to Bridlington, A614 Spalding Moor, A613 Driffield, A166 Bridlington through lights – across roundabout signed town centre, through lights, left second lights, ground on right.

BUXTON

Formed in 1877 and played in several leagues, including the Combination and the Manchester League before joining the Cheshire County League in 1932. In 1973 they joined the Northern Premier League.

Ground: The Silverlands, Buxton, Derbyshire
Phone: 0298-24733   **Nickname:** The Bucks   **Founded:** 1877
Manager: Ernie Oliver   **Secretary:** David Belfield   **Chairman:** Geoff Worth
Colours: All White   **Change:** All Yellow

5-Year Record		P	W	D	F	A	Pts	Psn	Cup	FAT
88-89	HFSP	42	12	14	61	63	50	15	2q	1
89-90	HFSP	42	15	8	59	72	53	16	3q	3q
90-91	HFSP	40	17	11	66	61	59	8	2q	1q
91-92	HFSP	42	21	9	65	47	72	5	2q	2q
92-93	HFSP	42	13	10	60	75	49	14	1q	2q

Capacity: 4,000 (654)   **Record:** 6,000 v Barrow, FAC1 11/62
Rail: Buxton (½ mile from ground).
Directions: 200 yards from Buxton Market Place, directly opposite County Police Headquarters.

CHORLEY

Formed in 1883 and joined the Lancashire League in 1894. Founder members of the Lancashire Combination Second Division from which they were promoted in 1907 and again in 1909. In 1968 they were founder members of the Northern Premier League, only to be relegated in 1969, then promoted back in 1970. In 1972 they were relegated to the Cheshire County League, but in 1982 they returned to the Northern Premier. They were promoted to the Conference in 1988 but relegated in 1990.

Ground: Victoria Park, Duke Street, Chorley, PR7 3DU
Phone: 02572-63406   **Nickname:** Magpies   **Founded:** 1883
Manager: Glen Buckley   **Secretary:** Alan Robinson
Chairman: David Murgatroyd
Colours: Black and White Stripes, White, Black   **Change:** All Yellow

5-Year Record		P	W	D	F	A	Pts	Psn	Cup	FAT
88-89	CONF	40	13	6	57	65	45	17	4q	1
89-90	CONF	42	13	6	42	67	45	20	4q	3q
90-91	HFSP	40	12	10	55	55	46	14	2	1
91-92	HFSP	42	11	9	61	82	42	21	4q	3q
92-93	HFSP	42	10	10	52	93	40	18	1q	1q

Capacity: 9,900 (700) **Record:** 9,679 v Darwen 1931/2
Rail: Chorley (400 yards from ground). **Directions:** M61 to Westhoughton, follow A6 to Chorley. M6 to Standish, follow signs to Chorley.

COLWYN BAY

Formed in 1886, they were a prominent North Wales side and members of, among others, the National League of 1921-30. Founder members of the reformed Welsh League (North) in 1945, they moved to the North West Counties League in 1984 and to the HFS in 1991.

Ground: The Drill Field, Drill Field Road, Northwich, Cheshire, CW9 5HN
Phone: 0606-41450 **Nickname:** Bay **Founded:** 1886
Manager: Bryn Jones **Secretary:** Alan Banks **Chairman:** G. Owens
Colours: Sky Blue, Maroon, Blue **Change:** Maroon, Sky Blue, Maroon

5-Year Record		P	W	D	F	A	Pts	Psn	Cup	FAT
88-89	NWC1	34	19	9	77	45	47	4	1q	1
89-90	NWC1	34	16	12	79	50	60	3	3q	1q
90-91	NWC1	36	22	10	85	37	76	2	4q	3q
91-92	HFS1	42	30	4	99	49	94	1	4q	1q
92-93	HFSP	42	16	6	80	79	54	12	3q	2q

Capacity: 16,000 (600) **Record:** –
Rail: Northwich (1 mile).
Directions: M6 Junction 19. Take Chester road to roundabout and head for Bus Station (6 miles from M6). Ground adjacent to Bus Station.

DROYLSDEN

Formed in 1866. Lancashire Combination members in the 1930s, they joined the Cheshire County League in 1939, only to return to the Combination in 1949. In 1968 they re-entered the Cheshire County League and in 1982 were founder members of the North West Counties League Division Two. They became founder members of the Northern Premier League Division One in 1987 and were promoted to the Premier Division in 1990.

Ground: Butchers Arms, Market Street, Droylsden, Manchester
Phone: 061-370-1426 **Nickname:** The Bloods **Founded:** 1866
Manager: Stan Allan **Secretary:** Gordon Hargreaves **Chairman:** Dave Pace
Colours: All Red **Change:** All Yellow

5-Year Record		P	W	D	F	A	Pts	Psn	Cup	FAT
88-89	HFS1	42	25	9	84	48	84	4	1q	(V2)
89-90	HFS1	42	27	6	81	46	80*	2	2q	(V3†)
90-91	HFSP	40	12	11	67	70	47	13	2q	2
91-92	HFSP	42	12	14	62	72	50	15	3q	3q
92-93	HFSP	42	10	7	47	84	37	20	1q	1q

Seven points deducted †Tie awarded to opponents.
Capacity: 3,500 (200) **Record:** 4,250 v Grimsby T, FAC1 11/76
Rail: Fairfield (1½ miles from ground).
Directions: Market Street off Ashton New Road.

EMLEY

Joined the Yorkshire League from the Huddersfield League in 1969. In 1982 became founder members of the Northern Counties East League and in 1989 were promoted to the First Division of the HFS Loans League. Promoted to Premier Division 1991.
Ground: Emley Welfare SG, Emley, Huddersfield, West Yorkshire
Phone: 0924-848398/840087 **Nickname:** not known **Founded:** 1903
Manager: Steve Codd **Secretary** Gordon Adamson
Chairman: Peter Mathews
Colours: Sky Blue, Maroon, Sky Blue **Change:** Amber, Black, Amber

5 Year Record		P	W	D	F	A	Pts	Psn	Cup	FAT
88-89	NCEP	32	25	5	80	18	80	1	3q	(V4)
89-90	HFS1	42	20	9	70	42	69	5	1q	(V5)
90-91	HFS1	42	24	12	78	37	84	2	2q	(VQF)
91-92	HFSP	42	18	11	69	47	65	6	1	3q
92-93	HFSP	42	13	6	62	91	45	16	1q	3q

Capacity: 2,600 (230) **Record:** 5,134 v Barking, FAAC 2/69
Rail: Huddersfield (7 miles from ground).
Directions: M1 Junction 38. Follow signs to Huddersfield to roundabout, then left on Denby Dale Road A636 for approximately ¾ mile, then turn right for Emley.

FLEETWOOD TOWN

Formed in 1977, following the disbanding of former Northern Premier League team Fleetwood. Joined the Cheshire County League in 1978. Founder members of the North West Counties League Division Two in 1982, they were promoted to Division One after two seasons. Founder members of the Northern Premier League Division One in 1987 and promoted to the Premier Division in 1988.
Ground: Highbury Stadium, Park Avenue, Fleetwood, Lancs
Phone: 03917-6443 **Nickname:** Fishermen **Founded:** 1977
Manager: Steve Edwards **Secretary:** **Chairman:** Paul Murfin
Colours: Red and White, White, Red **Change:** Black and White, Black, Black

5-Year Record		P	W	D	F	A	Pts	Psn	Cup	FAT
88-89	HFSP	42	19	16	58	44	73	7	4q	1
89-90	HFSP	42	17	12	73	66	63	8	1q	1q
90-91	HFSP	40	20	9	69	44	69	4	1	1
91-92	HFSP	42	8	17	67	64	59	10	2q	1
92-93	HFSP	42	10	7	50	77	37	19	2q	3q

Capacity: 9,700 (200) **Record:** 6,000 v Rochdale, FAC1 1965
Rail: Poulton le Fylde (7 miles from ground).

Directions: M55 Junction 3. A585 to Fleetwood – ground is behind fire station on left just before town centre. Turn back on yourself for 100 yards at the point where the tramtracks cross the road.

FRICKLEY ATHLETIC

Formed as Frickley Colliery. Joined the Midland League from the Yorkshire League in 1924. In 1960 joined the Cheshire County League, moving back to the Midland Counties League in 1970. In 1976 they joined the NPL and moved up to the Conference in 1980. Relegated in 1987.
Ground: Westfield Lane, South Elmsall, West Yorkshire
Phone: 0977-642460/644453   **Nickname:** The Blue   **Founded:** 1910
Manager: Ronnie Glavin **Secretary:** Bob Bates **Chairman:** Mike Twiby
Colours: Blue and White, Blue, Blue **Change:** All Yellow and Red

5-Year Record		P	W	D	F	A	Pts	Psn	Cup	FAT
88-89	HFSP	42	17	10	64	53	61	9	1	2
89-90	HFSP	42	16	8	56	61	56	12	2q	3q
90-91	HFSP	40	16	6	64	62	54	10	4q	2
91-92	HFSP	42	12	16	61	57	52	14	3q	1
92-93	HFSP	42	21	6	62	52	69	7	3q	1

Capacity: 8,000 (900)   **Record:** 7,000 v Rotherham U, FAC1 1971
Rail: South Elmsall (2 miles from ground).
Directions: M62 to A1 Junction 33. Follow A1 (South) towards Doncaster. Leave A1 at first exit after Trusthouse Forte. Follow signs for South Kirby, then South Elmsall. In town centre near Market Place, travel along Westfield Lane into Oxford Street; ground at bottom of Oxford Street on right.

GAINSBOROUGH TRINITY

One-time Football League Second Division Club, and founder members of the Midland League. They re-joined the Midland League in 1912 and, apart from the 1960-61 season spent in the Central Alliance, they stayed there until being founder members of the NPL in 1968.
Ground: The Northolme, North Street, Gainsborough
Phone: 0427-613295   **Nickname:** The Blues   **Founded:** 1873
Manager: Gary Simpson **Secretary:** Frank Nicholson **Chairman:** John Davis
Colours: Royal Blue with White Trim, White, Blue and White
Change: White, Black, Red

5-Year Record		P	W	D	F	A	Pts	Psn	Cup	FAT
88-89	HFSP	42	12	11	56	73	47	17	1q	2q
89-90	HFSP	42	16	8	59	55	53*	15	1q	1q
90-91	HFSP	40	9	11	57	84	38	20	1q	2q

| 91-92 | HFSP | 42 | 11 | 13 | 48 | 63 | 46 | 18 | 1q | 2q |
| 92-93 | HFSP | 42 | 17 | 8 | 63 | 66 | 59 | 11 | 4q | 1q |

Three points deducted

Capacity: 9,950 (350) **Record:** 9,600 v Scunthorpe, 1948
Rail: Gainsborough (2 miles from ground).
Directions: Ground is situated near the town centre, 250 yards from the General Post Office and Magistrates' Court.

HORWICH RMI

Joined the Lancashire Combination during the First World War and stayed until 1968 when they moved to the Cheshire County League. Were founder members of the North West Counties League in 1982 and after one season moved to the Northern Premier League.

Ground: Grundy Hill, Victoria Road, Horwich
Phone: 0204-696908 **Nickname:** Railwaymen **Founded:** 1896
Manager: **Secretary:** Brian Hart **Chairman:** Garry Culshaw
Colours: Blue and White Stripes, Blue, Blue **Change:**

5-Year Record		P	W	D	F	A	Pts	Psn	Cup	FAT
88-89	HFSP	42	7	14	42	70	35	20	2q	1q
89-90	HFSP	42	15	13	66	69	55 *	13	1q	1q
90-91	HFSP	40	13	6	62	81	45	16	3q	QF
91-92	HFSP	42	13	14	44	52	53	16	2q	3q
92-93	HFSP	42	14	10	72	79	52	13	2q	3q

Three points deducted

Capacity: 5,000 (500) **Record:** not known
Rail: Blackrod (3 miles from ground).
Directions: M61 Junction 6. Follow Horwich signs at roundabout, bear left, just prior to second zebra crossing turn right (Victoria Road). Ground along side-road on left.

HYDE UNITED

Joined the Cheshire County League in 1930. Founder members of the Northern Premier League in 1968, they returned first to the Cheshire County in 1970 and then to the Northern Premier in 1982.

Ground: Tameside Stadium, Walker Lane, Hyde, Cheshire, SK14 2SB
Phone: 061-368-1031 **Nickname:** Tigers **Founded:** 1919
Manager: Ged Coyne **Secretary:** Alan Slater **Chairman:** Steve Hartley
Colours: Red White and Black, White, Black **Change:** White and Blue

5-Year Record		P	W	D	F	A	Pts	Psn	Cup	FAT
88-89	HFSP	42	24	8	77	44	80	2	3q	SF
89-90	HFSP	42	21	8	73	50	71	4	3q	2

90-91	HFSP	40	14	11	73	63	53	11	3q	2
91-92	HFSP	42	17	9	69	67	60	9	1q	1
92-93	HFSP	42	17	13	87	71	64	9	1q	1

Capacity: 4,000 (400) **Record:** 9,500 v Nelson, FAC 1952
Rail: Newton (400 yards from ground).
Directions: On entering Hyde follow signs for Tameside Leisure Park, and on Walker Lane take second car park entrance near Leisure Pool. Follow road round to Stadium.

KNOWSLEY UNITED

Founded as Kirkby Town in 1984, joining the North West Counties League, where an earlier Kirkby Town had played. Promoted in their first and second seasons, they changed their name in 1988 and, after five seasons in the top division, were promoted to the Northern Premier League First Division in 1991. Promoted from there in their second season.

Ground: Alt Park, Endmoor Road, Huyton, Merseyside
Phone: 051-480-2529 **Nickname:** The Reds **Founded:** 1984
Manager: Paul J. Orr **Secretary:** J. Williams **Chairman:** Paul G. Orr
Colours: Red & Black Hoops, Black, Red & Black **Change:** Grey, White

5-Year Record	P	W	D	F	A	Pts	Psn	Cup	FAT
88-89	NWC1	34	21	8	85	43	50	2	-	-
89-90	NWC1	34	21	6	68	45	69	2	-	(V1)
90-91	NWC1	36	25	8	95	37	83	1	1q	(V5)
91-92	HFS1	42	18	10	69	52	64	8	4q	(V5)
92-93	HFS1	40	23	7	86	48	76	2	2q	(V4)

Capacity: 5,000 (300) **Record:** 900 v Everton, Liverpool Snr Cup 1986
Rail: Huyton.
Directions: M62 Junction 6. M57 to Junction 3. Towards Huyton. At roundabout take Huyton Link Road. Ground on left-hand side.

LEEK TOWN

Formed in 1945 as Abbey Green Rovers and later known as Leek Lowe Hamil, the club played local football before joining the Staffs County League. They became Leek Town in 1951 on joining the Manchester League. Moved to the Birmingham League in 1954 but returned to the Manchester in 1957, later falling back into the Staffs County. Re-emerged to join the Cheshire County League in 1973 and become North West Counties League founder members in 1982. Founder members of the Northern Premier League Division One in 1987 and promoted to the top division in 1990.

Ground: Harrison Park, Macclesfield Road, Leek, Staffs, ST13 8LD
Phone: 0538-399278 **Nickname:** The Blues **Founded:** 1945

Manager: Neil Baker **Secretary:** Michael Rowley **Chairman:** Godfrey Heath
Colours: Blue, Blue & White, Blue & White **Change:** Red, Yellow, Red

5-Year Record		P	W	D	F	A	Pts	Psn	Cup	FAT
88-89	HFS1	42	25	11	74	41	85*	3	4q	1q
89-90	HFS1	42	26	8	70	31	86	1	1q	F
90-91	HFSP	40	15	11	48	44	56	9	2	1
91-92	HFSP	42	21	10	62	49	73	4	4q	1
92-93	HFSP	42	21	11	86	51	74	5	2q	1

One point deducted

Capacity: 5,000 (200) **Record:** 3,500 v Macclesfield, FAC 1973/4
Rail: Stoke (13 miles from ground) or Macclesfield (13 miles from ground).
Directions: Situated on the A53 main Buxton to Macclesfield road about ½ mile outside Leek on north-west side of the town.

MARINE

Formed in 1894 as an off-shoot of Waterloo Melville, in 1935 they joined the Lancashire Combination from the Liverpool County Combination. In 1969 they transferred to the Cheshire County League and, in 1979, joined the Northern Premier League.

Ground: Rossett Park, College Road, Crosby, Liverpool
Phone: 051-924-1743 **Nickname:** Lilywhites **Founded:** 1894
Manager: Roly Howard **Secretary:** John Wildman **Chairman:** T. Culshaw
Colours: White, Black, Black **Change:** Yellow, Blue, Yellow

5-Year Record		P	W	D	F	A	Pts	Psn	Cup	FAT
88-89	HFSP	42	23	7	69	48	76	5	2q	1
89-90	HFSP	42	16	14	59	55	62	9	1	1
90-91	HFSP	40	18	11	56	39	65	6	4q	3q
91-92	HFSP	42	23	9	64	32	78	2	3q	SF
92-93	HFSP	42	26	8	83	47	86	4	3	3

Capacity: 4,000 (400) **Record:** 4,000 v Nigeria 1947
Rail: Blundellsands (½ mile from ground).
Directions: From North: M6-M58 (end) then follow Crosby and Marine signs. From South: M6-M62-M57 (end) then as before.

MATLOCK TOWN

Founder members of the new Central Alliance in 1947. In 1961 they were founders of the revived Midland Counties League, and in 1969 they moved on to the Northern Premier League.

Ground: Causeway Lane, Matlock, Derbyshire
Phone: 0629-55362 **Nickname:** The Gladiators **Founded:** 1886
Manager: David Vaughan **Secretary:** Keith Brown **Chairman:** Donald Carr

Colours: Royal Blue, White, Royal Blue **Change:** All Yellow

5-Year Record		P	W	D	F	A	Pts	Psn	Cup	FAT
88-89	HFSP	42	16	5	65	73	53	13	1q	1
89-90	HFSP	42	18	12	61	42	66	6	1	2q
90-91	HFSP	40	12	7	52	70	43	17	2q	2q
91-92	HFSP	42	12	9	59	87	45	19	3q	3q
92-93	HFSP	42	13	11	56	79	47*	15	2q	2q

* Three points deducted

Capacity: 7,500 (240) **Record:** 5,123 v Burton A, FAT 1975
Rail: Matlock (½ mile from ground).
Directions: On A615 – 500 yards from the town centre.

MORECAMBE

Joined the Lancashire Combination on their formation. Founder members of the Northern Premier League in 1968.

Ground: Christie Park, Lancaster Road, Morecambe, LA4 5TJ
Phone: 0524-832230/411797 **Nickname:** Shrimps **Founded:** 1920
Manager: Bryan Griffiths **Secretary:** Dermot Cooke **Chairman:** E. Weldrake
Colours: Red & Black stripes, White, Black **Change:** All White

5-Year Record		P	W	D	F	A	Pts	Psn	Cup	FAT
88-89	HFSP	42	13	9	55	50	47*	16	3q	3q
89-90	HFSP	42	15	9	58	70	54	14	1q	1q
90-91	HFSP	40	19	16	72	44	73	3	1q	3q
91-92	HFSP	42	21	13	70	44	76	3	1	3
92-93	HFSP	42	25	11	93	51	86	3	1q	2

* *One point deducted*

Capacity: 2,500 (1,300) **Record:** 9,383 v Weymouth, FAC3 1/62
Rail: Morecambe Promenade (2 miles from ground).
Directions: From South: M6 Junction 34 to Lancaster A589 to Morecambe. From North: M6 Junction 35 to Carnforth, A6 to Bolton-le-Sands, A5105 to Morecambe. Ground on main town-centre road.

WHITLEY BAY

Formed in 1958 as successors to Whitley Bay Athletic, a Northern Alliance and latterly North Eastern League Club. Joined the Northern League in 1958. Moved to the HFS Loans League Division One in 1988. Promoted to Premier Division as champions in 1991.

Ground: Hillheads Park, Hillheads Road, Whitley Bay, Tyne and Wear
Phone: 091-251-3680 **Nickname:** The Bay **Founded:** 1958
Manager: Bobby Graham **Secretary:** Robert Harding **Chairman:**

Colours: Blue and White stripes, Blue, Blue **Change:** All Yellow

5-Year Record	P	W	D	F	A	Pts	Psn	Cup	FAT
88-89	HFS1	42	23	6	77	49	75	5	3q	3q
89-90	HFS1	42	21	11	93	59	74	4	3	2q
90-91	HFS1	42	25	10	95	38	85	1	2	1q
91-92	HFSP	42	13	9	53	79	48	17	4q	2q
92-93	HFSP	42	11	8	57	96	41	17	4q	1q

Capacity: 4,500 (300) **Record:** 7,301 v Hendon, FAACqf 1965
Rail: Monkseaton (1 mile from ground). **Directions:** A1M or A19 through Tyne Tunnel, follow A1 Morpeth. Join A1059 to Tynemouth at first roundabout then A1058 Tynemouth. Pick up signs A192 Whitley Bay, then A191 Whitley Bay. Ground down Hillheads Road behind Ice Rink.

WINSFORD UNITED

Formed in 1883. Founder members of the Cheshire County League in 1919. On amalgamation of that League with the Lancashire Combination, were founder members of the North West Counties League in 1982. Founder members of the First Division of the Northern Premier League in 1987, promoted in 1992.

Ground: Barton Stadium, Wharton, Winsford, Cheshire, CW7 3EU
Phone: 0606-593021 **Nickname:** Blues **Founded:** 1883
Manager: Graham Heathcote **Secretary:** Peter Warburton
Chairman: Chris Clarke
Colours: Royal Blue, White, Royal Blue **Change:** Maroon, White, White

5-Year Record	P	W	D	F	A	Pts	Psn	Cup	FAT
88-89	HFS1	42	13	6	58	93	45	19	Pr	1q
89-90	HFS1	42	18	10	65	53	64	7	Pr	2q
90-91	HFS1	42	11	13	51	66	46	18	1q	1q
91-92	HFS1	42	29	6	96	41	93	2	1	1q
92-93	HFSP	42	27	9	91	43	90	2	1q	3

Capacity: 8,000 (300) **Record:** 7,000 v Witton Albion 1947
Rail: Winsford (1 mile from ground).
Directions: From North: M6 Junction 19; A556 towards Northwich to Davenham, then take A5018 to Winsford. From South: M6 Junction 18; A54 through Middlewich towards Chester.

FIRST DIVISION

Final Table 1992-93

	P	W	D	L	F	A	Pts
Bridlington Town	40	25	11	4	84	35	86
Knowsley United	40	23	7	10	86	48	76
Ashton United	40	22	8	10	81	54	74
Guiseley	40	20	10	10	90	64	70
Warrington Town	40	19	10	11	85	57	67
Gretna	40	17	12	11	64	47	63
Curzon Ashton	40	16	15	9	69	63	63
Great Harwood Town	40	17	9	14	66	57	60
Alfreton Town	40	15	9	16	80	80	54
Harrogate Town	40	14	12	14	77	81	54
Worksop Town	40	15	9	16	66	70	54
Radcliffe Borough	40	13	14	13	66	69	53
Workington	40	13	13	14	51	61	52
Eastwood Town	40	13	11	16	49	52	50
Netherfield	40	11	14	15	68	63	47
Caernarfon Town	40	13	8	19	66	74	47
Farsley Celtic	40	12	8	20	64	77	44
Lancaster City	40	10	12	18	49	76	42
Shepshed Albion	40	9	12	19	46	66	39
Congleton Town	40	10	7	23	58	95	37
Rossendale United	40	5	5	30	50	126	20

Leading First Division Goalscorers

Goals	Player	Club
27	Andy Whittaker	Netherfield
26	Peter Coyne	Radcliffe Borough
23	Chris Shaw	Ashton United
22	Steve French	Harrogate Town
21	Graeme Jones	Bridlington Town
	Gary Waller	Worksop Town
20	Dave Siddell	Knowsley United
	Liam Watson	Warrington Town
	Darren Washington	Congleton Town

Attendance Summaries for First Division 92-93

Club	Position	(91-92)	Att	(91-92)	Ave	(91-92)	%change
Guiseley	4	(4)	10,343	(11,441)	517	(545)	-5.1
Worksop Town	11	(3)	6,538	(2,308)	327	(110)	+197.2
Ashton United	3	(Bass NWC)	5,621	(n/a)	281	(n/a)	n/a
Bridlington Town	1	(6)	4,991	(3,462)	250	(165)	+51.2
Harrogate Town	10	(10)	4,814	(5,809)	241	(242)	-0.5
Warrington Town	5	(7)	4,411	(3,891)	221	(185)	+19.2
Workington	13	(22)	3,841	(2,654)	174	(126)	+38.1
Great Harwood Tn	8	(Bass NWC)	3,711	(n/a)	186	(n/a)	n/a
Shepshed Albion	19	(Prem Div)	3,608	(5,621)	180	(268)	-32.7
Rossendale United	21	(19)	3,492	(4,300)	175	(205)	-14.8
Netherfield	15	(9)	3,381	(3,448)	169	(164)	+3.1
Farsley Celtic	17	(12)	3,321	(3,225)	166	(154)	+7.8
Congleton Town	20	(17)	3,010	(3,506)	150	(167)	-9.9
Curzon Ashton	7	(11)	2,945	(3,089)	147	(147)	–
Gretna	6	(Northern)	2,889	(n/a)	144	(n/a)	n/a
Eastwood Town	14	(15)	2,836	(2,730)	142	(130)	+9.1
Alfreton Town	9	(20)	2,491	(2,489)	125	(119)	+4.7
Knowsley United	2	(8)	2,233	(2,059)	112	(98)	+13.9
Radcliffe Borough	12	(13)	2,215	(2,107)	111	(100)	+10.8
Lancaster City	18	(16)	2,211	(3,151)	111	(150)	-26.3
Caernarfon Town	16	(5)	2,054	(4,965)	103	(236)	-56.5
Total			80,956	(91,795)	193	(199)	-3.0

Mail On Sunday Manager of the Month Awards

Month	Manager	Club
September	Steve Waywell	Curzon Ashton
October	Colin Richardson	Bridlington Town
November	Gordon Raynor	Guiseley
December	Alan Tinsley	Fleetwood Town
January	Derek Brownbill	Warrington Town
February	Alan Cook	Workington
March	Tommy Spencer	Worksop Town
April	Max Thompson	Knowsley United

Mail On Sunday Player of the Month Awards

Month	Player	Club
September	Joey Dunn	Warrington Town
October	Peter Smith	Great Harwood Town
November	Martin Roderick	Shepshed Albion
December	Don Nicely	Congleton Town
January	Malcolm Jackson	Netherfield
February	Chris Shaw	Ashton United
March	Keith Evans	Curzon Ashton
April	Jason Priestley	Gretna
	Andy Whittaker	Netherfield

FIRST DIVISION RESULTS 1992-93

	Alfreton Town	Ashton United	Bridlington	Caernarfon	Congleton Tn	Curzon Ashton	Eastwood Tn	Farsley Celtic	Gt Harwood Tn	Gretna	Guiseley
Alfreton Town	•	1-2	2-3	1-0	4-1	0-1	1-2	1-3	4-0	2-3	3-5
Ashton United	6-2	•	1-1	2-0	1-2	5-1	1-4	3-1	0-0	1-1	5-2
Bridlington Town	1-4	6-2	•	0-0	5-1	1-0	2-0	1-1	1-0	1-0	2-1
Caernarfon Town	2-3	1-3	2-2	•	3-2	2-1	1-1	3-4	3-0	1-4	1-0
Congleton Town	3-2	1-0	3-3	0-2	•	0-3	0-0	2-1	2-4	0-1	4-3
Curzon Ashton	1-1	2-2	2-1	2-2	2-2	•	3-3	1-1	1-2	0-4	1-1
Eastwood Town	2-1	1-2	0-0	2-2	2-1	1-2	•	2-0	3-2	2-1	1-3
Farsley Celtic	2-3	1-1	1-2	0-4	3-2	0-1	0-1	•	0-2	1-3	0-3
Great Harwood Town	2-1	2-1	1-2	1-1	4-0	1-1	1-1	7-0	•	3-2	2-2
Gretna	2-3	3-0	1-3	4-2	5-1	0-0	2-2	3-2	2-1	•	0-1
Guiseley	1-1	4-1	2-2	3-1	5-1	1-3	2-1	3-2	2-0	0-0	•
Harrowgate Town	2-2	1-1	1-5	3-0	2-1	1-5	3-3	1-6	1-1	0-1	3-2
Knowsley United	0-1	3-2	3-1	3-1	5-0	5-0	0-1	2-0	2-0	0-1	4-2
Lancaster City	1-1	1-2	2-1	0-3	1-1	0-0	1-0	1-2	0-0	0-0	1-3
Netherfield	1-1	2-1	0-1	1-1	1-1	2-2	3-0	0-1	2-0	1-4	1-1
Radcliffe Borough	3-1	0-2	0-3	1-3	1-3	1-0	1-0	2-4	5-2	1-0	1-0
Rossendale United	1-1	1-7	0-1	1-4	1-4	1-1	0-2	3-2	0-4	1-0	0-1
Shepshed Albion	1-2	3-1	0-1	3-1	0-1	1-2	0-2	3-1	1-0	1-0	1-1
Warrington Town	4-2	0-0	0-1	3-1	6-1	3-3	1-0	3-1	1-0	0-0	2-0
Workington	2-1	3-2	0-1	3-1	2-1	1-1	3-0	3-0	0-0	0-0	3-2
Worksop Town	3-1	0-1	0-4	1-2	6-4	0-3	0-3	2-3	1-1	2-1	1-0

	Harrogate Town	Knowsley Utd	Lancaster City	Netherfield	Radcliffe Boro	Rossendale Utd	Shepshed Alb	Warrington Tn	Workington	Worksop Town
Alfreton Town	3-2	2-1	3-2	3-3	2-2	5-3	2-1	0-3	1-1	6-2
Ashton United	2-1	3-0	4-0	3-0	2-1	2-0	1-1	2-1	2-1	1-0
Bridlington Town	3-0	2-0	0-0	2-1	4-0	6-3	5-0	1-1	0-0	1-0
Caernarfon town	2-4	1-3	4-2	1-5	0-0	3-0	1-1	4-1	0-1	0-2
Congleton Town	3-3	1-2	1-2	0-4	1-2	0-1	1-2	2-1	0-3	1-3
Curzon Ashton	4-1	1-1	3-0	1-4	0-1	6-1	1-0	3-3	2-1	2-1
Eastwood Town	5-3	1-3	0-2	1-0	1-1	4-1	1-0	4-0	0-1	0-0
Farsley Celtic	0-1	0-3	3-0	1-1	1-1	1-3	2-2	1-1	1-2	2-2
Great Harwood Tn	2-2	1-3	2-1	0-3	3-0	7-1	5-2	3-2	2-2	4-2
Gretna	3-2	1-5	1-2	2-1	1-0	2-3	2-1	2-0	0-0	3-0
Guiseley	2-3	1-2	5-0	4-2	3-3	3-2	1-1	3-2	4-3	3-1
Harrogate Town	•	1-1	2-0	1-1	1-1	3-0	1-0	2-2	1-1	1-1
Knowsley United	3-0	•	1-2	0-1	2-3	2-0	2-2	4-3	4-1	1-0
Lancaster City	1-1	1-1	•	3-2	1-5	2-0	1-1	2-2	1-3	0-1
Netherfield	1-1	2-1	3-3	•	6-1	3-2	0-0	0-1	1-2	1-1
Radcliffe Borough	4-2	1-1	2-1	3-0	•	1-1	3-0	1-1	1-1	3-3
Rossendale United	1-6	3-8	2-2	1-2	4-3	•	1-2	2-7	2-2	0-1
Shepshed Albion	3-0	0-2	2-3	0-3	2-2	2-0	•	0-3	1-1	1-0
Warrington Town	4-3	3-0	0-2	2-0	2-0	4-1	5-0	•	2-1	1-1
Workington	2-1	3-2	1-1	3-1	6-1	3-3	3-0	0-1	•	2-3
Worksop Town	0-3	1-1	6-2	5-2	4-2	5-4	4-2	1-0	3-0	•

DIVISION ONE CLUBS

ALFRETON TOWN

Ground: North Street, Alfreton, Derby
Phone: 0773-832819 **Nickname:** The Reds **Founded:** 1959
Manager: Danny Hague **Secretary:** Roger Taylor **Chairman:** Sean Egan
Colours: Red & White & Black, Black, Red **Change:** All White
Capacity: 6,000 (120) **Record:** 5,200 v Matlock, Central All. 1961
Rail: Alfreton & Mansfield Parkway (½ mile from ground).
Directions: M1 Junction 28. A38 towards Derby, follow for 2 miles then take slip road on to B600, turn right at main road towards town centre ½ mile, turn left into North Street and ground is on the right-hand side.

ASHTON UNITED

Ground: Surrey Street, Hurst Cross, Ashton-under-Lyne, Tameside
Phone: 061-339-4158 **Founded:** 1878
Manager: Kevin Keelan **Secretary:** Ernie Jones **Chairman:** John Milne
Colours: Red, Black, Red **Change:** Blue, White, Blue
Capacity: 8,000 (300) **Record:** 11,000 v Halifax, FA Cup 1953
Rail: Ashton Charlstown (1 mile)
Directions: M62 Junction 20. A627(M) to Oldham/Ashton-under-Lyne. Leave at Ashton, follow Stalybridge (B6194) until Hurst Cross. Ground on right behind Royal Oak public house.

BAMBER BRIDGE

Ground: Irongate, Brownedge Road, Bamber Bridge, PR5 6UX
Phone: 0772-627387 **Founded:** 1952
Manager: Tony Greenwood **Secretary:** David Spencer
Chairman: Dennis Allen
Colours: White, Black, White
Capacity: 3,200 (200) **Record:** 2,241 v Preston NE 1988
Rail: Bamber Bridge (1 mile)
Directions: M6, J29. A6 (Bamber Bridge to Preston). Right at roundabout. Third exit at next roundabout to Bamber Bridge. First right. Ground on left in cul-de-sac.

CAERNARFON TOWN

Ground: National Park, Katherine Street, Ashton-under-Lyne, Lancashire
Phone: 061-330-6033   **Nickname:** Canaries   **Founded:** 1876
Manager: Roy Soule **Secretary:** W.Gray-Thomas **Chairman:** E. Price-Jones
Colours: Yellow, Green, Yellow   **Change:** Red, White, Red
Capacity: 8,000 (350)   **Record:** First year at Curzon Ashton FC
Rail: Ashton-under-Lyne (1½ miles from ground).
Directions: Behind Ashton Police Station, off A635 Manchester Road.

CONGLETON TOWN

Ground: Booth Street Ground, Crescent Road, Congleton, Cheshire
Phone: 0260-274460   **Nickname:** The Bears   **Founded:** 1901
Manager: Billy Wright **Secretary:** John Pullen **Chairman:** Cliff Salt
Colours: White, Black, Black   **Change:** All Red
Capacity: 5,000 (300)   **Record:** 7,000 v Huddersfield, Ches. Lg
Rail: Congleton (2 miles from ground).
Directions: On approach to Congleton via Clayton by-pass, take second turning right after Fire Station into Booth Street; ground off Booth Street.

CURZON ASHTON

Ground: National Park, Katherine Street, Ashton-under-Lyne, Lancashire
Phone: 061-330-6033   **Nickname:** Curzon   **Founded:** 1963
Manager: Dave Jones **Secretary:** Alun Jones **Chairman:** Harry Twamley
Colours: Blue, Blue, White   **Change:** All White
Capacity: 8,000 (350)   **Record:** 1,862 v Stamford, FAVsf2 1980
Rail: Ashton-under-Lyne (1½ miles from ground).
Directions: Behind Ashton Police Station, off A635 Manchester Road.

EASTWOOD TOWN

Ground: Coronation Park, Eastwood, Notts
Phone: 0773-2301/715823   **Nickname:** The Badgers   **Founded:** 1953
Manager: Brian Chambers **Secretary:** Paddy Farrell **Chairman:** George Belshaw
Colours: Black and White Stripes, Black, Red   **Change:** Yellow
Capacity: 6,000 (200)   **Record:** 2,500 v Wealdstone, FAAC 2/68
Rail: Nottingham (10 miles).
Directions: From North: M1 Junction 27 – follow Heanor signs via Brinsley to traffic lights in Eastwood, here turn left then first right past Fire Station. From South: M1 Junction 26 – B6010 to first exit, left at traffic lights; take first left at the Man in Space public house.

FARSLEY CELTIC

Ground: Throstle Nest, Newlands, Farsley, Pudsey, Leeds, LS28 3TE
Phone: 0532-561517   **Nickname:** Celts   **Founded:** 1908
Manager: Dennis Metcalf **Secretary:** Brian Whitehead **Chairman:** John Palmer
Colours: All Blue   **Change:** All White
Capacity: 5,000 (300)   **Record:** not known
Rail: New Pudsey (1 mile from ground).
Directions: M62 Junction 28. Follow the Leeds ring road to A647. Turn right at roundabout towards Leeds; after approx ½ mile turn left down New Street (Tradex warehouse on corner). After approx 400 yards turn right down Newlands, ground at bottom.

GREAT HARWOOD TOWN

Ground: The Showground, Wood Street, Great Harwood, Lancs
Phone: 0254-883913   **Founded:** 1978
Manager: Eric Whalley **Secretary:** Graham Snowden
Chairman: Chris Hickey
Colours: All Red
Capacity: 2,000 (200)   **Record:** 1,200 v Manchester United, 1987
Rail: Blackburn (6 miles from ground)
Directions: M66 Haslingden exit. A680 through Baxenden, Accrington, Clayton-le-Moors. Left at Hyndburn Bridge Hotel into Hyndburn Road, right into Wood Street.

GRETNA

Ground: Raydale Park, Dominion Road, Gretna, Carlisle
Phone: 0461-37602   **Nickname:** not known   **Founded:** 1946
Manager: Mick McCartney **Secretary:** Keith Rhodes **Chairman:** Ian Dalgliesh
Colours: Black and White Hoops, Black, Black and White   **Change:** All red
Capacity: 3,500 (200)   **Record:** 2,000 v Glasgow Rangers, 1989
Rail: Carlisle (8 miles from ground)
Directions: A74, north end of town, 8 miles north of Carlisle.

GOOLE TOWN

Ground: Victoria Pleasure Grounds, Carter St, Goole, North Humberside
Phone: 0405-762794   **Nickname:** Town   **Founded:** 1900
Manager: Tim Hotte **Secretary:** Graeme Wilson **Chairman:** C. Raywood
Colours: Blue and Red, Blue, Red   **Change:** Red and White Stripes
Capacity: 4,500 (200)   **Record:** 8,700 v Scunthorpe, Mid. Lg 1950

Rail: Goole (400 yards from ground).
Directions: M62 Junction 36, Goole exit. A614 to Goole centre and turn right at second set of traffic lights. Carter Street is sixth turning on the right.

GUISELEY

Ground: Nethermoor Ground, Otley Road, Guiseley, Yorks
Phone: 0493-72872 **Founded:** 1909
Manager: Ray McHale **Secretary:** Philip Rogerson
Chairman: Garry Douglas
Colours: All Yellow with Blue Trim **Change:** All White
Capacity: 4,000 (400) **Record:** 2,142 v Sudbury Town FAVsf 3/92
Rail: Guiseley (½ mile from ground)
Directions: M1, M62 Junction 26. Follow to Leeds, take Leeds Ring Road (A6110) to A65. On to A65 to Rawdon, then Guiseley. Ground 400 yards on right past traffic lights.

HARROGATE TOWN

Ground: Wetherby Road, Harrogate, North Yorkshire
Phone: 0423-883671 **Nickname:** not known **Founded:** 1919
Manager: Alan Smith **Secretary:** Roy Dalby **Chairman:** George Dunnington
Colours: Amber, Black, Amber **Change:** All Blue
Capacity: 3,800 (370) **Record:** 3,208 v Starbeck, Whitworth Cup Final 1948
Rail: Harrogate (¾ mile from ground).
Directions: From Leeds on A61 turn right at first traffic lights (Appleyards Garage) into Hook Stone Road, continue to Woodlands Hotel traffic lights then turn left into Wetherby Road – ground 300 yards on the right.

LANCASTER CITY

Ground: Giant Axe, West Road, Lancaster, Lancs
Phone: 0524-382238 **Nickname:** The Blues **Founded:** 1905
Manager: Alan Tinsley **Secretary:** Barry Newsham
Chairman: John Bagguley
Colours: All Blue **Change:** Yellow, Black, Yellow
Capacity: 5,000 (500) **Record:** 7,500 v Carlisle, FAC 1936
Rail: Lancaster Castle (400 yards from ground).
Directions: From South: M6 Junction 33. Follow into city, turn left at Waterstones Bookshop by traffic lights, following signs to railway station. Take second right and follow road down hill, ground on the right-hand side. From North: M6 Junction 34. Follow signs to railway station.

MOSSLEY

Ground: Seel Park, Market Street, Mossley, nr Ashton-under-Lyne, Lancs
Phone: 0457-832369   **Nickname:** Lilywhites   **Founded:** 1909
Manager: Steve Taylor **Secretary:** Les Fitton **Chairman:** Roger Finn
Colours: White, Black, Black   **Change:** Yellow and Red, Red, Red
Capacity: 3,000 (250)   **Record:** 7,000 v Stalybridge, Ches. Lg 1950
Rail: Mossley (½ mile from ground).
Directions: From M62: Oldham, Lees, Grotton Mossley. From M1 or Sheffield to Stalybridge, Mossley. From Manchester or Stockport to Ashton-under-Lyne, Mossley.

NETHERFIELD

Ground: Parkside Road, Kendal, Cumbria
Phone: 0539-722469   **Nickname:**   **Founded:** 1920
Manager: Tony Hesketh **Secretary:**   **Chairman:** David Willan
Colours: Black and White Stripes, Black, Red
Change: Yellow and Green, Green, Yellow and Green
Capacity: 6,000 (300)   **Record:** 5,184 v Grimsby, FAC1 11/55
Rail: Oxenholme (½ mile from ground).
Directions: M1 Junction 36. Follow Skipton sign for 200 yards, left at roundabout straight into Kendal, opposite K Shoes into Parkside Road, 400 yards on right.

RADCLIFFE BOROUGH

Ground: Stainton Park, Pilkington Road, Radcliffe, Manchester, M26 0PE
Phone: 061-725-9197   **Nickname:** Boro   **Founded:** 1949
Manager: Ken Bridge **Secretary:** Graham Fielding **Chairman:** Ian Wood
Colours: All Blue   **Change:** All Red
Capacity: 2,500 (270)   **Record:** 1,365 v Caernarfon, Bass Lg Div 2 1983
Rail: Radcliffe (½ mile from ground).
Directions: M62 Junction 17. Follow signs for Whitefield and Bury. Follow A665 to Radcliffe, through town centre to Bolton Road, turn right into Unsworth Street, ground on left, Colshaw Close.

SPENNYMOOR UNITED

Ground: Brewery Field, Durham Road, Spennymoor, Co. Durham.
Phone: 0388-811934   **Nickname:** The Moors   **Founded:** 1901
Manager: Matt Pearson **Secretary:** Jim Nutt **Chairman:** Barry Hindmarch
Colours: Black & White stripes, Black, Black

Capacity: 7,500 (300)   **Record:** 7,202 v Bishop Auckland, 1957
Rail: Durham (6 miles)
Directions: A167. At Thinford take A688. At roundabout, 3rd exit. Left at Church. Continue past Salvin Arms PH. Ground on left.

WARRINGTON TOWN

Ground: Common Lane, Latchford, Warrington, WA4 2RS
Phone: 0925-31932   **Nickname:** The Wires   **Founded:** 1961
Manager: Derek Brownbill **Secretary:** Graham Ost **Chairman:** Bob Smith
Colours: Yellow, Blue, Yellow   **Change:** Red and White
Capacity: 3,500 (200)   **Record:** 2,120 v Halesowen, FAVsf1 3/86
Rail: Bank Quay (2 miles from ground).
Directions: From town centre (Bridge Foot) via A49 South to Loushers Lane (1 mile) turn left at lights. From M6 via A50 to Latchford Swing Bridge, turn left into Station Road, ground ½ mile.

WHITBY TOWN

Ground: Turnbull Ground, Upgang Lane, Whitby.
Phone: 0947-604847   **Nickname:** Town   **Founded:** 1896
Manager: Bob Scaife Jnr **Secretary:** Charles Woodward
Chairman: Bob Scaife Snr
Colours: Royal Blue with White sleeves, Royal Blue, Royal Blue
Change: All White
Capacity: 4,000 (200)   **Record:** 5,000
Rail: Whitby (1 mile)
Directions: Ground on A174. Follow signs for West Cliff when entering Whitby.

WORKINGTON

Ground: Borough Park, Workington, Cumbria, CA14 2DT
Phone: 0900-602871   **Nickname:** Reds   **Founded:** 1884
Manager: Alan Cook **Secretary:** Tom Robson **Chairman:** Jackie Donald
Colours: Red, White, Red   **Change:** Sky Blue, Navy, Sky Blue
Capacity: 5,000 (200)   **Record:** 21,000 v Man. Utd, FAC3 1958
Rail: Workington (400 yards from ground).
Directions: From Penrith A66 to town, down hill to T-Junction – right. Approx ½ mile under bridge, first right – ground 200 yards on left.

WORKSOP TOWN

Ground: The Northolme, Gainsborough, Lincs
Phone: 0427-613295 **Nickname:** The Tigers **Founded:** 1861
Manager: Tommy Spencer **Secretary:** Wally Peace **Chairman:** Mel Bradley
Colours: Amber and Black stripes, Black, Black **Change:** Blue and White
Capacity: not known **Record:** 8,171 v Chesterfield, FAC 1925
Rail: Worksop.
Directions: The ground is situated near town centre, 250 yards from the General Post Office and Magistrates' Court. Car park opposite ground.

OFFICIAL FEEDER LEAGUES – DIADORA LEAGUE

The Isthmian League Division Two was expanded and regionalised into a North and South Division for the start of the 1984-85 season. For the 1991-92 season the division was altered again to create, without regionalisation, a Second and Third Division. Since 1985 clubs have joined the League from lower feeder leagues. Details of these, and their source leagues are listed below.

Season	Club(s) Joining	Division	Source and Position	
1986-87	Chertsey Town	South	Combined Counties	2nd
	Collier Row	North	London Spartan	1st
	Wivenhoe Town	North	Essex Senior	1st
1987-88	Southwick	South	Combined Counties	2nd
	Vauxhall Motors	North	South Midland	2nd
1988-89	Witham Town	North	Essex Senior	2nd
	Yeading	South	Greene King Spartan	1st
1989-90	Purfleet	North	Essex Senior	1st
1990-91	Abingdon Town	South	Greene King Spartan	1st
	Malden Vale	South	Dan Air	2nd
1991-92	Cove	South	Dan Air	3rd
	Edgware Town	North	Greene King Spartan	1st
19992-93	Aldershot Town	Div 3	Football League †	
	East Thurrock Utd	Div 3	Essex Senior	3rd
	Farnham Town	Div 3	Dan Air League	1st
	Leighton Town	Div 3	South Midlands	1st
	Northwood	Div 3	Spartan	1st
1993-94	Cheshunt	Div 3	Spartan	3rd
	Harlow Town	Div 3	Resigned from Div One	
	Oxford City	Div 3	South Midlands	1st

† *Reformed from Aldershot FC who resigned from the Football League during the 1991-92 season.*

Parasol Combined Counties League

The Surrey Senior League was formed in 1922 by 11 clubs. It became the Home Counties League in 1978 and the Combined Counties League in 1979.

	P	W	D	L	F	A	Pts
+ Peppard	36	27	3	6	111	39	85
Chipstead	36	19	10	7	78	47	67
Ashford Town (Middx)	36	18	13	5	67	36	67
Merstham	36	16	11	9	67	66	59
Viking Sports	36	15	10	11	67	56	55
Ash United	36	15	10	11	49	48	55
Sandhurst Town	36	14	11	11	48	52	53
Hartley Wintney	36	14	10	12	60	47	52
* Goldalming & G	36	14	8	14	51	61	49
Cranleigh	36	12	11	13	66	59	47
Steyning Town	36	12	8	16	55	69	44
Bedfont	36	10	13	13	51	46	43
+ DCA Basingstoke	38	11	8	17	50	67	42
* Horley Town	36	10	12	14	60	73	41
Frimley Green	36	11	7	18	43	55	40
Farleigh Rovers	36	11	5	20	46	65	38
Cobham	36	9	10	17	54	78	37
Ditton	36	9	9	18	48	71	36
Westfield	36	6	9	21	32	68	27

+ *One point added,* * *One point deducted*

5-Year One, Two, Three Records

Year	1st	Pts	2nd	Pts	3rd	Pts
1987-88	BAe Weybridge	72	Merstham	69	Farnham Town	69
1988-89	BAe Weybridge	77	Malden Vale	70	Merstham	66
1989-90	Chipstead	79	Merstham	78	Cove	67
1990-91	Farnham Town	76	Chipstead	74	Malden Town	72
1991-92	Farnham Town	85	Malden Town	70	Chipstead	64

Essex Senior League

Formed by nine clubs in 1971, the inclusion of a reserve team inhibited its full participation in the Pyramid. Now, however, it is a feeder to the Isthmian arm of the Pyramid.

	P	W	D	L	F	A	Pts
Canvey Island	32	23	7	2	66	20	76
Sawbridgeworth Town	32	19	7	6	82	41	64
Bowers United	32	18	9	5	56	27	63

Burnham Ramblers	32	17	6	9	80	53	57
Basildon United	32	16	7	9	65	37	55
Brentwood	32	13	9	10	58	49	48
Gt Wakering Rovers	32	13	8	11	50	43	47
* Ford United	32	14	10	8	47	26	46
Romford	32	12	9	11	48	42	45
Southend Manor	32	13	4	15	40	45	43
Concord Rangers	32	9	9	14	41	51	36
Maldon Town	32	8	10	14	45	59	34
East Ham United	32	10	4	18	46	67	34
Woodford Town	32	7	9	16	46	84	30
Eton Manor	32	7	8	17	32	75	29
Hullbridge Spartans	32	7	6	19	38	70	27
Stansted	32	2	6	24	27	87	12

* Six points deducted

5-Year, One, Two, Three

Year	1st	Pts	2nd	Pts	3rd	Pts
1986-87	Canvey Island	70	Witham Town	63	Purfleet	61
1987-88	Purfleet	73	Brentwood	71	Halstead Town	63
1988-89	Brightlingsea	68	East Thurrock U	65	Ford United	61
1989-90	Brightlingsea	68	Woodford Town	64	East Thurrock U	56
1990-91	Southend Manor	64	Brentwood	60	Burnham Rams	59
1991-92	Ford United	66	Brentwood	66	East Thurrock U	66

Spartan League

Formed in 1975 as the London Spartan League on the amalgamation of the Spartan League (1907) and the Metropolitan London League (itself a result of an amalgamation of leagues in 1971). The league originally comprised Divisions One and Two but in 1977 changed to a Premier Division and a Senior Division. Was known as the Greene King Spartan League for the period 1987-91.

Premier Division	P	W	D	L	F	A	Pts
Brimsdown Rovers	42	31	4	7	99	27	97
Corinthian Casuals	42	29	5	8	98	31	92
Cheshunt	42	27	8	7	92	29	89
Willesden	42	27	8	7	102	50	89
Hanwell Town	42	27	7	8	100	50	88
St Margotsbury	42	25	5	12	93	64	80
Walthamstow Penn	42	21	10	11	72	44	73
Cockfosters	42	21	6	15	84	65	69
St Andrews	42	15	12	15	70	85	57

Tower Hamlets	42	17	4	21	83	83	55
Croydon Athletic	42	13	15	14	72	59	54
Waltham Abbey	42	13	13	16	65	71	52
Beaconsfield United	42	14	9	19	68	85	51
Brook House	42	14	6	22	72	99	48
Haringey Borough	42	11	12	19	59	80	45
Barkingside	42	9	13	20	52	80	40
Hillingdon Borough	42	10	10	22	59	99	40
Eltham Town	42	11	6	25	50	95	39
North Greenford United	42	11	5	26	53	100	38
Amersham Town	42	8	11	23	49	93	35
Beckton United	42	9	5	28	68	117	32
Southgate Athletic	42	6	12	24	48	103	30

Division One	P	W	D	L	F	A	Pts
Metrogas	28	24	2	2	94	31	74
Craven	28	20	2	6	120	45	62
Clapton Villa	28	18	5	5	93	41	59
Old Roan	28	17	3	8	81	48	54
Leyton County	28	16	6	6	67	41	54
Lewisham Elms	28	16	4	8	89	46	52
Walthamstow Trojans	28	12	4	12	63	48	40
AFC Eltham	28	12	4	12	70	59	40
Cray Valley	28	11	6	11	50	46	39
Met Police Chigwell	28	10	3	15	66	67	33
Woolwich Town	28	7	7	14	58	71	28
Chingford Town	28	8	2	18	38	79	26
Catford Wanderers	28	5	6	17	41	60	21
South East Olympic	28	5	3	20	60	99	18
Swanley Town	28	0	1	27	15	224	1

5-Year, One, Two, Three

Year	1st	Pts	2nd	Pts	3rd	Pts
Premier Division						
1987-88	Edgware Town	68	Southgate Ath	66	Southwark Spts	58
1988-89	Abingdon Town	84	Wandsworth N	84	Northwood	79
1989-90	Edgware Town	86	Northwood	84	Southgate Ath	70
1990-91	Walthamstow P	81	Barkingside	80	Northwood	78
1991-92	Northwood	82	Brimsdown Rvrs	76	Haringey B	71
Division One						
1987-88	Catford Wands	53	Hackney D. Ath	50	Thamesmead T	48
1988-89	Newmont Travel	74	Metrogas	63	Catford Wands	62

1989-90	KPG Tipples	66	Royal George	64	Newmont Travel	60
1990-91	Sangley Sports	69	AFC Millwall	58	Royal George	57
1991-92	Willesden Hk	63	Tower Hamlets	60	Elms	60

Minerva South Midlands League

Formed by eight clubs in 1922 as the Bedfordshire County League. It later became the Bedfordshire & District League and, in 1929, the South Midlands League. A second division was added in 1925. The League was reconstituted into three divisions (Premier, One and Two) in 1948 but in 1955 Division Two was discontinued. Former sponsors were Benskins, Key Consultants and Campri.

Premier Division	P	W	D	L	F	A	Pts
Oxford City	42	32	4	4	141	44	106
Brache Sparta	42	29	7	6	97	41	94
Arlesey Town	42	26	9	7	99	40	87
Wingate & Finchley	42	23	11	8	84	54	80
Hatfield Town	42	21	11	10	114	71	74
Hoddesdon Town	42	21	11	10	80	48	71
Biggleswade Town	42	19	9	14	86	58	66
Shillington	42	19	9	14	63	58	66
Leverstock Green	42	19	7	16	62	62	64
Harpenden Town	42	18	9	15	67	47	63
Letchworth Garden City	42	18	8	16	79	63	62
Milton Keynes Borough	42	18	8	16	77	65	61
Potters Bar Town	42	17	9	16	81	82	60
Langford	42	14	13	15	75	63	55
Totternhoe	42	13	13	16	56	67	52
Luton Old Boys	42	15	7	20	57	75	49
Buckingham	42	11	8	23	73	103	41
Pitstone & Ivinghoe	42	11	5	26	50	99	38
Welwyn Garden City	42	9	10	23	47	88	37
The 61 FC	42	9	5	28	54	120	32
Pirton	42	4	8	30	32	115	20
New Bradwell	42	0	7	35	20	131	7

First Division	P	W	D	L	F	A	Pts
Bedford Town	42	36	4	2	163	40	112
London Colney	42	32	3	7	127	36	99
Bedford United	42	26	7	9	114	64	85
Risborough Rangers	42	25	9	8	86	55	84
Shenley & Loughton	42	24	10	8	98	56	82
Toddington Rovers	42	24	8	10	102	56	80

Winslow United 42	21	8	13	117	62	71
P B Crusaders................42	23	2	17	106	87	71
Caddington....................42	22	3	17	88	78	69
Tring Athletic.................42	18	12	12	83	72	66
Shefford Town................42	18	9	15	76	51	60
Ashcroft.........................42	17	9	16	80	79	60
Ampthill Town................42	17	7	18	76	74	58
Stoney Stratford.............42	16	4	22	85	97	52
Delco..............................42	12	5	25	63	103	41
Sandy Albion.................42	10	10	22	62	108	40
Cranfield United 42	9	11	22	59	94	38
Emberton........................42	8	8	26	51	117	32
Flamstead.......................42	7	10	25	57	124	31
De Havilland..................42	7	10	25	55	111	28
Walden Rangers.............42	7	4	31	44	129	25
Ickleford........................42	4	5	33	46	145	17

5-Year, One, Two, Three
Premier Division

Year	1st............................Pts	2nd............................Pts	3rd............................Pts
1987-88	Shillington........70	Selby....................69	Langford............66
1988-89	Langford............82	Thame United.......75	Selby....................66
1989-90	Pitstone & Iv........74	Thame United.......68	Leighton Town.....66
1990-91	Thame United....80	Wolverton AFC....80	Biggleswade Tn...75
1991-92	Leighton Town....95	Milton Keynes B..93	Biggleswade Tn...84

First Division

1987-88	Pitstone & Iv.........59	Brache Sparta........44	Caddington............43
1988-89	Welwyn G. City ...50	Buckingham A. 50	Caddington............42
1989-90	Harpenden Town..70	Wingate.................66	Caddington............59
1990-91	Buckingham A. 82	Shenley & L...........78	Oxford City...........69
1991-92	Ashcroft................95	Luton OB 91	Bedford United.....89

ADDITIONAL REGIONAL LEAGUES

Charrington Chiltonian League

Premier Division	P	W	D	L	F	A	Pts
Eton Wick 24	19	1	4	66	22	58
Finchampstead 24	16	4	4	56	32	52
Slough YCOB.................24	16	1	7	56	30	49
Reading Town................24	11	5	8	38	23	38
Holmer Green................24	11	3	10	45	47	36

Wraysbury Coopers	24	10	4	10	38	35	34
Binfield	24	8	9	7	37	32	33
Martin Baker Sports	24	9	5	10	37	42	32
Stocklake	24	8	5	11	40	49	29
Letcombe	24	6	5	13	30	41	23
Brill United	24	7	2	15	40	58	23
Penn & Tylers Green	24	5	6	13	28	56	21
Prestwood	24	5	0	19	24	68	15

Division One	P	W	D	L	F	A	Pts
Broadmoor Staff	24	17	3	4	69	36	54
Wooburn Athletic	24	15	6	3	69	29	51
Mill End Sports	24	13	3	8	58	33	42
Henley Town	24	12	5	7	59	40	41
Drayton Wanderers	24	11	7	6	47	33	40
Denham United	24	11	5	8	43	36	38
Kodak Harrow	24	11	5	8	49	43	38
Chinnor	24	9	5	10	48	57	32
Hazells Aylesbury	24	9	3	12	50	55	30
Stokenchurch	24	9	5	11	40	49	29
Chalfont Wasps	24	5	5	14	31	56	20
Iver	24	4	6	14	30	64	18
Wallingford United	24	1	2	21	21	83	5

5-Year, One, Two, Three

Year   1st ....Pts   2nd................Pts   3rd................Pts

Premier Division

1987-88	Finchampstead	77	Coopers Payen	68	Sonnong CP	66
1988-89	Coopers Payen	73	Finchampstead	64	Sonning CP	60
1989-90	Coopers Payen	67	Sonning CP	61	ITS Reading	52
1990-91	Peppard	67	Stocklake	57	Penn & Tylers G.	47
1991-92	Peppard	70	Binfield	60	Holmer Green	52

Division One

1987-88	Henley Town	57	Bromley Park R.	56	Stokenchurch	45
1988-89	Mill End Sports	70	Loudwater	60	Chalfont Wasps	58
1989-90	Binfield	65	Stocklake	59	Kodak Sports	56
1990-91	Letcombe Sports	60	Brill United	56	Kodak (Harrow)	54
1991-92	Eton Wick	56	Molins Sports	53	Slough YCOB	45

Herts Senior County League

Premier Division	P	W	D	L	F	A	Pts
Sun Sports	38	25	8	5	76	35	83
Bovingdon	38	22	12	4	59	23	78
Wormley Rovers	38	20	11	7	83	41	71
Chipperfield Corinth	38	20	11	7	68	49	71
Wellcome	38	29	8	10	71	49	68
Knebworth	38	19	8	11	65	49	65
Sandridge Rovers	38	18	10	10	79	49	64
Park Street	38	16	12	10	55	44	60
Colney Heath	38	17	7	14	67	49	58
Bushey Rangers	38	17	7	14	60	52	58
Elliott Star	38	17	6	15	73	61	57
Bedmond Social	38	15	8	15	74	67	53
Cuffley	38	13	9	16	55	55	48
Kings Langley	38	13	7	18	58	64	46
Lucas Sports	38	9	6	23	46	86	33
Walkern	38	9	6	23	47	89	33
Oxhey Jets	38	8	8	22	44	79	32
BAC Stevenage	38	9	2	27	48	109	29
Kodak Hemel Hempstead	38	7	7	24	37	73	28
Croxley Guild	38	6	7	25	46	88	25

5-Year, One, Two, Three

Year	1st	Pts	2nd	Pts	3rd	Pts
Premier Division						
1987-88	Sandridge Rvrs	55	Kings Langley	54	Sun Sports	53
1988-89	London Colney	71	Bedmond Soc.	64	Park Street	56
1989-90	London Colney	57	Bedmond Soc.	57	Sun Sports	57
1990-91	Mount Grace	62	Leverstock Green	61	Bedmond Social	60
1991-92	Hatfield Town	67	Kings Langley	54	London Colney	50

FCN Music Kent League

Premier Division	P	W	D	L	F	A	Pts
Sevenoaks Town	26	16	6	4	65	37	64
Aylesford PM	26	13	8	5	56	35	47
Knockholt	26	13	6	7	57	37	45
Scott Sports	26	13	4	9	50	44	43
Oakwood	26	9	11	6	47	42	38
Stansfield O&B	26	8	12	6	45	40	36
Teynham & Lynsted	26	8	11	7	49	49	37

Lordswood	26	7	11	8	38	38	32
Otford United	26	8	7	11	48	53	31
New Romney	26	9	4	13	31	42	31
Thames Polytechnic	26	8	6	12	51	63	30
Greenways	26	7	6	13	48	57	27
VCD Athletic	26	6	6	14	43	53	24
Woodnesborough	26	6	4	16	34	72	22

Surrey County League

	P	W	D	L	F	A	Pts
Virginia Water	30	20	7	3	66	27	67
Raynes Park	30	20	6	4	64	27	66
Chobham	30	17	8	5	65	42	59
Hersham RBL	30	18	4	8	73	54	58
Frinton Rovers	30	14	6	10	67	47	48
Netherne	30	14	6	10	73	59	48
Surbiton Town	30	13	9	8	55	43	48
Burpham	30	13	8	9	64	47	47
Croydon MO	30	12	4	14	52	64	40
Ottershaw	30	10	4	16	35	62	34
Vandyke	30	9	6	15	54	58	33
Walton Casuals	30	10	3	17	48	74	33
Springfield BI	30	6	13	11	51	53	31
British Telecom	30	6	7	17	34	61	25
Sheerwater	30	3	7	20	36	74	16
Ashtead	30	4	4	22	43	88	16

5-Year, One, Two, Three

Year	1st	Pts	2nd	Pts	3rd	Pts
1986-87	Bedfont	68	Frinton Rovers	65	Ditton F&SC	51
1987-88	Frinton Rovers	70	Ditton F&SC	60	British Telecom	50
1988-89	Ditton F&SC	47	Frinton Rovers	45	Springfield Hosp	44
1989-90	Frinton Rovers	51	Ashford Town	42	Springfield Hosp	42
1990-91	Ditton F & SC	52	Frinton Rovers	50	Surbiton Town	45
1991-92	At. Andrews	57	Chobham	55	Netherne	53

OFFICIAL FEEDER LEAGUES – BEAZER HOMES LEAGUE

The regionalised competition was reorganised for season 1982-83 with the return of the Premier Division and the establishment of a Division One (South) and a Division One (Midland). These leagues are generally referred to as the Southern and Midland Divisions. Several clubs have moved 'sideways' to and from the other arms of the Pyramid but the following clubs have joined from the Southern League's own 'feeders'.

Season	Club(s) Joining	Division	Source and Position	
1983-84	Bridgnorth Town	Midland	Midland Combination	1st
	Chatham Town	Southern	Kent	7th
	Coventry Sport	Midland	W. Midlands (Regional)	16th
	Moor Green	Midland	Midland Combination	2nd
	Rushden Town	Midland	United Counties	2nd
	VS Rugby	Midland	W. Midlands (Regional)	7th
1984-85	Hednesford Town	Midland	W. Midlands (Regional)	2nd
	Sheppey United	Southern	Kent	2nd
1985-86	Bilston	Midland	W. Midlands (Regional)	2nd
	Hastings Town	Southern	Sussex County	9th
	Mile Oak Rovers	Midland	Midland Combination	1st
	Ruislip	Southern	Middlesex County	11th
	Burnham & Hil.	Southern	Green King Spartan (as Burnham)	1st
1986-87	Buckingham Town	Midland	United Counties	1st
	Halesowen Town	Midland	W. Midlands (Regional)	1st
1987-88	Atherstone Utd	Midland	W. Midlands (Regional)	1st
	Baldock Town	Southern	United Counties	1st
	Bury Town	Southern	Jewson Eastern	3rd
	Paget Rovers	Midland	Midland Combination	3rd
1988-89	Ashtree Highfield	Midland	Midland Combination	3rd
	Spalding United	Midland	United Counties	1st
1989-90	Bashley	Southern	Wessex	1st
	Hythe Town	Southern	Kent	1st
	RC Warwick	Midland	Midland Combination	2nd
	Yate Town	Midland	Hellenic League	1st
1990-91	Hinckley Town	Midland	W. Midlands (Regional)	1st
	Newport IOW	Southern	Wessex	2nd
	Newport AFC	Midland	Hellenic	1st
	Sudbury Town	Southern	Jewson Eastern	1st

1991-92	Braintree Town	Eastern Counties	1st
	Havant Town	Wessex League	1st
	Sittingbourne Town	Kent League	1st
	Solihull Borough	Midland Combination	1st
1992-93	Evesham United	Midland Combination	1st
	Gresley Rovers	West Midlands (Regional)	1st
	Weston-super-Mare	Western League	1st
1993-94	Armitage '90	West Midlands	1st
	Tonbridge AFC	Winstonlead Kent	1st
	Clevedon Town	Great Mills	1st

Boddingtons West Midlands League

This League is a successor to the Birmingham and District League which was formed in 1889. It adopted the name of the West Midlands (Regional) League in 1962. In 1965 a second division was formed (Premier and First) and another division, Division Two, was added in 1977. Banks's Brewery were recent sponsors.

Premier Division	P	W	D	L	F	A	Pts
Oldbury United	36	24	8	4	80	39	80
Chasetown	36	23	11	2	66	28	80
Paget Rangers	36	21	7	8	84	54	70
Rocester	36	20	9	7	71	41	69
Stourport Swifts	36	19	9	8	69	38	66
Ilkeston Town	36	19	8	9	73	38	66
Rushall Olympic	36	17	7	12	61	53	58
Wednesfield	36	14	10	12	58	47	52
Alvechurch	36	14	5	17	58	65	47
West Bromwich Town	36	13	6	17	55	86	45
Pelsall Villa	36	10	12	14	60	54	12
Blakenall	36	9	13	14	57	75	40
Willenhall	36	12	4	20	49	69	40
Hinckley Athletic	36	11	6	19	56	68	39
Halesowen Harriers	36	8	9	19	44	62	33
Cradley Town	36	9	6	21	42	71	33
Oldswinford	36	9	6	21	39	80	33
Westfields	36	8	6	21	47	72	29
Lye Town	36	7	8	21	47	72	29

Division One	P	W	D	L	F	A	Pts
Knypersley Victoria	36	26	3	7	105	34	81
Darlaston	36	25	6	5	69	27	81
Lichfield	36	23	6	7	75	42	75
Ettingshall	36	20	11	5	69	34	71
Gornal Athletic	36	17	8	11	75	52	59
Cannock Chase	36	16	4	16	50	59	52
Wolverhampton United	36	14	7	15	60	69	49
Great Wyrely	36	12	12	12	44	53	48
Tividale	36	14	5	17	76	67	47
Hill Top Rangers	36	13	8	15	58	62	47
Donnington Wood	36	12	11	13	647	77	47
Malvern Town	36	12	10	14	56	71	46
Oldbury United Reserves	36	10	13	13	52	67	43
Moxley Rangers	36	11	11	14	48	53	41
Ludlow Town	36	10	9	17	55	78	39
Wolverhampton Casuals	36	11	5	20	57	72	38
Tipton Town	36	9	11	16	42	63	38
Gornal Spots	36	7	6	23	42	75	27
Wem Town	36	4	6	26	39	84	18

Division Two	P	W	D	L	F	A	Pts
Rushall Olympic Reserves	32	23	4	5	87	42	73
Bloxwich Strollers	32	23	2	7	99	39	71
Chasetown Reserves	32	21	5	6	81	28	68
Rocester Reserves	32	20	6	6	104	49	66
Manders	32	20	5	7	83	40	65
Blackheath Motors	32	17	5	10	69	56	56
Mitchells & Butlers	32	14	9	9	70	53	51
Hinckley Athletic	32	14	9	9	57	48	51
Lye Town Reserves	32	14	5	13	61	71	47
Albright & Wilson	32	13	5	14	53	62	44
Oldswinford Reserves	32	10	4	18	40	67	34
Halesowen Harriers Res	32	9	6	17	49	86	32
Cradley Reserves	32	8	4	20	38	68	28
Wolves Casuals Reserves	32	7	5	20	44	87	26
Park Rangers	32	6	5	21	34	80	23
Cheslyn Hay	32	4	6	22	44	87	18
Tividale Reserves	32	5	3	24	38	88	18

5-Year, One, Two, Three

Year	1st	Pts	2nd	Pts	3rd	Pts

Premier Division
1987-88	Tamworth	57	Oldbury United	56	Lye Town	52
1988-89	Blakenhall	86	Gresley Rovers	85	Halesowen Har.	78
1989-90	Hinckley Town	82	Rochester	82	Gresley Rovers	80
1990-91	Gresley Rovers	101	Chasetown	85	Oldbury United	83
1991-92	Gresley Rovers	79	Paget Rangers	65	Stourport Swifts	64

Division One
1987-88	Rochester	62	Stourport Swifts	51	Millfields	51
1988-89	Newport Town	78	Donnington	72	Ettingshall HT	69
1989-90	Darlaston	73	Springvale-T.	63	Pelsall Villa	63
1990-91	Cradley Town	66	Ludlow Town	57	Cannock Chase	52
1991-92	Ilkeston Town	99	Darlaston	77	Donnington Wd	75

Great Mills League

Formed by nine clubs in 1892, with a second division added in 1894. Many Southern League clubs, including some from London, participated in early competition, most games being played midweek. Division Two was disbanded in 1909 but the League emerged from the First War again with two divisions. Division Two was disbanded between 1922 and 1925 and again in 1960. In 1976 Division One was added with the top section becoming the Premier Division.

Premier Division	P	W	D	L	F	A	Pts
Clevedon Town	38	34	4	0	137	23	106
Tiverton Town	38	28	8	2	134	30	92
Saltash United	38	22	8	8	98	51	74
Taunton Town	38	22	8	8	62	37	74
Mangotsfield	38	20	8	10	89	47	68
Torrington	38	17	10	11	69	44	61
Westbury United	38	18	7	13	50	45	61
Paulton Rovers	38	15	10	13	76	51	55
Torquay United	38	16	7	15	58	62	55
Plymouth Argyle Reserves	38	15	9	14	72	64	54
Exmouth Town	38	14	9	15	47	59	51
Elmore	38	14	5	19	54	71	47
Bristol Manor Farm	38	10	13	15	49	59	43
Bideford	38	11	8	19	59	66	41
Frome Town	38	9	12	17	57	75	39
Chippenham Town	38	8	14	16	65	86	38

Minehead	38	10	8	20	59	88	38
Liskeard Athletic	38	8	9	21	61	87	33
Chard Town	38	6	3	29	37	119	21
Dawlish Town	38	2	2	34	17	186	8

First Division

	P	W	D	L	F	A	Pts
Odd Down	40	27	10	3	87	26	91
Calne Town	40	23	12	5	97	47	81
Crediton Utd	40	23	11	6	79	43	80
Brislington	40	22	8	10	77	41	74
Warminster Topwn	40	22	7	11	70	50	73
Clyst Rovers	40	18	13	9	75	48	67
Keynsham Town	40	19	10	11	66	50	67
Backwell United	40	16	14	10	68	52	62
Barnstaple Town	40	15	10	15	62	58	55
Bridport	40	14	13	13	67	66	55
Heavitree United	40	14	9	17	64	69	51
Devizes Town	40	15	6	19	61	84	51
Bishop Sutton	40	14	8	18	55	55	50
Welton Rovers	40	12	11	17	69	65	47
Wellington	40	11	14	15	53	65	47
Glastonbury	40	13	5	22	52	70	44
Larkhall Athletic	40	11	5	24	59	81	38
Ilfracombe Town	40	8	9	23	47	94	33
Ottery St Mary	40	9	5	26	53	116	32
Radstock Town	40	7	10	23	38	60	31
Melksham Town	40	6	12	22	39	98	30

5-Year, One, Two, Three

Year	1st	Pts	2nd	Pts	3rd	Pts

Premier Division

Year	1st		2nd		3rd	
1987-88	Liskeard Athletic	68	Saltash United	60	Mangotsfield Utd	60
1988-89	Saltash United	62	Exmouth Town	62	Taunton Town	56
1989-90	Taunton Town	92	Liskeard Athletic	91	Mangotsfield Utd	88
1990-91	Mangotsfield Utd	92	Torrington	82	Plymouth A. Res	79
1991-92	Weston-S-M	98	Clevedon Town	89	Tiverton Town	85

First Division

Year	1st		2nd		3rd	
1987-88	Welton Rovers	54	Chard Town	53	Tiverton Town	49
1988-89	Larkhall Ath	61	Tiverton Town	60	Bridport	55
1989-90	Ottery St Mary	85	Backwell United	73	Ilfracombe Tn	71
1990-91	Minehead	93	Elmore	78	Calne Town	77
1991-92	Westbury Utd	91	Torquay Utd	89	Crediton Utd	72

Spectre Hellenic League

Formed in 1953 by 16 clubs. A second division was added three years later and the divisions became the Premier and First Divisions. Despite being a feeder to the Beazer Homes League, few teams have moved up. Former sponsors have been Halls Brewery and Federated Homes.

Premier Division	P	W	D	L	F	A	Pts
Wollen Sports	34	25	4	5	75	31	79
*Moreton Town	34	22	4	8	79	43	70
Milton United	34	21	7	6	67	33	70
Cirencester Town	34	20	8	6	54	28	68
Cinderford Town	34	15	10	9	64	44	55
Almondsbury Picksons	34	15	7	12	62	50	52
Shortwood United	34	12	10	12	63	58	46
Swindon Supermarine	34	11	13	10	46	43	46
Bicester Town	34	12	9	13	45	45	45
Rayners Lane	34	13	4	17	53	63	43
*Banbury United	34	10	10	14	50	66	40
Fairford Town	34	8	13	13	55	48	37
Headington Amateurs	34	10	6	18	40	67	36
Kintbury Rangers	34	9	8	17	35	51	35
Abingdon United	34	9	7	18	49	67	34
Wantage Town	34	8	8	18	47	70	32
Pegasus Juniors	34	7	9	18	52	78	30
Didcot Town	34	6	9	19	42	94	27

record excludes one game ordered to be replayed

Division One	P	W	D	L	F	A	Pts
Tuffley Rovers	30	25	2	3	90	24	77
North Leigh	30	21	4	5	113	43	67
Wallingford Town	30	17	9	4	84	47	60
Lambourn Sports	30	16	6	8	73	61	54
Purton	30	17	3	10	64	53	54
Kidlington	30	13	9	8	49	41	48
Yarnton	30	12	4	14	48	61	40
Cheltenham Saracens	30	12	2	16	48	47	38
Carterton Town	30	11	4	15	58	63	37
Clanfield	30	9	10	11	47	66	37
Highworth Town	30	9	6	15	48	62	33
Wootton Bassett Town	30	8	6	16	41	53	30
Bishops Cleve	30	9	3	18	44	76	30
Cirencester United	30	8	4	18	41	78	28

Chipping Norton 30	7	5	18	51	82	26
Easington Sports 30	5	5	20	34	76	20

5-Year, One, Two, Three

Year	1st.............Pts	2nd.............Pts	3rd.............Pts
Premier Division			
1987-88	Yate Town 82	Abingdon Town ...74	Shortwood Utd 68
1988-89	Yate Town 83	Sharpness 71	Abingdon Town ...60
1989-90	Newport AFC 75	Shortwood Utd 67	Abingdon Utd.......67
1990-91	Milton United 71	Fairford Town.......71	Bicester Town.......63
1991-92	Shorton Utd..........79	Cirencester Town .78	Almondsbury........64
First Division			
1987-88	Chelt.Town Res....66	Wantage Town 58	Kintbury Rangers .57
1988-89	Almondsbury P.....64	Headington A 62	Lanbourn Sports ...49
1989-90	Carterton Town 76	Milton Utd 66	Chelt. Town Res...59
1990-91	Cinderford Town..75	Cirencester Town .71	Purton 60
1991-92	Wollen Sports.......82	Wantage Town 75	Tuffley Rovers......68

Hereward Sports United Counties League

Formed in 1895 as the Northamptonshire League with a second division added in 1896 although it has not always operated. The competition became the United Counties League in 1934. In 1968 a third division was added and in 1972 the divisions became the Premier, First and Second. In 1980 Division Two became the Reserve Division. Former sponsors are Nene Group. Hereward Sports have been sponsors since 1990.

Premier Division	P	W	D	L	F	A	Pts
Rothwell Town 42	30	8	4	97	28	98
Northampton Spencer 42	29	6	7	96	37	93
Raunds Town 42	28	6	8	93	41	90
Potton United 42	26	7	9	107	56	85
Daventry Town 42	24	7	11	91	60	79
Cogenhoe 42	23	9	10	101	56	78
S & L Corby.......................42	24	6	12	97	62	78
Bourne Town 42	22	6	14	94	59	72
Eynesbury Rovers 42	22	6	14	92	71	72
Long Buckby 42	19	6	17	91	65	63
Boston 42	17	7	18	80	74	58
Stamford.............................42	18	3	21	81	76	57
Spalding United 42	17	4	21	66	70	55
Newport Pagnell 42	15	9	18	65	79	54
Kempston Rovers................42	14	11	17	60	60	53

Mirrlees Blackstone	42	14	8	20	69	82	50
Stotfold	42	15	3	24	90	82	48
Wootton	42	11	10	21	51	76	43
Holbeach United	42	12	3	27	59	91	39
Desborough Town	42	5	10	27	61	127	25
Wellingborough Town	42	4	8	30	44	143	20
Brackley Town	42	0	3	39	20	210	3

Division One	P	W	D	L	F	A	Pts
Ford Sports	34	37	3	4	134	48	84
Higham Town	34	22	9	3	97	28	75
Bugbrooke	34	21	4	9	78	43	67
Ramsey Town	34	18	10	6	76	49	64
Whitworths	34	14	8	12	68	49	50
Burton Park Woods	34	13	11	10	60	52	50
St Ives Town	34	13	9	12	72	52	48
Cottingham	34	13	9	12	70	64	48
Olney Town	34	12	11	11	61	38	47
Thrapston	34	12	9	13	61	70	45
Peterborough City	34	13	5	16	70	78	44
Harrowby United	34	11	10	13	57	60	43
ON Chenecks	34	10	11	13	69	61	41
Blisworth	34	11	7	16	51	67	40
Sharnbrook	34	11	6	17	64	74	39
British Timken	34	9	6	16	68	100	36
Irchester United	34	6	6	22	58	95	24
Towcester Town	34	1	1	31	18	204	4

5-Year, One, Two, Three

Year	1st	Pts	2nd	Pts	3rd	Pts

Premier Division

1987-88	Spalding United	90	Rothwell Town	76	Raunds Town	71
1988-89	Potton United	78	Brackley Town	68	Holbeach Utd	64
1989-90	Holbeach Utd	92	Rothwell Town	89	Raunds Town	70
1990-91	Bourne Town	93	Rothwell Town	85	Eynesbury Rvrs	81
1991-92	Northampton S	101	Raunds Town	95	Rothwell Town	93

First Division

1987-88	British TD	91	M. Blackstone	84	Blisworth	83
1988-89	Ramsey Town	88	Burton Pk Wds	76	Sharnbrook	75
1989-90	Daventry Town	81	Higham Town	80	Ramsey Town	72
1990-91	Bourne Town	93	Rothwell Town	85	Eynesbury Rvrs	81
1991-92	Harrowby Utd	80	Newport Pagnell	80	Ramsey Town	75

Jewson (Eastern) League

This League was formed in 1935 with 12 clubs. Membership was increased to 16 clubs in 1948, and for several seasons Football League 'A' teams and some reserve sides took part. A second division was added in 1988. The League is in the Beazer Homes League arm of the Pyramid.

Other sponsors of this League have been Magnet & Planet; Town & Country; and Building Scene. Jewson has been the sponsor since 1988.

Premier Division	P	W	D	L	F	A	Pts
Wroxham	42	32	4	6	106	36	100
Wisbech Town	42	28	6	8	109	48	90
Newmarket Town	42	27	9	6	87	37	90
Cornard United	42	32	9	11	99	68	75
Diss Town	42	24	2	16	65	52	74
Harwich & Parkeston	42	20	10	12	75	51	70
Fakenham Town	42	19	10	13	68	50	67
Norwich United	42	16	14	12	66	57	62
Felixstowe Town	42	15	12	15	66	62	57
Gorleston	42	16	9	17	64	89	57
Gt Yarmouth Town	42	16	8	18	41	62	56
Tiptree United	42	15	8	19	64	76	53
Stowmarket Town	42	14	9	19	54	59	51
Haverhill Rovers	42	14	8	20	65	80	50
Halstead Town	42	14	8	20	60	83	50
Chatteris United	42	15	4	23	64	73	49
Lowestoft Town	42	12	12	18	55	56	48
March Town United	42	13	9	20	56	67	48
Watton United	42	12	8	22	51	84	44
*Histon	42	10	13	19	60	90	42
Brantham Athletic	42	8	12	22	47	73	36
Brightlingsea United	42	2	12	28	35	104	18

One point deducted

First Division	P	W	D	L	F	A	Pts
Sudbury Wanderers	36	26	5	5	96	37	83
Soham Town Rangers	36	24	4	8	119	45	76
Woodbridge Town	36	24	4	8	82	40	76
Hadleigh United	36	19	9	8	95	59	66
Clacton Town	36	20	6	10	78	53	66
Somersham Town	36	21	3	12	68	52	66
Cambridge City Reserves	36	16	7	13	104	77	55
Ely City	36	14	11	11	59	48	53

Long Sutton Athletic............36	15	8	13	69	75	53
Stanway Rovers 36	15	6	15	73	76	51
Ipswich Wanderers 36	14	6	16	63	72	48
Mildenhall Town..................36	14	5	17	76	98	47
Sudbury Town Reserves 36	13	7	16	70	72	46
Warboys Town.....................36	10	12	14	63	72	38
Kings Lynn Reserves............36	11	5	20	49	63	38
Downham Town...................36	11	4	21	64	84	37
*Swaffham Town..................36	12	4	20	58	97	36
Bury Town Reserves.............36	6	1	29	46	122	19
Thetford Town.....................36	2	3	31	24	114	9

Six points deducted

5-Year, One, Two, Three

Year	1st.......................Pts	2nd.....................Pts	3rd.....................Pts
1987-88	March Town U....67	Braintree Town......64	Sudbury Town......63

Premier Division
1988-89	Sudbury Town......93	Braintree Town......85	Wisbech Town.....84
1989-90	Sudbury Town......88	Thetford Town.....76	Braintree Town.....75
1990-91	Wisbech Town.....91	Braintree Town.....85	Halstead Town......82
1991-92	Wroxham............99	Stowmarket Tn.....87	Cornard United.....80

First Division
1988-89	Wroxham............62	Halstead Town......62	Diss Town............59
1989-90	Cornard United.....71	Norwich United....69	Soham Town R....68
1990-91	Norwich United....84	Brightlingsea Utd.77	Fakenham Town...74
1991-92	Diss Town............90	Fakenham Tn........82	Woodbridge Tn....67

Jewson Wessex League

Formed for season 1984-85 for clubs in the Chiltern and Thames Valley region. A second division was added for season 1985-86.

First Division
	P	W	D	L	F	A	Pts
AFC Lymington...................40	30	7	3	111	27	97
Wimborne Town..................40	30	5	5	101	27	95
Bemerton Heath H'lequins .40	27	7	6	77	33	88
Thatcham Town...................40	24	10	6	104	45	82
Gosport Borough..................40	20	12	8	83	48	72
Ryde Sports........................40	21	4	15	79	61	67
Bournemouth 40	18	11	11	83	58	65
Fleet Town.........................40	17	10	13	79	51	61
Eastleigh............................40	17	9	14	68	54	60

Brockenhurst	40	17	7	16	60	56	58
Horndean	40	15	9	16	63	66	54
Aerostructures	40	13	14	13	55	57	53
Christchurch	40	14	7	19	60	73	49
Swanage & Herston	40	11	11	18	65	78	44
Whitchurch United	40	12	6	22	57	80	42
AFC Totton	40	12	6	22	56	82	42
Portsmouth Royal Navy	40	10	10	20	52	83	40
BAT	40	9	9	22	59	83	36
Sholing Sports	40	7	10	23	46	94	31
East Cowes Vics	40	8	4	28	52	106	28
Romsey Town	40	3	2	35	20	168	11

5-Year, One, Two, Three

Year	1st	Pts	2nd	Pts	3rd	Pts
1987-88	Bashley	84	Havant Town	80	Romsey Town	69
1988-89	Bashley	82	Havant Town	71	Newport IoW	66
1989-90	Romsey Town	81	Newport IoW	79	BAT	70
1990-91	Havant Town	80	Swanage & Her	78	Bournemouth	76
1991-92	Wimborne Town	80	AFC Lymington	74	Thatcham Town	70

Ansells Midlands Combination

Formed in 1927 as the Worcestershire Combination, the League became the Midland Combination in 1968. A second division was added in 1961 and a third in 1979. For season 1983-84 the divisions were renamed Premier, One and Two. Few teams have moved up to the Beazer Homes League.

Premier Division	P	W	D	L	F	A	Pts
Armitage '90	38	26	6	6	91	32	84
Stapenhill	38	25	4	9	105	45	79
Stratford Town	38	21	13	4	70	33	76
Sandwell Borough	38	21	9	8	89	47	72
Pershore Town '88	38	21	8	9	74	38	71
West Midlands Police	38	20	10	8	77	39	70
Coleshill Town	38	21	6	11	63	44	69
Boldmere St Michaels	38	17	12	9	74	48	63
Bolehall Swifts	38	15	10	13	66	56	55
Knowle	38	15	10	13	70	71	55
Barnwell	38	14	12	12	63	70	54
Northfield Town	38	13	12	13	58	59	51
Meir	38	9	12	17	47	60	39

Mile Oak Rovers	38	9	9	20	37	72	36
Studley	38	7	14	17	39	71	35
Chelmsley Wood	38	7	13	18	51	75	34
Highgate United	38	8	10	20	47	80	34
Bloxwich Town	38	5	11	22	28	74	26
Barlestone St Giles	38	5	5	28	40	104	20
Alcester Town	38	3	10	25	30	102	19

Division One

	P	W	D	L	F	A	Pts
Wellesbourne	40	27	8	5	89	41	89
Kings Heath	40	24	7	9	100	44	79
Kenilworth Rovers	40	23	7	10	86	49	76
West Heath United	40	23	4	13	92	64	73
Handraham Timbers	40	19	10	11	66	52	67
Kings Norton	40	20	6	14	71	54	66
Southam United	40	17	13	10	66	45	64
Becketts Sporting	40	17	13	10	69	61	64
Sherwood Celtic	40	19	6	15	76	63	63
WM Fire Service	40	18	7	15	71	58	61
Badsey Rangers	39	16	8	15	64	62	56
Hams Hall	40	15	11	14	68	68	56
Solihull Reserves	40	15	10	15	65	64	55
Marston Green	40	14	8	18	69	75	50
Wilmcote	40	12	10	18	67	85	46
Polesworth N. Warwick	40	12	8	20	68	95	44
Triplex	40	11	10	19	41	57	43
Dudley Sports	40	11	3	26	55	84	36
Wigston Fields	39	9	8	22	57	80	35
Upton Town	40	9	8	23	45	84	35
Ledbury Town '84	40	5	1	34	31	130	16

Division Two

	P	W	D	L	F	A	Pts
Ansell	40	32	4	4	137	41	100
Shirley	40	29	5	6	142	57	92
Colletts G	40	27	5	8	122	52	83
Monica Star	40	26	5	9	104	41	83
Coleshill Town Reserves	40	24	3	13	92	57	75
Fairfield	40	22	8	10	96	60	74
Enville	40	20	9	11	93	67	69
Meir KA Reserves	40	20	9	11	75	57	69
Archdales	40	15	12	13	87	78	57
Holly L	40	16	9	15	90	82	57
Swift P P	40	70	5	18	78	647	56
Pershore	40	15	10	15	76	59	55

Thimblemill	40	60	7	17	86	78	55
Burntwood	40	15	6	19	65	75	51
Kenilworth	40	13	10	17	65	89	49
Studley Reserves	40	12	8	20	67	86	44
Earlswood	40	10	5	25	65	110	35
Wigston Reserves	40	7	6	27	49	119	27
Barlestone	40	6	4	30	42	168	22
Wellsbo Reserves	40	6	2	32	42	133	20
Dudley Sports	40	3	6	31	45	141	15

5-Year, One, Two, Three

Year	1st	Pts	2nd	Pts	3rd	Pts
Premier Division						
1987-88	RC Warwick	56	Boldmere St M.	50	Ashtree High	50
1988-89	Boldmere St M.	55	RC Warwick	52	Evesham United	49
1989-90	Boldmere St M.	81	Northfield Town	74	Evesham United	73
1990-91	W. Mid. Police	80	Solihull Borough	78	Evesham United	74
1991-92	Evesham Utd	91	Armitage 90	88	West Mids Pol.	80
Division One						
1987-88	Chelmsley Town	39	Shirley Town	38	Bloxwich Strol.	32
1988-89	Bloxwich AFC	40	Streetly Celtic	39	West Heath Utd	36
1989-90	Stapenhill Res	66	Kings Norton E	61	Studley BKL	60
1990-91	Alcester Town	64	Wilmcote	60	Pershore Town	57
1991-92	Studley BKL	76	Badsley Rangers	73	Wellesbourne	71

Unijet Sussex County League

Formed in 1920 by 12 clubs. A second division was added in 1952 and a third in 1983. Unijet have been sponsors since 1990.

Division One	P	W	D	L	F	A	Pts
Peacehaven & Telscombe	34	27	6	1	89	23	87
Pagham	34	25	5	4	103	32	80
Wick	34	25	3	6	81	35	78
Langney Sports	34	20	5	9	77	42	65
Whitehawk	34	18	9	7	55	32	63
Newhaven	34	16	5	13	63	51	53
Littlehampton Town	34	15	7	12	64	58	52
Oakwood	34	14	9	11	55	52	51
Three Bridges	34	14	6	14	50	50	48
Hallsham Town	34	13	6	15	64	53	45
Bexhill Town	34	10	6	18	43	61	36

Arundel	34	10	6	18	42	75	36
Portfield	34	8	10	16	39	60	34
Burgess Hill Town	34	7	8	19	39	59	29
Ringmer	34	8	5	21	44	73	29
Chichester City	34	8	5	21	41	85	29
Eastbourne Town	34	8	4	22	35	78	28
Midhurst & Easebourne	34	5	5	24	26	91	20

Division Two

	P	W	D	L	F	A	Pts
Crowboro' Athletic	36	26	6	4	948	34	84
Stamco	36	26	4	6	94	36	82
East Grinstead	36	21	10	5	78	40	73
Lancing	36	18	10	8	73	37	64
Worthing United	36	19	6	11	70	60	63
Horsham YMCA	36	18	8	10	71	46	62
Shoreham	36	16	11	9	74	56	59
Hassocks	36	16	7	13	61	49	55
Mile Oak	36	14	10	12	69	65	52
Southwick	36	14	10	12	59	56	52
Selsey	36	12	3	21	55	65	39
Redhill	36	10	9	17	55	71	39
Little Common Athletic	36	10	8	18	42	77	38
Sidley United	36	9	8	19	57	80	35
Broadbridge Heath	36	9	8	19	43	84	35
Eastbourne United	36	9	6	21	48	76	33
Saltdean United	36	9	6	21	44	76	33
Seaford Town	36	8	5	23	38	79	29
Hayward Heath	36	7	7	22	49	91	28

Division Three

	P	W	D	L	F	A	Pts
Withdean	26	18	5	3	69	21	59
Storrington	26	16	4	6	62	27	52
Bosham	26	15	4	7	52	51	49
Sidlesham	26	12	7	7	51	49	43
Forest	26	11	8	7	51	40	41
Hurstpierpoint	26	9	10	7	45	42	37
Ifield	26	10	7	9	44	43	37
St Francis H	26	9	8	9	42	40	35
Lindfield Rangers	26	9	6	11	38	43	33
Franklands Village	26	7	6	13	22	45	27
Shinewater	26	6	7	13	39	49	25
East Preston	26	6	7	13	34	49	25
Buxted	26	6	6	14	45	66	24
Ferring	26	3	5	18	27	56	14

5-Year, One, Two, Three

Year	1st	Pts	2nd	Pts	3rd	Pts

First Division
1987-88	Pagham	67	Three Bridges	61	Wick	58
1988-89	Pagham	81	Three Bridges	66	Whitehawk	65
1989-90	Wick	79	Littlehampton T	76	Langney Sports	66
1990-91	Littlehampton T	77	Peacehaven & T	77	Langney Sports	74
1991-92	Peacehaven & T	91	Langney Sports	76	Littlehampton T	76

Second Division
1987-88	Langney Sports	66	Bexhill Town	55	Oakwood	52
1988-89	Seaford Town	52	Ringmer	51	Midhurst & E	48
1989-90	Bexhill Town	69	Oakwood	60	Chichester City	57
1990-91	Newhaven	64	Chichester City	62	Horsham YMCA	58
1991-92	Portfield	74	Midhurst & E	66	Stamco	61

Winstonlead Kent League

The Kent League was formed in 1894 with two divisions. The second division later regionalised and the competition was abandoned altogether in 1959. It was reformed in 1968 and a Second Division was added in 1978. Winstonlead have been sponsors since 1985.

Division One	P	W	D	L	F	A	Pts
Tonbridge FC	40	27	9	4	107	39	90
Herne Bay	40	26	6	8	96	44	84
Sheppey United	40	25	9	7	65	29	81
Deal Town	40	24	7	9	128	58	79
Alma Swanley	40	24	4	12	83	65	76
Chatham Town	40	19	11	10	79	52	68
Danson Furness United	40	18	13	9	58	40	67
Thamesmead Town	40	17	9	14	62	56	60
Beckenham Town	40	17	8	15	64	60	59
Whitstable Town	40	18	4	18	77	64	58
Slade Green	40	15	13	12	71	60	58
Ramsgate	40	17	5	18	78	76	56
Folkestone Invicta	40	16	5	19	78	95	53
Tunbridge Wells	40	13	6	21	66	102	45
Faversham Town	40	11	10	19	44	71	43
Greenwich Borough	40	12	5	23	49	75	41
Cray Wanderers	40	10	8	22	64	79	38
Kent Police	40	10	7	23	56	121	37
Darenth Heathside	40	9	7	24	54	104	34
Corinthian	40	6	8	26	50	95	26

OFFICIAL FEEDER LEAGUES – NORTHERN PREMIER LEAGUE

An additional division, the First Division, was added for season 1987-88. In 1988-89 three clubs plus one from a 'feeder' brought the new division up to strength and, thereafter, the two 'feeder' League champions were promoted. The Northern League champions now also gain automatic promotion along with those of the Bass North West Counties League and Northern Counties East League, while for 1992-93 an additional club was promoted in order to retain a full complement of clubs.

Season	Club(s) Joining	Source and Position	
1988-89	Bishop Auckland	Northern	6th
	Colne Dynamoes	North West Counties	1st
	Newtown	Central Wales	1st
	Whitley Bay	Northern	4th
1989-90	Emley	North West Counties	1st
	Rossendale United	Northern Counties East	1st
1990-91	Bridlington Town	Northern Counties East	1st
	Warrington Town	North West Counties	1st
1991-92	Guisley	Northern Counties East	1st
	Knowsley	North West Counties	1st
1992-93	Ashton United	North West Counties	1st
	Gt Harwood Town	North West Counties	2nd
	Gretna	Northern Counties East	1st
	North Shields	Northern League	1st
1993-94	Spennymoor United	Northern Counties East	1st
	Whitby Town*	Northern League	1st
	Bamber Bridge	North West Counties	2nd

* Subject to FA decision.

Bass North West Counties League

Formed in 1982 on the amalgamation of the Cheshire County League and Lancashire Combination clubs not moving into the Northern Premier League. Originally comprising three divisions, the League was reduced to two divisions in 1987.

The champions are normally promoted to the NPL (with a team relegated) while other regional leagues serve the bottom division. Bass have been the sponsors since 1986.

First Division	P	W	D	L	F	A	Pts
Atherton LR	42	33	7	2	75	25	106
Bamber Bridge	42	24	11	7	81	37	83
Chadderton	42	24	11	7	99	64	83
Prescot	42	20	12	10	68	44	72
Newcastle Town	42	20	8	14	70	57	68
Bradford Park Avenue	42	19	8	15	54	43	65
Clitheroe	42	17	8	17	61	40	59
St Helens Town	42	16	11	15	79	62	59
Salford City	42	15	13	14	58	61	58
Burscough	42	16	10	16	58	68	57
Flixton	42	14	15	13	50	42	57
Blackpool Rovers	42	16	9	17	66	64	57
Nantwich Town	42	14	15	13	60	60	57
Penrith	42	15	11	16	62	67	56
Bacup Borough	42	14	13	15	66	59	55
*Glossop North End	42	16	9	17	70	67	54
Darwen	42	14	10	18	54	61	52
Eastwood Hanley	42	14	10	18	45	57	52
Maine Road	42	12	9	21	55	63	45
Kidsgrove Athletic	42	9	8	25	53	94	35
Skelmersdale United	42	7	10	25	45	84	31
Blackpool Mechs	42	2	4	36	27	137	10

* Three points deducted

Second Division	P	W	D	L	F	A	Pts
Maghull	34	21	9	4	77	26	72
Bootle	34	20	8	6	89	49	68
Oldham Town	34	20	6	8	79	47	66
Ellesmere Port	34	16	9	9	65	46	57
Stantondale	34	16	9	9	59	49	57
Castleton Gabriels	34	15	10	9	61	48	55
North Trafford	34	14	9	11	67	63	51

Formby	34	14	9	11	49	49	51
Atherton Colliery	34	14	7	13	63	67	49
Burnley BH	34	14	4	16	87	77	46
* Westhoughton Town	34	14	3	17	65	75	42
* Cheadle Town	34	12	7	15	44	48	40
Squires Gate	34	11	5	18	56	73	38
K Chell	34	10	8	16	52	72	38
Holker Old Boys	34	8	13	13	57	60	37
Ashton Town	34	8	8	18	51	74	32
Nelson	34	7	7	20	47	82	28
Irlam Town	34	4	5	25	47	110	17

* *Three points deducted*

5-Year, One, Two, Three

Year	1st	Pts	2nd	Pts	3rd	Pts
First Division						
1987-88	Colne Dynamoes	55	Rossendale Utd	55	Clitheroe	46
1988-89	Rossendale Utd	56	Knowsley Utd	50	St Helens Town	48
1989-90	Warrington T	72	Knowsley Utd	69	Colwyn Bay	60
1990-91	Knowsley Utd	83	Colwyn Bay	76	Ashton United	67
1991-92	Ashton United	77	Gt. Harwood Tn	74	Eastwood Hnly	63
Second Division						
1987-88	Ashton United	70	Flixton	64	Wren Rovers	61
1988-89	Vauxhall GM	58	Maine Road	51	Chadderton	49
1989-90	Maine Road	70	Bacup Borough	68	Blackpool Mech.	57
1990-91	Great Harwood T	86	Blackpool Rovers	78	Bradford PA	69
1991-92	Bamber Bridge	78	Newcastle Town	75	Blackpool Mech	69

Northern Counties East League

Formed in 1982 on the amalgamation of the Yorkshire and Midland Leagues. With a huge number of clubs involved, the League originally had a Premier Division and regionalised Divisions One and Two (each North and South). In 1984 Division Two disappeared and Division One was split into three leagues – North, Central and South. In 1985 the format was changed to a Premier and three (non-regionalised) divisions. In 1986 the size of the League was reduced and Division Three was disposed of.

The champions are now normally promoted to the Northern Premier League (with a team relegated) while additional leagues serve the bottom division.

Premier Division

	P	W	D	L	F	A	Pts
Spennymoor United	36	26	7	5	102	33	85
Pickering Town	38	27	4	7	90	48	85
North Ferriby United	38	23	7	8	90	40	76
Maltby Miners Welfare	38	21	11	6	69	40	74
Thackley	38	20	7	11	62	39	67
Brigg Town	38	16	14	8	55	39	62
Denaby United	38	15	11	12	71	63	56
Ossett Albion	38	16	7	15	68	60	55
Eccleshill United	38	16	6	16	65	65	54
Winterton Rangers	38	14	7	17	61	72	49
Ashfield United	38	12	11	15	69	88	47
Ossett Town	38	13	7	18	69	71	46
Belper Town	38	11	12	15	56	62	45
Liversedge	38	12	8	18	56	77	44
Sheffield	38	12	6	20	55	70	42
Stockbridge Park Steel	38	10	11	17	54	70	41
Pontefract Colliery	38	11	8	19	62	88	41
Glasshoughton Welfare	38	9	9	38	46	77	36
Armthorpe Welfare	38	8	8	22	49	81	32
Harrogate Railway	38	3	9	26	49	115	18

Division One

	P	W	D	L	F	A	Pts
Lincoln United	20	17	5	4	62	31	56
Hucknall Town	26	15	6	5	54	32	51
Hallam	26	15	5	6	50	23	50
Yorkshire Amateurs	26	14	3	9	42	29	45
RES Parkgate	26	12	9	5	39	38	45
Tadcaster Albion	26	12	5	9	51	43	41
Rossington Main	26	9	7	10	33	31	34
Hall Road Rangers	26	9	6	11	48	43	33
Garforth Town	26	8	8	10	34	38	32
Worsbrough Bridges	26	7	8	11	33	48	29
Hatfield Main	26	6	6	14	40	63	24
Immingham Town	26	5	8	13	38	51	23
Brodsworth MW	26	6	4	16	41	65	22
Selby Town	26	5	4	17	34	64	19

Bradley Rangers records expunged

5-Year, One, Two, Three

Year	1st	Pts	2nd	Pts	3rd	Pts

Premier Division

| 1987-88 | Emley | 68 | Armthorpe Wel | 68 | Denaby United | 61 |
| 1988-89 | Emley | 80 | Hatfield Main | 72 | Bridlington T | 68 |

1989-90	Bridlington Town.75	North Shields.........69	Denaby United......62
1990-91	Guiseley 76	North Shields........71	Spennymoor Utd..61
1991-92	North Shields........96	Sutton Town 72	Denaby Utd...........68

First Division

1987-88	York Railway In...68	Rowntree Mac 65	Maltby MW 60
1988-89	Sheffield................68	Rowntree Mac 60	Woolley MW.........59
1989-90	Rowntree Mack....61	Liversedge.............54	Ossett 54
1990-91	Sheffield................64	Hallam...................55	Liversedge.............47
1991-92	Stocksbridge PS...62	Pickering Town 61	Bradley Rangers...61

Northern League

Formed by ten clubs in 1889 with a second division added in 1897. The second division lasted just three seasons. In this early period several Football League reserve teams participated in the competition. In 1982, however, the second division was reinstated. Several clubs in recent years have moved elsewhere in search of the advantages of the Pyramid and the League finally joined the Pyramid system itself for the 1991-92 season feeding into the HFS Loans League First Division. Past sponsors have included Skol and Dryboroughs.

Division One

	P	W	D	L	F	A	Pts
Whitby Town	38	26	10	2	104	30	88
Billingham Synthonia	38	25	10	3	98	41	85
Guisborough	38	25	9	4	91	35	84
Blyth Spartans	38	26	4	8	83	35	82
Seaham Red Star	38	21	10	7	76	45	73
Durham City	38	21	10	7	73	51	73
Stockton	38	14	15	9	65	59	57
Murton	38	14	12	12	72	65	54
Chester-le-Street	38	15	8	15	82	82	53
Consett	38	15	7	16	54	54	52
* Northallerton	38	13	14	11	54	47	50
West Auckland	38	12	9	17	64	76	45
Newcastle Blue Star	38	12	6	20	64	81	42
Tow Law	38	11	8	19	65	73	41
Brandon	38	11	5	22	47	81	38
** Hebburn	38	8	11	19	74	94	29
Ferryhill	38	6	10	22	51	97	28
Easington	38	6	8	24	51	94	26
Peterlee	38	3	9	26	40	105	18
* South Bank	38	3	11	24	34	95	17

Three points deducted **Six points deducted*

Division Two

	P	W	D	L	F	A	Pts
Dunston Fed Brewery	38	30	5	3	139	31	95
Eppleton CW	38	27	7	4	116	51	88
Shildon	38	25	6	7	93	24	81
Billingham Town	38	24	8	6	89	36	80
Prudhoe East End	38	18	7	13	65	53	61
Evenwood	38	18	7	13	75	68	61
Whickham	38	19	3	16	71	62	60
Ashington	38	17	5	16	77	70	56
Alnwick	38	16	7	15	51	61	55
* Ryhope CA	38	16	8	14	67	61	53
* Darlington Cleve. Bridge	38	14	11	13	48	54	50
Norton	38	13	5	20	54	79	44
Esh Winning	38	13	4	21	70	82	43
Shotton	38	11	10	17	53	74	43
Washington	38	10	9	19	54	74	39
Willington	38	12	3	23	61	106	39
* Bedlington	38	11	3	24	64	76	33
* Crook Town	38	9	9	20	45	78	33
Horden	38	6	8	24	48	99	26
Langley Park	38	5	7	26	52	141	22

* Three points deducted

5-Year, One, Two, Three

Year	1st	Pts	2nd	Pts	3rd	Pts

First Division

1987-88	Blyth Spartans	92	Newcastle BS	87	Billingham Syn	77
1988-89	Billingham Syn	84	Tow Law Town	77	Gretna	73
1989-90	Billingham Syn	91	Gretna	75	Tow Law Town	73
1990-91	Gretna	95	Guisborough T	75	Blyth Spartans	68
1991-92	Gretna	85	Murton	78	Whitby Town	78

Second Division

1991-92	Stockton	88	Durham City	87	Chester-le-St Tn	86
1987-88	Stockton	73	Seaham RS	71	Durham City	63
1988-89	Consett	93	Alnwick Town	84	Whickham	84
1989-90	Murton	89	Northallerton T	87	Peterlee	82
1990-91	West Auckland T	79	Langley Park	76	Easington Collry	68

McEwan's Northern Alliance

Founded in 1890 with seven clubs and often included League club reserve or 'A' teams. It grew to just short of 20 members but in 1926 amalgamated with the North Eastern League. Reformed with 13 clubs in 1935. In 1964-65 there was no competition, but otherwise the Alliance continued with a one division format until major growth and the formation of Premier, First and Second divisions in 1988.

Premier Division

	P	W	D	L	F	A	Pts
Seaton Delaval	30	20	6	4	79	34	66 †
West Allotment Celtic	30	21	3	6	86	35	66 †
Carlisle City	30	19	6	5	80	41	63
Morpeth Town	30	20	3	7	67	37	63
Seaton Terrace	30	18	1	11	74	46	55
Walker	30	15	5	10	75	52	50
Gilford Park	30	13	9	8	72	56	48
Ponteland United	30	13	6	11	71	59	45
Haltwhistle CP	30	12	5	13	43	41	41
Winlaton Hallgarth	30	12	4	14	58	64	40
Spittal Rovers	30	12	3	15	55	54	39
Heaton Stanhope	30	9	4	17	489	68	31
Wark	30	8	2	20	45	79	26
Blyth Kitty Brewster	30	7	5	18	50	100	26
Westerhope	30	5	7	18	36	66	22
Forest Hall	30	1	1	28	24	132	4

Playoff Seaton Delavale Amateurs won 4-3 on agg (2-2, 2-1)

Division One

	P	W	D	L	F	A	Pts
Longbenton	30	21	4	5	105	38	67
Newbiggin Central Welfare	30	21	2	7	80	36	65
Benfield Park	30	19	3	8	84	42	60
North Shields St Columbas	30	16	6	8	63	50	54
NEI Reyrolle	30	14	7	9	76	60	49
Wylam	30	14	7	9	66	59	49
Swalwell	30	12	7	11	53	48	43
Procter & Gamble	30	11	8	11	61	59	41
Dudley Welfare	30	10	8	12	60	69	38
Percy Rovers	30	11	5	15	57	68	38
** Northern Counties	30	10	6	14	52	74	33
New York	30	8	8	14	49	61	32
Percy Main Amateurs	30	9	5	16	52	72	32
Ryton	30	7	7	16	41	69	28
Hexham Swinton	30	5	6	19	36	94	21
Northern Electric	30	5	5	20	48	94	20

Division Two

	P	W	D	L	F	A	Pts
Amble Town	30	24	3	3	132	42	75
Gosforth Bohemians	30	23	3	4	101	43	72
Ashington Hirst	30	23	3	4	104	52	72

Shankhouse	30	20	2	8	92	46	62
County Kitchens	30	18	3	9	119	68	57
Marden Athletic	30	16	6	8	69	49	54
Highfields United	30	13	3	14	73	76	42
* Monkseaton Kosa	30	12	7	21	58	69	40
Shalwell Crowley	30	12	3	15	70	74	39
DHSS	30	10	5	15	58	87	35
Newcastle University	30	9	6	15	58	57	33
Norgas United	30	8	4	18	79	100	28
Stobswood Welfare	30	7	5	18	52	106	26
Heddon Institute	30	6	7	17	43	73	25
New Winning	30	5	3	22	73	126	18
Wallsend Rising Sun	30	2	1	27	32	144	7

* Three points deducted.

5-Year, One, Two, Three

Year	1st	Pts	2nd	Pts	3rd	Pts
1987-88	SD Seaton Ter	43	Prudhoe East	39	Gosforth St N	39

Premier Division
1989-89	SD Seaton Ter	69	W Allotment	62	Seaton Delaval	58
1989-90	Seaton Delaval	59	W Allotment	58	Forest Hall	57
1990-91	W. Allotment C	62	Seaton Terrace	54	Heaton Stann	49
1991-92	W. Allotment C.	64	Walker	58	Gilford Pk	56

Division One
1988-89	Ashington HP.	63	Haltwhistle	61	Westerhope W	59
1989-90	Westerhope W	73	Walker	62	Hexham	62
1990-91	Blyth KB	64	Spittal Rovers	60	Heaton Corner H	56
1991-92	Carlisle City	75	Winlaton Hall'	65	Longbenton	61

Vaux Wearside League

Founded in 1892 with 10 clubs and often included League club reserve or 'A' teams. There was a major increase of membership in the early 1970s but it was not until 1988-89 that a Second Division, comprising 12 clubs was introduced.

Division One	P	W	D	L	F	A	Pts
South Shields	28	20	5	3	84	36	65
Hartlepool Town	28	19	6	3	70	30	63
Silkworth	28	18	5	5	59	29	59
Jarrow Roofing	28	16	5	7	51	39	53
Marske United	28	12	11	5	55	37	47
Annfield Plain	28	11	7	10	57	58	40

Roker	28	12	3	13	54	42	39
Boldon CA	28	12	3	13	42	50	39
Cleadon South Shields	28	9	7	12	51	49	34
Wolviston	28	9	5	14	47	50	32
Ryhope CW	28	8	6	14	50	64	30
Newton Aycliffe	28	6	9	13	33	63	27
Cleator Moor	28	6	5	17	41	59	23
Herrington CW	28	5	6	17	36	76	21
Windscale	28	5	1	22	36	82	16

Northern Premier Additional Regional Leagues

Websters Bitter Central Midlands League

Supreme Division	P	W	D	L	F	A	Pts
Arnold Town	30	22	4	4	76	32	70
Heanor Town	30	22	4	4	80	42	70
Blidworth Welf	30	18	7	5	45	22	61
Harworth Colliery	30	18	2	10	60	42	56
Priory (Eastwood)	30	12	11	7	47	35	47
Mickleover RBL	30	14	4	12	51	48	46
Gedling Town	30	14	3	13	64	55	45
Shirebrook Colliery	30	13	4	13	78	65	43
Louth United	30	11	7	12	60	46	40
Glapwell	30	11	5	14	53	60	38
Borrowash Victoria	30	11	5	14	59	71	38
Kimberley Town	30	8	8	14	43	57	32
Sheffield Aurora	30	8	6	16	48	69	30
Nettleham United	30	7	7	16	53	76	28
Oakham United	30	4	5	21	26	64	17
Wombwell Town	30	4	4	22	28	87	16

Premier Division	P	W	D	L	F	A	Pts
Sandiacre Town	36	31	4	1	127	24	97
Rossington	36	25	7	4	91	49	82
Kiveton Park	36	20	4	12	80	49	64
Norton Woodseats	36	20	2	14	79	68	62
Long Eaton United	36	19	4	13	80	58	61
Derby C&W Reckitts	36	16	11	9	65	46	59

S Normanton Athletic	36	16	10	10	62	58	58
Derby Rolls Royce	36	15	6	15	60	62	51
Askern Miners Welfare	36	13	9	14	79	71	48
Stanton Ilkeston	36	14	4	18	61	64	46
Kilburn Miners Welfare	36	13	7	16	63	82	46
Mexborough Town	36	13	6	17	61	58	45
Biwater	36	12	7	17	63	70	43
Newhall United	36	13	4	19	69	88	43
Radford	36	12	4	20	63	106	40
Blackwel Miners Welfare	36	9	7	20	41	84	34
Bulwell United	36	7	10	19	63	91	31
Nuthall	36	8	7	21	42	79	31
Shardlow St James	36	6	7	23	40	82	25

5-Year, One, Two, Three

Year	1st	Pts	2nd	Pts	3rd	Pts
Supreme Division						
1987-88	Harworth Col	66	Hinckley Town	64	Ilkeston Town	58
1988-89	Boston	65	Arnold	60	Gainsborough T	57
1989-90	Hucknall Town	93	Heanor Town	81	Arnold	76
1990-91	Hucknall Town	75	Heanor Town	67	Lincoln United	66
1991-92	Lincoln United	83	Hucknall Town	69	Louth United	66
Premier Division						
1987-88	Huthwaite	80	Derby Prims	68	Melton Town	61
1988-89	Priory	83	Mickleover	80	Highfield Rangers	74
1989-90	Mickleover	91	Highfield Rangers	81	Nettleham	74
1990-91	Mickleover	78	Highfield Rangers	76	Blackwell	72
1991-92	Fryston CW	62	Kiverton park	55	Norton Woodseats	49
First Division						
1987-88	Stanton	57	Priory	54	Blackwell	46
1988-89	Brailsford	66	Swanwick PR	65	West Hallam	65
1989-90	Glapwell	68	Leicester Nirvana	67	Bulwell United	63
1990-91	Gedling Town	54	Derby C & W	49	Nuthall	46
1991-92	Slack & Parr	75	Gedling Town	63	Kimberley Town	57

Liverpool County Combination

First Division	P	W	D	L	F	A	Pts
St Dominics	30	24	4	2	111	40	76
Lucas Sports	30	22	5	3	100	46	71
Crawford UB	30	20	5	5	82	34	65
Ayone	30	18	7	5	71	44	61
Waterloo Dock	30	18	4	8	80	38	58

	P	W	D	L	F	A	Pts
Electric Supply	30	15	9	6	85	38	54
YCT	30	14	4	12	77	63	46
Ford Motors	30	11	8	11	60	67	41
Earle	30	9	8	13	67	76	35
Crystal Villa	30	8	6	16	51	72	30
Littlewoods Athletic	30	6	9	15	57	93	27
Speke	30	6	8	16	56	82	26
BRNESC	30	7	4	19	65	102	25
Mossley Hill	30	5	6	19	48	86	21
Eldonians	30	6	3	21	47	96	21
Bootle Reserves	30	3	6	21	43	123	15

Second Division	P	W	D	L	F	A	Pts
Beesix	26	16	6	4	94	47	54
* Cheshire Lines SL	26	17	4	5	75	36	52
Stockbridge	26	15	5	6	72	43	50
Royal Seaforth	26	15	2	9	50	49	47
* BRNESC Reserves	26	14	4	8	77	51	43
Plessey (GPT)	26	12	4	10	59	56	40
* Knowsley United Res	26	12	5	9	64	61	38
Halewood Town	26	9	8	9	43	49	35
Elec Supply Reserves	26	8	9	9	46	46	33
* MDHC	26	8	8	10	53	51	29
Camadale	26	7	7	12	51	67	28
Speke Reserves	26	5	4	17	46	76	19
Mersey Bus	26	3	6	17	41	94	15
Mossley Hill Reserves	26	3	4	19	32	77	13

Three points deducted

5-Year, One, Two, Three

Year	1st	Pts	2nd	Pts	3rd	Pts
1987-88	Uniasco	53	Waterloo Dock	44	Earle	38
1988-89	Waterloo Dock	46	St. Dominics	43	Ayone	40
1989-90	Waterloo Dock	72	St. Dominics	64	Stanton Dale	57
1990-91	Stanton Dale	64	St. Dominics	63	Crawfords UB	63
1991-92	Yorkshire CT	70	St Dominics	69	Stanton Dale	61

West Lancashire League

Division One	P	W	D	L	F	A	Pts
Vickers Sports Club	34	25	4	5	102	36	79
Feniscowles	34	22	7	5	72	39	73
BAC Preston	34	21	6	7	95	37	69
Eagley	34	20	8	6	91	58	68

	P	W	D	L	F	A	Pts
Poulton Town	34	9	9	6	70	47	66
Turton	34	20	5	9	84	59	65
Wigan College	34	16	4	14	88	57	52
Freckleton	34	14	8	12	66	70	50
* Burnley United	34	14	8	12	66	66	47
* Vernon Carus	34	14	3	17	57	69	42
Lytham St Annes	34	11	7	16	61	68	40
Springfields	34	11	6	17	49	90	39
Glaxo	34	11	4	19	71	80	37
Dalton United	34	10	7	17	58	77	37
Thorton Int	34	8	9	17	70	76	33
Colne RBL	34	8	7	19	62	71	31
Norcross & Warbreck	34	3	8	23	38	106	17
Blackpool Rangers	34	1	6	27	33	127	9

* Three points deducted

Division Two

	P	W	D	L	F	A	Pts
Leyland DAF	34	25	7	2	102	30	82
Haslingden	34	26	4	4	113	42	82
Kirkham & Wesham	34	16	12	6	56	38	60
Tempest United	34	17	5	12	74	61	56
Lansil	34	15	9	10	75	57	54
* Blackrod Town	34	16	8	10	82	57	53
* BAe Canberry	34	16	8	10	70	52	53
Multipart	34	15	8	11	72	58	53
Wyre Villa	34	13	9	12	80	65	48
Fleetwood Hesketh	34	12	9	13	52	67	45
Blackpool Rovers Reserves	34	12	6	16	60	73	42
Barrow Wanderers	34	11	8	15	70	78	41
Hesketh Bank	34	11	5	18	59	77	38
Londridge United	34	11	4	19	73	111	37
Carnforth Rangers	34	8	10	16	35	62	34
Padiham	34	9	5	20	47	83	32
BAe Warton	34	5	6	23	54	107	21
Wigan Rovers	34	4	5	25	39	95	17

* Three points deducted

5-Year, One, Two, Three

Year	1st	Pts	2nd	Pts	3rd	Pts
1987-88	BAC Preston	72	Holker OB	63	Squires Gate	59
1988-89	BAC Preston	74	Vickers SC	67	Holker OB	67
1989-90	Colne Dy. Res.	89	Wigan College	74	BAC Preston	69
1990-91	BAC Preston	79	Vickers SC	74	Burnley Bnk Hall	70
1991-92	Burnley Bank H.	88	Vickers SC	81	BAC Preston	74

Manchester League

Premier Division	P	W	D	L	F	A	Pts
Wythenshawe Amateur	34	24	4	6	82	37	76
Woodley Sports	34	21	4	9	92	57	67
East Manchester	34	19	10	5	67	37	67
Dukinfield Town	34	19	7	8	62	41	64
Abbey Hey	34	17	9	8	66	42	60
Springhead	34	15	9	10	97	69	54
Little Hulton	34	15	6	13	80	85	51
Prestwich Heys	34	13	9	12	54	52	48
Mitchell Shackleton	34	12	10	12	61	50	46
Highfield United	34	13	5	16	50	57	44
Ramsbottom United	34	13	1	19	56	78	43
Stockport Georgians	34	12	5	17	55	72	41
BT Cables Leigh	34	12	5	17	61	81	41
Whitworth Valley	34	11	6	17	45	57	35
Gt Man Police	34	9	8	17	45	57	35
Wythenshawe Town	34	9	7	18	59	77	34
Silcoms Woodside	34	6	8	20	50	84	26
ICI Blackley	34	5	7	22	43	91	22

5-Year, One, Two, Three

Year	1st	Pts	2nd	Pts	3rd	Pts
1987-88	Stockport Geo.	60	Little Hulton	55	E. Manchester	49
1988-89	Abbey Hey	54	Little Hulton	54	Prestwich H	51
1989-90	Wythenshawe Am	57	E. Manchester	55	Springhead	50
1990-91	Abbey Hey	75	Springhead	65	E. Manchester	63
1991-92	E. Manchester	76	Wytheshaw Ams	72	Abbey Hey	68

Roger Smith Insurance Notts Football Alliance

Senior Division	P	W	D	L	F	A	Pts
Clipstone Miners Welfare	30	19	6	5	73	31	63
GPT FC	30	18	8	4	80	35	62
Worthington Simpsons	30	18	4	8	54	39	58
Dunkirk FC	30	17	2	11	82	62	53
Rainworth Miners Welfare	30	15	8	7	48	37	53
Boots Athletic	30	14	5	11	67	47	47
Hucknall Rolls Royce	30	14	5	11	63	52	47
Notts Police	30	12	7	11	47	41	43
Pelican FC	30	13	4	13	46	53	43
Ruddington FC	30	9	8	13	43	60	35
Greenwood Meadows	30	9	7	14	33	51	34

Thoresby CW	30	7	11	12	49	53	32
Bulwell Forest Villa	30	7	10	13	27	50	31
Cotgrave Miners Welfare	30	7	5	18	47	77	26
Radcliffe Olympic	30	7	3	20	47	75	24
John Player FC	30	6	3	21	44	87	21

Division One

	P	W	D	L	F	A	Pts
Sneinton FC	30	23	4	3	73	34	73
Wollaton FC	30	22	6	2	97	33	72
Keyworth United	30	18	5	7	68	35	59
Basford United	30	17	5	8	59	42	56
Gedling CW	30	16	6	8	91	45	54
Worthington Simpson Res	30	14	7	9	74	65	49
Southwell City	30	14	6	10	47	35	48
Hucknall RR Welfare Res	30	11	5	14	51	58	38
City & Sherwood Hospital	30	10	8	12	59	76	38
Awsworth Villa	30	10	6	14	66	65	36
Carlton Athletic	30	9	5	16	52	64	32
Clipstone MW Reserves	30	8	7	15	43	61	31
Bilsthorpe CW	30	7	5	18	47	69	26
Stapleford Villa	30	7	5	18	37	67	26
Rainworth MW Reserves	30	5	5	20	38	96	20
Clifton AW	30	2	5	21	40	97	17

Division Two

	P	W	D	L	F	A	Pts
Ollerton B/Cotes	32	22	8	2	79	26	74
Linby CW	32	21	7	4	88	28	70
Abacus	32	20	5	7	81	45	65
Retford United	32	20	6	7	82	49	65
GPT Reserves	32	19	5	8	100	68	62
Teversal Grange	32	15	12	5	81	50	57
Attenborough FC	32	15	7	10	69	36	52
Calverton CW	32	13	5	14	56	66	44
John Player Reserves	32	12	4	16	71	72	40
Bestwood Miners Welfare	32	11	5	16	71	64	38
Fairham FC	32	10	7	15	49	57	37
Dunkirk FC	32	10	7	15	59	68	37
Greenwood Meadow Res	32	10	2	20	52	102	32
British Rail Newark	32	7	8	17	58	99	29
Ruddington FC Reserves	32	7	7	18	48	95	28
Basford United Reserves	32	6	3	23	51	114	21
Carlton Athletic Reserves	32	3	5	24	30	85	14

5-Year, One, Two, Three

Year   1st.................Pts   2nd.................Pts   3rd.................Pts

Senior Division
1987-88	Hucknall Town.....48	Rainworth MW 43	Notts Police............41
1988-89	Hucknall Town.....47	Dunkirk.................43	Worthington S 40
1989-90	John Player.........43	Dunkirk.................41	Notts Police............37
1990-91	Rainworth Mines..51	Dunkirk.................44	Worthington S 38
1991-92	GPT Plessey.........49	Notts Police...........47	Rainworth MW 44

Tetley Walker West Cheshire League

Division One

	P	W	D	L	F	A	Pts
Christleton	30	22	6	2	65	19	50
Merseyside Police	30	21	4	5	84	35	46
Vauxhall Motors	30	18	5	7	76	40	41
Bromborough Pool	30	17	6	7	65	43	40
Heswall	30	17	4	9	73	37	38
Poulton Victoria	30	14	9	7	55	39	37
Cammell Laird	30	14	8	8	71	39	36
Capenhurst	30	13	5	12	58	55	31
Ashville	30	12	6	12	68	57	30
Mersey Royal	30	12	5	13	39	50	29
Stork	30	9	7	14	35	61	25
Shell	30	8	4	18	46	95	20
General Chemicals	30	6	4	20	34	63	16
Upton Athletic Association	30	5	5	20	41	73	15
Newton	30	5	5	20	31	75	15
Moreton	30	2	7	21	27	87	11

Division Two

	P	W	D	L	F	A	Pts
Cammell Laird Reserves	34	21	9	4	91	45	51
Poulton Victoria Reserves	34	22	5	7	96	42	49
Mond Rangers	34	21	6	7	89	43	48
Christleton Reserves	34	20	7	7	76	38	47
West Kirby	34	20	6	8	69	37	46
Blacon Youth Club	34	18	6	10	85	67	42
Vauxhall Motors Reserves	34	14	11	9	61	58	39
Stork Reserves	34	14	8	12	70	63	36
Manor Athletic	34	12	10	12	74	68	34
Bromsborough Pool Res	34	13	8	13	72	75	34
Ashville Reserves	34	12	8	14	55	63	32
St. Werburghs	34	13	5	16	74	79	31

Heswall Reserves..................34	8	12	14	55	64	28
Mersey Royal Reserves 34	6	10	18	43	70	22
Willaston............................34	6	7	21	40	92	19
Shell Reserves......................34	6	5	23	47	109	17
Rivacre Rossfield.................34	4	7	23	55	100	15

5-Year, One, Two, Three

Year	1st	Pts	2nd	Pts	3rd	Pts
1987-88	Heswall Res	41	Gen. Chemicals	40	Cammell Laird	38
1988-89	Cammell Laird	46	Mersey Police	42	Gen. Chemicals	40
1989-90	Cammell Laird	42	Mersey Royal	42	Heswall Res	38
1990-91	Cammell Laird	49	Mersey Royal	39	Mersey Police	37
1991-92	Cammell Laird	49	Shell	41	Heswall Res	40

Whitbread County Senior League

Premier Division	P	W	D	L	F	A	Pts
Frecheville CA 26	18	4	4	66	23	58
Ash House............................26	17	3	6	54	23	54
Mexborough Main St...........26	16	5	5	52	32	53
Goldthorpe Colliery 26	16	2	8	68	40	50
White Rose Throstles...........26	15	3	8	64	38	48
Parramore Sports..................26	10	8	8	36	31	38
Hallam Reserves...................26	10	7	9	48	45	37
Phoenix 26	10	5	11	31	46	35
Denaby & Cadeby MW 26	9	6	11	57	50	33
Worsbrough Bridge Res.......26	8	4	14	34	48	28
Wath Saracens Athletic........26	8	3	15	36	51	27
RES Parkgate Reserves........26	8	3	15	33	64	27
ABM 26	5	5	16	42	73	20
Oughtibridge WM SC..........26	1	4	21	26	83	7

5-Year, One, Two, Three

Year	1st	Pts	2nd	Pts	3rd	Pts
1987-88	Ash House	37	Davy McKee	31	Windsor	30
1988-89	Ash House	40	Aurora United	38	Mexboro' Main	36
1989-90	Ash House	42	Aurora United	36	Mexboro' Main	30
1990-91	Ash House	60	Denaby-Cadeby	54	Parramore Sports	46
1991-92	Pheonix	63	Ash House	57	Mexboro' Main	46

MISCELLANEOUS LEAGUES

The Konica League of Wales

	P	W	D	L	F	A	Pts
Cwmbran Town	38	26	9	3	69	22	87
Inter Cardiff	38	26	5	7	79	36	83
Aberystwyth Town	38	25	3	10	85	49	78
Ebbw Vale	38	19	9	10	76	61	66
Bangor City	38	19	7	12	77	58	64
Hollywell Town	38	17	8	13	65	48	59
Conwy United	38	16	9	13	51	51	57
Connah's Quay Nomads	38	17	4	17	66	67	55
Porthmadog	38	14	11	13	61	49	53
Haverfordwest County	38	16	5	17	66	66	53
Caersws	38	14	10	14	64	60	52
Afan Lido	38	14	10	14	64	65	32
*Mold Alexandra	38	16	4	18	63	69	48
Llanelli	38	11	8	19	49	64	41
Maesteg Park Athletic	38	9	13	164	52	59	40
Flint Town United	38	11	6	21	47	67	39
Briton Ferry Athletic	38	10	9	19	61	87	39
Newtown	38	9	9	20	55	87	36
Llanidloes Town	38	7	9	22	48	93	30
Abergavenny Thursdays	38	7	7	24	36	76	28

Three points deducted

Cymru Alliance

	P	W	D	L	F	A	Pts
Llansantffraid	28	23	3	2	89	34	72
Welshpool Town	28	21	2	5	92	34	65
Rhyl	28	20	4	4	74	22	64
Wrexham	28	19	4	5	81	34	61
Lex XI	28	14	8	6	60	62	50
Carno	28	9	11	8	44	56	38
Cefn Druids	28	10	5	13	46	41	35
Penryncoch	28	10	5	13	56	71	35
Ruthin Town	28	9	7	12	43	58	34

	P	W	D	L	F	A	Pts
Rhos Aelwyd	28	7	6	15	37	67	27
Knighton Town	28	7	6	15	48	82	27
Mostyn	28	7	3	18	35	64	24
Rhyader	28	6	5	17	32	66	23
Gresford Athletic	28	6	1	21	36	76	19
Brymbo	28	3	8	17	40	66	17

2-Year, One, Two, Three

Year	1st	Pts	2nd	Pts	3rd	Pts
1990-91	Flint Town U	67	Caersws	60	Connah's Quay	51
1991-92	Caersws	55	Llansartffraid	53	Porthmadog	52

(League formed in 1990)

Dorset Football Combination League

	P	W	D	L	F	A	Pts
Westland Sports	38	28	6	4	118	28	90
Sherborne Town	38	24	7	7	108	45	79
Hamworthy Eng	38	22	9	7	81	37	75
** Hamworthy United	38	23	4	11	112	74	70
Bournemouth Sports	38	21	3	14	72	59	66
* Flight Refuelling	38	17	10	11	84	61	60
** Portland United	38	19	6	13	68	62	60
Dorchester Town Reserves	38	17	7	14	79	57	58
Shaftesbury	38	17	6	15	84	71	57
Parley Sports	38	14	15	9	64	56	57
Poole Town Reserves	38	16	8	14	68	58	56
Swan'ge Town&H Res	38	15	9	14	67	61	54
Sturminster Newton	38	14	9	15	68	59	51
Blandford United	38	13	12	13	55	50	51
Holt United	38	13	5	20	61	91	44
Gillingham Town	38	13	3	22	55	78	42
Weymouth Reserves	38	11	7	20	51	83	40
* Wareham Rangers	38	7	3	28	58	121	23
Bridport Reserves	38	5	6	27	36	113	21
Cranborne	38	2	3	33	37	162	9

** 3 Points deducted   * 1 point deducted

5-Year, One, Two, Three

Year	1st	Pts	2nd	Pts	3rd	Pts
1987-88	Bridport	60	Flight Refuelling	52	Westland Sports	51
1988-89	Shaftesbury	53	Westland Sports	48	Parley Sports	44
1989-90	Weymouth Res	56	Flight Refuelling	46	Westland Sports	41

| 1990-91 | Dorchester T. Res..54 | Flight Refuelling...51 | Westland Sports....47 |
| 1991-92 | Blandford United..76 | Westland Sports....71 | Parley Sports.........70 |

Everards Brewery Leicestershire Senior League

Premier Division

	P	W	D	L	F	A	Pts
Holwell	34	23	6	5	115	43	75
Friar Lane	34	23	7	5	85	30	73
Oadby Town	34	23	4	7	85	45	73
Anstey Nomads	34	21	5	8	103	46	68
St Andrews	34	19	8	7	66	30	65
Burbage Old Boys	34	17	5	12	71	56	56
N Kilworth	34	16	7	11	60	68	55
Birstall United	34	15	7	12	76	65	52
Highfield Rangers	34	14	8	12	46	51	50
Constbulary	34	14	7	13	64	66	49
Syston	34	11	8	15	55	75	41
Lutterworth	34	11	7	16	54	63	40
Newfoundpool	34	11	7	16	41	67	40
Ibstock	34	9	6	19	52	65	33
Downes	34	9	4	21	50	78	31
Petfoods	34	8	4	22	43	95	28
Houghton	34	6	4	24	32	89	22
Narborough	34	2	6	26	28	94	10

First Division

	P	W	D	L	F	A	Pts
Barrow Town	34	26	2	6	91	27	80
Sileby Town	34	24	5	5	81	37	77
Cottesmore	34	23	3	8	91	49	72
Kirby Muxloe	34	23	3	8	85	39	70
Thringstone	34	19	6	9	94	53	63
Asfordby	34	18	8	8	105	54	62
Fosse Imps	34	18	5	11	70	44	59
Quorn	34	16	7	11	67	60	55
Ravenstone	34	15	7	12	68	71	52
L'boro Dyn	34	11	8	15	8	72	41
Anstey	34	13	2	19	51	68	41
Harborough	34	13	2	19	60	63	41
Hillcroft	34	11	2	21	55	82	35
YMCA	34	9	5	20	59	102	32
East Shilton	34	6	8	20	51	89	26
Huncote	34	7	5	22	38	92	26
Ayleston PK	34	8	2	24	55	114	26
Whetstone Athletic	34	4	5	25	35	78	17

5-Year, One, Two, Three
Premier Division

Year	1st	Pts	2nd	Pts	3rd	Pts
1987-88	Holwell Works	46	Stapenhill	42	St. Andrews SC	41
1988-89	Stapenhill	53	Wigston Town	38	Birstall United	38
1989-90	St Andrews SC	67	Syston St Peters	64	Lutterworth Tn	55
1990-91	Lutterworth Tn	57	Anstey Nomads	57	Oadby Town	56
1991-92	Holwell Sports	69	St Andrews SC	61	Birstall United	53

Jewson South Western League

First Division

	P	W	D	L	F	A	Pts
Truro City	32	23	3	6	72	2	49
Bodmin Town	32	20	6	6	84	46	46
Newquay	32	20	5	7	76	39	45
Launceston	32	17	10	5	81	41	55
St Blazey	32	14	9	9	71	65	37
Falmouth Town	32	15	6	11	77	51	36
Holsworthy	32	12	8	12	49	54	30
Tavistock	32	11	7	14	53	77	30
Mulion	32	9	10	13	51	61	28
Appledore	32	10	8	14	556	73	28
Penzance	32	10	6	16	65	69	26
* Devon & Cornwall Police	32	12	5	15	61	69	26
Porthleven	32	9	7	16	69	82	25
Wadebridge Town	32	8	9	15	49	87	25
Milbrook	32	8	8	16	50	69	24
Torpoint Athletic	32	8	7	17	44	68	23
St Austell	32	7	4	21	61	89	18

* Three points deducted

5-Year, One, Two, Three

Year	1st	Pts	2nd	Pts	3rd	Pts
1987-88	Newquay	65	Falmouth Town	62	St Blazey	56
1988-89	Falmouth Town	55	St Blazey	53	Bodmin Town	53
1989-90	Falmouth Town	54	St Blazey	50	Bodmin Town	44
1990-91	Bodmin Town	55	St. Blazey	52	Falmouth Town	45
1991-92	Falmouth Town	57	Newquay	51	Bugle	41

Hampshire League

Division One

	P	W	D	L	F	A	Pts
Pirelli General	32	23	5	4	71	26	74
Bishops Waltham Town	32	22	6	4	101	40	72
Dowton	32	20	7	5	72	33	67
Fleetlands	32	19	5	8	58	44	62
Cowes Sports	32	18	6	8	79	49	60
Blackfield & Langley	32	16	9	7	63	40	57
Overton United	32	15	6	11	56	46	51
New Milton	32	14	7	11	55	49	49
Colden Common	32	13	6	13	63	51	45
Bass Alton Town	32	13	5	14	68	57	44
Winchester City	32	10	6	16	47	69	36
Malshanger	32	9	7	16	32	48	34
AC Delco	32	8	9	15	33	51	33
Locks Heath	32	6	7	19	48	78	25
Alresford Town	32	6	7	19	40	73	25
Awbridge	32	6	5	21	39	82	23
Midanbury	32	1	3	28	30	119	6

5-Year, One, Two, Three

Division One

Year	1st	Pts	2nd	Pts	3rd	Pts
1987-88	BAT	55	Basing Rovers	49	Blackfield & L	47
1988-89	BAT	53	Blackfield & L	47	Pirelli Gen	46
1989-90	Ryde Sports	70	Arton Town	63	Netley CS	61
1990-91	Locksheath	81	DCA Basingstoke	74	Blackfield & L	69
1991-92	Coldon Common	70	Blackfield & Lgly	68	Whitchurch Utd	64

Green Insulation Mid-Cheshire League

Division One

	P	W	D	L	F	A	Pts
Grove United	30	22	4	4	87	28	70
Winnington Park	30	19	5	6	67	32	62
Chorlton Town	30	18	4	8	68	49	58
Barnton	30	15	9	6	57	49	54
Knutsford	30	16	5	9	59	45	53
The Beeches	30	15	5	10	62	44	50
Linotype	30	14	6	10	57	51	48
Wilmslow Albion	30	11	6	13	51	65	39
Hanley Town	30	10	6	14	39	43	36
Whitchurch Alport	30	10	4	16	46	59	34
Rylands	30	9	6	15	41	57	33

Broadheath Central	30	9	6	15	55	72	33
Poynton	30	9	5	16	47	61	32
Garswood United	30	7	5	18	48	69	26
Bramhall	30	7	4	19	42	69	25
Newcastle Town	30	6	6	18	28	61	24

Division Two

	P	W	D	L	F	A	Pts
Malpas	34	28	5	1	116	35	89
Middlewich Athletic	34	24	5	4	90	49	77
Pilkington	34	20	7	7	83	51	67
Littlemoor	34	18	4	12	88	63	58
Bollington Athletic	34	16	5	13	71	65	53
I.C.I. Pharms	34	16	4	14	80	67	52
The Beeches	34	14	10	10	71	64	52
Warrington Town Reserves	34	11	12	11	63	58	45
Alsager	34	12	7	15	59	59	43
Knutsford Reserves	34	11	9	13	45	53	42
Rylands Reserves	34	11	6	17	56	77	39
Linotype Reserves	34	9	12	13	50	61	39
Chorlton Town Reserves	34	11	6	17	65	77	39
Poynton Reserves	34	9	9	16	52	66	36
Barswood Unt Reserves	34	8	12	14	41	63	36
Styal	34	7	10	17	52	67	31
Bramhall Reserves	34	8	5	21	41	100	29
Wilmslow Reserves	34	4	7	23	53	104	19

5-Year, One, Two, Three

Year	1st	Pts	2nd	Pts	3rd	Pts
Divsion One						
1987-88	Kidsgrove Ath	53	Alsager United	47	Hanley Town	46
1988-89	Barnton	44	Grove United	40	Linotype	39
1989-90	Grove United	65	Linotype	63	Bramhall	62
1990-91	Linotype	57	Bramhall	54	Knutsford	50
1991-92	Grove United	71	Knutsford	60	Linotype	59

Sportscene International Senior League

First Division

	P	W	D	L	F	A	Pts
Redgate Clayton	32	25	4	3	99	30	79
Norton United	32	24	6	2	74	30	78
Stafford Town	32	2	4	6	89	36	20
Walsall Wood	32	18	6	8	61	38	60
Milton United	32	17	6	9	59	45	57

	P	W	D	L	F	A	Pts
Goldenhill Wanderers	32	14	11	7	61	46	53
Brocton	32	16	4	12	62	50	52
Leek CSOB	32	13	7	12	60	52	46
Staffordshire Police	32	11	9	12	55	55	42
Congleton Hornets	32	12	5	15	55	72	41
Heath Haynes	32	10	8	14	37	55	38
Audley	32	10	5	17	40	66	35
Brereton Social	32	8	4	20	46	71	28
Eccleshall	32	7	6	19	40	60	27
Rists United	32	6	7	19	41	66	25
Ball Haye Green	32	5	7	20	36	78	22
Hanford	32	3	3	26	29	94	12

5-Year, One, Two, Three

Year	1st	Pts	2nd	Pts	3rd	Pts
1987-88	Redgate Clayton	45	Knypersley Vic	42	Meir Kings Arms	38
1988-89	Meir Kings A	46	Redgate Clayton	42	Hanford	40
1989-90	Eccleshall	58	Hanford	50	Knypersley Vic	49
1990-91	Meir Kings A	54	Staffs. Police	50	Eccleshall	47
1991-92	Redgate Clayton	78	Stafford MSHD	78	Meir Kings A	75

Gloucestershire County League

	P	W	D	L	F	A	Pts
Hallen	34	26	2	6	91	35	80
Old Georgians	34	24	5	5	77	37	77
Ellwood	34	21	4	9	94	50	67
DRG (FP)	34	20	3	11	74	42	63
Wotton Rovers	34	16	9	9	61	56	57
Harrow Hill	34	16	6	12	68	54	54
Patchway Town	34	14	11	9	59	43	53
Cadbury Heath	34	15	6	13	52	51	51
Hedbury OB	34	13	11	10	52	49	50
Pucklechurch Sports	34	14	4	16	46	56	46
St Phillips MAS	34	12	7	15	53	53	43
St Marks CA	34	12	6	16	43	52	42
Campden Town	34	10	10	14	39	56	40
Winterbourne United	34	10	7	17	47	70	37
Dowty Dynamos	34	8	8	18	49	63	32
Smiths Athletic	34	8	8	18	42	62	32
Stapleton	34	6	5	23	42	87	23
Hambrook	34	2	6	26	20	93	12

Ceiling System Reading League

Senior Division

	P	W	D	L	F	A	Pts
Woodley Arms	22	16	3	3	61	26	51
Mortimer	22	IS	3	4	53	22	48
Reading Exiles	22	13	6	3	47	20	45
Forest Old Boys	22	11	7	4	47	20	37
Marlow United	22	10	7	5	49	33	37
South Reading	22	9	6	7	54	36	33
Remr	22	10	1	11	62	65	31
Cookham Dean	22	8	4	10	35	42	28
West Reading	22	6	4	12	37	53	22
Newton Henley	22	4	4	14	30	60	16
Tilehurst	22	2	5	15	20	53	11
Old Prestonians	22	3	0	19	28	93	9

Premier Division

	P	W	D	L	F	A	Pts
Reading Old Blues	20	12	4	4	51	24	40
Checkendon	20	11	6	3	55	25	39
Reading University	20	11	4	5	57	40	34
Theale	20	9	5	6	64	41	32
Thames Vale	20	9	5	6	52	48	32
Berks Co Sports	20	9	3	8	41	42	30
Ibis	20	8	5	7	46	43	29
Sonning	20	7	4	9	34	58	25
Earlbourne	20	6	5	9	30	43	23
CS Reading	20	4	4	12	36	56	16
Nettlebed	20	0	3	17	21	67	3

Colborne Trophies Somerset Senior League

Premier Division

	P	W	D	L	F	A	Pts
Long Sutton	34	22	8	2	106	41	80
Clevedon United	34	23	5	6	85	38	74
Bridgewater T84	34	15	9	10	67	53	54
Shepton Mallet	34	16	6	12	72	63	54
Portishead	34	15	7	12	60	53	52
Fry's Club	34	14	9	11	64	58	51
Shirehampton	34	13	10	11	60	54	49
Brislington	34	14	6	14	56	54	48
** Mang'ld United	34	15	4	15	60	61	47
Imperial United	34	12	10	12	54	43	46
Weston-Super-Mare	34	14	4	16	67	61	46

	P	W	D	L	F	A	Pts
Avon/Som Const.............34		11	10	13	58	66	43
Bristol MF.......................34		10	9	15	59	59	39
Castle Cary.....................34		10	9	15	65	71	39
Peasedown Athletic............34		11	5	18	60	77	38
Longwell Green.................34		10	6	18	51	99	36
Weston St John 34		10	3	21	51	86	33
Frome Town.....................34		7	4	23	44	109	25

** *Two points deducted*

First Division	P	W	D	L	F	A	Pts
Cleveland Town..............34		24	7	3	85	30	78
Portishead Reserves 34		24	5	5	86	35	77
Burnam United................34		19	7	8	78	49	64
Westland United 34		18	6	10	77	56	60
Wells City.......................34		13	14	7	70	45	53
Keynsham Town...............33		15	6	12	55	62	51
* Bishop Sutton................34		15	6	13	59	47	50
Stockwood Green..............34		14	7	13	65	66	49
Hengrove Athletic.............33		14	5	14	61	69	47
Larkhall Athletic..............34		12	7	15	64	64	43
* Dundry Athletic '82........34		12	8	14	51	61	43
Congresbury....................34		11	6	17	51	64	39

* *One point deducted*

Hampshire League

Division One	P	W	D	L	F	A	Pts
Pirelli General................32		23	5	4	71	26	74
Bishops Waltham Town.......32		22	6	4	101	40	72
Dowton..........................32		20	7	5	72	33	67
Fleetlands......................32		19	5	8	58	44	62
Cowes Sports..................32		18	6	8	79	49	60
Blackfield & Langley.........32		16	9	7	63	40	57
Overton United................32		15	6	11	56	46	51
New Milton.....................32		14	7	11	55	49	49
Colden Common...............32		13	6	13	63	51	45
Bass Alton Town 32		13	5	14	68	57	44
Winchester City...............32		10	6	16	47	69	36
Malshanger.....................32		9	7	16	32	48	34
AC Delco........................32		8	9	15	33	51	33
Locks Heath...................32		6	7	19	48	78	25
Alresford Town................32		6	7	19	40	73	25
Awbridge.......................32		6	5	21	39	82	23
Midanbury......................32		1	3	28	30	119	6

GM VAUXHALL CONFERENCE

	Altrincham	Bath City	Bromsgrove R	Dagenham & R	Dover Athletic	Gateshead	Halifax Town	Kettering Town	Kidderminster	Macclesfield	Merthyr Tydfil
Altrincham	•	28/8	5/2	2/10	26/2	27/11	30/4	2/5	11/9	27/12	15/1
Bath City	19/2	•	20/11	7/5	26/4	18/9	30/10	2/10	30/8	21/8	9/4
Bromsgrove Rovers	30/8	30/4	•	22/3	13/11	16/10	8/1	19/3	27/12	29/1	27/11
Dagenham & Redbridge	29/1	13/11	21/2	•	25/9	26/3	16/10	27/12	6/11	8/1	12/3
Dover Athletic	18/9	27/11	1/1	3/1	•	4/9	18/12	12/2	21/8	5/3	6/11
Gateshead	1/2	16/4	15/1	20/11	30/4	•	4/4	12/3	19/2	2/4	19/3
Halifax Town	1/1	26/3	6/11	9/4	12/3	27/12	•	21/8	4/12	26/4	26/2
Kettering Town	30/10	4/12	7/5	26/2	4/4	11/12	23/4	•	8/1	26/3	11/9
Kidderminster	7/5	1/1	4/4	5/2	11/12	5/3	3/1	23/8	•	11/10	25/9
Macclesfield	3/1	12/3	24/8	4/9	28/8	6/11	19/3	18/9	16/4	•	18/12
Merthyr Tydfil	21/8	24/8	2/5	11/12	30/11	29/1	9/10	2/4	1/3	13/11	•
Northwich Victoria	29/3	26/2	12/10	4/9	8/1	23/11	2/4	9/4	29/1	7/5	4/12
Runcorn	20/11	23/4	26/3	23/4	16/10	15/3	11/9	27/11	12/2	30/8	4/4
Slough Town	23/4	9/10	26/2	5/3	24/8	2/5	28/8	5/3	30/10	12/2	12/10
Southport	12/10	11/9	28/8	1/1	30/10	28/9	24/8	9/10	18/12	15/3	19/2
Stafford Rangers	5/3	15/1	3/1	15/1	16/10	9/4	5/2	6/11	2/10	30/10	30/4
Stalybridge Celtic	4/12	29/1	30/10	28/8	19/2	30/8	28/9	4/9	16/10	1/1	8/1
Telford United	4/4	6/11	25/9	30/4	16/4	8/1	29/1	13/11	15/3	26/2	27/12
Welling United	4/9	4/4	23/4	18/12	26/3	19/2	19/2	15/1	30/4	27/11	30/8
Witton Albion	18/12	25/9	4/9	9/10	27/12	12/2	27/11	4/9	14/9	9/10	28/8
Woking	12/3	11/12	15/3	30/10	12/10	24/8	25/9	3/1	27/11	11/9	5/10
Yeovil Town	9/10	27/12	11/12	2/4	20/11	23/4	16/4	29/1	2/4	25/9	26/4

280

FIXTURES 1993-94

	Northwich V	Runcorn	Slough Town	Southport	Stafford R	Stalybridge C	Telford Utd	Welling Utd	Witton Albion	Woking	Yeovil Town
Altrincham	13/11	12/4	16/10	2/4	25/9	24/8	16/4	11/12	12/2	8/1	19/3
Bath City	18/12	5/2	30/11	8/1	16/10	4/9	2/4	28/9	5/3	19/3	3/1
Bromsgrove Rovers	19/2	12/3	2/4	16/4	7/9	18/12	4/12	2/10	9/4	18/9	21/8
Dagenham & Redbridge	27/11	16/4	30/8	21/8	2/5	19/2	18/9	25/4	19/3	4/12	4/4
Dover Athletic	2/5	7/5	4/12	9/4	29/1	19/3	15/1	29/3	2/10	30/8	23/4
Gateshead	1/1	21/8	2/10	7/5	4/12	3/1	28/8	2/5	27/10	18/12	5/2
Halifax Town	11/12	15/1	7/5	12/2	30/8	26/10	2/10	26/2	18/9	23/10	4/9
Kettering Town	28/8	25/9	15/3	20/11	16/4	5/2	1/1	20/11	30/8	19/2	16/10
Kidderminster	25/10	9/10	4/9	12/3	26/2	18/9	23/4	18/12	20/11	26/3	15/1
Macclesfield	5/2	19/2	20/11	2/10	4/4	11/12	26/10	2/5	23/4	15/1	30/4
Merthyr Tydfil	30/10	18/9	5/2	4/9	20/11	23/4	3/1	16/4	7/5	5/3	1/1
Northwich Victoria	•	6/11	18/9	30/8	19/3	5/3	20/11	15/1	27/12	21/8	2/10
Runcorn	4/9	•	8/1	4/12	27/12	2/10	24/8	30/10	29/1	9/4	26/2
Slough Town	26/3	11/12	•	30/4	11/9	15/1	19/3	3/1	6/11	4/4	21/9
Southport	3/1	2/5	25/9	•	23/4	4/4	11/12	5/2	26/2	9/10	27/11
Stafford Rangers	24/8	1/1	18/12	6/11	•	27/11	12/2	2/4	11/12	4/9	18/9
Stalybridge Celtic	12/2	30/11	21/8	27/12	12/3	•	22/2	7/5	2/4	20/11	9/4
Telford United	30/4	27/11	29/1	16/10	23/11	13/11	•	9/4	21/8	2/5	30/8
Welling United	16/10	19/3	19/2	18/9	21/8	26/3	5/3	•	8/1	1/1	6/11
Witton Albion	4/4	3/1	16/4	1/1	15/1	2/5	12/10	12/3	•	30/4	19/2
Woking	16/4	28/8	27/12	29/1	7/5	26/2	30/10	24/8	16/10	•	29/3
Yeovil Town	12/3	23/10	5/3	26/3	8/1	28/8	7/5	14/9	11/9	12/2	•

DIADORA PREMIER LEAGUE

	Aylesbury Utd	Basingstoke Tn	Bromley	Carshalton Ath	Chesham Utd	Dorking	Dulwich Ham	Enfield	Grays Athletic	Harrow Boro	Hayes
Aylesbury United......	•	18/12	4/9	5/10	4/4	26/2	16/4	18/9	30/4	26/3	12/2
Basingstoke Town......	9/4	•	31/8	23/4	28/9	27/12	30/10	11/12	12/3	8/1	27/11
Bromley....................	5/2	1/1	•	19/2	16/4	28/8	4/4	5/10	4/12	12/10	19/3
Carshalton Athletic....	12/3	20/11	25/9	•	16/10	30/10	5/3	21/8	6/11	2/10	4/9
Chesham United........	27/12	19/2	13/11	26/2	•	7/5	13/10	23/4	28/8	11/12	8/1
Dorking....................	16/10	4/4	29/1	26/3	4/12	•	6/11	15/1	18/12	23/10	25/9
Dulwich Hamlet........	13/11	26/3	27/12	9/10	12/2	8/1	•	19/10	2/10	23/4	21/8
Enfield.....................	19/2	14/9	12/3	22/1	20/11	24/8	30/4	•	5/2	28/8	16/10
Grays Athletic..........	30/11	5/10	7/5	8/1	29/1	9/4	19/3	4/9	•	9/10	31/8
Harrow Borough........	30/10	6/11	12/2	19/3	1/9	2/4	29/1	29/1	5/3	•	15/1
Hayes......................	9/10	30/4	2/10	5/2	6/11	19/2	22/1	26/2	1/1	24/8	•
Hendon....................	11/12	24/8	23/4	9/4	12/3	27/11	28/8	7/5	25/1	14/9	27/12
Hitchin Town............	2/10	9/10	2/10	23/10	1/1	12/3	18/12	12/2	16/4	26/2	29/1
Kingstonian..............	22/1	16/4	21/8	24/8	18/12	7/9	4/12	19/3	18/9	5/2	26/10
Marlow....................	11/9	28/8	26/3	11/12	2/4	2/10	5/2	12/10	19/2	27/11	13/11
Molesey...................	7/5	22/1	9/4	24/1	2/10	15/9	19/2	13/11	25/8	12/3	9/4
St Albans City..........	5/3	19/3	9/10	13/11	21/8	23/4	16/10	27/12	2/4	9/4	7/5
Stevenage Borough....	2/4	5/2	23/11	22/1	30/10	11/12	23/8	9/4	27/9	7/5	23/4
Sutton United...........	8/1	26/2	8/1	13/9	11/12	2/4	2/4	31/8	30/10	13/11	11/12
Wivenhoe Town........	23/8	25/9	15/1	27/12	4/9	12/10	2/4	23/10	4/4	19/2	26/3
Wokingham Town.....	28/8	4/12	26/2	28/8	30/4	22/1	13/9	26/3	20/11	22/1	5/10
Yeading...................	23/4	23/10	23/10	28/9	5/3	5/2	1/1	8/1	16/10	27/12	5/3

FIXTURES 1993-94

	Hendon	Hitchin Town	Kingstonian	Marlow	Molesey	St Albans City	Stevenage Boro	Sutton United	Wivenhoe Tn	Wokingham Tn	Yeading
Aylesbury United.....	31/8	19/3	21/8	1/1	4/12	12/10	26/10	6/11	15/1	29/1	20/11
Basingstoke Town.....	15/1	5/3	13/11	29/1	21/8	2/10	4/9	16/10	12/2	7/5	2/4
Bromley...................	20/11	22/1	30/10	18/12	5/3	30/4	6/11	24/8	16/10	2/4	14/9
Carshalton Athletic...	18/12	2/4	15/1	30/8	30/4	16/4	1/1	4/4	29/1	12/2	4/12
Chesham United........	6/10	15/9	9/4	27/10	19/3	26/1	26/3	5/2	18/9	9/10	25/8
Dorking....................	30/4	5/10	12/2	19/3	1/1	20/11	31/8	5/3	21/8	4/9	16/4
Dulwich Hamlet........	29/1	9/4	7/5	4/9	25/9	26/2	4/4	28/9	11/12	31/8	12/3
Enfield.....................	4/12	28/9	2/10	5/3	16/4	4/4	18/12	1/1	2/4	30/10	6/11
Grays Athletic..........	21/8	13/11	11/12	25/9	15/1	23/10	12/2	26/3	27/12	23/4	26/2
Harrow Borough.......	1/1	16/10	4/9	30/4	6/10	18/12	4/12	16/2	29/9	21/8	4/4
Hayes......................	4/4	28/8	2/4	16/4	18/12	4/12	2/10	11/9	30/10	12/3	12/10
Hendon....................		30/10	8/1	16/10	2/4	5/2	2/10	19/2	5/3	13/11	28/9
Hitchin Town............	26/3		25/9	4/12	31/8	6/11	4/4	20/11	4/9	15/1	30/4
Kingstonian.............	6/11	19/2		20/11	4/4	28/8	9/10	30/4	5/10	26/2	1/1
Marlow.....................	26/2	7/5	23/4		30/10	24/8	12/3	9/10	8/1	27/12	22/1
Molesey....................	23/10	11/12	27/12	26/3		29/9	26/2	28/8	23/4	8/1	5/2
St Albans City..........	4/9	8/1	29/1	15/1	12/2		25/9	5/10	31/8	11/12	30/10
Stevenage Borough...	19/3	27/12	5/3	4/10	16/10	19/2		6/9	13/11	27/11	28/8
Sutton United...........	25/9	23/4	14/9	12/2	29/1	12/3	21/8		7/5	9/4	2/10
Wivenhoe Town........	9/10	5/2	12/3	6/11	20/11	1/1	16/4	4/12		2/10	18/12
Wokingham Town.....	16/4	24/8	16/10	4/4	6/11	14/9	30/4	18/12	19/3		19/2
Yeading...................	12/2	27/11	31/8	21/8	4/9	26/3	29/1	19/3	9/4	25/9	

BEAZER HOMES LEAGUE

	Atherstone Utd	Bashley	Burton Albion	Cambridge City	Chelmsford C	Cheltenham	Corby Town	Crawley Town	Dorchester Tn	Farnborough	Gloucester City
Atherstone United......	•	19/2	3/1	8/9	27/10	13/11	4/4	26/2	7/5	21/8	16/4
Bashley....................	5/3	•	16/4	30/10	29/1	7/5	12/2	8/2	4/4	12/12	3/1
Burton Albion............	9/4	8/1	•	15/1	4/9	23/4	12/10	29/1	26/2	27/12	26/10
Cambridge City.........	19/3	30/4	5/3	•	3/1	4/9	27/12	18/12	12/2	2/10	6/11
Chelmsford City........	23/8	23/10	19/3	9/4	•	11/12	15/11	1/1	28/8	13/9	2/10
Cheltenham..............	20/11	12/3	4/12	29/1	21/8	•	26/3	11/9	3/1	12/2	4/4
Corby Town..............	1/1	4/9	5/2	2/4	30/8	18/9	•	8/1	5/3	30/4	21/8
Crawley Town...........	30/4	15/1	20/11	26/3	4/4	9/10	16/4	•	18/9	26/10	30/8
Dorchester Town.......	6/11	1/1	22/1	13/11	18/12	25/9	2/10	19/2	•	30/8	4/12
Farnborough Town....	11/12	2/4	26/3	19/2	8/2	1/1	30/10	24/8	16/11	•	20/11
Gloucester City.........	8/1	9/4	24/8	23/4	15/1	5/2	11/12	16/11	30/10	12/3	•
Gresley Rovers.........	16/11	26/3	27/12	24/8	12/3	24/8	7/9	28/8	11/12	16/4	30/4
Halesowen Town.......	23/4	11/12	19/2	5/2	6/11	8/1	28/8	12/3	20/11	15/1	7/9
Hastings Town..........	4/9	24/8	28/8	16/11	26/3	7/2	7/5	2/4	8/2	27/11	12/2
Hednesford Town......	12/2	28/8	4/4	12/3	9/10	16/4	23/8	30/10	20/11	18/9	13/11
Moor Green...............	23/10	2/10	7/9	11/12	16/4	16/11	3/1	7/5	4/9	5/2	5/3
Nuneaton Borough....	2/4	26/2	16/11	1/1	20/11	28/8	23/4	11/12	15/1	6/11	23/10
Sittingbourne............	15/1	6/11	30/4	23/10	27/11	19/2	29/1	2/10	9/10	3/1	18/12
Solihull Borough........	9/2	16/10	9/10	8/1	16/4	30/10	13/11	23/4	26/3	26/2	26/3
Trowbridge Town......	2/10	5/2	11/12	28/8	30/4	2/4	16/10	9/4	29/1	13/11	26/2
Waterlooville.............	28/8	23/11	6/11	7/5	15/1	19/2	12/2	19/3	24/8	4/4	29/1
Worcester City..........	29/1	20/11	30/10	2/10	12/2	19/3	19/3	13/11	16/4	16/10	27/12